MW00629512

THE KLEINMAN EDITION

A Torah theme for every day of every week,
blending profound perspectives
from all areas of Torah literature –
Scripture, Mishnah, Jewish Law, Mussar/Ethics,
Tefillah/Prayer, and Hashkafah/Jewish Thought –
collected for daily study.

ArtScroll Series®

THE KLEINMAN EDITION

A TORAH THEME FOR EVERY DAY OF EVERY WEEK FROM ALL AREAS OF TORAH LITERATURE — COLLECTED FOR DAILY STUDY.

Rabbi Yosaif Asher Weiss
General Editor

OF TORAH

VOLUME 8

DAILY STUDY FOR THE WEEKS OF

אחרי-בחקתי

ACHAREI – BECHUKOSAI

Published by

ArtScroll · Mesorah Publications, ltd

FIRST EDITION
First Impression ... April 2007

Published and Distributed by
MESORAH PUBLICATIONS, LTD.
4401 Second Avenue / Brooklyn, N.Y 11232

Distributed in Europe by
LEHMANNS
Unit E, Viking Business Park
Rolling Mill Road
Jarow, Tyne & Wear, NE32 3DP
England

Distributed in Australia and New Zealand by
GOLDS WORLDS OF JUDAICA
3-13 William Street
Balaclava, Melbourne 3183
Victoria, Australia

Distributed in Israel by
SIFRIATI / A. GITLER — BOOKS
6 Hayarkon Street
Bnei Brak 51127

Distributed in South Africa by
KOLLEL BOOKSHOP
Ivy Common
105 William Road
Norwood 2192, Johannesburg, South Africa

ARTSCROLL SERIES®
THE KLEINMAN EDITION — LIMUD YOMI / A DAILY DOSE OF TORAH
VOL. 8: ACHAREI–BECHUKOSAI

4401 Second Avenue / Brooklyn, N.Y. 11232 / (718) 921-9000 / www.artscroll.com

---

ISBN 10: 1-4226-0147-1 (hard cover)

ISBN 13: 978-1-4226-0147-1 (hard cover)

Typography by CompuScribe at ArtScroll Studios, Ltd.

Printed in the United States of America by Noble Book Press Corp.
Bound by Sefercraft, Quality Bookbinders, Ltd., Brooklyn N.Y. 11232

DEDICATION OF THIS VOLUME

This volume is dedicated in honor of

R' Zvi Ryzman שליט"א

מחבר ספרי „רץ כצבי"

He is a unique example of the classic
תורה וגדולה במקום אחד, a man
who combines greatness in Torah scholarship
with commercial success, and uses both
to benefit countless causes throughout the world.

As a teacher, lecturer, author, and philanthropist,
he has made an indelible mark
on his Los Angeles community
and the Torah world at large.

R' Zvika and his *eishes chayil* **Betty** שתחי'
have built a family in their image of sensitivity,
integrity, generosity, and love of Torah.

He is a dear friend and source of
inestimable counsel, help, and encouragement
to all who know, revere, and admire him.

The Kleinman Edition

**To our fathers and grandfathers, daily Torah study was the first priority.
It is fitting, therefore, that we dedicate this Limud Yomi Series in their memory**

Avrohom Kleinman ז"ל
ר' אברהם אייזיק ב"ר אלכסנדר ז"ל

נפ' י"ב שבט תשנ"ט

After years of slave labor and concentration camps — years when he risked his life to put on *tefillin* every day! — he courageously rebuilt. Wherever he was — in DP camps, Poughkeepsie, Borough Park, or Forest Hills — he was a one-man *kiruv* movement, before "*kiruv rechokim*" was a familiar phrase. Everyone was drawn to his enthusiasm for Yiddishkeit.

His home was open to anyone in need, even when there was barely enough for family.

All his life he felt close to his Rebbe, the Nitra Rav, and to the father-in-law he never knew; their *sefarim*, *Naos Desheh* and *Lechem Abirim*, were part of our Shabbos table. He was a caring and gentle man whose life was defined by his love of learning Torah, *gemillas chasadim*, *kiruv* work, *hachnasas orchim*, *askanus*, and love for his family. He left a noble legacy that we are honored to perpetuate.

Mendel Indig ז"ל
ר' מנחם דוד ב"ר מרדכי שמואל ז"ל

נפ' ט' אדר ב' תשס"ג

"It was as if a *maloch* protected us," he used to say about the dark years of Churban Europa. He lost almost everything — even the *tefillin* that he put on every day until the very end — but he kept his spirit, his *emunah*, his dedication to Torah, and his resolve to rebuild.

He became a living legend of Torah, *chesed*, and service to his Bensonhurst community. His home was open to anyone in need, and there was always enough room for guests. His *succah* was the largest in the neighborhood, and he always found a way to bring endangered relatives to America and help them become established.

After he retired, he devoted himself to learning and bringing others close to Yiddishkeit, especially immigrants from the former Soviet Union, teaching them to put on *tefillin* and reuniting them with the Judaism of their ancestors. It is our privilege to carry on his glorious legacy.

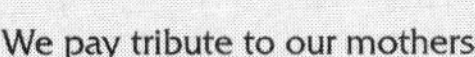

We pay tribute to our mothers

Ethel Kleinman תחי'

Rose Indig תחי'

To us and our children and grandchildren — and to all who know them — they are role models of *emunah*, *chesed*, love and wisdom.

Our mothers שיחיו and our fathers ז"ל planted seeds of Torah in America and produced magnificent *doros* of children, grandchildren, and great-grandchildren following their example. May Hashem continue to bless our mothers with good health and many nachas-filled years.

Elly and Brochie Kleinman and their children

Deenie and Yitzy Schuss   Yossie Kleinman   Aliza and Lavey Freedman

and families

PATRONS OF LIMUD YOMI / A DAILY DOSE OF TORAH

With dedication to the principle that Torah study should always be available,
the following generous and visionary patrons
have dedicated volumes of this series:

VOL. 1: BEREISHIS-VAYEIRA / בראשית-וירא

Elly and Brochie Kleinman and family

In memory of their fathers

ר׳ אברהם אייזיק ב״ר אלכסנדר ז״ל – Avrohom Kleinman ז״ל

ר׳ מנחם דוד ב״ר מרדכי שמואל ז״ל – Mendel Indig ז״ל

and יבלח״ט in tribute to their mothers שתחי׳ לאוי״ט

Ethel Kleinman

Rose Indig

VOL. 2: CHAYEI SARAH-VAYISHLACH / חיי שרה-וישלח

Motty and Malka Klein

for the merit of their children שיחיו

Esther and Chaim Baruch Fogel   Dovid and Chavie   Binyomin Zvi

Elana Leah and Natan Goldstein   Moshe Yosef   Yaakov Eliyahu

In honor of his mother שתחי׳

Mrs. Suri Klein לאוי״ט

In memory of his father

ר׳ יהודה ב״ר דוד הלוי ז״ל נפ׳ כ״ז אדר ב׳ תשס״ג – Yidel Klein

In memory of her parents

ר׳ אשר אנשיל ב״ר משה יוסף ז״ל נפ׳ ג׳ שבט תשנ״ט – Anchel Gross

שרה בת ר׳ חיים אליהו ע״ה נפ׳ כ״ד סיון תשס״א – Suri Gross

And in memory of their grandparents who perished על קידוש השם in the Holocaust

ר׳ דוד ב״ר יעקב הלוי ע״ה ופערל בת ר׳ צבי ע״ה הי״ד – Klein

ר׳ מרדכי ב״ר דוד הלוי ע״ה ולאה בת ר׳ יעקב הלוי ע״ה הי״ד – Klein

ר׳ משה יוסף ב״ר בנימין צבי ע״ה ומלכה בת ר׳ יחיאל מיכל ע״ה הי״ד – Gross

ר׳ חיים אליהו ב״ר מרדכי ע״ה ויוטא בת ר׳ שלמה אליעזר ע״ה הי״ד – Gartenberg

VOL. 3: VAYEISHEV-VAYECHI / וישב-ויחי

Leon and Agi Goldenberg

Mendy and Estie Blau – Efraim, Rivka, and Chava

Shiffie Grossman – Chanie, and Rikki

Abi and Shoshana Goldenberg – Yehudis

Tzvi and Leilie Fertig

and Yitzy Goldenberg

In memory of their fathers and uncle

ר׳ אברהם אבא ב״ר צבי ז״ל – Abba Goldenberg ז״ל

ר׳ יוסף אליעזר ב״ר יעקב יצחק ז״ל – Joseph Brieger ז״ל

ר׳ יעקב שלמה ב״ר משה הלוי ז״ל – Yaakov Shlomeh Lebovits ז״ל

and יבלח״ט in tribute to their mothers שתחי׳ לאוי״ט

Chaya (Sicherman) Goldenberg   Malka (Karfunkel) Brieger

and their aunt – Faiga (Sicherman) Lebovits

VOL. 4: SHEMOS-BESHALACH / שמות-בשלח
Yossi and Bella Essas (Los Angeles)
Noam Zvi Hillel Avraham Adina Batya Ashira Miriam
In honor of his parents
Rabbi Eliyahu and Anya Essas שליט״א

VOL. 5: YISRO-TETZAVEH / יתרו-תצוה
Edward J. and Rose F. Leventhal
in honor of their children,
Alison, Martin and Bonnie,
and in honor of their parents
Eddie and Irma Muller,
and Ruth Leventhal,
and in beloved memory of his father,
ברוך בן משה ז״ל – Bernard E. Leventhal ז״ל

VOL. 6: KI SISA-VAYIKRA / כי תשא-ויקרא
Drs. Mark and Barbara Bell (Shavertown, PA)
in honor of their children,
Ben, Mory and Adina Kayla,
and in honor of their parents
Drs. Isadore and Viola Evelyn Kreel שיחי׳
Rabbi Tzvi Alexander and Renah Bell שיחי׳
and grandparents
Rabbi Moses and Magda Mescheloff שיחי׳
and in memory of their grandparents
בן ציון בן אליה ז״ל ונחמה רבקה בת דוד ע״ה – Kreel
יוסף חיים ז״ל וטאניה ע״ה – Hornstein
הרב אליעזר בן הרב משה ז״ל וקיילא שרה בת אפרים ע״ה – Schonfeld
ראובן בן יחזקאל ז״ל ואיידל בת יעקב שמשון ע״ה – Bell

VOL. 7: TZAV-METZORA / צו-מצורע
Lawrence Uri and Barbara Skolnik (Toronto)
Brian Benjamin and Marni Skolnik
Allen and Mindy Smith
and families
in honor of their mother and grandmother
Mrs. Masha Skolnik שתחי׳
in memory of their parents and grandparents
יוסף בן משה ז״ל – Joe Skolnik ז״ל
ניסן בן מנחם מענדל ז״ל – Norman Chousky ז״ל
מאטל גיטל בת בנימן ליפא ע״ה – Mildred Chousky ע״ה
and in memory of their brother and uncle
ברוך ירחמיאל בן יוסף ז״ל – Prof. Barry Skolnik ז״ל

VOL. 8: ACHAREI-BECHUKOSAI / אחרי־בחקתי
in honor of
R' Zvi and Betty Ryzman (Los Angeles)

VOL. 9: BAMIDBAR-SHELACH / במדבר־שלח
Mark and Chani Scheiner
Dr. Jonathan and Vicki Scheiner
in memory of
שלמה טוביה בן יהושע מנחם הלוי ע״ה — Sol Scheiner
אליהו ב״ר חיים ע״ה — Elihu Brodsky
יונה בת ר׳ פינחס ע״ה — Vera (Greif) Brodsky

VOL. 10: KORACH-PINCHAS / קרח־פינחס
Jeffrey and Leslie Bernstein
for the merit of their children
Gideon and Hadassah
And in memory of all those who have perished *Al Kiddush Hashem* defending the Children of Israel and the Land of Israel,
with a special tribute to
Major Ro'i Klein הי״ד and
Lieutenant Colonel Emanuel Moreno הי״ד

VOL. 14: THE FESTIVALS / מועדי השנה
The Teichman Family (Los Angeles)
In memory of their parents and grandparents
שמואל ב״ר יששכר דוב ז״ל — Sam Teichman ז״ל
ליבה בריינדל בת ר׳ יהושע הלוי ע״ה — Lujza Teichman ע״ה
רחל בת ר׳ אלכסנר סנדר ע״ה — Rose Teichman ע״ה
יצחק אייזיק ב״ר אברהם חיים ז״ל — Isaac Nae ז״ל

DEDICATION OPPORTUNITIES

We are gratified by the
very enthusiastic response to this
new program for daily Torah study.
It is yet another demonstration
of the strong and growing desire
to make Torah part of every Jew's life,
seven days a week, fifty-two weeks a year.

Each volume of the

KLEINMAN EDITION

A DAILY DOSE OF TORAH

will carry individual dedications.
Many visionary families have already
undertaken to dedicate volumes
in memory or in honor of loved ones.
Additional dedication opportunities are available.

For further information, please call:
718-921-9000,
write to:

ArtScroll · Mesorah Publications, ltd

4401 Second Avenue · Brooklyn, NY 11232

or e-mail: DailyDose@artscroll.com

Publisher's Preface

King David said: גַּל עֵינַי וְאַבִּיטָה נִפְלָאוֹת מִתּוֹרָתֶךָ, *Unveil my eyes that I may perceive wonders from your Torah* (*Psalms* 119:18).

Shammai said: עֲשֵׂה תוֹרָתְךָ קֶבַע, *Make your Torah study a fixed practice* (*Avos* 1:15).

Rav Saadiah Gaon said: The Jewish people is a nation only by virtue of the Torah.

The Torah is the essence of the Jewish people, and not a day should go by without Torah study. How much learning should there be? Just as the Torah itself is infinite, there is no limit to the effort to master its contents. The task does not end when one bids farewell to the academy and enters the world of work and business. All over the world, study halls are filled before dawn and after dark with men plumbing the depths of the Talmud and other works. Before and after their workdays, they overcome fatigue with a relentless desire to absorb more and more of God's word.

To such people, **The Kleinman Edition: Limud Yomi / A Daily Dose of Torah** will be a welcome supplement, an enrichment that offers glimpses of additional topics and a means of filling the day's spare minutes with nourishment for the mind and spirit.

To those who as yet have not been able to savor the beauty of immersion in the sea of study, this new series will be a vehicle to enrich their every day with an assortment of stimulating Torah content.

We are gratified that the previous volumes of this new series have been phenomenally well received. Many people have told us how they are filling once-empty gaps in their day with these "daily doses," and how this work has stimulated them to do further research in these subjects. As King Solomon said, תֵּן לְחָכָם וְיֶחְכַּם־עוֹד הוֹדַע לְצַדִּיק וְיוֹסֶף לֶקַח, *Give the wise man and he will become wiser; make known to the righteous and he will add [to his] learning* (*Proverbs* 9:9).

Each "Daily Dose of Torah" includes selections from a broad spectrum of Torah sources (see below); in combination they provide a multi-dimensional study program. Each selection can stand on its own, or, ideally, serve as a vehicle for further research and enrichment. These components are as follows:

- ❑ ***A Torah Thought for the Day***, focusing on a verse in the weekly *parashah*. The discussion may revolve around various classic interpretations, or it may offer a selection of insights and lessons that are derived from the verse. This section will draw from a wide gamut of early and later commentators, and will enhance the reader's appreciation for the wealth of Torah interpretation and its lessons for life.
- ❑ ***The Mishnah of the Day,*** presenting a Mishnah selection every day, with text, translation, and concise commentary, adapted from the classic ArtScroll Mishnah Series and the Schottenstein Edition of the Talmud. This daily dose will begin with Tractate Shabbos, and continue through Seder Moed.
- ❑ ***Gems from the Gemara,*** presenting some of the Talmud's discussion of the daily Mishnah. Thus the reader will "join the academy" of the Talmud's question-and-answer clarification of the laws and underlying principles of the Mishnah.
- ❑ ***A Mussar Thought for the Day,*** building upon the theme of the *Torah Thought for the Day*, by presenting an ethical or moral lesson drawn from the masters of Mussar, Hashkafah, and Chassidus. This selection will stimulate thought and growth — and be a welcome source of uplifting ideas for times when the reader is called upon to speak at a *simchah*.
- ❑ ***The Halachah of the Day,*** presenting a practical, relevant halachic discussion, beginning with the thirty-nine forbidden categories of Shabbos labor. The selections are adapted from Rabbi Simcha Bunim Cohen's popular and authoritative works, which are part of the ArtScroll Series. [These brief discussions are not intended to be definitive. Questions should be directed to a qualified rav.]
- ❑ ***A Closer Look at the Siddur,*** broadening the reader's understanding of the rich tapestry of *tefillah*/prayer. The Shabbos Daily Dose will focus on the Shabbos prayers. And once a week, this section will discuss such universal themes as the Thirteen Principles of Faith or the Six Constant Commandments.

❑ ***A Taste of Lomdus,*** a special weekly feature that will present a brief but in-depth discussion of a Talmudic subject, in the tradition of the Torah giants whose reasoning and novellae are the basis of research and study in advanced yeshivas. Every day, there will be a challenging "Question of the Day," related to the theme of the day. The answers for the questions will come at the end of each week.

Each volume of the Daily Dose of Torah Series will present a capsule study program for twenty-eight days. The annual cycle will be comprised of thirteen four-week volumes, covering all fifty-two weeks of the year, and a fourteenth volume devoted to Rosh Hashanah, Yom Kippur, and the festivals. We are confident that the complete series will bring the excitement of Torah study to countless people, and that many of them will use it as a springboard to further learning, both independently and by joining *shiurim.*

The Kleinman Edition: Limud Yomi / A Daily Dose of Torah is dedicated by **ELLY AND BROCHIE KLEINMAN,** in memory of their fathers ז"ל and in honor of their mothers שׁיחיו. The Kleinmans have long distinguished themselves as generous and imaginative supporters of Torah and *chesed* causes. With warmth and kindness, they have opened their home countless times to help institutions and individuals. They have richly earned the respect and affection of all who know them, and we are honored to count them not only as major supporters of our work, but as personal friends. They and their family bring honor to the legacy of their parents.

This volume is dedicated to **R' ZVI RYZMAN** of Los Angeles, one of the truly remarkable people of our time. A native of Israel and an accomplished *talmid chacham* who has made his mark in the American and international world of commerce, Torah remains his first love. His brilliant scholarship earns the respect of *admorim,* roshei yeshivah, rabbis, and the multitudes who attend his Torah lectures and study the volumes of his *Ratz KaTzvi.* To anyone who claims that the pressures of business prevent him from learning, Reb Zvika is living refutation. A man of judicious vision and enormous generosity, he is involved in too many causes to enumerate, not only to help those who are needy and deserving, but with a view to what will be to the long-term benefit of Klal Yisrael. He and his wife, **BETTY**, are much admired fixtures of the Los Angeles community, and their family is living and eloquent testimony to their values and perspectives. We are proud that he is a personal friend and an important supporter of our work.

The editor of this new series is **RABBI YOSAIF ASHER WEISS**, Rosh Yeshivas Ohr Hadaas, Staten Island, who is also a distinguished editor of the Schottenstein Editions of the Talmud Bavli and Yerushalmi. Rabbi Weiss' reputation as a noted scholar and educator will be justly embellished by the Daily Dose Series.

We are grateful to **RABBI RAPHAEL BUTLER**, the dynamic and innovative founder and president of the Afikim Foundation, who conceived of this concept and had a significant role in its development. We are proud to enjoy his friendship.

We are grateful to the outstanding *talmidei chachamim* who are contributing to this series: **RABBI YOSEF GAVRIEL BECHHOFER, RABBI REUVEN BUTLER, RABBI ELIYAHU COHEN, RABBI ASHER DICKER, RABBI MAYER GOLDSTEIN, RABBI MOSHE YEHUDA GLUCK, RABBI BERYL SCHIFF, RABBI MORDECHAI SONNENSCHEIN, RABBI MOSHE UNGAR, AND RABBI YISROEL DOV WEISS.** The quality of their scholarship shines through every page. We thank **RABBI SIMCHA SHAFRAN** for allowing us to use his *sefer Maadanei Simchah* as a source for some of the Questions of the Day.

The beauty and clarity of the book's design is yet another tribute to the graphics genius of our friend and colleague **REB SHEAH BRANDER**. As someone once said in a different context, "I can't put it into words, but I know it when I see it." It is hard to define good taste and graphics beauty in words, but when one sees Reb Sheah's work, one knows it.

ELI KROEN, a master of graphics in his own right, designed the cover with his typical creativity and good taste. **MOSHE DEUTSCH** had an important hand in the typesetting and general design. **MRS. CHUMIE LIPSCHITZ**, a key member of our staff, paginated the book. **TOBY GOLDZWEIG, SURY REINHOLD, AND SARA RIFKA SPIRA** typed and corrected the manuscript. **MRS. ESTHER FEIERSTEIN** proofread the final copy.

MRS. MINDY STERN proofread and made many important suggestions. **AVROHOM BIDERMAN** was involved in virtually every aspect of the work from its inception, and **MENDY HERZBERG** assisted in shepherding the project to completion.

As this new series continues to take shape, we express our great appreciation to our long-time friend and colleague **SHMUEL BLITZ**, head of

ArtScroll Jerusalem. His dedication and judgment have been indispensable components of virtually every ArtScroll/Mesorah project.

We are grateful to them all. The contributions of ArtScroll/Mesorah to the cause of Jewish life and Torah study are possible because of the skill and dedication of the above staff members and their colleagues.

It is an enormous privilege to have been instrumental in bringing Torah knowledge to the people of Torah. There are no words to express our gratitude to Hashem Yisbarach for permitting us to disseminate His Word to His children.

Rabbi Meir Zlotowitz / Rabbi Nosson Scherman

Nissan 5767 / April 2007

פרשת אחרי

Parashas Acharei

פרשת אחרי

SUNDAY

PARASHAS ACHAREI

A TORAH THOUGHT FOR THE DAY

וַיְדַבֵּר ה׳ אֶל־מֹשֶׁה אַחֲרֵי מוֹת שְׁנֵי בְּנֵי אַהֲרֹן בְּקָרְבָתָם לִפְנֵי־ה׳ וַיָּמֻתוּ . . . בְּזֹאת יָבֹא אַהֲרֹן אֶל־הַקֹּדֶשׁ

HASHEM spoke to Moshe after the death of Aharon's two sons, when they approached before HASHEM, and they died . . . With this shall Aharon come into the Sanctuary (*Vayikra* 16:1,3).

The question may be asked: Why does the Torah juxtapose the death of the sons of Aharon with the description of the service of Yom Kippur? The *Yerushalmi* (*Yoma* 1:1) learns from this that just as Yom Kippur atones for sins, so does the death of the righteous. *R' Meir Simchah of Dvinsk* (in his *Meshech Chochmah*) notes, however, that one must keep in mind that the atonement afforded by the death of the righteous is subject to the same rules as the atonement of Yom Kippur. Just as one who does not recognize the holiness of Yom Kippur does not benefit from the atonement it affords, so too, one who did not appreciate the righteous person, and does not feel a loss at his passing, is not granted atonement as a result of that death.

R' Yitzchak Elchanan Spector, Rav of Kovno, points out another parallel between the atonement of Yom Kippur and that of the death of the righteous, citing an incident related in the Gemara (*Kesubos* 103b). On the day of the death of Rebbi (R' Yehudah HaNasi), a Heavenly voice proclaimed: "Whoever was present at the death of Rebbi is made ready for the World to Come" (i.e., he will face no preparatory judgment or punishment prior to receiving his portion in the World to Come) (*Tosafos*). Why was Rebbi singled out in that only the participants in *his* funeral merited so great a reward?

R' Spector explains that with regard to the atonement of Yom Kippur, it is the view of Rebbi that one can be granted atonement even without repentance (*Yoma* 85b). The *Chachamim* (Sages) disagree, and hold that the atonement of Yom Kippur is provided only when one repents. Since the atonement effected by the death of the righteous is parallel to that of Yom Kippur, it follows that the same two views prevail there as well. According to Rebbi, one would receive atonement by merely participating in the funeral of the departed *tzaddik* even without repentance, while the *Chachamim* hold that only when the *tzaddik's* death was the cause of introspection and repentance would one be granted atonement in its wake.

Just as with regard to Yom Kippur the final ruling follows the opinion of the *Chachamim* that one does not receive atonement without repentance, so too does this ruling apply with regard to the death of the righteous. One must therefore repent at the death of a *tzaddik* in order to benefit from the special atonement of that time. However, while this is the case regarding the deaths of all righteous people, an exception was made in the case of Rebbi himself. At this occasion, it was decreed in Heaven that the ruling should follow his view. Thus, everyone attending the funeral, even if they did not make a special effort to repent, were guaranteed — if they would but guard themselves from future sin — direct entry into their portion in the World to Come.

MISHNAH OF THE DAY: ERUVIN 6:10

The Mishnah continues to discuss the case of two courtyards that are one within the other. It now deals with cases where both courtyards had *eruvin,* but not necessarily valid ones:[1]

שָׁכַח אֶחָד מִן הַחִיצוֹנָה וְלֹא עֵירַב — If ***one*** resident ***of the outer [chatzeir] forgot and did not join in the eruv*** of his *chatzeir,* **הַפְּנִימִית מוּתֶּרֶת** — ***the inner one is permitted*** **וְהַחִיצוֹנָה אֲסוּרָה** — ***and the outer one is restricted.***[2] **מִן הַפְּנִימִית וְלֹא עֵירַב** — If one person ***from the inner [chatzeir]*** forgot ***and did not join in the eruv,*** **שְׁתֵּיהֶן אֲסוּרוֹת** — ***both of them are restricted.***[3]

Until now, the Mishnah has discussed cases in which each courtyard had its own *eruv.* The Mishnah now discusses cases where the two courtyards had joined together in one common *eruv*:[4]

NOTES

1. The rulings in this section of the Mishnah where some, but not all, of the residents joined in an *eruv* are identical to the rulings in the previous Mishnah, where no *eruv* at all was made in one of the *chatzeiros* (see *R' Yehonasan*).

2. The negligent resident of the outer *chatzeir* restricts his colleagues, but cannot restrict the members of the inner *chatzeir,* who are separated from them by a partition.

3. The inner *chatzeir* is restricted because of the failure of one of its members to participate in the *eruv.* As a consequence, they restrict the outer one because of their right of passage (*Rashi*). This is in accord with the opinion of the Tanna Kamma in the previous Mishnah — that the right of passage of a person who is restricted in his own *chatzeir* restricts the outer one.

4. In order to carry from one *chatzeir* to another, they joined together in a common *eruv,* to merge their *chatzeiros* into a single incorporated entity. The food that is collected for this common *eruv* is placed in a house in one of the *chatzeiros,* so that all the residents of both *chatzeiros* are considered residents of that same house.

נָתְנוּ עֵירוּבָן בְּמָקוֹם אֶחָד — If ***they placed their*** joint *eruv* ***in one place,*** i.e., in the outer *chatzeir,* **וְשָׁכַח אֶחָד בֵּין מִן הַפְּנִימִית בֵּין מִן הַחִיצוֹנָה** — ***and one*** resident ***of either the inner [chatzeir] or outer one forgot*** **וְלֹא עֵירַב** — ***and did not join in the eruv,*** **שְׁתֵּיהֶן אֲסוּרוֹת** — ***both of [the chatzeiros] are restricted.***[5]

The Mishnah concludes with a case of two courtyards, one within the other, where a joint *eruv* is not even required: **וְאִם הָיוּ שֶׁל יְחִידִים** — ***If [the two chatzeiros] were*** inhabited ***by individuals,***[6] **אֵינָן צְרִיכִין לְעָרֵב** — ***they need not join in an eruv.***[7]

NOTES

5. The *chatzeir* in which the negligent resident dwelled is certainly restricted. The Mishnah teaches that even the residents of the adjoining *chatzeir* are restricted, as follows: The inner *chatzeir* is restricted even if a member of the outer *chatzeir* forgot to join in the *eruv,* because the inner *chatzeir* cannot dissociate itself from the outer one and dissolve their joint *eruv* merger, because its *eruv* bread was placed in the outer *chatzeir.* And the outer *chatzeir* would be restricted if one of the members of the inner *chatzeir* forgot to join the *eruv,* because of the right of passage through this *chatzeir,* which is itself restricted (*Rashi*).

See *Gems from the Gemara* for why this is true only in a case where the *eruv* was placed in the outer *chatzeir.*

6. Each *chatzeir* contained only one inhabited house.

7. Since the inner *chatzeir* is permitted, its right of passage does not restrict the outer *chatzeir* according to the Rabbis who disagree with R' Akiva. If either of the *chatzeiros* contained two residents, however, the outer *chatzeir* would be restricted. [If the inner *chatzeir* contained two residents it would be restricted, and consequently would restrict the outer one because of its right of passage.] Even if the outer *chatzeir* contained two residents and the inner *chatzeir* only one [who should not restrict the outer *chatzeir*], we ban the outer *chatzeir* in order not to come to permit a case when the inner *chatzeir* has two residents and the outer one has one (*Rashi*).

GEMS FROM THE GEMARA

The Mishnah taught that if they placed their joint *eruv* in one place, and one resident of either *chatzeir* forgot and did not join in the *eruv,* both of them are restricted. The Gemara explains that the Mishnah refers specifically to a case in which the joint *eruv* was placed in the *outer chatzeir.* [The Mishnah refers to the outer *chatzeir* as "one place" because it is the one place that is designated for the residents of both *chatzeiros* (as even the residents of the inner *chatzeir* have a right of passage through it).] Only in that case would each *chatzeir* be restricted in the event that a member of the *other chatzeir* forgot to join in its own *eruv* (see above, note

5). If, however, the joint *eruv* was placed in the inner *chatzeir,* the inner *chatzeir* would not necessarily be prohibited if a member of the outer *chatzeir* forgot to contribute to the *eruv,* as the Gemara proceeds to explain.

As taught in a Baraisa, where the two *chatzeiros* placed their joint *eruv* in the inner *chatzeir,* if one member of the inner *chatzeir* forgot and did not join in the *eruv,* indeed both *chatzeiros* would be restricted. The inner *chatzeir* is certainly restricted because one of its residents did not join in the *eruv.* Since the outer *chatzeir* cannot unilaterally terminate the inner *chatzeir's* right of passage, it too is restricted. In addition, even if the outer *chatzeir* could dissociate itself from the inner *chatzeir,* it would still be restricted, because the *eruv* is not available to it, having been placed in the inner *chatzeir* (*Rashi*).

But if a member of the outer *chatzeir* forgot and did not join in the *eruv,* the outer *chatzeir* is certainly restricted, because one of its residents did not join in the *eruv.* Concerning the inner *chatzeir,* the Baraisa cites a Tannaic dispute. R' Akiva holds that the inner *chatzeir* is also restricted; the inner *chatzeir* may not dissociate itself from the outer one, because the *eruv* that is placed in the inner *chatzeir* accustoms the members of the outer *chatzeir* to use the inner one. However, the Sages say that in this case, the inner *chatzeir* is permitted; the inner *chatzeir* does not become restricted because of the forgetfulness of a resident of the outer *chatzeir,* since those in the inner *chatzeir* can figuratively "close its door," i.e., bar passage, and dissociate itself from the outer *chatzeir* (*Rashi*).

[This figurative "closing the door" is not possible in any other case. If the *eruv* was placed in the outer *chatzeir,* the inner *chatzeir* cannot "close its door," because it must remain associated with the outer *chatzeir* where its *eruv* is located. If the *eruv* was placed in the inner *chatzeir* and one of its residents had forgotten to join in the *eruv,* the inner *chatzeir* would be restricted even if it could close its door. Only if the *eruv* was placed in the inner *chatzeir* and one of the residents of the outer *chatzeir* had forgotten to join in the *eruv* is it possible for the inner *chatzeir* to close its door and be used.]

The Gemara further explains that the Sages allow the inner *chatzeir* to dissociate itself, even though the *eruv* accustomed the outer *chatzeir* to use the inner one, because [a resident of] the inner *chatzeir* can say to [a resident of] the outer *chatzeir,* "I merged with you to improve my situation, and not to detract from it." Therefore, since in this case the *eruv* would cause the inner *chatzeir* to be restricted, the Sages permit it to dissociate itself from the outer *chatzeir* and dissolve the *eruv.*

And R' Akiva, who does not let the inner *chatzeir* say, "I merged with you to improve my situation, and not to detract from it," maintains that

the outer *chatzeir* can say to the inner one, "We, the residents of the outer *chatzeir,* relinquish back to you the rights that we gained in your inner *chatzeir* through the *eruv.*" In this manner the inner *chatzeir* would again become solely the province of its own residents, and would no longer be restricted by the residents of the outer *chatzeir.* Since it is possible to restore the inner *chatzeir's* rights in this manner, they cannot simply annul the *eruv.* [According to this, R' Akiva's ruling that the inner *chatzeir* is restricted applies only until the outer *chatzeir* relinquishes the rights it acquired from the *eruv* back to the inner *chatzeir* (*Rashi*).]

A MUSSAR THOUGHT FOR THE DAY

Rashi explains that the verse at the beginning of our *parashah* mentions the death of Nadav and Avihu to underscore to Aharon the severity of improper entry into the Sanctuary. R' Elazar ben Azaryah compared this to a sick person who had to be cautioned not to eat cold food or sleep in a damp place. One doctor merely gave him the instructions, while the second doctor told him, "Unless you avoid these things you will die, as did So-and-so." The second warning is clearly much more effective than the first.

R' Yehudah Leib Chasman, in his *Ohr Yahel,* learns an important lesson from this. We are speaking here of Aharon HaKohen, the brother of Moshe and a great prophet in his own right. Was it really necessary to use such vivid imagery to enforce Hashem's warning? Would he not have listened to Hashem's instructions even unaccompanied by the example of the death of his sons? Consider, in the above comparison, if it were a doctor who fell ill. Would he also need to be given a strong version of the warning for it to be heeded?

We learn from here that the pull of the physical side of man must never be underestimated. No matter what level a person reaches in his life, he must realize that he is still attached to the body, to that which desires only physical pleasures and seeks to hide from truth and live in fantasy and indulgence. And it can always be the cause of one's fall.

It is true that *avodas Hashem* based on fear of punishment is only the very first step in the service of Hashem. After this level, a person should progress to serving Hashem from an appreciation of His greatness and power. From there a person can reach the highest level of service and be motivated by pure love of Hashem. However, even after he has

reached these heights, he must never forget the original fear of punishment with which he started, for a person is made up of a combination of the angelic and the animal, and the animal portion of man understands nothing but the stick and the rod. Thus, even one on as high a level as Aharon should not disregard the warnings that are directed at the body: If you disobey, you will die as did your sons.

This method of exhorting a person to stay on the proper path — using such bold imagery — is called *mussar.* The word *mussar* is cognate to the word *yissurim* (afflictions). Its job is to teach a person that this life is not the goal, and that there is a world that is more important than this one. And it cautions a person not to do that which will cause him harm. If even Aharon HaKohen had to be warned in such a stark manner through the use of such *mussar,* we must recognize *our* great need for it and never think that we are above it.

HALACHAH OF THE DAY

Continuing our discussion of creating temporary roofs on Shabbos, we will now turn to a discussion of cases where creating a temporary roof is permissible.

The prohibition against creating a temporary roof applies only when the supports of the roof are erected prior to the creation of the roof itself. If, however, the roof is put in place before the walls that will be used to support it, the roof may be erected without violating the prohibition. This leniency applies both to cases where erecting the roof is prohibited only in concert with the erection of walls (as is true of a roof not used for the benefit of people or animals), as well as cases where erecting a roof is prohibited even without the presence of walls (as in the case of a roof intended for the benefit of people or animals).

Thus, if one person were to hold the roof in the air while another placed walls or supports beneath it, they would not violate the prohibition of creating a temporary *ohel,* since the roof was assembled in reverse order.

To illustrate this point: We have said that it is generally prohibited to spread a mosquito net over a baby carriage, since this creates a protective roof over the baby. However, if one person holds up the net while another wheels the carriage under the net, there is no violation of the *melachah,* since the roof was erected before its supports.

The Rabbinic prohibition against creating a temporary roof is limited

to the creation of a *new* roof. The Sages did not prohibit the extending of a pre-existing roof. To illustrate: If one has a tarpaulin that is rolled open in order to cover an area (or closed in order to expose an area), as long as an area of a *tefach* was covered prior to the onset of Shabbos, the tarpaulin may be unrolled completely closed on Shabbos. Since a *tefach* was already covered prior to Shabbos, unrolling the tarpaulin is seen as extending a pre-existing roof — an act not prohibited by the Sages.

It is important to emphasize that a roof is considered to be halachically viable only if it measures at least a *tefach.* Any covering smaller than this minimal measurement is not considered a roof; therefore, extending it would be prohibited.

A common application of these laws presents itself on the Yom Tov of Succos. Many people use tarpaulins to protect their *succah* from the elements when it is not being used. In order for it to be permissible to unroll a tarpaulin over the *succah* on Shabbos, one must make sure that at least one *tefach* of the tarpaulin was unrolled before Shabbos. If this was done, he may unroll the tarpaulin to cover the *succah* completely on Shabbos.

This applies to cases where the tarpaulin does not rest directly on the *s'chach,* and there is a *tefach* of empty space between the underside of the tarpaulin and the *s'chach.* If, however, the tarpaulin does rest directly on the *s'chach,* it is not necessary to have a *tefach* covered before Shabbos. Since, as we have explained, there must be a *tefach* of space underneath a roof in order for it to be considered a halachic "roof," spreading out the tarp over the *s'chach* does not create a roof, and is thus not prohibited. [Note that where the covering is wound onto a roll and the roll itself is a *tefach* wide, the roll cannot be counted as the minimum 1 *tefach* that must be covered before Shabbos. This is because the roll itself is not seen as a valid roof. Rather, the permit applies only where a *tefach* of the covering was spread out before Shabbos.]

We will continue this discussion tomorrow.

A CLOSER LOOK AT THE SIDDUR

The Yom Kippur service, as the beginning of our *parashah* makes clear, is of paramount importance and is central to the goal of achieving the atonement of Yom Kippur. Ever since the destruction of the Temple, the Jewish people have accessed the atonement of Yom Kippur through the recitation of the service of the day in their prayers.

This follows the well-known rule that in the absence of the ability to actually carry out the service, our learning about the service and our speaking of it is accepted by Hashem in its stead (see *Rashi* to *Yoma* 36b).

Over the years this recitation has taken many forms. In an earlier time, there were those who recited the Mishnayos of *Maseches Yoma,* which describes the service of Yom Kippur from beginning to end (*Shibbolei HaLeket* §320). In general, however, *piyutim* were composed to be recited as part of the *Mussaf* prayer, the prayer that corresponds to the special services of the day.

Although many versions of such *piyutim* were composed at different times of our history, today there are two that are recited by most congregations. They are אַמִּיץ כֹּחַ (*O Vigorously Strong One*), composed by R' Meshullam ben Klonimos and recited by *Nusach Ashkenaz;* and אַתָּה כּוֹנַנְתָּ (*You have established*), composed by Yose ben Yose Kohen Gadol (High Priest), which was accepted by *Nusach Sefard.* The latter is an extremely early composition. According to *Abudraham,* Yose ben Yose may have actually served in the Second Temple, or he may have been a descendant of one who served there. According to others, he was simply referred to as "Kohen Gadol" due to his greatness and the fact that he was of Priestly descent (see also *Responsa* of *Noda BiYehudah, Orach Chaim* §113).

While the language of the אַתָּה כּוֹנַנְתָּ *piyut* is simpler and clearer, there are few substantive differences between it and the אַמִּיץ כֹּחַ *piyut.* One difference pertains to the process of the פְּיָיסוֹת, *lots,* which determined which Kohanim were to do the various daily services. In אַמִּיץ כֹּחַ the composer adds the following line: עָלְצוּ תְּרוֹם דֶּשֶׁן בְּפַיִס רִאשׁוֹן, *Joyously [the Kohanim] drew the first lot for the privilege of removing the ash.* However, according to most commentaries, no lots were performed on Yom Kippur, since all the services of the day were performed by the Kohen Gadol. Indeed, in אַתָּה כּוֹנַנְתָּ this reference does not appear.

Matteh Ephraim writes that it is proper for one to take time before Yom Kippur to study the *piyut* describing the *avodah,* in order to understand what he is going to be saying on Yom Kippur. This *piyut* should be recited with a sense of sorrow for the glory that once was, for which we must now substitute our words, accompanied by the hope that we will soon merit the rebuilding of the *Beis HaMikdash.*

QUESTION OF THE DAY:

In what "cloud" does Hashem appear?

For the answer, see page 59.

פרשת אחרי

MONDAY

PARASHAS ACHAREI

A TORAH THOUGHT FOR THE DAY

וְהִתְוַדָּה עָלָיו אֶת־כָּל עֲוֹנֹת בְּנֵי יִשְׂרָאֵל
וְאֶת כָּל־פִּשְׁעֵיהֶם לְכָל־חַטֹּאתָם

And he shall confess upon it all the iniquities of the Children of Israel, and all their rebellious sins, among all their [unintentional] sins (*Vayikra* 16:21).

From the simple reading of the verse, it would seem that in the actual confession of the Kohen Gadol, the iniquities are mentioned first, followed by the rebellious sins, followed by the unintentional sins. This indeed is the opinion of R' Meir, in *Yoma* 36b; the *Chachamim* (Sages), however, disagree with him. Since unintentional sins are less severe than the others, it is illogical to first confess the egregious sins and afterward to add the lesser ones. Therefore, they hold that the actual order of the confession was first for the unintentional sins, and only then for the iniquities (intentional sins), followed by the most severe rebellious sins.

Although the *Chachamim* explain their position according to logic, the question of the order of the types of sins in the verse remains. Why, if the Kohen Gadol mentions the unintentional sins first, are they written last in the verse? *Maharsha* answers this question by calling attention to the exact wording of the end of the verse. The verse does not state: עֲוֹנֹת בְּנֵי יִשְׂרָאֵל וְאֶת־כָּל פִּשְׁעֵיהֶם **וְאֶת כָּל** חַטֹּאתָם, which would translate as: *the iniquities of the Children of Israel, and all their rebellious sins, and all their [unintentional] sins.* If the verse had been written this way, it would surely be implying the order of the confession. However, the actual words used by the Torah are **לְכָל**־חַטֹּאתָם, which mean *among,* or *in addition to* their unintentional sins. Thus, the verse is actually implying that the unintentional sins had already been mentioned by the time the other classes of sins are confessed.

Our question about the *Chachamim's* reading of the verse is thus resolved. However, with this answer another question is brought into sharper focus: Why is the verse written in such a manner? Would it not have been more forthright to simply write the sins in the order that the Kohen Gadol is to recite them: אֶת־כָּל חַטֹּאתָם וְאֶת־כָּל עֲוֹנֹתָם וְאֶת־כָּל פִּשְׁעֵיהֶם, *all their [unintentional] sins, and all their iniquities, and all their rebellious sins*? Why first introduce the other sins, and then, at the end of the verse, inform us that the unintentional sins had to have already been mentioned?

Shaarei Aharon explains that the Torah is teaching us here an important lesson regarding unintentional sins. *Alshich* writes that one who is

totally free of sin will not be allowed by Heaven to sin unintentionally. It is only one who has already sinned, whether in deed or in thought, who is allowed to sin in an unintentional fashion. Thus, he explains, the order in our verse alludes to the order in which the sins were *committed.* If one is guilty of unintentional sin, it must be that he has already committed intentional sins. Only after one has sinned intentionally is he in danger of stumbling by committing unintentional sins.

MISHNAH OF THE DAY: ERUVIN 7:1

The previous chapter dealt with cases where several *chatzeiros* joined together in one communal *eruv.* The first five Mishnayos of this chapter now delineate the following three possible situations:

(a) When two *chatzeiros* cannot join in one *eruv,* but must each make their own *eruv*: Where the two *chatzeiros* are totally separated from one another by means of a partition, the residents of one *chatzeir* may not make a joint *eruv* with the residents of the other *chatzeir* for the purpose of passing objects back and forth over the partition.

(b) When they cannot make independent *eruvin,* but *must* join in *one eruv*: Where the two *chatzeiros* adjoin each other, and are not adequately separated, they are considered one *chatzeir,* and the residents of both *chatzeiros* must share one communal *eruv* before they may carry from their homes even into their respective areas. There is no option for each *chatzeir* to make its own *eruv.*

(c) When they are afforded the choice of an independent or joint *eruv*: There are instances when a partition is judged sufficient to separate two *chatzeiros,* yet it does not preclude the making of a common *eruv* by the two *chatzeiros.*

Our Mishnah discusses this last situation, the case of two *chatzeiros* that are separated by a wall at least 10 *tefachim* high;[1] however, the wall has a window, through which objects might be passed. The Mishnah discusses the conditions under which these two *chatzeiros* may be joined together by a communal *eruv*:

חַלּוֹן שֶׁבֵּין שְׁתֵּי חֲצֵירוֹת — In a case of ***a window***[2] ***between two***

NOTES

1. The minimum height for a partition is 10 *tefachim.* If the wall is of lesser height, the two *chatzeiros* are considered one unit and a mutual *eruv* is required (Gemara 79a).

2. The window discussed in our Mishnah is an opening in the wall permitting transfer between the two *chatzeiros.* [There is no windowpane (of glass) to seal the window.]

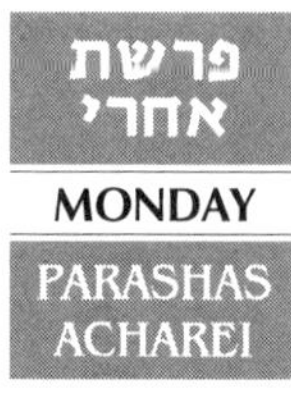

chatzeiros אַרְבָּעָה עַל אַרְבָּעָה — that is at least ***four*** *tefachim* ***by four*** *tefachim* in size בְּתוֹךְ עֲשָׂרָה — and located ***within ten*** *tefachim* of the ground,[3] מְעָרְבִין שְׁנַיִם — ***they*** [the residents of the two *chatzeiros*] ***may join in two*** independent ***eruvin,*** because the *chatzeiros* are still considered separate areas,[4] וְאִם רָצוּ מְעָרְבִין אֶחָד — ***or if they desire they may join in one*** communal ***eruv,*** because the window connects them.[5]

פָּחוֹת מֵאַרְבָּעָה עַל אַרְבָּעָה — However, if the window is ***less than four by four*** *tefachim* in size, אוֹ לְמַעְלָה מֵעֲשָׂרָה — ***or*** is entirely ***above ten*** *tefachim* from the ground, מְעָרְבִין שְׁנַיִם — ***they must join in two*** independent ***eruvin*** וְאֵין מְעָרְבִין אֶחָד — ***but may not join in one*** common ***eruv,*** because in this case the *chatzeiros* are considered two completely separated areas.[6]

NOTES

3. The window begins at a point in the wall that is within 10 *tefachim* of the ground. It is sufficient for even a minute portion of the window opening to be within these 10 *tefachim.*

4. Since most of the wall is intact, it constitutes a valid partition between the two *chatzeiros,* even though it does not reach 10 *tefachim* at the place of the window. This small breach is considered a portal (פֶּתַח), which is a feature common to walls.

Each *chatzeir* may then make its own *eruv* and need not participate with the other *chatzeir.* In this case, they may carry only from their houses into their *chatzeir,* but not from one *chatzeir* to the other (*Rashi*).

5. Since the height of the wall to the window is less than the 10-*tefach* minimum height of a partition, and since the window's size qualifies it as a portal, the two *chatzeiros* are considered connected, and so may join in a mutual *eruv.* The *eruv* permits transfer of objects between the *chatzeiros,* either through the window, over the wall, or through cracks or holes in the wall (*Rashi*).

6. Either of two factors disqualify a window from attaining the status of a פֶּתַח, *portal,* that serves to connect two *chatzeiros*: (1) if it lacks the requisite size of a portal (4 *tefachim* by 4 *tefachim*), or (2) it is not located anywhere in the area of the essential, 10-*tefachim* high wall. In either case, the remaining wall is a solid, if minimal, partition that completely divides the two *chatzeiros* (*Rashi*).

GEMS FROM THE GEMARA

Our Mishnah ruled that a window between two *chatzeiros* must measure at least 4 *tefachim* by 4 *tefachim,* and be partially within 10 *tefachim* of the ground, in order to permit the *chatzeiros* to join in a communal *eruv.* Rav Nachman explained that this latter ruling is limited to a window that is between two *chatzeiros.* But if a window is between

two houses, even if it is completely above 10 *tefachim,* the occupants of the two homes may join in one mutual *eruv,* and objects may then be transferred between the two houses. The Gemara explained that this is because a house is regarded as being "full of objects." Hence, the window is considered as though it were not higher than 10 *tefachim* from the floor.

The Gemara seeks to understand Rav Nachman's principle, and wonders in which sense a house is regarded as being "full." The concept has two possible interpretations. It can mean that a house or other enclosed structure is ordinarily filled with furniture or other objects. As applied to our case, this interpretation suggests that these objects can serve as platforms that make a high window more accessible and convenient to use. Alternatively, the concept may mean that since the air inside a house is filled with vapor, the interior airspace is as though it were a solid mass, and therefore non-existent. Hence, it is halachically impossible to measure height within the structure, and so a window can never be regarded as exceeding the height limitation of 10 *tefachim.*

Now, in the case of a window in a wall, a house is considered "full" according to either interpretation. The Gemara gives another case in which there is a practical difference between these interpretations. Does an overhead window that opens from a house to an attic require a permanent ladder to serve as a portal in order to permit the joining in a common *eruv* by the owners of the house and attic? Or does it not require a permanent ladder to permit them to join in an *eruv*? [As explained in our Mishnah, two areas may join in a common *eruv* as long as the areas are not totally separated. Rav explains (on 59b) that a ladder 4 *tefachim* wide can serve as a portal between two areas even when no other opening exists between them, thereby making feasible a common *eruv.* However, only one of the two interpretations is appropriate if an overhead window is to be judged a valid portal, as we will explain.]

For if, as in the first interpretation, a house is regarded as being "full" in that a window in a wall above 10 *tefachim* is accessible and convenient to use, this is true only in reference to a window in the wall of the house [since benches and crates are ordinarily placed along the walls of the house, and one can stand upon them to reach the window (*R' Yehonasan*)]. But an overhead window, which is not readily accessible or convenient to use [since furniture is not customarily placed in the middle of a room], might not be able to serve as a connecting portal between the attic and the house. And so, an overhead window that opens from a house to an attic would require a permanent ladder to serve as a portal.

But if, as in the second interpretation, airspace inside a house is "filled" with vapor as though it were a solid mass, it is halachically impossible to measure height within the structure. If so, it makes no difference where the window is located, since in any event the interior airspace of an enclosed structure is regarded as non-existent. And so, even an overhead window is a valid portal, and a permanent ladder is unnecessary.

The Gemara concludes that a ladder is not required (apparently following the second interpretation).

A MUSSAR THOUGHT FOR THE DAY

In a talk given before Yom Kippur, *R' Shimshon Pincus* used the mitzvah of *viduy,* confession, to bring out the importance of serving Hashem from within the framework of a relationship with Him.

One may have thought that the confession, which is an integral part of repentance, could be recited independently of the prayers of Yom Kippur. In practice, however, the confession is recited only as part of the *Shemoneh Esrei,* or as part of the *Selichos* prayers. This is due to the fact that the essence of *viduy* is not merely a listing of our sins. Let us explain: The word *viduy,* besides meaning *confession,* is also used to describe words spoken to Hashem that tell of the fulfillment of His commandments by the one speaking (see *Devarim* 26:13). *Viduy* is a term that can describe any words spoken before Hashem that have the effect of bringing the person closer to Him. Our *viduy* — confession of our sins — is in essence a turning to Hashem, with the words, "Master of the World! There exists a barrier between us in the form of my sins. Please grant that I can return and once again become close to You." [Indeed, the root of the word *teshuvah,* repentance, means *to return.*]

As an introduction to the confession prayer, we say: אֵין אָנוּ עַזֵּי פָנִים וּקְשֵׁי עֹרֶף לוֹמַר לְפָנֶיךָ . . . צַדִּיקִים אֲנַחְנוּ וְלֹא חָטָאנוּ, *We are not so brazen and obstinate as to say before You that we are righteous and have not sinned.* The question may be asked: Why is it necessary for us to begin by stating what we are *not* about to say? Furthermore, why would anyone think that we are about to claim innocence? For what purpose have we come to pray, if not to confess our sins?

According to what we have explained, however, the prayer becomes clear, for *viduy* need not be only for confession of sins. Here, we are comparing the *viduy* that could have been with the *viduy* that now has to be. In essence we are saying: Hashem, if only we could come before You to speak a *viduy* containing words of closeness, borne of complete fulfillment of Your laws. Alas, we have sinned and that is impossible, but we are not so brazen as to deny our faults. We now have to speak different words, and rebuild this closeness through confession of our misdeeds and a declaration of our intention to repair what we have damaged.

Thus, the confession must always be a part of prayer. When a person stands in prayer, he is at the point of his closest connection with Hashem. It is this time that must be used for the *viduy,* the words of closeness and connection to Hashem.

There are many people whose service of Hashem, although encompassing their entire life, is only one-sided. A person can know that Hashem exists, and expend much effort to live according to His "rules," but this does not mean that there is a relationship between that person and Hashem. A person can share a room with someone, and take care not to engage in any activity that would bother that person, without there being any real connection between the two.

The most basic aspect of true *avodas Hashem* is that there exist a bond and relationship between the person and Hashem. This is the lesson that we must seek to learn from the *viduy.*

HALACHAH OF THE DAY

We spoke yesterday of the permissibility of extending a roof on Shabbos. While it is permissible to extend a pre-existing roof on Shabbos, one may add to an existing roof only in a manner that actually extends the existing roof. Thus, while it is permissible for one to extend the roof indefinitely from the point where it ends and cover as much additional area as he desires, he may not begin spreading out a tarpaulin from the opposite side of the structure that was not covered before Shabbos.

The Rabbinic prohibition against creating a temporary *ohel* does not apply to opening a folding canopy that was assembled before Shabbos. Since the Rabbinic decree forbids only the assembly of a roof, this canopy, which was already assembled prior to Shabbos, is not included in the decree.

According to many *poskim,* the above holds true even when the folding canopy will be used to benefit people. Thus, one is permitted to

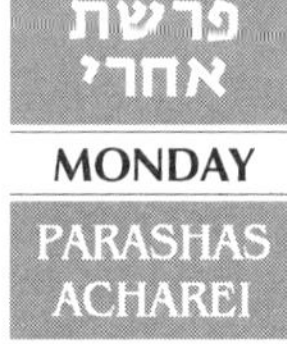

unfold the hood of a baby carriage on Shabbos in order to protect the child from the sun or rain, provided that it was attached to the carriage before Shabbos. [There are other *poskim* who rule that if the canopy protects a person, it may not be unfolded on Shabbos.]

The prohibition against construction of a temporary *ohel* applies only when the covering is independently supported through the use of poles, walls, or other support structures. An *ohel* that has no support other than a person holding it in place is therefore not prohibited. Thus, one is permitted to protect himself from the rain by holding his coat a *tefach* above his head.

As we stated earlier, the two parts of a temporary *ohel* — the roof and the walls — are viewed from the standpoint of halachah as being two different entities.

We have completed our discussion of the guidelines governing the creation of a temporary roof. We will now discuss the laws of creating a temporary wall. In most cases, it is permissible to erect a temporary wall (one intended to stand for only a few days) on Shabbos. Since walls are not seen as being the primary part of an *ohel,* the Sages did not extend their prohibition to them.

For example, it is permissible to divide a room using free-standing folding or portable partitions in order to create a *mechitzah* separating men and women during davening.

A CLOSER LOOK AT THE SIDDUR

There is a requirement on Yom Kippur to confess our sins. The Gemara rules that this requirement can be fulfilled by saying the words: אֲבָל אֲנַחְנוּ חָטָאנוּ, *in fact we have sinned.* We add to these words the word וַאֲבוֹתֵינוּ, *and our fathers,* following the advice of *Rabbeinu Yonah* (*Shaarei Teshuvah* 1:40) that we are to confess the sins of our fathers as well.

In addition to these words, we add two sets of confessions — אָשַׁמְנוּ and עַל חֵטְא, both in the order of the *aleph-beis. Chayei Adam* (143) explains that the sinner, through his actions, has brought destruction to the world that was created with the letters of the Torah; he must therefore confess using all these letters.

R' Yonasan Eibeshitz (in *Yaaros Devash*) gives another reason for the alphabetical setup of the words of the confession. He explains that it is comparable to one who approached a very great king and was faced with

the task of addressing him with titles befitting his greatness. Seeing that he would not be able to do the king justice, he took a large piece of paper and started to write titles for the king on the bottom of the page. He was thus demonstrating that the greatness of the king was so limitless that he did not wish to fill up the top of the page with the titles that he could think of. He therefore left it blank, in case more appropriate titles would be found. In a similar way, when we confess using every letter of the *aleph-beis,* we are expressing the thought that our transgressions are so numerous that any sins able to be expressed with the letters of the *aleph-beis* are applicable to us.

In addition to this general confession, there are some who maintain that a person is required to enumerate his own individual sins. Doing this increases one's shame over his sins, and this shame brings atonement (see *Yoma* 86b and *Tosafos* to *Gittin* 35b). Although we rule that a person need not enumerate his sins (*Shulchan Aruch, Orach Chaim* 607:2), *Chayei Adam* (143) writes that it is preferable to do so. The detailed list of sins in the עַל חֵטְא listing does not constitute an enumeration of one's sins, since everyone says the same set text. It is therefore no more than part of the order of the prayers (*Rama* to *Shulchan Aruch* ibid.).

Chayei Adam therefore advises that one insert his individual sins in their appropriate place in the order of the *aleph-beis.* For example, after אָשַׁמְנוּ, he should add, if applicable, אָכַלְתִּי דְּבָרִים הָאֲסוּרִים, אָכַלְתִּי בְּלֹא בְּרָכָה (I have eaten forbidden things, I have eaten without the proper blessings, etc.). [If a person is unfamiliar with the Hebrew language and cannot articulate his personal sins in the *aleph-beis* order, he may add them at any point in the confession where they are appropriate.]

QUESTION OF THE DAY:

Why does the verse say that the chatas goat atones "for [Israel's] sins," but the goat that is sent away to Azazel atones "for all [Israel's] sins"?

For the answer, see page 59.

פרשת אחרי

TUESDAY

PARASHAS ACHAREI

A TORAH THOUGHT FOR THE DAY

כִּי־בַיּוֹם הַזֶּה יְכַפֵּר עֲלֵיכֶם לְטַהֵר אֶתְכֶם
מִכֹּל חַטֹּאתֵיכֶם לִפְנֵי ה׳ תִּטְהָרוּ

For on this day he shall provide atonement for you to cleanse you from all your sins before HASHEM you shall be cleansed (*Vayikra* 16:30).

The punctuation for the verse above, according to *Maharsha* to *Yoma* 85b, is the basis of a disagreement between R' Elazar ben Azaryah and R' Akiva. In the last Mishnah in *Yoma,* R' Elazar ben Azaryah learns from this verse that the atonement of Yom Kippur serves to cleanse only sins between man and Hashem. In his view, Yom Kippur atones only for כֹּל חַטֹּאתֵיכֶם לִפְנֵי ה׳, *all your sins that are before HASHEM,* not those sins between man and his fellow (for which atonement cannot be granted until he appeases the one against whom he sinned). Thus, the words לִפְנֵי ה׳, *before HASHEM,* are read as the conclusion of the previous phrase — *to cleanse you from all your sins before HASHEM.*

Cited immediately after the words of R' Elazar ben Azaryah are the words of R' Akiva: "Fortunate are you, O Israel! Before Whom do you cleanse yourself? Who cleanses you? Your Father in Heaven!" From where in this verse does R' Akiva see the special role of Hashem in cleansing the Jewish people? The answer is that R' Akiva reads the words לִפְנֵי ה׳ as the beginning of a new sentence: לִפְנֵי ה׳ תִּטְהָרוּ, *Before HASHEM you shall be cleansed.* R' Akiva explains that the verse is informing us of the fact that the Jewish people are assured that Hashem Himself will cleanse them. According to R' Akiva, then, there is no indication in the verse that Yom Kippur atones only for sins between man and Hashem.

Netziv (in his *Haamek Davar*) provides a different understanding of R' Akiva's exposition of the verse. He explains that R' Akiva maintains that the position of the phrase לִפְנֵי ה׳ lends itself to be interpreted both as the conclusion of the words preceding it, *and* as the opening of the next clause. In the first interpretation, we are being told that on Yom Kippur one is cleansed and made fit to stand "before Hashem" and to serve Him. In the latter interpretation, we are enjoined to cleanse ourselves "before" or prior to, Hashem's cleansing. *Netziv* explains this with a parable:

A child soiled himself, and his father was approaching to clean him. A bystander turned to the child and told him, "Take care to cleanse yourself as well as you can before your father comes; do not leave the entire task to him. After you do what you can, your father will come and complete the job."

Similarly, Yom Kippur atones at the conclusion of the day. The Torah is telling us that before the moment of Hashem's cleansing comes, we should repent and atone for whatever we can. After we do what is in our power, Hashem will complete the cleansing. This is the lesson in the words of R' Akiva: "Fortunate are you, O Israel! Before Whom do you cleanse yourself? Who cleanses you? Your Father in Heaven!" We should therefore try our best to cleanse ourselves before He comes and cleanses us: לִפְנֵי ה׳, תִּטְהָרוּ, *Before HASHEM comes, cleanse yourselves!*

MISHNAH OF THE DAY: ERUVIN 7:2

The Mishnah continues its discussion of the status of two *chatzeiros* that are separated by a wall:

כּוֹתֶל שֶׁבֵּין שְׁתֵּי חֲצֵירוֹת — If ***a*** solid ***wall*** standing ***between two chatzeiros*** **גָּבוֹהַּ עֲשָׂרָה וְרוֹחַב אַרְבָּעָה** — is ***ten*** tefachim ***high and four*** tefachim ***wide,*** i.e., thick, **מְעָרְבִין שְׁנַיִם** — ***they*** [the residents of the two *chatzeiros*] ***may join in two*** independent ***eruvin,*** **וְאֵין מְעָרְבִין אֶחָד** — ***but they may not join in one*** common ***eruv.*** Since there is no portal in the wall, the two *chatzeiros* are completely separate areas.[1] **הָיוּ בְּרֹאשׁוֹ פֵּירוֹת** — If ***there was fruit on top of*** the wall, **אֵלּוּ עוֹלִין מִכָּאן וְאוֹכְלִין** — ***these*** residents ***may ascend from here*** [i.e., from their *chatzeir*] ***and eat*** the fruit, **וְאֵלּוּ עוֹלִין מִכָּאן וְאוֹכְלִין** — ***and those*** residents ***may ascend from here*** [i.e., from the other *chatzeir*] ***and eat*** the fruit — **וּבִלְבַד שֶׁלֹּא יוֹרִידוּ לְמַטָּן** — ***provided that they do not bring*** any fruit ***down*** into their respective *chatzeiros.*[2]

NOTES

1. A wall of even nominal thickness effectively divides the *chatzeiros* and precludes a communal *eruv*. The Mishnah mentions a thickness of 4 *tefachim* because of its relevance to the Mishnah's second case. In fact, this first ruling is not at all novel in itself; it can be derived from the previous Mishnah. This clause serves only to introduce the following one concerning the placing of objects on top of the wall (*Rashi*).

2. Since the top of the wall is 4 *tefachim* wide and 10 *tefachim* high, it qualifies as a separate and distinct area. Hence, carrying on top of the wall is unrestricted, but to carry from atop the wall to either *chatzeir* below is forbidden (according to the Rabbis cited in Mishnah 9:1). According to R' Shimon (ibid.), however, one may transfer from the wall to each *chatzeir,* and from *chatzeir* to *chatzeir.* He therefore explains that the Mishnah prohibits carrying from atop the wall to the houses of the courtyards.

נִפְרְצָה הַכּוֹתֶל — If *the wall was breached* עַד עֶשֶׂר אַמּוֹת — *up to* a length of *ten amos,* מְעָרְבִין שְׁנַיִם — *they may join in two* independent *eruvin,* וְאִם רָצוּ מְעָרְבִין אֶחָד — *or if they desire they join in one* communal *eruv,* מִפְּנֵי שֶׁהוּא כְּפֶתַח — *because [the breach] is like a portal* and so the partition remains valid.[3] יוֹתֵר מִכַּאן — However, if the breach *is more than that,* i.e., wider than 10 *amos,* מְעָרְבִין אֶחָד — *they may join in one* common *eruv,* וְאֵין מְעָרְבִין שְׁנַיִם — *but may not join in two* independent *eruvin.* A breach wider than 10 *amos* is too large to be considered a portal, and thus nullifies the partition.[4] Therefore, the *chatzeiros* are considered one area, and if the residents desire an *eruv* they must join in one common *eruv* for both *chatzeiros.*[5]

NOTES

3. The two *chatzeiros* are now in the category of areas separated by the wall between them, but which still have easy access to each other because of the entranceway in that wall. Therefore, they may elect to have two *eruvin* (one for each *chatzeir*), in which case carrying is prohibited from one *chatzeir* to the other, or they may make one joint *eruv* and thus be permitted to carry from one courtyard to the other.

4. Ibid.

5. Therefore, should each *chatzeir* make its own *eruv,* the residents are prohibited from carrying even into their own *chatzeiros* (*Rashi*).

GEMS FROM THE GEMARA

The Mishnah had discussed the case of a wall 4 *tefachim* thick. The Gemara wonders what the law would be if the wall were less than 4 *tefachim* thick. Rav said that the two unmerged *chatzeiros* control the top of the wall; therefore, one may not move anything on it, even as much as the fullness of a hair. [Although it is sufficiently tall, the top surface of the wall is too narrow to be considered a separate domain. Rav therefore understands that the wall is subsumed by both *chatzeiros,* so that any carrying on the top is deemed a transfer from one *chatzeir* into another (*Rashi*).] But R' Yochanan said that the residents of both *chatzeiros* may bring food up from their *chatzeiros* to the top of the wall, or from the top of the wall down to their *chatzeiros.*

The Gemara explains that R' Yochanan's ruling differentiating between the two types of walls is based on a similar ruling of his taught in the matter of הוֹצָאָה, the Biblically prohibited act of *transferring* between public and private domains. The law is that an area less than 4 *tefachim* by 4 *tefachim* that is situated between a *reshus harabim* and a *reshus*

hayachid is considered a מְקוֹם פְּטוּר, *an exempt area,* into which one may carry from either the *reshus harabim* or the *reshus hayachid,* provided that one does not transfer an object from the *reshus harabim* to the *reshus hayachid* (or the reverse) via this exempt area. [That is, one may not take an object from the *reshus hayachid,* place it in the exempt area, and then remove it to the *reshus harabim* (or vice versa). Although each of these two actions is in itself permissible, when performed together they appear to constitute the *melachah* of carrying from a *reshus hayachid* to a *reshus harabim.* The Rabbis therefore prohibited it, so that people would not mistakenly conclude that the actual *melachah* was permitted.] If, however, this intervening area measured 4 by 4 *tefachim* or more, its status would be that of a *karmelis,* a separate and distinct domain, and one would be forbidden to carry between it and the *reshus harabim* or *reshus hayachid.*

R' Yochanan thus holds that just as it is permitted to transfer objects to an area whose dimensions are less than 4 *tefachim* by 4 *tefachim,* he also permits food to be transferred onto the wall between neighboring *chatzeiros* as long as it is not 4 *tefachim* wide. However, if the top of the wall exceeds that measure, it is considered a separate area, and transferring onto it from the *chatzeiros* is prohibited.

The Gemara asks how it is that Rav does not accept this ruling of R' Yochanan (inasmuch as it is supported by a Baraisa in *Shabbos* 6a). The Gemara answers that if we were speaking of domains prescribed by Biblical law [i.e., a *reshus harabim* and a *reshus hayachid,* as in the case of Rav Dimi], Rav would indeed concur with Rav Dimi's ruling, which permitted carrying from a *reshus harabim* or a *reshus hayachid* into an exempt area. The Sages were not concerned that from this leniency people would conclude that carrying directly between a *reshus harabim* and a *reshus hayachid* is permissible. However, here in the dispute between Rav and R' Yochanan, we dealing with a case that involves domains between which transfer is prohibited by Rabbinic decree. [Since each *chatzeir* is a *reshus hayachid,* carrying between the two (either between the two *chatzeiros* according to the Rabbis, or between a house and the opposite *chatzeir* according to R' Shimon) is prohibited only by Rabbinic decree (*Rashi*).] And the Sages strengthened their own enactments more than they would in cases where carrying between domains is prohibited by Biblical law, prohibiting one to carry even atop the narrow wall. [In Rav's view, the Sages were concerned that if carrying from a *chatzeir* to the exempt area atop the wall were permitted, people would eventually carry from one *chatzeir* into another, since people tend to be more conscientious about observing Biblical law than observing Rabbinic law (*Ritva*).]

Not in all cases of Rabbinic law do the Sages "strengthen their own enactments" by adding stringencies. Only when the likelihood that people will violate the Rabbinic law is reasonably strong, such as here where only the *reshus hayachid* (i.e., the two *chatzeiros*) is involved, will they do so. However, in the case of an exempt area situated between a *karmelis* and a *reshus hayachid,* Rav would agree that one may carry between the exempt area and either domain, even though carrying directly between a *reshus hayachid* and a *karmelis* is Rabbinically prohibited. Since in that case two different types of domains are involved, one would not mistakenly come to carry directly between them if the leniency were granted (*Tosafos*).

A MUSSAR THOUGHT FOR THE DAY

In his introduction to the laws of *Aseres Yemei Teshuvah* (Days of Repentance) and Yom Kippur, *Chayei Adam* (§143) also alludes to the above-mentioned interpretation of the verse לִפְנֵי ה׳ תִּטְהָרוּ, *prior to Hashem's cleansing, you shall cleanse yourselves* (see above, *A Torah Thought for the Day*). He applies it to the days preceding Yom Kippur, which must be filled with added Torah study and kindness, as well as careful introspection. In this way, one will arrive at the day of Yom Kippur already in a pure state.

In addition, one must be sure to appease those whom he has wronged, for Yom Kippur cannot atone for those sins until he is forgiven. If one stole money, before Yom Kippur can atone for this sin the money must be returned and one must also seek the forgiveness of the one from whom he stole.

Chayei Adam warns that a person must not delude himself into thinking that due to the numerous mitzvos that he fulfills daily he will surely emerge unscathed from the judgment of Yom Kippur, for he must remember that a person stumbles constantly and performs many sins without even noticing that he is sinning. This is most prevalent with sins associated with speech, which are numerous and often committed unthinkingly.

There are people who spend the Days of Repentance in intense prayer and repentance, and then do as they wish throughout the year, sure that their sins will be forgiven the next Yom Kippur. This is a grave error. The Mishnah in *Yoma* (8:9) states that one who says, "I will sin and Yom Kippur will atone for my sin," does not benefit from the atonement of

Yom Kippur. One who does what he wishes the entire year, relying on his repentance and the power of Yom Kippur to atone, will not find atonement in Yom Kippur. To the contrary: One must be careful to live the entire year as if it is the period of the Days of Repentance, and during the actual Days of Repentance he must increase his observance even more.

Chayei Adam writes that not even one day in the year should go by in which one does not spend at least some time learning from the *sefarim* that teach about fear of Heaven (*yiras Shamayim*). This must be done even at the expense of other Torah studies. While it is very important for every person to study the laws of the Torah so that he knows how to execute Hashem's will, it is still better to remain a relative ignoramus and retain one's fear of Heaven than to become a great Torah scholar lacking in this most important of qualities — fear of Heaven.

HALACHAH OF THE DAY

Yesterday, we began discussing the guidelines that govern the erection of temporary walls on Shabbos.

While it is generally permissible to erect temporary partitions on Shabbos, there are exceptions to this rule.

A temporary partition that bears too strong a resemblance to a permanent one may be forbidden. For example, we have learned previously that one may not set up a curtain to divide a room if the curtain is secured both on top and on bottom. Even though the intent in hanging the curtain is strictly for its temporary use, since the curtain is firmly fixed in position, this resembles permanent construction and is forbidden.

Another exception to the rule allowing for the erection of temporary walls is the case of a partition that is required for halachic reasons. In such cases, since the construction of the partition has halachic effect, the wall is by its very definition a significant construct, and putting it up is therefore forbidden.

To illustrate: One may not set up a partition in a bedroom in order to cut off an area where there is a *Sefer Torah* or *sefarim* (whose presence in a bedroom create certain halachic restrictions). Since the presence of the *Sefer Torah* creates a halachic need to have a divider between it and the bedroom proper, such a halachically dictated partition is seen as a substantial construction and is forbidden. This type of prohibited partition is known as a מְחִיצָה הַמַּתֶּרֶת, *a partition that permits.*

Despite this rule, we have written above that a temporary partition may be erected in order to act as a *mechitzah* between men and women for the purpose of davening. This is because the *mechitzah* required for the purposes of davening does not halachically serve as a wall that divides the room in two; rather, it need only serve as a tool that prevents men and women from mingling.

Even in the case of a מְחִיצָה הַמַּתֶּרֶת described above, if a *tefach* of the required wall was erected prior to Shabbos, it may be extended on Shabbos. For example, in the case of the divider required to separate a part of a bedroom that contains a *Sefer Torah,* one may completely close off the temporary dividers on Shabbos, as long as they were already blocking an area of a *tefach* prior to the onset of Shabbos.

A CLOSER LOOK AT THE SIDDUR

Three times a day, in the *Shemoneh Esrei* prayer, we request of Hashem: סְלַח לָנוּ אָבִינוּ כִּי חָטָאנוּ, *Forgive us, our Father, for we have sinned.* The *Shemoneh Esrei* prayer was instituted for all Jewish people, among them the greatest saints. Can it be that every one of them has sinned daily and is in need of forgiveness?

Furthermore, we recite this request at the *Maariv* prayer after the conclusion of Yom Kippur. Have we not, just moments before, achieved complete forgiveness for all our sins? Why must we ask for forgiveness immediately afterward, as if we have already sinned in the few minutes since Yom Kippur ended?

Rav Schwab (in *Maayan Beis HaSho'eivah*) addresses these questions and answers them by explaining that there are two levels of repentance. A person can repent out of fear of Hashem's punishment, either in this world or the next. In His kindness, Hashem accepts such repentance and the sin is hidden from sight. However, it does not disappear. The repentant is freed from any punishment as a result of the sin, but he is not free of all its effects. The distance that was created between the person and Hashem has yet to be bridged; his personal spiritual level that existed prior to the sin has yet to be regained.

The second, higher level of repentance is that performed out of a sense of love for Hashem. In this scenario, a person, by recognizing the greatness of Hashem and realizing that his sin has created a chasm between himself and his Creator, is moved to repent and come closer to Him. There is no limit to the levels of this repentance. The higher one's understanding of Hashem and His ways, the more one is motivated to become close to Him. This repentance is a constant process, emanating from a person's continued growth in the service of Hashem.

The power of Yom Kippur to atone for sins is similar to the way sin is removed when one repents out of fear. The blessing of Yom Kippur is: מַעֲבִיר אַשְׁמוֹתֵינוּ בְּכָל שָׁנָה וְשָׁנָה, *He removes our sins each and every year.* This is a mere removal of our sins from open sight. Our real responsibility starts after Yom Kippur, when, freed from the shackles of our sins, we are able to pursue the higher level of *teshuvah* out of our love for Hashem and a deeper understanding of His ways. Thus, at the very close of Yom Kippur, we immediately ask: סְלַח לָנוּ, *Forgive us,* הֲשִׁיבֵנוּ, *Help us to come closer to You.*

Indeed, every person at every time, after he has prayed for increased understanding in אַתָּה חוֹנֵן (the blessing of understanding), is in a new position to request a deeper connection to Hashem in the following blessings of תְּשׁוּבָה, *Repentance,* and סְלִיחָה, *Forgiveness.*

QUESTION OF THE DAY:

Why does the verse stress that the atonement will be for sins that were committed "before Hashem"?

For the answer, see page 59.

פרשת אחרי

WEDNESDAY

PARASHAS ACHAREI

A TORAH THOUGHT FOR THE DAY

וְכָל־נֶפֶשׁ אֲשֶׁר תֹּאכַל נְבֵלָה וּטְרֵפָה בָּאֶזְרָח וּבַגֵּר
וְכִבֶּס בְּגָדָיו וְרָחַץ בַּמַּיִם וְטָמֵא עַד־הָעֶרֶב וְטָהֵר

Any person who will eat [a bird] that died or was torn — the native or the proselyte — he shall immerse his garments and immerse himself in the water; he shall remain contaminated until evening, and then become pure (*Vayikra* 17:15).

Although the Torah does not clearly identify what creature it is that, having *died or was torn,* contaminates a person who eats it, *Toras Kohanim* (see *Rashi* to our verse and to *Vayikra* 11:40) explains that the subject of this verse can be readily divined when it is read closely and contrasted with other verses in the Torah. This unique *tumah* that comes from eating a carcass, explains *Toras Kohanim,* cannot result from eating a dead unslaughtered *animal,* for earlier (ibid. vs. 38-40) the Torah already taught that an animal carcass contaminates a person who merely *handles* it, even if he does not eat from its flesh. Consequently, the *tumah* described as transmitted by eating can be referring only to something that, since it is not included in the laws of *tumah* transmitted by touching or carrying, does not otherwise transfer *tumah* — and this is a dead bird. Additionally, the Torah is clear that this *tumah* transmitted through eating comes only when the bird *died* — on its own — *or was torn* — instead of being slaughtered — implying that if not for these problems, this bird would be permissible to be eaten. This is not the case with a bird from a nonkosher species, which is of course forbidden to be eaten even when properly slaughtered. Thus, concludes *Toras Kohanim,* the verse decreeing *tumah* on a person who eats a carcass that *died or was torn* can be speaking only of someone who eats a נִבְלַת עוֹף טָהוֹר, *the carcass of a kosher species of bird that died without being properly slaughtered.*

The *Klausenburger Rebbe* suggests that this *tumah* may be considered a סְיָג (*s'yag*), *a protective fence* that the Torah ordained in order that we should not come to eat this form of forbidden food. This *s'yag,* explains the Rebbe, is necessary only in regard to bird carcasses; since the Torah previously commanded us regarding the *tumah* of animal carcasses, there is no fear that people — who are in any case careful not to handle them in order not to become *tamei* — will come to eat them. However, since, as we explained, a bird carcass does not transmit *tumah* when touched, an extra protection — the decree of *tumah* when swallowed — is needed in order to make sure that people will not eat this forbidden food.

R' Yaakov Kamenetsky points out that the context of our *parashah* does not seem to be the proper place for a commandment that introduces a new form of *tumah.* This Torah passage begins (17:1) with the prohibition of שְׁחוּטֵי חוּץ (*shechutei chutz*), *slaughtering korbanos outside the Beis HaMikdash.* Having established that slaughtering an animal for an offering in a place where it may not be used as a *korban* is so severe that: דָּם יֵחָשֵׁב לָאִישׁ הַהוּא דָּם שָׁפָךְ, *it shall be considered as bloodshed for that man, he has shed blood* (17:4), the Torah then proceeds to teach us other laws that are based on the importance of blood: the prohibition against consuming blood and the mitzvah of *kisui hadam,* covering the blood [when slaughtering a wild animal (*chayah*) or a fowl in order to eat from its flesh, the blood must immediately be covered with earth]. Why is a *tumah* that is based on eating a *nivlas ohf tahor* — the carcass of a kosher species of bird that died without being properly slaughtered — included in our Torah passage?

R' Yaakov answers that the reason behind this sequence becomes clearer based on the *Ramban's* (*Bereishis* 1:29) explanation of the prohibition against eating an animal that has not been properly slaughtered. Originally, explains the *Ramban,* mankind was not permitted to slaughter an animal for food. It was only after the Flood, when all of animal life owed their physical survival to man — Noach — that mankind was allowed to slaughter and eat animals. However, although man was now allowed to eat an animal's physical body, he was not given authority over its more esoteric *nefesh,* life force. This is the reason we are not allowed to consume the blood of an animal; the Torah, in our *parashah,* tells us (17:14): נֶפֶשׁ כָּל בָּשָׂר, *the life of any creature,* דָּמוֹ בְנַפְשׁוֹ, *its blood represents its life,* דַּם כָּל־בָּשָׂר לֹא תֹאכֵלוּ, *you shall not consume the blood of any creature,* כִּי נֶפֶשׁ כָּל־בָּשָׂר דָּמוֹ הִוא, *for the life of any creature is in its blood*.

Continuing, *Ramban* explains that this prohibition against consuming blood is also the reason behind the Torah's requirement to properly slaughter an animal before eating its flesh, for only by doing so will the blood satisfactorily leave the body.

With this in mind, we may now understand why the *tumah* transmitted to someone who swallows a *nivlas ohf tahor* belongs in the Torah passage that centers on the importance of blood. Unlike other forms of *tumah,* which are transmitted by *handling* a contaminated item, this contamination is unique in the sense that it is transmitted by eating a forbidden food — a bird carcass that was not slaughtered. Accordingly, the reason this food is prohibited — and causes *tumah* to a person who

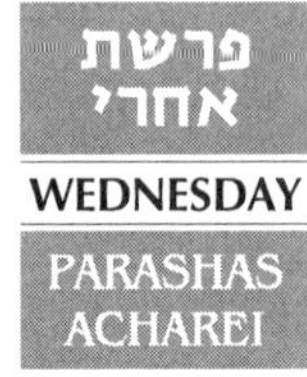

swallows it — is because it contains blood. We can therefore see, concludes R' Yaakov, that the underlying reason for this *tumah* is based on the same principle as the other mitzvos commanded in this Torah passage — the role of blood as a creature's life force requires that it be treated with special regard, and does not allow it to be consumed in any form.

MISHNAH OF THE DAY: ERUVIN 7:3

The Mishnah continues its discussion of two neighboring *chatzeiros,* discussing under what circumstances a ditch running between them will prevent them from joining in one *eruv*:

חָרִיץ שֶׁבֵּין שְׁתֵּי חֲצֵירוֹת — If ***a ditch between two chatzeiros***[1] עָמוֹק עֲשָׂרָה וְרוֹחַב אַרְבָּעָה — is ***ten*** *tefachim* ***deep and four*** *tefachim* ***wide,***[2] מְעָרְבִין שְׁנַיִם — ***they*** (i.e., the residents of the two *chatzeiros*) ***may make two*** independent ***eruvin,*** וְאֵין מְעָרְבִין אֶחָד — ***but may not make one*** common ***eruv,***[3] אֲפִילוּ מָלֵא קַשׁ אוֹ תֶּבֶן — ***even if*** the ditch ***is filled with stubble or straw.***[4] מָלֵא עָפָר אוֹ צְרוֹרוֹת — However, if it ***is filled with earth or pebbles,*** מְעָרְבִין אֶחָד וְאֵין מְעָרְבִין שְׁנַיִם — ***they may make one*** common ***eruv, but may not make two*** independent ***eruvin.***[5]

NOTES

1. Two adjoining *chatzeiros* are separated by a ditch that runs along the entire length of their boundary (*Rashi*). If the ditch does not extend along the entire boundary, leaving a segment 4 *tefachim* or more in width between the two *chatzeiros* uncut by the ditch, or if the ditch itself lacks the minimum dimensions along a span of 4 *tefachim,* that space is considered an entrance between the two *chatzeiros,* and they make either one *eruv* together or two *eruvin* separately (*Rama, Orach Chaim* 372:17 and *Mishnah Berurah* there §118).

2. If it is shallower than this minimum, it is considered as if it were level and they must make one joint *eruv* (*Ritva*). If the ditch is less than 4 *tefachim* wide, it is easy to step over, and so is not considered a partition (*Rashi*).

3. Since at these dimensions the ditch separates the two areas totally, it precludes them from joining in a common *eruv.*

4. It is assumed that the stubble or straw is being stored temporarily in the ditch, and that the owner will eventually remove it (for use as fodder). Hence, the ditch is not considered filled in (*Rashi*).

Our Mishnah refers to stubble and straw that are not *muktzeh* (*Tosafos*) and may therefore be removed even on the Sabbath (see Gemara 77a).

5. Since the earth or pebbles will likely remain in the ditch permanently, and thus become a part of it, the ditch no longer constitutes a partition between the two *chatzeiros;* hence, they must be regarded as one and cannot make two separate *eruvin.*

GEMS FROM THE GEMARA

Our Mishnah taught that if the ditch is filled with earth, it is considered permanently filled, presumably even if one has not declared his intention to leave the earth there. The Gemara argues that this apparently contradicts another Mishnah (*Oholos* 15:7) that deals with the *tumah* of a corpse. According to Biblical law, a corpse radiates *tumah* above and below itself. The *tumah* even penetrates a covering to contaminate people above it. However, if there is at least a *tefach* of empty space between the corpse and the covering, the covering is classified as an אֹהֶל, *tent,* and in most cases the *tumah* does not penetrate the covering (*Berachos* 19b). The Mishnah discusses a case in which a house was filled to the ceiling with straw or pebbles, and one abandoned them by declaring that he will not remove them, so that they become a permanent filling of the building. That Mishnah taught that since the space is negated, the effectiveness of the roof as a barrier is also negated, and if a corpse is inside, the *tumah* penetrates through the roof.

That Mishnah thus indicates that straw or pebbles are considered permanently in place only if one has abandoned them. But if one did not abandon the straw and pebbles, they are not considered permanently in place. [Therefore, in the absence of an express declaration of abandonment, the roof of the house still covers a space at least a *tefach* high underneath, and intervenes to prevent *tumah* from rising above it (*Rashi*).] Why, then, does our Mishnah rule that pebbles close the ditch even without a declaration of abandonment?

The Gemara gives a number of answers to this question:

(1) Our Mishnah follows the opinion of R' Yose, who maintains that although we are not aware of the owner's plans, he probably has no use for the pebbles, and it is considered abandoned as a matter of course, even without any declaration of abandonment. However, the Mishnah in *Oholos* records a dissenting opinion stating that pebbles are not ordinarily considered abandoned, but must be declared abandoned.

(2) In this discussion of whether pebbles or earth are ordinarily considered abandoned, the laws of *tumah,* discussed in the Mishnah in *Oholos,* cannot be compared with the laws of the Sabbath, discussed in our Mishnah. In the case of the laws of the Sabbath, the prohibition of *muktzeh,* which proscribes the movement of certain objects on the Sabbath, will cause a person to abandon on the Sabbath (at least

temporarily) even a purse filled with money, because it may not be moved. Similarly, although pebbles and earth ordinarily are not considered abandoned (as we see from the Mishnah in *Oholos*), they are so considered for the duration of the Sabbath because they may not be moved.

(3) A house and a ditch cannot be compared. It is acceptable, in the case of a ditch, to presume that the pebbles that fill it are abandoned, because a ditch is customarily filled in. [Therefore, even those who, in the Mishnah of *Oholos,* maintain that earth that fills a house is considered abandoned only when an express declaration to that effect has been made, agree that earth or pebbles that fill a ditch are considered abandoned without a declaration (*Rashi*).] However, it is certainly not customary to fill up a house, and therefore, the Mishnah in *Oholos* teaches that the pebbles are not presumed to be abandoned.

A MUSSAR THOUGHT FOR THE DAY

The *Klausenburger Rebbe* explains (see *A Torah Thought for the Day*) that the Torah decreed *tumah* (contamination) on someone who swallows a *nivlas ohf tahor* as a *s'yag,* a protective fence, to ensure that people will not come to inadvertently eat this forbidden food. [The Klausenburger Rebbe (*Divrei Yatziv* 6:124) in fact notes that the relationship between these two elements — *tumah* and forbidden foodstuffs — is the focus of a dispute between *Rambam* and *Ramban. Ramban* (*Vayikra* 22:8) maintains that the *nivlas ohf tahor* is forbidden only so people will not become *tamei* and contaminate sanctified items or places. A close reading of the *Rambam,* however, implies the opposite view, that the *tumah* is present only in order to ensure that people will not consume this foodstuff. See also *Rivash,* cited in *Shaarei Aharon.*]

At first glance, the effect that a decree of *tumah* will have in deterring a person who wants to eat forbidden foodstuffs is puzzling. If a person desires to transgress the sin of consuming nonkosher food, why would he care if he becomes *tamei*? Moreover, this question is strengthened when we realize that for a person who does not plan on entering the *Beis HaMikdash* or eating sanctified food (*kodashim*), there is in fact no general prohibition against becoming *tamei*! [Of course, a Kohen is forbidden from contracting corpse-*tumah.* However, no inherent restriction exists against his contracting other forms of *tumah,* as long as he does not handle sanctified foods.]

R' Chaim Shmulevitz asks a similar question on the Gemara (*Berachos* 22a) that speaks about a person who was driven to sin with a married woman, and was deterred only when he realized that he would not have a *mikveh* to immerse in after his adulterous deed. Asks R' Chaim: Why should a person who is ready to violate the cardinal sin of adultery care about Rabbinic impurity? In answer to this question, he explains that this Gemara is providing us with a great insight into human nature; the reason people do things that they clearly know are wrong is because they convince themselves that their actions do not really matter. A person tempted by sin will rationalize: "Committing this sin will not change who I am; an action, as soon as it is over, is history." Of course, if a person would realize the everlasting effect that every action — good or bad — has on his *neshamah,* he would never sin. However, since this spiritual impact is not tangibly apparent, we allow ourselves to be persuaded by temptation. This lesson, explains R' Chaim, is in fact taught in the Gemara's statement (*Sotah* 3a) that a person sins only when a רוּחַ שְׁטוּת, *a spirit of foolishness,* enters his body. If a person were to rationally look at the action that he is going to do, he would realize that he is going to permanently blemish himself. The only way to sin is by *foolishly* ignoring this reality.

This is the reason, explains R' Chaim, why the would-be adulterer, by realizing that his sin would make him *tamei,* was deterred from committing it. Even the Rabbinic requirement to immerse in a *mikveh* showed him that his action was a reality that, even on a physical level, would change who he is. Thus, once he was conscious of some of the impact an *aveirah* has on a person, he was unable to rationalize that what he wanted to do would not really matter and that he would remain the same person afterwards. Once he realized that what a person does really matters, sin was no longer possible.

Perhaps this idea taught by R' Chaim may be used to understand the Klausenburger Rebbe's explanation that the *tumah* that comes from consuming a *nivlas ohf tahor* is a *s'yag* to ensure that people will not come to eat this food. It is true that there is nothing wrong with being *tamei* if the person does not handle sanctified objects, while eating nonkosher food is a serious sin. However, a person who becomes *tamei* sees a tangible change — he knows that he must now immerse in the *mikveh* to purify himself — which he does not see when he eats forbidden foods. Thus, a person will be careful to ensure that he does not become *tamei.* Understanding this, the Torah decreed *tumah* to ensure that people do not eat the forbidden *nivlas ohf tahor.*

פרשת
אחרי

WEDNESDAY

PARASHAS
ACHAREI

HALACHAH OF THE DAY

The next of the thirty-nine labors forbidden on Shabbos is the *melachah* of סוֹתֵר, *demolishing.* As in the case of the other forbidden *melachos,* this one is based on an activity that took place in the Mishkan. When the Bnei Yisrael broke camp in the Wilderness they had to dismantle the Mishkan in order to travel to their next destination.

The *melachah* of *demolishing* is defined as the dismantling of any object, or any part of an object, whose creation would be a violation of the *melachah* of *building.*

As we have mentioned several times previously, as a general rule the *melachos* that are forbidden on Shabbos are forbidden only when they are done for some beneficial purpose. Acts that are simply destructive, for no benefit, are not forbidden on Shabbos.

Accordingly, the Biblical prohibition against demolishing includes only acts of demolishing that are done for some beneficial reason. A primary example of a Biblically forbidden act of demolishing would be the demolishing of a building in order to make way for new construction. However, we shall see that certain acts of demolition that are done for other beneficial reasons are also Biblically forbidden.

It is forbidden by Biblical law to demolish a structure in order to replace it with an improved structure in the very same place. An obvious example of this would be demolishing a house in order to replace it with a larger structure on the same lot. Less obvious examples of the same prohibition would be removing a carpet in order to replace it with a new one, or removing a burnt-out bulb from a socket in order to replace it with a new one.

It is also forbidden by Biblical law to do an act of demolishing for beneficial purposes that are not connected to any future plans of building. For example, one who removes a nail that is protruding from a wall in order to prevent anyone from harming themselves violates the *melachah* of *demolishing.*

While the Biblical prohibition against demolishing applies only to cases where there is some constructive purpose behind the act, the Sages extended this prohibition to cover even purely destructive acts on Shabbos. As we have seen in regard to other *melachos,* the Sages were concerned that allowing destructive (i.e., non-beneficial) acts of *demolishing* would lead one to inadvertently transgress the *melachah* by performing constructive acts of *demolishing.*

We will discuss the Rabbinic prohibition tomorrow.

A CLOSER LOOK AT THE SIDDUR

R' *Chaim Shmulevitz* (see *A Mussar Thought for the Day*) explains that the reason a person, who knows intellectually that what he is about to do is wrong, is nevertheless able to transgress is because he rationalizes that his doing this action will not affect him. The person concludes that since he will remain the same person even after he sins, there is no reason why he should not give in to the temptation of the moment. R' Chaim cites a Midrash that states that the only way Yosef was able to withstand the temptation to sin with Potiphar's wife was by realizing the unalterable change that the sin would bring about. What will happen, Yosef thought, if Hashem will soon appear to me as He has appeared to my forefathers? He will find me impure, and I will not be fit to fully serve Him!

The Midrash relates another example that Yosef used to convince himself of the immeasurable impact that every action makes: he thought about Adam who, although he had committed a relatively minor transgression, was banished from Gan Eden. If I commit the serious crime of adultery, thought Yosef, I too will be punished severely! Only by thinking of the impact that transgressing Hashem's word would have on him, concludes R' Chaim, was Yosef able to avoid sinning.

The *Mesillas Yesharim* (Chs. 3-4) comments that the awareness that transgressing Hashem's commandments will have permanent impact does not come automatically. In fact, this perspective requires much thought, as we may understand from a phrase that is part of the וְהוּא רַחוּם prayer recited during *Shacharis* on Monday and Thursday: נַחְפְּשָׂה דְרָכֵינוּ וְנַחְקֹרָה וְנָשׁוּבָה אֵלֶיךָ, *we will search our ways and examine them and return to You!* (based on *Eichah* 3:40). It is only through much introspection that a person will become fully aware of the impact his actions will have on him; only then will he be able to avoid sinning and thereby attain closeness to Hashem.

Mesillas Yesharim explains that there are several things a person may concentrate on to make himself aware that the actions he performs will have long-term effects. The very righteous, who are already conscious of their lifelong goal of achieving perfection, need only realize that their spiritual perfection will be tarnished by not following Hashem's word. With this on their minds, they will not give in to sin. *Mesillas Yesharim* counsels lesser people, who are not so altruistically driven, to think about the level of reward that they desire in *Olam Haba,* and how embarrassed they will be — for eternity — if someone whom they consider as lesser than themselves will earn a greater portion.

Before every challenge, they should realize that the decision they make now will affect them forever. For a person who is not able to rouse himself to perform mitzvos for the sake of his portion in the World to Come, *Mesillas Yesharim* offers a different suggestion: Realize that Hashem's reward and punishment — even in this world — is meted out מִדָּה כְּנֶגֶד מִדָּה (*middah keneged middah*), *measure for measure.* Anything that you do will come back to you in a similar manner. Although these three motivations vary, they are all based on one idea — a person must concentrate on maintaining an awareness that his actions are not momentary, but have the power to change who he is and to affect the quality of his life both in *Olam Hazeh* and in *Olam Haba.* Once a person becomes cognizant of the fact that every action has a consequence, it will be immeasurably easier for him to overcome challenge; he will come to the conclusion that he does not wish to be hampered by the negative consequences of sin.

A TASTE OF LOMDUS

When stating the laws of the *tumah* (contamination) that results from eating a *nivlas ohf tahor,* the carcass of a kosher species of bird that died without being properly slaughtered, *Rambam* (*Hilchos Avos HaTumah* 3:1) rules that the person who eats a *kezayis*-size piece of this carcass becomes impure when the food reaches his throat. This is understood, explains *Rambam* (based on *Toras Kohanim*), from the description that the Torah uses to refer to a person who ate from this bird: נֶפֶשׁ, which, literally translated, means *life force.* Thus, the Torah is telling us that the throat — which is the part of the body that, by swallowing food, sustains life — is the place that the dead bird must reach to cause *tumah.*

R' Chaim Soloveitchik (*Chidushei Rabbeinu Chaim HaLevi al HaRambam, Hilchos Avos HaTumah* 3:3) observes that it is unusual for the Torah to specify the part of the body that the food must reach in order to fulfill a mitzvah or violate a transgression. For example, when commanding us to eat matzah on the first night of Pesach, the Torah simply commands: בָּעֶרֶב תֹּאכְלוּ מַצּוֹת, *in the evening you shall eat matzos* (*Shemos* 12:18), without explaining to us how this eating is to be performed. Similarly, the prohibitions against eating forbidden foods also do not contain a warning — such as the use of the word נֶפֶשׁ — that the food is not to reach our throat, or any other part of the body; we are simply told not to eat certain items. Why does the Torah, through the use of נֶפֶשׁ, emphasize the place where *nivlas ohf tahor* contaminates the body?

R' Chaim also points out something else — food reaching the throat is in fact *not* the determining factor in the other mitzvos or prohibitions that involve eating. In all other areas of the Torah, the act of "eating" is considered to have been completed when the food reaches the stomach; a person who chews a *kezayis* of matzah and is unable to fully swallow does not fulfill his mitzvah. Similarly, the Gemara in *Kesubos* (30b) rules that a non-Kohen who eats *terumah* is not liable if he spits it out while it is still in his throat, before it reaches his stomach. The only exception to this rule is the *tumah* transmitted by eating *nivlas ohf tahor,* where a person who unsuccessfully attempts to swallow a piece of bird carcass will nevertheless become *tamei* as soon as the *kezayis* has reached his throat. Why are the laws of the *tumah* transmitted from eating a bird carcass different from the other laws in the Torah that involve eating?

In answer to these questions, R' Chaim explains that *Rambam* has a slightly different perspective in understanding the Torah's instruction regarding the *tumah* generated when a *nivlas ohf tahor* is eaten. The Torah is not, strictly speaking, telling us about a *tumah* that comes from *eating* something. Rather, a clearer definition of the Scriptural decree of *tumah* that is generated when the bird carcass reaches the throat is just that — a new type of *tumah* that contaminates a person when a certain substance (a *nivlas ohf tahor*) is contained by a certain part of the body (the throat). Accordingly, unlike regarding the commandments to eat matzah and refrain from eating nonkosher foodstuffs, where the Torah did not have to give further instruction beyond commanding "eat" or "refrain from eating" — for the basic act of eating is obvious to all — the *tumah* transmitted from ingesting a kosher bird carcass is not related to the act of eating. Therefore, the Torah, by employing the word נֶפֶשׁ, is telling us which part of the body must contain the *nivlas ohf tahor* in order to trigger this *tumah;* it is not the mouth or the stomach, rather, it is the throat.

R' Chaim points out that this perspective of what the Torah is instructing us in regard to the *tumah* of *nivlas ohf tahor* — not that *eating* a bird carcass makes one *tamei,* rather, this *tumah* is caused by the food being *contained* in one's throat — explains why *Rambam* omitted one apparently basic law from his otherwise comprehensive list of the laws of this *tumah* — the qualification of *kedei achilas pras* (i.e., the time span it takes to eat a half-loaf of bread). When the Torah speaks of eating, it does not mean that the full amount of food should be ingested

instantaneously. Rather, every food mentioned in the Torah — whether mitzvah or prohibition — is seen as having been "eaten" as long as a full *kezayis* (olive's volume) is eaten in the close proximity of the time span of *kedei achilas pras.* [The exact period of time is disputed by the authorities, and ranges from 2 to as many as 9 minutes.] Thus, a person fulfills the mitzvah of eating matzah as long as he eats the full *kezayis* of matzah in this time span, and someone who eats a *kezayis* of nonkosher food is liable if it was eaten in this amount of time. [If, however, the food is eaten spread out over a longer period of time — e.g., after consuming the first half-*kezayis,* the person pauses for 10 minutes before continuing with the second half — no act of "eating" has been accomplished.] Why, asks R' Chaim, does *Rambam* not tell us, as he does concerning the many other mitzvos of eating, that eating a *kezayis* of *nivlas ohf tahor* causes *tumah* even when the entire *kezayis* was not swallowed at once, but is spread out over *kedei achilas pras*?

This question falls away, answers R' Chaim, for we explained that Rambam understood that the *tumah* that comes from swallowing a bird carcass is not a *tumah* transmitted through *eating,* but is a *tumah* that the Torah decreed when the throat *contains* a *kezayis* of *nivlas ohf tahor.* Thus, since the time span of *kedei achilas pras* is applied only to combining two otherwise separate acts of eating, and does not serve to combine other types of actions (for example, if a person touches a half-*kezayis* of animal carcass, removes his hand, and then touches another half-*kezayis,* he has not become *tamei*), the rule of *kedei achilas pras* does not apply to *tumah* that comes from a bird carcass being *contained* in the throat; as long as the full *kezayis* is not present in the throat at one time, the person remains uncontaminated.

QUESTION OF THE DAY:

If a person is dangerously ill and he requires meat, is it better to slaughter an animal for him on Shabbos, or should he be given meat from a nonkosher animal?

For the answer, see page 59.

A TORAH THOUGHT FOR THE DAY

כְּמַעֲשֵׂה אֶרֶץ־מִצְרַיִם אֲשֶׁר יְשַׁבְתֶּם־בָּהּ לֹא תַעֲשׂוּ
וּכְמַעֲשֵׂה אֶרֶץ־כְּנַעַן אֲשֶׁר אֲנִי מֵבִיא אֶתְכֶם
שָׁמָּה לֹא תַעֲשׂוּ וּבְחֻקֹּתֵיהֶם לֹא תֵלֵכוּ

Do not perform the practices of the land of Egypt, in which you dwelled; and do not perform the practices of the land of Canaan, to which I am bringing you; and do not follow their traditions (*Vayikra* 18:3).

Rashi, citing *Toras Kohanim* (13:6-7), explains that the Egyptians and the Canaanites were the most depraved of all the nations. Thus, the Torah singled them out when warning the Jewish people not to follow the pagan and idolatrous practices of the nations.

Be'er BaSadeh adds that the fact that these nations were the greatest offenders in matters of idolatry was in fact because of the Jews. He explains that while the Jews were in Egypt, the Egyptians worshiped their deities with extra fervor, in the hope that this would allow them to retain the Jews as slaves. And when the Jews were liberated from Egypt and began making their way to Eretz Yisrael, it was the nations of Canaan that became the most zealous idolaters, in the hope that they could thereby prevent the Jews from inheriting Eretz Yisrael.

Kli Yakar, however, finds *Rashi's* explanation problematic. He asks: Why would the Torah warn against following the practices of the *worst* idolaters, thereby implying that following the practices of lesser idolaters would not be forbidden? Surely *any* hint of idolatry is forbidden by the Torah!

Kli Yakar therefore interprets the verse in the opposite manner. He maintains that the Egyptians and the Canaanites were *not* the most zealous of idolaters. In fact, it was for this reason that Hashem arranged that the exile of the Jews would happen in Egypt, and that the land they would inherit was occupied by the Canaanites. Since these nations were *not* such fervent idolaters, there was less concern that the Jews, when coming into contact with them, would learn from their idolatrous ways. Nevertheless, the Torah warns against following after even the ways of the Egyptians and the Canaanites — and certainly it is forbidden to follow after the ways of more fervent idolaters.

This, explains *Kli Yakar,* is why the verse identifies Egypt as *the land in which you dwelled,* and Canaan as *the land to which I am bringing you.* One might have thought that since these were the lands that Hashem

had selected, it could be deduced that contact with their citizens and learning their ways would not be injurious. Thus, the Torah states explicitly: In spite of the fact that you dwelled there, you may not follow the practices of the Egyptians. And in spite of the fact that I am bringing you there, you may not follow the ways of the Canaanites.

For a defense of *Rashi's* explanation, see *A Mussar Thought for the Day*.

MISHNAH OF THE DAY: ERUVIN 7:4

The Mishnah continues its discussion of two neighboring *chatzeiros* with a ditch running between them, explaining how the two courtyards, or a similar case of neighboring balconies, might be easily connected, allowing them to join in one *eruv*:

נָתַן עָלָיו — If ***one placed over*** the ditch **נֶסֶר שֶׁרָחָב אַרְבָּעָה טְפָחִים** — ***a board that is four tefachim wide,***[1] **וְכֵן שְׁתֵּי גְזוּזְטְרָאוֹת זוֹ כְּנֶגֶד זוֹ** — ***and, similarly, two balconies*** whose sides ***face each other precisely,***[2] that are bridged with a 4-*tefach* board,[3] **מְעָרְבִין שְׁנַיִם** — ***they***[4] ***may make two*** independent ***eruvin,*** **וְאִם רָצוּ מְעָרְבִין אֶחָד** — ***or, if they desire*** they ***may make one*** mutual ***eruv,*** because the board serves as a portal connecting the two areas. **פָּחוֹת מִכַּאן** — But if the board is ***less than this*** (i.e., less than 4 *tefachim* wide), **מְעָרְבִין שְׁנַיִם וְאֵין מְעָרְבִין אֶחָד** — ***they may make two*** separate ***eruvin, but they may not make one*** common ***eruv,*** because the board is too narrow to serve as a portal.

NOTES

1. He bridged the ditch with a board 4 *tefachim* wide, creating a portal to connect the two *chatzeiros.*

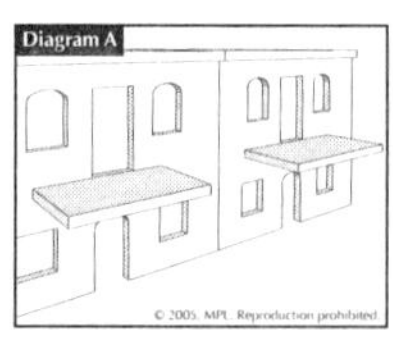

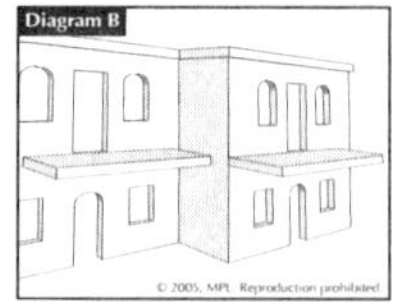

2. זוֹ כְּנֶגֶד זוֹ describes two balconies from two adjoining residences situated on the same side of a *reshus harabim* (*Rashi;* see diagram A). זוֹ שֶׁלֹּא כְּנֶגֶד זוֹ describes two balconies, alongside each other on the same side of the *reshus harabim,* that are not vertically or horizontally aligned see (diagram B). Such balconies may not be joined by means of a board spanning from one to the next.

3. I.e., if the board placed between them as a bridge measures 4 *tefachim* in width, it qualifies as a portal (*Rashi*).

4. I.e., the residents of the *chatzeiros* on both sides of the ditch or the residents of the adjoining houses with the balconies (according to *Rashi*).

GEMS FROM THE GEMARA

Our Mishnah said that if one placed over the ditch a board that is 4 *tefachim* wide, it connects the *chatzeiros*. Rava qualified this ruling by saying that a board 4 *tefachim* wide is required only when one placed the length of the board across the width of the ditch, to serve as a bridge across the ditch. However, if he placed it along the length of the ditch [with the board supported by pegs (*Rashi;* see diagram)], even a board of minimal width suffices to permit the *chatzeiros* to join in a mutual *eruv,* since he reduced the width of the ditch to less than 4 *tefachim.* Hence, this section of the ditch is considered a portal between the two *chatzeiros.* [If the board is at least 4 *tefachim* long, the length of this narrowed section of ditch corresponds to the minimum width of a portal (*Rashi*).]

The Mishnah taught that neighboring balconies that are זו כְּנֶגֶד זו may be joined by means of a board stretching from one to the next, implying that two balconies that are זו שֶׁלֹּא כְּנֶגֶד זו cannot be joined by a board. Now, as explained above, *Rashi* describes the case of זו כְּנֶגֶד זו as two balconies from two adjoining residences situated on the same side of a *reshus harabim,* and זו שֶׁלֹּא כְּנֶגֶד זו as two balconies, alongside each other on the same side of the *reshus harabim,* that are not vertically or horizontally aligned. [Since the connecting board must be placed at an angle, a board even 4 *tefachim* wide is not adequate (*Rashi*), since people are afraid to cross a board that runs at an angle or is inclined (*R' Yehonasan*).]

There is a difficulty with this interpretation, for as stated in the Mishnah (*Shabbos* 96a), one is Biblically prohibited from handing objects (מוֹשִׁיט) from one balcony to another so situated. Moreover, even when the Biblical prohibition does not apply (e.g., the object is thrown rather than handed), it is Rabbinically forbidden to transfer objects between two such balconies in all instances. *Pri Megadim* (*Mishbetzos Zahav* 373:1) suggests that in this case one may carry objects from balcony to balcony because the space over the connecting bridge is not considered to be "over the public domain" (although it would then follow that one would not be able to transfer objects through the airspace between the two balconies).

Most other *Rishonim* understand the two cases of זו כְּנֶגֶד זו and זו שֶׁלֹּא כְּנֶגֶד זו as follows: זו כְּנֶגֶד זו describes two balconies on two sides of the

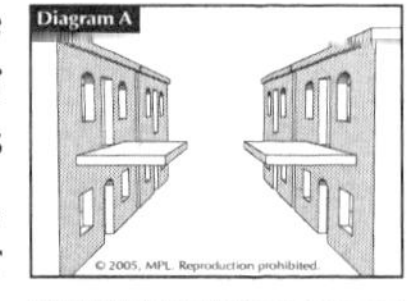

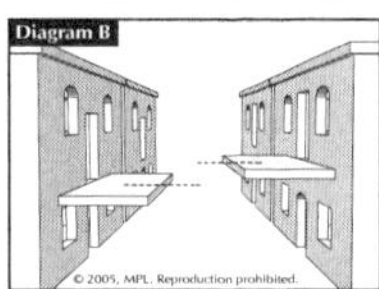

reshus harabim directly opposite each other (see diagram A), and זו שֶׁלֹּא כְּנֶגֶד זו describes two balconies not directly opposite each other, i.e., they are not at the same height, or are separated on a horizontal plane (see diagram B). Indeed, *Ritva's* version of *Rashi* concurs with this interpretation.

Now, Rava added that the rule that a board does not connect two balconies זו שֶׁלֹּא כְּנֶגֶד זו is true only when there are at least 3 *tefachim* of space between the balconies. However, if there is not a space of 3 *tefachim* between them, the two balconies are considered one crooked balcony, and the two residences may join in a mutual *eruv* even if the balconies do not face each other precisely. [A board 4 *tefachim* wide would suffice to bridge the gap between the balconies, since people are not afraid to cross at such a slight angle or slope (*R' Yehonasan*).]

A MUSSAR THOUGHT FOR THE DAY

In *A Torah Thought for the Day,* we explained that according to *Rashi,* the Egyptians and the Canaanites were the most depraved of the idolatrous nations. *Kli Yakar* asks: Why would the Torah single out the most depraved nations as the ones whose practices may not be followed? Surely any idolatrous practices are forbidden!

R' Moshe Feinstein (in *Darash Moshe*) notes that the verse does not forbid us from practicing the *depraved acts* (תּוֹעֲבוֹת) that were practiced in Egypt; it simply tells us not to act as the Egyptians and Canaanites did. He therefore understands that the Torah is cautioning us not to make the mistake of thinking that it is permitted to act as the Egyptians did, if we emulate the "good" people among the Egyptians. Rather, we must not follow *any* of the practices of the Egyptians or Canaanites — even the "good" ones.

Why is this so? R' Moshe explains that the correct way to avoid falling into sin is not simply to avoid the sinful behavior; one must distance himself from all things that are likely to *lead* to the sin. This is the way that a Jew who serves Hashem must live. The Egyptians and Canaanites, however, had no such aspirants among them. Even their noblest citizens were content with simply attempting to abstain from sin; they did not guard themselves from behavior that would increase their desire to sin.

THURSDAY

PARASHAS ACHAREI

And, of course, their attempts at refraining from sin were ultimately futile.

Thus, R' Moshe explains, the Torah is telling us: Learn the lesson from the nations that are the most zealous idolaters, and do not even act as the good among them did. For if you will act as they did, and simply avoid sin itself, in the end you will come to be as depraved as they are. According to this approach, we can understand why the Torah singles out Egypt and Canaan, the worst offenders. The Torah focuses on the worst of nations to tell us not to be complacent and sure of ourselves. Once a person relaxes his vigilance and does not guard himself against taking even the first step down the slippery slope that leads to sin, he is in danger of becoming every bit as depraved as the idolaters of Egypt and Canaan. The only way to ensure that one will not succumb to sin is by not emulating the nations at all. Rather, one must always strive to distance himself from places, people, and situations in which his desire to sin might be inflamed.

HALACHAH OF THE DAY

As we learned yesterday, the Biblical prohibition against *demolishing* applies to acts of demolishing that have constructive purpose. The Sages forbade even purely destructive acts of demolition as well.

For example, one may not break the window of an abandoned vehicle on Shabbos even if there is no beneficial purpose behind the act at all. As another example, one may not break down the door of a locked room on Shabbos. [This is *not* a Biblical violation, however. While a benefit is derived from the removal of the door, the benefit is not from the *destruction* of the door — opening the door without destroying it would accomplish the same objective.] Therefore, the act of destruction is seen as being purely destructive, and is forbidden only by Rabbinic decree.

However, if a young child who is unable to unlock the door becomes locked in a room on Shabbos, it is permitted to break down the door and free the child. The halachah views this as a potentially life-threatening situation; therefore, one may break down the door or take any other action deemed necessary to free the child.

According to most *poskim,* demolishing a structure in order to make use of its components to build another structure elsewhere is forbidden by Rabbinic decree. However, others maintain that this too is Biblically forbidden.

The *melachah* of *demolishing* is, in essence, the converse of the *melachah* of *building.* It therefore follows that any structure that may not be erected on Shabbos is also subject to the restrictions against *demolishing* on Shabbos. If the erection of a particular type of structure violates Biblical law, its demolition violates the Biblical law as well; if the erection constitutes a violation of Rabbinic decree, the demolition also violates Rabbinic decree. By the same token, a structure that may be built on Shabbos may also be destroyed on Shabbos.

As we have seen in our discussion of the *melachah* of *building,* making improvements to the ground is forbidden on Shabbos. Conversely, one is forbidden as part of the *melachah* of *demolishing* to reverse any improvements that have been made to the ground.

For example, packing down earth in order to create a firm, level pathway or floor is a violation of the *melachah* of *building.* It therefore follows that tearing up the packed-down earth on Shabbos is forbidden as well, for it is a violation of the *melachah* of *demolishing.*

A CLOSER LOOK AT THE SIDDUR

We continue our discussion of the first of the *Sheish Zechiros,* the Six Remembrances, which bids us to remember daily the occurrence of *Yetzias Mitzrayim,* the Exodus from Egypt, by reciting the verse: לְמַעַן תִּזְכֹּר אֶת־יוֹם צֵאתְךָ מֵאֶרֶץ מִצְרַיִם כֹּל יְמֵי חַיֶּיךָ, *That you remember the day of your departure from the land of Egypt all the days of your life* (*Devarim* 16:3).

Last week, we discussed the nature of this remembrance, that it is primarily that of the heart, and that it is to be a constant realization. Now we will discuss some of the meanings and implications of the Exodus for the nation and for the individual.

The most basic significance of the Exodus from Egypt is that it is the foundation of our obligation to serve Hashem. When Hashem revealed Himself to the entire nation at Sinai, He introduced Himself, not as the Creator of the heavens and the earth, but as the One Who redeemed us from Egypt. The special relationship between Hashem and the Jewish people does not trace itself to the creation of the world, but to Hashem's acquiring us as His own by redeeming us from servitude. [See *Rashi* to *Shemos* 20:2 with *Re'em* and *Gur Aryeh; Ramban* ad loc.]

In addition, the events surrounding the Exodus served at the time as

a refutation of the contentions of those who denied the existence of Hashem or His involvement in the world. When a prophet declares that a certain miracle will occur, and it occurs exactly as foretold, it is clear that there is an All-powerful God, Who by virtue of having created the world is in full control of its every aspect. It also becomes apparent that He takes a great interest in what is happening in this world.

Now, Hashem will not make such miracles for every generation, or for the benefit of every denier. Instead, He commanded us to perpetuate the memory of these events for all generations and for all times. In this way we will always know His greatness, and the basic tenets of our faith will be clear to all (*Ramban* to *Shemos* 13:16).

In a different vein, *R' Tzadok HaKohen* (*Pri Tzaddik, Pesach* 24) writes that this mitzvah is to serve as a source of personal encouragement. There are times when a person finds himself sunk into some impure desire or sin, and feels that he cannot, try as he may, rid himself of it. The more he attempts to stop or disengage from it, the more entrapped he feels. As his situation seems hopeless, he is inclined to simply give up. In this state, it becomes important that he keep in mind the Exodus from Egypt.

The Jewish people in the land of Egypt had sunk to the lowest possible level of impurity — so much so that it was nearly impossible to distinguish between Jew and gentile. And then, suddenly, Hashem pulled them out from beneath all their impurity, and they were free — ready for a new beginning and spiritual greatness.

One must remember that no matter how far he has sunk, and as hopeless as his situation may seem, he has still not descended to the level of his forefathers in Egypt. His spiritual predicament cannot be worse than theirs. He must remind himself of the Exodus and internalize its meaning. He can then look toward the time when Hashem, in His mercy and in His kindness, will simply lift him up, freeing him from his seemingly hopeless state, and allowing him to begin his spiritual ascent anew.

QUESTION OF THE DAY:

Why does the verse repeat the words "you shall not do"?

For the answer, see page 59.

פרשת אחרי

FRIDAY

PARASHAS ACHAREI

A TORAH THOUGHT FOR THE DAY

וּשְׁמַרְתֶּם אֶת־חֻקֹּתַי וְאֶת־מִשְׁפָּטַי אֲשֶׁר
יַעֲשֶׂה אֹתָם הָאָדָם וָחַי בָּהֶם אֲנִי ה׳

You shall observe My decrees and My laws, which man shall carry out and by which he shall live — I am H*ASHEM* (*Vayikra* 18:5).

The plain sense of this verse, according to *Ramban,* refers to the framework of Torah laws, spelled out in *Parashas Mishpatim* as well as in other places, that govern the fiscal relationships between people. These include torts, pecuniary measures, and many aspects of civil law (מִשְׁפָּטִים). It is this part of the legal system of the Torah that ensures the peaceful running of society; hence, these mitzvos are described in this verse as laws *by which [man] shall live.*

Ramban writes that *Chazal* interpreted the "life" mentioned at the end of the verse as the reward for the person who keeps all the Torah's mitzvos. However, just as each person's service of Hashem is different, so, correspondingly, is the "life" that he receives. Following is a description of the four levels of reward that *Ramban* lists, with a few added words of explanation from *R' Dovid Kviat* in his *Succas Dovid.*

(1) The first level is the reward given to a person who keeps the Torah for the sole purpose of receiving his reward in this world. Although the optimal place for receiving reward is in the World to Come — for all the good of this world cannot measure up to the pleasures of the next world — one who desires his reward in this world is granted his wish. He thus receives his "life" in the form of long years, filled with wealth and honor.

(2) One who serves Hashem, not for the reward of this world but out of fear of punishment in the next, receives his primary reward in the next world. The conditions of his life in this world will not reflect his good deeds, for the only true place to receive reward for keeping the Torah is in the next world.

(3) The ideal motivation for serving Hashem is that of love. One who, while involved in all the necessary functions of life, such as planting and reaping, still serves Hashem in the elevated manner that is an outgrowth of love, receives his complete reward in the next world. However, such a person is also granted success in this world. This is not a form of reward for his actions, but the result of the special assistance that Hashem gives to His most loyal servants, to enable them to continue to serve Him in the most complete way.

(4) The highest level of attachment to Hashem results in the most rare and exalted form of "life." This is one who completely cleaves to his Creator, to the extent that he totally abandons all things worldly, such as earning a living or tending to physical needs, striving only to attach himself in every thought and action to Hashem. This true servant of Hashem elevates his life to such a level that he, as the prophet Eliyahu, rises above the clutches of death. He continues to live, both in body and soul, forever.

The observance of the Torah carries with it the promise of life. As we see from the words of the *Ramban,* the level and quality of that life depends on the level and quality of one's individual observance.

MISHNAH OF THE DAY: ERUVIN 7:5

The Mishnah teaches the final case involving two neighboring *chatzeiros* separated by a temporary wall, again dealing with the question of whether they may make one joint *eruv* or separate *eruvin:* מַתְבֵּן שֶׁבֵּין שְׁתֵּי חֲצֵירוֹת — If ***a haystack between two chatzeiros***[1] גָּבוֹהַּ עֲשָׂרָה טְפָחִים — is ***ten tefachim high,*** it completely separates the *chatzeiros* and מְעָרְבִין שְׁנַיִם — ***they*** (i.e., the residents of the two *chatzeiros*) ***may make two*** independent ***eruvin,*** וְאֵין מְעָרְבִין אֶחָד — ***but they may not make one eruv.***[2] אֵלּוּ מַאֲבִילִין מִכָּאן — ***These*** (i.e., the residents of one of the *chatzeiros*) ***may feed*** their livestock ***from here,***[3] וְאֵלּוּ מַאֲבִילִין מִכָּאן — ***and those*** (i.e., the residents of the other *chatzeir*) ***may feed*** their livestock ***from here.***[3],[4] נִתְמַעֵט הַתֶּבֶן מֵעֲשָׂרָה טְפָחִים — If before the

NOTES

1. Two adjoining *chatzeiros* are separated by a haystack that runs the entire length of their boundary (*Rashi*).

2. The law of the haystack is identical to the law of a dividing wall — transfer between the two *chatzeiros* is prohibited.

[Although the haystack separates the *chatzeiros* only temporarily, it is nevertheless a valid partition since, at least for the present, the two *chatzeiros* are in fact separate. This is in contrast to Mishnah 3 in which the hay, because it was placed in a trench on a temporary basis, does not invalidate the trench's status as a partition.]

3. I.e., from their side of the haystack.

4. The residents need not be concerned that their animals will consume so much straw without anyone noticing that the height of the haystack will shrink to below 10 *tefachim* (in which case the two *chatzeiros* become one domain into which none of the residents may carry), since a partition is not considered breached until its height has been reduced to under 10 *tefachim* along a continuous 10-*amah* stretch, and it is highly unusual for an animal to eat so much during one Sabbath (*Rashi*).

Sabbath[5] *the* height of the *straw was reduced from ten tefachim,*[6] מְעָרְבִין אֶחָד — *they may make one* common *eruv,* וְאֵין מְעָרְבִין שְׁנַיִם — *but they may not make two eruvin.* Since a legal breach has been created in the partition, the two *chatzeiros* are considered one area.

NOTES

5. *Rashi.* If the breach occurred on the Sabbath, it is too late for the two *chatzeiros* to make a common *eruv.*

6. Either along a 10-*amah* section of the haystack, or along the entire common boundary of the *chatzeiros* if it is not 10 *amos* long (*Rashi*).

GEMS FROM THE GEMARA

Our Mishnah allowed one to have his animals eat on the Sabbath from a haystack that divides the *chatzeiros.* In the Gemara, Rav Huna qualifies this leniency by saying that the owner may have his animals eat from the haystack only if he does not put straw into his basket and feed them from it. *Rashi* gives two explanations for this. First, in such a case we are concerned that he may unwittingly take too much straw and invalidate the partition; this would combine the two *chatzeiros* into one domain into which none of the residents are permitted to carry, and the residents may unwittingly carry there. However, when the animals feed themselves, they do not generally eat enough to invalidate the partition. Alternatively, the owner himself may not handle the straw because it was designated before the Sabbath as a partition, and so it is *muktzeh.* But the *muktzeh* prohibition does not apply to livestock.

Now, Rav Huna prohibited the owner only from "taking" the straw, implying, however, that one may lead his animal to the straw to eat. Apparently, then, Rav Huna is not concerned that the owner will unintentionally transgress the Rabbinic prohibition against taking the straw. The Gemara questions this from Rav Huna's own ruling elsewhere that a person may lead his animal to grass on the Sabbath, because we are not concerned that he might uproot the grass for his animal. [As this is the Biblically forbidden *melachah* of קוֹצֵר, *reaping,* we assume that people are scrupulous when a Biblical prohibition is involved, and would not err in this matter (*Rashi*).] But a person may not stand his animal over fodder that is *muktzeh* on the Sabbath [e.g., straw that has been designated for building purposes (*R' Yehonasan*)]. Since the prohibition of *muktzeh* is only Rabbinic in origin and is perceived to be less severe, we are concerned that he might be less scrupulous and err, inadvertently handling the *muktzeh* himself. Similarly here, the Gemara concludes its question, since the prohibition of taking the straw from the partition is also only Rabbinic in origin — either because he might thereby invalidate the partition or because the haystack is *muktzeh* — leading an animal to the straw should also be prohibited, because he might come to remove the straw himself.

The Gemara then cedes this point, saying that the Mishnah does not speak of his physically leading the animal to the haystack. Rather, it allows the owner only to stand in front of the animal to block it from going elsewhere, and the animal will go to the straw of its own accord and eat from it. Thus, since he may not actually lead the animal to the haystack, he will not inadvertently handle the straw himself.

The Gemara challenges Rav Huna's qualification (that one may not put straw from the haystack into his basket) from a Baraisa that teaches about a house that is between two *chatzeiros* [and one house from each *chatzeir* opens into this house (*Rashi*)], and it is filled with straw that forms a partition between the two *chatzeiros.* The Baraisa teaches that the residents of the two *chatzeiros* may make two independent *eruvin,* but may not make one mutual *eruv,* since there is no connection between them. The Baraisa further teaches that the residents of each *chatzeir* may put straw into their baskets and feed it to their animals, but if the height of the straw was reduced from 10 *tefachim,* the residents of both *chatzeiros* are prohibited from taking more straw. [This is because at a height of less than 10 *tefachim,* the haystack can no longer function as a partition between the two houses. Hence, the entire area of the three houses becomes one large unmerged *chatzeir,* into which the residents of neither house may carry (*Ritva*).]

The Baraisa clearly permits the residents of the *chatzeiros* to put straw into their baskets and feed it to their animals. This contradicts Rav Huna's contention that straw that divides two *chatzeiros* may not be handled!

The Gemara resolves this contradiction by distinguishing between the cases as follows: In the Baraisa's case, it was a house that was filled with straw, and since there is a ceiling, when the haystack becomes diminished it is noticeable, since the space between the top of the haystack and the ceiling increases. Therefore, should the haystack be reduced to a height of less than 10 *tefachim,* people will notice and refrain from removing any more straw, lest they destroy the partition. And according to the alternative explanation of Rav Huna's prohibition (that the straw is *muktzeh* — see above), since only the lower 10 *tefachim* of straw have

FRIDAY

PARASHAS ACHAREI

been designated as a partition, people in a house may take from the straw above, which is not *muktzeh*, since they will notice when the 10-*tefach* level has been reached (*Rashi*).

Here, however, in the case of our Mishnah, it is not noticeable when the haystack becomes diminished, since it stands outside and there is no ceiling. Therefore, Rav Huna prohibited the owner from removing the straw by hand, lest the height of the haystack be reduced inadvertently to under 10 *tefachim*.

A MUSSAR THOUGHT FOR THE DAY

People have the impression that *kiddush Hashem* (sanctifying the Name of Hashem) means dying or getting killed for the sake of Hashem. *Rav Elazar Menachem Man Shach* develops the theme, based on the verse וָחַי בָּהֶם, *and by which he shall live,* that it is no less important, and perhaps even more important, for man to *live* with *kiddush Hashem.*

The Torah values life over death, as we see in the verse cited in *A Torah Thought for the Day.* The *kiddush Hashem* that one must perform with his life is to rise to every occasion, face every obstacle, and live — according to the mitzvos of the Torah.

In a certain sense, to die for a cause is easier than to live a difficult life for it. Throughout history, millions have given their lives for one cause or another. Many of these, however, could not stand up to the challenges of the simplest of their desires. The charge of the Torah is the exact opposite of this. The goal is not to die, but to live one's life with dedication and a readiness to give up whatever he must in the pursuit of adherence to the laws of the Torah.

R' Akiva was killed in an extremely cruel fashion for teaching Torah in public. It is a well-known story: As his flesh was being raked with combs of iron, R' Akiva recited the *Shema,* accepting upon himself the sovereignty of Hashem. His soul left as he said the word *echad.* On the surface, this seems to be a story of supreme self-sacrifice, of willingness to die for Hashem and accept His decree.

However, a careful reading of this narrative in the Gemara (*Berachos* 61b) reveals another angle. "It happened that the time that R' Akiva was led out to be executed was the time for the recitation of *Shema.*" R' Akiva did not recite *Shema* as a part of his glorious death for the sake

of Hashem. R' Akiva recited the *Shema* because the appropriate time for its reading had arrived. And in this, as in all other situations in R' Akiva's life, he reacted by fulfilling the commandments incumbent upon him at that time. The Gemara is relating the greatness of R' Akiva, not in his dying, but in his living for the sake of Hashem, even in the most extreme of circumstances.

A Jew is obligated to keep the Torah's commandments in all situations and at all times. Up to the very end of one's life, one is obligated to keep whatever mitzvos he still can. This is the lesson that we must learn from R' Akiva.

HALACHAH OF THE DAY

Just as one is forbidden to erect a structure upon the ground on Shabbos, so too one may not demolish any structure that has been built upon the ground. The prohibition applies irrespective of whether the structure is attached to the ground or merely standing upon it; and it applies no matter what the style of the structure and no matter what types of materials are used in its construction.

Included in this prohibition would be the destruction of a wall, fence, or even the removal of a protective border around a garden that has been created out of bricks or pavers firmly set in place in the ground. Just as is true of the prohibition against *building,* it is forbidden to destroy a structure built upon the ground even if the components of the structure are not tightly joined.

Removing objects that are attached to a structure is likewise forbidden under the *melachah* of *demolishing.* Even if the objects are only loosely attached to the structure — for instance, a doorknob assembly that has become loose — their removal is a violation of Biblical law. If, however, the items being removed are entirely unsecured, their removal is a violation of Rabbinic law only.

There are cases where the removal of an item attached to a structure is permissible. The prohibition of *demolishing* does not apply to the removal of an object whose normal use entails detaching it from and reattaching it to the structure. Detaching such an item is not an act of *demolishing,* for it simply represents the normal use of this item and is therefore permissible.

For example, one may remove the spring-loaded holder that holds a roll of bathroom tissue in place on its dispenser. Since the tube is meant to be removed and replaced, removing it does not constitute an act of *demolishing,* and, as we have stated previously, replacing it is not a violation of *building.*

Something that is attached to a structure only in a flimsy manner is not seen as truly being a part of the structure, and it therefore may be removed from the structure on Shabbos. For example, we have stated previously that a curtain may be hung on Shabbos in order to divide a room provided that it is held in place only on top and not on the bottom. Since the curtain may be hung on Shabbos without violating the *melachah* of *building,* on account of its not being seen as truly attached to the structure, it may also be removed on Shabbos without violating the *melachah* of *demolishing.*

A CLOSER LOOK AT THE SIDDUR

During the Days of Repentance, and especially on Rosh Hashanah and Yom Kippur, we repeatedly pray to merit being judged for "life." Primary among these prayers is the זָכְרֵנוּ לְחַיִּים request added to the first blessing of the *Shemoneh Esrei*: זָכְרֵנוּ לְחַיִּים מֶלֶךְ חָפֵץ בַּחַיִּים וְכָתְבֵנוּ בְּסֵפֶר הַחַיִּים לְמַעַנְךָ אֱלֹהִים חַיִּים, *Remember us for life, O King Who desires life; and inscribe us in the Book of Life, for Your sake, O Living God. R' Moshe Chaim Luzzato* explains that the "life" we pray for in this short prayer is not favorable circumstances (such as riches and prosperity) in the life of this world. Here we are asking that we be counted among the righteous who are inscribed in the Book of Life (see *Rosh Hashanah* 16a).

This, however, is difficult to understand. How can one request to be designated as a righteous person and be inscribed as such, if he is in fact not righteous? And if he already falls into that category, why must he pray to be so inscribed? *R' Chaim Friedlander* (in his *Sifsei Chaim*) answers this question in his detailed explanation of this prayer.

זָכְרֵנוּ לְחַיִּים, *Remember us for life* — We ask to be remembered, not for the transient "life" of the physical world, not even for the illusory "life" of keeping the Torah out of habit, but for a true life — a life filled with behavior in accordance with our full recognition of our responsibilities, and in the light of genuine fear of Heaven.

Our honest plea for life of this quality is in itself cause for Hashem to define our spiritual essence as being among the *tzaddikim.*

מֶלֶךְ חָפֵץ בַּחַיִּים, *O King Who desires life* — We want to live the kind of life that our King would desire us to live. This is a life lived to bring increased honor to His Name.

וְכָתְבֵנוּ בְּסֵפֶר הַחַיִּים, *And inscribe us in the Book of Life* — As a result of this very request to live life in such a manner, inscribe us in the Book of those who are truly considered alive — the righteous.

לְמַעַנְךָ, *for Your sake* — Just as a soldier receives all his needs from the army in which he serves, for his life is in the service of his king, so do we ask to receive a full measure of spiritual and even physical assistance, for we wish to live our life for Your sake.

אֱלֹהִים חַיִּים, *O Living God* — We stress that we wish to receive life only from the true Source of life — Hashem. A person may be granted the power and ability to rebel against Hashem, as part of his free will. Thus, we proclaim that we want nothing at all to do with "life" from these sources. We reject such a life, for Hashem does not desire that life. Our sole purpose is to receive from, and live for, the Living God.

QUESTION OF THE DAY:

What practical halachah do we learn from the words וָחַי בָּהֶם, and by which he shall live?

For the answer, see page 59.

פרשת אחרי

SHABBOS

PARASHAS ACHAREI

A TORAH THOUGHT FOR THE DAY

וּשְׁמַרְתֶּם אֶת־מִשְׁמַרְתִּי לְבִלְתִּי עֲשׂוֹת מֵחֻקּוֹת הַתּוֹעֵבֹת אֲשֶׁר נַעֲשׂוּ לִפְנֵיכֶם וְלֹא תִטַּמְּאוּ בָּהֶם אֲנִי ה׳ אֱלֹהֵיכֶם

You shall safeguard My charge not to do any of the abominable traditions that were done before you and [you shall] not contaminate yourselves through them; I am H*ASHEM your God* (*Vayikra* 18:30).

As *Rashi* explains, this verse is addressing the courts and commanding them to enact safeguards around the laws of the Torah, to prevent any transgression. For example, to distance a person from any of the forbidden relationships, the Sages forbade a number of relationships that are even further removed than those listed in this chapter.

Ohr HaChaim explains that these safeguards are important because without them one may come to violate one of the laws of the Torah unintentionally. And, while a person is not punished for his unintentional violations, he is affected by them. This is explained in the end of the verse: *and [you shall] not contaminate yourselves through them.* I.e., the actions themselves, however they are done, cause you to be impure.

The verse's conclusion, *I am* H*ASHEM your God,* underscores this message. It is only when we are free from any form of immorality that Hashem identifies His Name with us. In the presence of immorality, intentional or not, the Divine Presence cannot remain.

Another explanation of the function of these safeguards is offered by *Alshich.* Often, the desire of a person for that which is forbidden is not primarily based upon the item that is prohibited *per se.* It is rather the very fact that it is *forbidden* that is so attractive. [This thought is expressed in the verse (*Mishlei* 9:17): מַיִם־גְּנוּבִים יִמְתָּקוּ, *Stolen waters are sweet.*] Therefore, the Sages set up other prohibitions that one will encounter before violating the actual Torah prohibition. In this way, even if a person will be unable to control himself, he will be "satisfied" with the violation of the Rabbinic prohibition and will not need to proceed to the actual sin.

Thus, the verse reads as follows: *You shall safeguard My charge,* i.e., you shall enact Rabbinic prohibitions surrounding the actual sins; [so that] *you will not come to do any of the [actual] abominable traditions.*

One may claim that such enactments will not be enough to prevent a sinner from violating even the Torah laws. To this claim, the verse responds: *You will not contaminate yourselves through them;* you are assured that as a result of enacting such legislation and creating distance between yourselves and the actual prohibitions of the Torah, you will not fall prey to these sins. For, *I am* H*ASHEM your God,* and those who fear Me I will protect from sin.

MISHNAH OF THE DAY: ERUVIN 7:6

The Mishnah now discusses the particulars of making a *shitufei mevo'os.* One way to accomplish this is to collect adequate amounts of food from each household in each of the courtyards. Obviously, this is a very cumbersome procedure, and so the Mishnah considers a more practical solution:

כֵּיצַד מִשְׁתַּתְּפִין בַּמָּבוֹי — ***How do we make a shituf for a mavoi?***[1] **מַנִּיחַ אֶת הֶחָבִית** — ***One places a barrel,*** containing his own food,[2] **וְאוֹמֵר הֲרֵי זוֹ לְכָל בְּנֵי מָבוֹי** — ***and declares, "Let this*** belong ***to all the residents of the mavoi,"*** **וּמְזַכֶּה לָהֶן** — ***and he confers ownership upon them***[3] **עַל יְדֵי בְּנוֹ וּבִתּוֹ הַגְּדוֹלִים** — ***through his adult son or daughter,***[4] **וְעַל יְדֵי עַבְדּוֹ וְשִׁפְחָתוֹ הָעִבְרִים** — ***or through his Jewish manservant or maidservant,***[5]

NOTES

1. I.e., what is a practical way of establishing a *shituf*?

2. The barrel contains an amount sufficient for everyone's contribution. [The required amount will be discussed in the Mishnah below (7:8).] In order to satisfy the requirement that each resident own his share of the *shituf,* he transfers ownership to them in the manner described below.

3. The formal act of taking possession consists of transferring an object from the hand of the current owner to the hand of the recipient or his proxy. The current owner cannot be the proxy for the recipient, since physically placing the object into his own hand is not considered a legal transfer from the hand of one person to the hand of another. As will be seen below, certain other people, such as the young children of the current owner who are still under their father's control, are also disqualified from acting as a proxy, for their "hand" is considered the "hand" of the owner. Since a man does not have monetary control over his adult children, they may act as proxies vis-a-vis their own father (see *Meiri*). Actually, anyone may serve as the proxy — not only the people mentioned here. These are mentioned only in contradistinction to those categories disqualified in the second part of the Mishnah.

The act of transferring ownership of the *shituf* consists of a declaration by its owner to the proxy, charging him to accept the *shituf* and to confer its ownership upon all the residents of the *mavoi* (*Rashi*), and of the proxy's lifting the barrel 1 *tefach* from the ground (Gemara below).

4. There is a dispute between Amoraim (*Bava Metzia* 12b) whether even an adult child is considered subject to his father's monetary control (regarding some aspects) if his board is provided by his father. The *Rishonim* differ as to whether the Amoraic dispute has any relevance concerning *eruv* law. Some assert that according to all Amoraim an adult child may confer ownership, even if he is dependent on his father for his board (see *Tosafos* and *Ritva* here; *Beis Yosef Orach Chaim* §366). In addition, there is some dispute as to the precise age of majority for a girl, relevant to this law (see *Tosafos* ד"ה ומזכה).

5. A Jewish servant is not the common property of his master, but is more like an indentured servant. Therefore, although one has placed himself in servitude, he nevertheless retains legal control over his own possessions.

SHABBOS

PARASHAS ACHAREI

אֲבָל אֵינוֹ מְזַכֶּה וְעַל יְדֵי אִשְׁתּוֹ — *or through his wife.*[6] לֹא עַל יְדֵי בְּנוֹ — *But he may not confer ownership* וּבִתּוֹ הַקְּטַנִּים — *through his minor son or daughter,* וְלֹא עַל יְדֵי עַבְדּוֹ וְשִׁפְחָתוֹ הַכְּנַעֲנִים — *or through his Canaanite slave or slavewoman,*[7] מִפְּנֵי שֶׁיָּדָן כְּיָדוֹ — ***because their hand is like his hand,*** and he cannot confer ownership of the *shituf* upon the other residents of the *mavoi* if it is still under his control.

NOTES

6. Although the husband exercises some control over his wife's possessions, this is not sufficient to preclude her from acquiring the *eruv* food for others.

The Talmud (*Nedarim* 88b) implies that the status of a wife in regard to this law is the subject of a disagreement between R' Meir and the Sages. The halachah is also in question, as some authorities rule in accordance with R' Meir and others with the Sages. Both views are represented in *Shulchan Aruch* (*Orach Chaim* 366:10); see also *Tosafos* ד״ה ועל.

7. The term "Canaanite" embraces slaves of all nationalities. According to Torah law, the master owns all his slave's belongings. Since whatever the slave acquires automatically reverts to his master, the donor cannot use his own slave as the proxy since that is the equivalent of being the proxy himself.

GEMS FROM THE GEMARA

Our Mishnah stated that food donated for a *shituf* must be acquired by the other residents of the *mavoi* through a proxy. The Gemara (80a) cites a dispute regarding this matter.

Rav (who has the status of a Tanna, and therefore has authority to disagree with the opinion of a Mishnah or Baraisa) said that someone donating food for a *shituf* does not need to confer ownership upon the other residents. [Rav maintains that since without a *shituf* the owner would not be permitted to carry into the *mavoi,* the owner definitely resolves to make a unilateral transfer of ownership to the other residents of the *mavoi,* thereby obviating the need for a formal act of acquisition (*Rashi*).] But Shmuel said that he must confer ownership upon the other residents (as indicated by our Mishnah).

In regard to food donated for an *eruv techumin,* the Gemara says that these two opinions are reversed: Rav said that he must confer ownership upon each beneficiary of the *eruv;* since an *eruvei techumin* benefits each of its owners individually, the donor is unaffected by his neighbors' status vis-a-vis the *eruv.* Hence, he is not motivated to confer ownership upon the others unilaterally, as in the case of *shituf* (see previous paragraph), and so a formal acquisition is necessary to entitle the others. But Shmuel said that he does not need to confer ownership. *Tosafos* (ד״ה רב) advance three explanations of Shmuel's opinion: (1) Joining in a *shituf* involves a quasi-acquisition of another's domain, whereas joining in an *eruvei techumin* does not. Hence, in the case of *shituf* the donor must actually confer ownership upon the other residents, while in the case of *eruvei techumin* that is not necessary. (2) Since an *eruvei techumin* may be made only to facilitate the performance of mitzvos outside of the *techum* (see *Eruvin* 31a), the donor is definitely willing to transfer ownership in the *eruv* to enable others to perform mitzvos. (3) Since a donor cannot compel others to accept membership in an *eruvei techumin* (since perhaps they wish to go in other directions on the Sabbath), the expression of their desire to be included serves in lieu of a formal act of acquisition.

For all practical purposes, Rav Nachman rules, on the basis of an accepted tradition from our teachers, that the donor must formally confer ownership of the food upon the people for whom the *eruv* or *shituf* is made, in the cases of *eruvei techumin, eruvei chatzeiros* and *shitufei mevo'os.*

The Gemara questions whether a donor of food for an *eruvei tavshilin* must also formally transfer ownership. [According to Biblical law, one may cook and make other preparations for the Sabbath on Yom Tov, just as one may prepare on that day for the Yom Tov itself. However, as a preliminary to preparing for the Sabbath on Yom Tov, the Sages required that one set aside a special dish before Yom Tov. This dish serves a symbolic function and is called עֵרוּבֵי תַבְשִׁילִין, *eruvei tavshilin* (lit., *blending* or *mingling of dishes*).]

The Gemara notes that in this case Shmuel presents an undisputed opinion — when one wishes to donate food for an *eruvei tavshilin,* he must confer ownership upon each of the people for whom the *eruv* is being made.

A MUSSAR THOUGHT FOR THE DAY

The second "gate" of *Shaarei Teshuvah* (Gates of Repentance) by *Rabbeinu Yonah* arranges the various Torah laws into ten levels of severity, ranging from the Rabbinic enactments to safeguard the Torah, to the most severe — those that carry the penalty of losing one's portion in the World to Come.

In explaining the first, and apparently least severe, of the levels, *Rabbeinu Yonah* explains that in fact there is an aspect of Rabbinic law that is more severe than the actual Torah law. *Chazal* tell us that one who violates the words of the Sages is liable to death (imposed from Heaven), while many Torah prohibitions do not carry such a penalty. There are two points that make the willful violator of the words of the Sages worse than one who violates a Torah law.

First of all, one who violates a commandment of the Torah generally does so under the influence of his *yetzer hara* (evil inclination), which succeeded in causing him to sin. After he has sinned, and the desire has faded, he will usually regret his actions and feel bad about what he did. This is not so with one who violates Rabbinic law. Usually, one who willfully transgresses these laws does so out of disregard for the importance of the words of the Sages. He either does not appreciate, or does not believe in, the gravity of these prohibitions, and therefore does not trouble himself to fulfill them. With these actions he puts himself into the same category as the *zakein mamrei,* who rebels against the ruling of the *Sanhedrin* and is liable to the death penalty.

Second, a person who violates Rabbinic law is generally not inclined to repent his actions or desist from them in the future, while one who fell into a Torah sin will usually try to rectify what he has done or at least abstain from such sins in the future. Thus, through repetition, the Rabbinic violation, albeit less severe, can become more severe than the once-violated Torah prohibition.

There is another aspect to the special status that these enactments have. Just as a person makes fences around the parts of a field that are most dear to him, the Sages have made "fences" around the laws of the Torah to protect that which is most dear to us — the laws of the Torah. When one is careful to avoid something that may bring him to violate a Torah law, he is demonstrating his fear of Heaven, which is the foundation for all the mitzvos in the Torah. The reward for one who keeps these mitzvos is therefore commensurate with the reward for the all-encompassing mitzvah of fearing Hashem.

QUESTION OF THE DAY:

***According to some Rishonim, what mitzvah finds its source in this verse* (18:30)?**

For the answer, see page 59.

HALACHAH OF THE DAY

As we taught in regard to the *melachah* of *building*, large utensils are seen by halachah as having the same law as structures that have been built upon the ground. It therefore follows that just as one may not demolish a structure even if its components are not tightly joined together, so too it is forbidden by Biblical law to disassemble a large utensil even if its components are not tightly joined together.

For example, one may not remove the sliding door of a large bookcase from its track on Shabbos. Since such a bookcase is treated by halachah in the same manner as a building, the removal of the loose-fitting door is a violation of the *melachah* of *demolishing.*

One who assembles a small utensil whose components are tightly joined together also violates the *melachah* of *building.* The converse is therefore also true — one who disassembles a small utensil of this type violates the *melachah* of *demolishing.* For example, one may not unscrew the the head of a broom from its broomstick. One who does this in order to reattach the head in a tighter, more effective way, violates the Biblical prohibition against *demolishing,* since the act is being done for a constructive purpose.

Just as is the case in regard to the building of small utensils, there are cases where small utensils may be disassembled on Shabbos. A utensil whose parts are not made to be tightly joined together may be disassembled on Shabbos. Since the parts of the utensil are never firmly attached one to the other, they are not regarded as comprising a single object; the *melachah* of *demolishing* therefore cannot apply to such a utensil. Examples of this would be the removal of a pendant from its necklace, or the removal of a loose-fitting door from a small curio cabinet.

Many *poskim* maintain that where a utensil's normal use involves its being assembled and disassembled, one may disassemble it even though its parts have been tightly assembled. For example, one may unscrew the top of a salt shaker in order to refill it, since this is done in the course of the normal use of the shaker.

A CLOSER LOOK AT THE SIDDUR

We continue our study of some of the *zemiros* that are sung at the Friday night meal.

One of the *zemiros* that is somewhat less well-known is the *zemer* of

יוֹם זֶה לְיִשְׂרָאֵל, *Yom Zeh L'Yisrael.* Some attribute it to *Arizal,* based on the fact that the acrostic of the six stanzas most commonly included in the *zemer* spells Yitzchak, followed by ל״ח which some translate as *Luria, Chazak* (the *Arizal's* name was R' Yitzchak Luria, and *Chazak* [May he be strong!] was commonly appended to such signatures). Indeed, later versions of the song have additional stanzas, filling in the acrostic so that it reads *Yitzchak Luria Chazak.* However, this *zemer* is written in Hebrew, which militates against its having been written by *Arizal,* who composed mainly in Aramaic.

The *zemer* begins by focusing on the special nature of the Sabbath day, from its ability to soothe pained souls through its festive meals, to the presence of the *neshamah yeseirah,* "the additional soul" that every Jew receives on the Sabbath.

Then, the *zemer* speaks of the great reward in store for those who observe the Sabbath. It states: אֶזְכֶּה הוֹד מְלוּכָה אִם שַׁבָּת אֶשְׁמֹרָה, *I will merit royal glory if I keep the Sabbath.* This is possibly a reference to the coming of Mashiach, in line with the well-known Midrash stating that proper observance of the Sabbath by the entire Jewish nation can trigger the ultimate redemption. The *zemer* then continues: אַקְרִיב שַׁי לַמּוֹרָא מִנְחָה מֶרְקָחָה, *I will bring near a tribute to the Fearsome One, a perfumed minchah-offering.* This is a reference to the passage in *Tehillim* (Ch. 76) where Dovid HaMelech states that Hashem will punish the nations who disobey Him. In gratitude for being spared Hashem's wrath, one will bring an offering to *the Fearsome One,* Who causes all those who are evil to fear His retribution. Since this retribution will occur upon the ultimate redemption, which in turn can be brought about by the observance of the Sabbath, the *zemer* connects them in this stanza.

In the closing of the standard version of this *zemer,* we conclude with a plea: חַדֵּשׁ מִקְדָּשֵׁנוּ זָכְרָה נֶחֱרֶבֶת, *Renew our Sanctuary, and remember the destroyed* (city of Jerusalem). We ask that this boon be granted to: נֶעֱצֶבֶת בְּשַׁבָּת יוֹשֶׁבֶת בְּזֶמֶר וּשְׁבָחָה, *the saddened one who* (nevertheless) *spends the Sabbath in song and praise.* Although we are currently in exile, the joy of the Sabbath is for us a ray of light, which we must use as a window to the redemption of the future. And we ask Hashem, in the merit of our not losing hope, to bring the redemption soon.

ANSWERS TO QUESTIONS OF THE DAY

Sunday:

Hashem "appears" in the cloud created by the incense offered by the Kohen Gadol (*Rashi*).

Monday:

The atonement of the *chatas* goat applies to sins involving the *Beis HaMikdash* and the *korbanos,* while the atonement of the Azazel goat is more inclusive.

Tuesday:

Sins that are committed only before Hashem — that is, in private — can always receive atonement on Yom Kippur. For sins done in public, however, if they involve desecration of Hashem's Name, Yom Kippur alone does not atone (*Panim Yafos*).

Wednesday:

If he requires the meat immediately, he should be given the nonkosher meat; if he can wait, the animal should be slaughtered for him (*Orach Chaim* 328:14).

Thursday:

The repetition forbids doing both the things that you have already seen (from the Egyptians), and the things that you will see in the future (from the Canaanites).

Friday:

We learn that a danger to life overrides the Sabbath, for one should not die in order to observe a mitzvah (with the exception of the three cardinal sins).

Shabbos:

This verse is the source for the mitzvah to make safeguards to protect ourselves from transgressing the Torah's laws (see *Ramban* and *Sforno*).

פרשת קדושים

Parashas Kedoshim

פרשת קדושים

SUNDAY

PARASHAS KEDOSHIM

A TORAH THOUGHT FOR THE DAY

קְדשִׁים תִּהְיוּ כִּי קָדוֹשׁ אֲנִי ה׳ אֱלֹהֵיכֶם
You shall be holy, for holy am I, Hashem, your God (*Vayikra* 19:2).

Ramban explains that the commandment to be holy is not a general prohibition to abstain from the forbidden (see *Rashi*), but is a positive commandment to withhold oneself from an excess of the permitted. It thus defines how one must live according to Torah values and it embraces all aspects of life.

In the absence of such a commandment, *Ramban* continues, it would be possible for one to adhere to all the laws of the Torah and still lead a degenerate life. For it is not necessary to violate any Torah prohibition to allow one's physical desires to drive all of his actions, and even to cause him to wallow in them. To eat to the point of gluttony, the food need not be forbidden; to drink to the point of drunkenness, the wine need not be proscribed. Likewise, one can marry women who are permitted to him and indulge in carnal pleasure to excess. And there is no specific prohibition in the Torah dictating that one's speech be of refined content and manner. In *Ramban's* famous phrase, he bestows upon such a person the epithet: נָבָל בִּרְשׁוּת הַתּוֹרָה, *a degenerate within the permits of Torah law.*

Therefore, after spelling out in the previous *parashah* specific actions that are forbidden, the Torah here gives a sweeping injunction as a summation of all those laws, enjoining one to practice moderation in all physical pursuits. One should be refined in his speech, and limit all actions involving physical pleasures to those that are necessary. *Chazal* even saw the mitzvah of washing before and after meals, while clearly of Rabbinic ordinance, to be hinted at in the mitzvah to practice "*kedushah.*" The overall sense of this mitzvah is that we practice restraint in all of our actions and comport ourselves in a way that is refined and pure, rising above the conduct of the masses who indulge in excess and indecency.

Shelah writes, in reference to this mitzvah, that if all people and situations were exactly alike, the Torah would have been able to write exact measures of how much of the permitted pleasures one is allowed to experience. Food, drink and other physical actions would be limited to defined amounts for each. Since, however, every person and every situation is different, what is considered necessary for one may be deemed excessive for another. The Torah therefore wrote a general rule: *You shall be holy.* It is the responsibility of each person to make an assessment of those things that for him, in his circumstances, are unnecessary indulgence. And with regard to them, he must apply the full force of the Torah's prohibition to abstain.

MISHNAH OF THE DAY: ERUVIN 7:7

The Mishnah discusses additional laws of *shituf,* specifically in the case of *shituf* food that became insufficient, either because the food itself was diminished or because more residents were added to the *chatzeir*:[1]

נִתְמַעֵט הָאוֹכֶל — ***If the shituf food became diminished*** from the required amount before the onset of the Sabbath,[2] **מוֹסִיף וּמְזַכֶּה** — ***one may add*** his own food to complete the required amount ***and confer ownership*** thereof upon the other residents,[3] **וְאֵין צָרִיךְ לְהוֹדִיעַ** — ***and***

NOTES

1. The laws of this Mishnah, and the laws of *shituf* in general, are identical to those of *eruvei chatzeiros* (*Orach Chaim* 386:3, from Mishnah 73b; see also *Mishnah Berurah* 368:15).

2. That is, if the quantity of food originally set aside for the *shituf* was adequate at the time, but was later found to have diminished to less than the minimum amount specified in the next Mishnah.

Further (Mishnah 9), R' Yose states that in regard to "remnants of the *eruv,*" i.e., an *eruv* that was valid at the beginning of the first Sabbath and was subsequently diminished, any amount is sufficient, so that it is not necessary to "add." There is a question among the commentators whether the Tanna Kamma here disagrees with this or not. *Maharshal's* version of *Rashi* [which appears in our editions in brackets] assumes that the Tanna Kamma disagrees. If so, the Tanna Kamma refers to an *eruv* that was diminished either before the first Sabbath or after its onset; in either case, one must add to the *eruv* in order for it to be valid for subsequent Sabbaths (according to the Tanna Kamma). Others maintain (see *Bach's* lengthy gloss to *R' Yehonasan;* see also *Bach, Orach Chaim* §368) that there is no disagreement between the Tanna Kamma and R' Yose, and that the Tanna Kamma speaks only about an *eruv* that was diminished before the onset of the *first* Sabbath. If it were diminished thereafter, he agrees with R' Yose that it is not necessary to add to it.

Moreover, everyone agrees that an *eruv* that was diminished after the onset of the Sabbath is valid for that Sabbath. The question is only whether the Tanna Kamma rules that such an *eruv* is not valid for subsequent Sabbaths.

3. As described in the previous Mishnah. *Rashi* (80a ד״ה צריך) explains that when a person donates his own food, he need not solicit the approval of the other residents, since they benefit from the *shituf* without any personal expense.

he need not notify them, even if he uses their food.[4] נִתּוֹסְפוּ עֲלֵיהֶן — If more residents ***were added to them*** [i.e., to the original residents],[5] so that the *shituf* food is insufficient for all the residents,[6] מוֹסִיף וּמְזַכֶּה — ***one may add*** his own food to reach the required amount, ***and confer ownership*** thereof upon the new residents, וְצָרִיךְ לְהוֹדִיעַ — ***but he must notify them*** and solicit their approval if he desires to use their food.[7]

NOTES

4. Although, according to our Mishnah, residents must approve the use of their food for the *shituf,* their consent need not be solicited in this case, since they have already approved the *shituf* (*Rashi*).

5. I.e., new residents moved in.

6. However, if there is enough food to cover the new residents as well, they are automatically included in the *eruv* (*Beis Yosef, Orach Chaim* §366, from *Ramban* and *Ritva*). *Ritva* explains that the original residents intended to include all future residents in the *shituf* (ibid.).

7. All the residents of the *mavoi* must be permitted to eat any of the *shituf* food. Thus, the new residents must contribute willingly, for otherwise their food would be prohibited to the veteran members (*Rashi*). However, *Rambam* (*Hilchos Eruvin* 5:6) and *Rif* explain that the consent of the new residents is required even if ownership of the *eruv* food is conferred upon them, because their inclusion in the *shituf* limits their options. They assume (based on the Gemara below, 81b) that the Mishnah refers to a case where the new residents moved into a *chatzeir* that opens into two *mevo'os.* Hence, since the newcomers have the choice of which *mavoi* to join, their consent to inclusion in either *mavoi* is necessary.

GEMS FROM THE GEMARA

The Gemara analyzes the first ruling of the Mishnah that taught that if the *shituf* (or *eruv*) food dwindled below the minimum requirement, it can be replenished from the stock of one of the residents without obtaining prior consent from the others. The Mishnah thereby implies that if the food were *totally consumed,* the residents' consent *would* be required. The Gemara seeks to understand in which case this rule could apply. For if you say that the supplemental food is of the same type as the original *shituf* food, why does the Mishnah mention only the case of the *diminished shituf*? Even if the original food were completely consumed, one also may replenish the *shituf* without the other residents' knowledge. And if you say that he replenishes the *shituf* with an altogether different type of food, then even if the *shituf* only dwindled, new food should not be appropriated without the other residents' knowledge. [When the same type of food is used to replenish the *shituf,* it does not appear as though he is making a new *shituf,* and the approval of the other residents is not required. However, if a different type of food is being used, it appears to be a new *shituf,* and their permission is required (*Ritva*).] The Gemara bases this on a Baraisa that teaches that if the *eruv* (or *shituf*) food was completely consumed (and presumably even if it was diminished to below the minimum requirement), and it is being replaced by food of a different type, it is necessary to notify the other residents and solicit their approval.

The Gemara offers two ways to resolve this problem, corresponding to the two possible types of replacement food the Mishnah can be discussing — either the same type as the original *shituf* food or a different type than the original *shituf* food.

In our Mishnah, if the replacement food is of the *same type* as the original *shituf* food, when the Mishnah says that the *shituf* "dwindled," it may actually mean that the *shituf* became totally consumed. And the Mishnah is coming to teach that since the same type of food is used, even if the *shituf* must be totally replaced, the original consent of the other residents is still valid (*Rashi;* cf. *Ritva*).

However, if our Mishnah is discussing a case where the replacement food and the original *shituf* food are of *two different types,* there is still no question, for it is different when the *shituf* is totally consumed. Only then did the Baraisa require the prior approval of the other residents before replacing the *shituf* food with a different type of food. However, our Mishnah refers only to a depleted *shituf,* which may be replenished even with a different food without the consent of the other residents. [Heretofore, the Gemara understood the Baraisa to include even the case of a diminished *shituf* — i.e., if two types of food were involved, the residents' approval was necessary. Now the Gemara distinguishes between the case of a diminished *shituf* and the case of a totally consumed *shituf,* requiring consent only for the latter (*Rashi*).]

QUESTION OF THE DAY:

Why was this parashah said to all the Jews as a group (בְּקָהָל)?

For the answer, see page 118.

A MUSSAR THOUGHT FOR THE DAY

The Torah explains that we are to be holy *"for holy am I, HASHEM."* Above (see *A Torah Thought for the Day*), we have seen that this mitzvah is a directive to abstain from excess physical pleasures. If so, asks *R' Shimon Shkop* (in the introduction to his *Shaarei Yosher*), how can this quality possibly pertain to Hashem, Who is entirely removed from the physical? R' Shimon therefore redefines the meaning of *kedushah,* explaining that it involves a comprehensive approach to life's goals and that abstention from pleasure is only one aspect of this approach.

The root of the word קְדֻשָּׁה (*kedushah*) means designation (הֶקְדֵּשׁ, *hekdesh,* for example, refers to any item that is designated for the use of the Sanctuary). The meaning of the commandment to be "*kedoshim*" is that we must live our lives dedicated to a higher cause. All of our goals, both short- and long-term, must be directed outwards. The true *kadosh* does not engage in any activity where he is the sole beneficiary. Thus, the pursuit of pleasure for its own sake is the direct antithesis of *kedushah,* for no one benefits from this pleasure except the person himself.

This mitzvah is all-encompassing. It defines what the general thrust of our lives should be, as well as demanding an assessment of our every action. One must constantly ask himself: How will the immediate or ultimate result of this action benefit another? A person should engage in activities that are directed toward his health or well-being only with the ultimate objective that he be healthy so that he can continue to benefit others.

In this quality, Hashem is the ultimate *kadosh.* The Creator of the world is inherently self-sufficient and wants for nothing. All of His actions are directed only for the good of others, never for His own needs. It is this type of *kedushah* that we are bidden to emulate.

There is, however, an operative difference between our *kedushah* and that of Hashem. While Hashem is ultimately selfless, people cannot be. It is built into the makeup of man's psyche to be self-centered and self-loving. While self-centeredness should not be the goal of one's actions, it can and must be their foundation. We are told to love our fellow *as we love ourselves.* We are to use our self-love and expand it to include others as well.

The difference between a selfish individual and a selfless one is not one of essence, but one of focus. While the selfish person defines his "self" only in terms of his own physical body, the selfless person has developed his definition of "self" to include, in concentric circles, his family, his community, his nation, and ultimately the entire world. In this way, he can direct the intrinsic drive to satisfy his "self" to benefit all of creation.

HALACHAH OF THE DAY

As we have previously discussed, there is a Biblical prohibition against the construction of a permanent *ohel* on Shabbos, and a Rabbinic prohibition against the construction of even a temporary *ohel.* Since the *melachah* of *demolishing* is the converse of the *melachah* of *building* upon which the prohibition of *ohel* is based, it follows that the demolishing of an *ohel* — whether permanent or temporary — is also forbidden.

The general rule is that any *ohel* that may not be constructed on Shabbos may also not be demolished. As we saw in the case of the prohibition against constructing an *ohel,* in many instances an *ohel* may consist of nothing more than a roof, in others cases both walls and a roof are present, and in still other cases walls alone may constitute a halachically viable *ohel.* Since we have already discussed the various permutations of *ohel* at length, we will only briefly review the main points here.

The prohibition against dismantling a temporary roof applies only to a roof that covers an area measuring at least 1 square *tefach.* [According to *Rav Moshe Feinstein,* a *tefach* measures approximately 3.55 inches.]

There must be empty space of at least 1 *tefach* in height beneath a covering in order for it to be seen as a roof in the eyes of halachah. Any covering with less than this amount of space beneath it is not halachically regarded as a roof, and it therefore may be dismantled on Shabbos.

This prohibition applies only to coverings that have their own independent supports. A covering that is being held in place by people is not considered to be a roof, and the prohibition against demolishing it therefore does not apply.

The prohibition against the construction of a roof does not apply in cases where the construction is done in a reverse order. For example, if one first erects the roof and then builds the necessary supports, he does not violate the *melachah* of building an *ohel.* Likewise, one who demolishes an *ohel* in the reverse of the typical order, for example by first disassembling the support structure and only then lowering the roof, is not in violation of the *melachah* of *demolishing.*

A roof that is used for the benefit of people or animals may not be dismantled on Shabbos even if the area that it covers is not surrounded by walls. For the laws that govern the demolishing of roofs used for other purposes, see our discussion of the laws governing the erection of such roofs. The simple rule is, once again, if it is forbidden for one to erect the roof on Shabbos, it is likewise forbidden to demolish it on Shabbos.

A CLOSER LOOK AT THE SIDDUR

While one must always be conscious of the obligation of *kedushah,* there is a time during the daily prayers in which one should specifically accept this obligation upon himself — in the third blessing of the *Shemoneh Esrei, Kedushas Hashem* (Holiness of God's Name).

In *Yaaros Devash, R' Yonasan Eibeshitz* provides a brief summary of the proper intentions one should have in mind while reciting each of the blessings of *Shemoneh Esrei.* He writes that although each word and phrase of this prayer alludes to deep and esoteric ideas, these intentions are not accessible to all. He therefore lists those ideas to which everyone can relate while praying. Below is a paraphrase of the thoughts we should have in mind while saying the words of the third blessing:

(1) We must reflect on the awe and trembling that seize the angels at the time they come to say the *Kedushah* and sanctify the Name of Hashem. The holy angels approach to say the *Kedushah* only after preparing themselves extensively. Even then, they say it with great awe and trepidation. We must consider that if the holy angels require such preparation, certainly we must not say the words of *Kedushah* without preparing ourselves, purifying ourselves, and making ourselves holy.

(2) While saying the words אַתָּה קָדוֹשׁ, *You are Holy,* one should fill his mind with the desire to sanctify the Name of Hashem with his very life. One should imagine that he is being called to give his life for the sake of any Torah commandment for which one must die rather than transgress, thereby testifying with his blood to the truth of Hashem and His Torah. He should also consider the joy that one must experience upon being given the opportunity to sanctify the Name of Hashem; this feeling is ordinarily only the lot of the angels on High.

(3) While saying this blessing, one should also accept upon himself the obligation to sanctify himself by abstaining from that which is permitted, as *Ramban* explains in the mitzvah of קְדֹשִׁים תִּהְיוּ (see above, *A Torah Thought for the Day*). It is not the case, as certain people think, that one who refrains from indulging in a bit of pleasure is to be considered an extra pious individual. It is, in fact, an obligation that is incumbent upon all, not an act of added righteousness. When one properly prepares himself during this blessing to abstain from pleasures that are unnecessary, he is then counted among the camp of the Holy, regarding whom the blessing states: וּקְדוֹשִׁים בְּכָל יוֹם יְהַלְלוּךָ סֶּלָה, *And holy ones praise You every day, forever!*

A TORAH THOUGHT FOR THE DAY

לֹא־תְקַלֵּל חֵרֵשׁ וְלִפְנֵי עִוֵּר לֹא תִתֵּן
מִכְשֹׁל וְיָרֵאתָ מֵּאֱלֹהֶיךָ אֲנִי ה׳

You shall not curse a deaf man, and you shall not place a stumbling block before the blind; and you shall fear your God — I am HASHEM (*Vayikra* 19:14).

Although the simple translation of this verse would appear to prohibit the physical act of placing a stumbling block before a blind person, many *Rishonim,* including *Rashi* and *Rambam* in *Sefer HaMitzvos,* explain the verse to be referring to one who is blind in a non-literal sense; that is, he is without knowledge and comes to seek advice. The Torah forbids the person whose counsel is being sought from dispensing advice that is based on self-interest rather than on what is best for the person seeking help. For example, one may not counsel a person to sell his property when the real reason he does so is because he wishes to acquire it for himself. *Rambam* also adds another dimension to this prohibition; it forbids a person from causing someone to sin by assisting him in obtaining what he needs in order to transgress, or by telling him that a forbidden act is permitted.

Other *Rishonim* (see, for example, *Ralbag* to the verse) understand that while these interpretations are correct, the prohibition certainly also includes the literal meaning of the verse; thus, placing a physical stumbling block would also be a violation.

What must be explained is: What indication is there in the verse that causes the *Rishonim* to explain it in a non-literal fashion? How do we know that the Torah is not simply prohibiting the physical act of placing an obstacle before a blind man?

Several approaches to resolve this difficulty are offered by the commentators. *Sifsei Chachamim* notes that the end of the verse states, *and you shall fear your God. Toras Kohanim* (cited by *Rashi*) explains that the Torah includes this warning to deter a person who feels that he is safe in dispensing selfish advice, for his transgression is not evident and he will be able to feign innocence. To him, the Torah says: Fear your God, Who knows your true intentions. From this, *Sifsei Chachamim* explains, it is clear that the Torah is not addressing exclusively the placement of a physical obstacle, for such an act is clearly malevolent, and no such warning would be necessary.

Malbim to the verse offers another possible proof. He notes that the

verb תִּתֵּן, *give,* is usually used to describe a situation where there is both a giver and a receiver, and one gives an item or report to another. When speaking of *placing* an item, the verb form שים, which means *to place,* would be more appropriate. Thus, he says, if the Torah meant to forbid merely placing a physical stumbling block, it would have stated לֹא תָשִׂים מִכְשֹׁל rather than לֹא תִתֵּן מִכְשֹׁל. The use of the verb תִּתֵּן thus directs us to interpret the verse as referring to the dispensing of advice, in which case there is a giver and a taker.

A third approach is suggested by *Maskil LeDavid,* who notes that the prohibition in the beginning of the verse, *you shall not curse a deaf man,* is also not meant only in the literal sense, for it is forbidden to curse any Jew. Thus, just as the beginning of the verse is more inclusive than its literal meaning, the end of the verse is as well.

MISHNAH OF THE DAY: ERUVIN 7:8

The Mishnah describes the requisite measure of food needed to make a *shituf* or an *eruv chatzeiros*:

כַּמָּה הוּא שִׁיעוּרָן — ***What is their measure*** (i.e., how much food must the residents contribute for the *shituf*)?[1] בִּזְמַן שֶׁהֵן מְרוּבִּין — ***When they*** (i.e., the residents) ***are numerous,*** מְזוֹן שְׁתֵּי סְעוּדוֹת לְכוּלָּם — ***provisions*** equivalent to ***two meals*** for one person satisfies the requirement ***for all of them.***[2] בִּזְמַן שֶׁהֵן מוּעָטִין — ***When they are few,***[3] כִּגְרוֹגֶרֶת לְהוֹצָאַת שַׁבָּת לְכָל אֶחָד וְאֶחָד — food ***equivalent to*** the volume of ***a dried fig,*** as required ***for*** liability in the case of ***transferring on the***

NOTES

1. Again, the minimum quantity requirements for *eruvei chatzeiros* are the same as those for *shitufei mevo'os; eruv* and *shituf* differ only in the types of food that may be used for them.

2. Although the individual contributions may be minuscule (depending on the number of residents involved), since the *shituf* or *eruv* itself contains the significant amount of food for two meals, that is sufficient (*R' Yehonasan*).

The measure indicated here, food for two meals, is relevant only to food that is eaten by itself, e.g., bread or grains. For food eaten as an accompaniment to bread (such as roasted meat), the required measure is the amount of that food that would be eaten with bread during two meals (Gemara 29b; *Orach Chaim* 386:6-7).

3. The Gemara will explain that this refers to less than eighteen residents. It is sufficient for each participant to contribute an amount of food equivalent to the volume of a dried fig, although the total will not add up to "two meals."

Sabbath,[4] ***for each one*** of the residents is the requisite measure.

NOTES

4. In order to be liable to a *chatas* for inadvertently violating the Sabbath by carrying from a *reshus harabim* to a *reshus hayachid* on the Sabbath, one must carry a minimum quantity of that substance. For most foodsuffs the minimum is the volume of a dried fig (*Shabbos* 7:4).

GEMS FROM THE GEMARA

The Mishnah distinguished between a *chatzeir* with numerous residents and one with few residents. The Gemara wonders how many residents are considered "numerous." Rav Yehudah said in the name of Shmuel that this refers to eighteen people, that is, eighteen or more. Even a large number of residents may join in an *eruv* that contains enough food for only two meals.

The Gemara explains that Shmuel chose eighteen because the Mishnah means to teach a leniency. If the residents are מְרוּבִּין, *numerous,* so that their individual contributions total more than the equivalent of two meals, an equivalent of two meals is sufficient. That is, the Mishnah teaches that if the residents are so numerous that if each contributed a dried fig the total would exceed the size of two meals, it is sufficient to collect only the equivalent of two meals from them, although each individual contribution will be less than a dried fig.

But if they are מוּעָטִין, *few,* so that their individual contributions do not total two meals, it is sufficient for each resident to contribute the size of a dried fig. That is, if there are not so many participants, so that if a two-meal equivalent were divided between them each resident's portion would be more than the size of a dried fig, they are considered few and it is sufficient for each person to contribute only the equivalent of a dried fig.

Incidentally, Rav Yehudah informs us in Shmuel's name that the amount of food for two meals is equal to the volume of eighteen dried figs. There is disagreement among the authorities what the amount of eighteen dried figs (i.e., food for two meals) is when the egg-volume system prevalent in the Talmud is used to calculate the amount. Some maintain that sufficient food for two meals is equivalent to the volume of six eggs, while others contend that eight eggs is the correct figure. Both views are cited in *Orach Chaim* (368:3). *Mishnah Berurah* advises

that ideally, one should make sure that there is enough food to conform with the more stringent view of eight eggs, but he rules that after the fact (בְּדִיעֲבַד), even if there was only the volume of six eggs, the *eruv* may be relied upon (see *Tosafos* ד״ה אגב for yet another view concerning this subject).

A MUSSAR THOUGHT FOR THE DAY

As we learned in *A Torah Thought for the Day,* according to many *Rishonim* the prohibition of placing a stumbling block before the blind applies to causing another Jew to sin, or giving him bad advice. *Sefer HaChinuch* explains that giving people harmful advice causes distrust and hatred among people, and destroys the *achdus* — unity — that is so essential to the prosperity of the Jewish nation.

Elsewhere (§243), *Chinuch* goes even further, stating that as part of the mitzvah for every person to love his fellow Jew, it is incumbent upon a person to think of ways that he can *help* his fellow Jew, and to always have his welfare in mind. It is important to note that from the Torah's insistence that one is forbidden to help another Jew sin, we learn that the need to help another Jew is not limited to physical assistance. It is equally, if not more, important to assure that one's fellow Jew is getting the spiritual support he needs to enable him to fulfill his obligations as a Jew.

How does one reach the level where he will not be tempted to advance his own interests over that of his fellow? One of the key thoughts to keep in mind is that כָּל יִשְׂרָאֵל עֲרֵבִים זֶה לָזֶה, *all of Israel are responsible for one another.* The Jewish nation is not a collection of individuals; it is a whole consisting of many parts. Every time a Jew sins, *all* Jews suffer, as the entity that is Klal Yisrael moves a bit further away from its Father in Heaven as a result. The problem of your fellow Jew is thus your own. One who succeeds in internalizing this message will never treat the needs of another Jew as secondary to his own, just as he would not favor one of his hands at the expense of the other.

This realization can also serve as a powerful deterrent to the *yetzer hara.* The Gemara in *Kiddushin* (40b) tells us that one should always regard the world as being exactly balanced between good and evil, so that his deed can determine the fate of the entire world. When one makes himself aware of the scope and power of his actions, he is much more likely to make reasoned choices and refrain from the rash or impulsive judgments that often result in sin.

By warning us not to take advantage of a person who is asking us for advice, the Torah reminds us that we are not to put our own interests before those of another Jew — because we are all one. And by warning us not to help another Jew sin, the Torah reminds us that every sin affects us all. Heeding these two reminders will allow us to strengthen both the unity of Klal Yisrael and the level of *avodas Hashem* that we can all reach in partnership.

HALACHAH OF THE DAY

One who folds up a folding canopy on Shabbos is not in violation of the *melachah* prohibiting the demolishing of a temporary *ohel.* The Rabbinic decree forbids the *disassembly* of an *ohel;* a folding *ohel,* however, remains fully *assembled* even after it has been folded closed. The mere act of folding is not seen by halachah as being equivalent to an act of *demolishing.* According to many *poskim,* the above holds true even in regard to canopies used for the benefit of a person.

One may dismantle a temporary *ohel* on Shabbos if he is careful to leave a *tefach* of the roof standing. For example, one may remove a mosquito net from a baby carriage on Shabbos if he takes care to leave at least a *tefach* of the net in place covering the carriage.

In most cases, one is permitted to erect or dismantle a temporary wall on Shabbos. If, however, the wall is needed to divide a room in order to fulfill a halachic requirement, one may neither erect nor dismantle it.

We will now discuss some practical applications of the prohibition of *demolishing.*

One may not remove a window screen from a window on Shabbos. Since the screen is intended to remain in its place and not be frequently removed, it is regarded as being part of the structure. Its removal on Shabbos is therefore a violation of the *melachah* of *demolishing.*

Shards of glass that remain in a window frame after a window has been broken are also regarded as being a part of the larger structure, and may not be removed.

One may not remove a door from its hinges. This remains true even if the door can be removed without resorting to the removal of screws or nails.

If a child becomes locked in a room and is unable to unlock the door, it is permitted to break the door down in order to free the child. According to halachah, this situation is seen as potentially life-threatening;

therefore one may take any action necessary to free the child.

On Shabbos one may not remove any object that is embedded in the wall of a structure — for example, nails, screws, thumbtacks, etc. These objects are considered to be a part of the structure; their removal is therefore a violation of the *melachah* of *demolishing.*

The *poskim* permit one to remove a picture from the nail upon which it is hanging.

Once again, as a general rule, anything that may not be constructed on Shabbos may also not be demolished on Shabbos. This concludes our discussion of the *melachah* of *demolishing.*

A CLOSER LOOK AT THE SIDDUR

This week, we will begin to discuss the second of the Six Remembrances, which bids us to remember daily the Giving of the Torah at Mount Sinai, by reciting the verse:

> רַק הִשָּׁמֶר לְךָ וּשְׁמֹר נַפְשְׁךָ מְאֹד פֶּן־תִּשְׁכַּח אֶת־הַדְּבָרִים אֲשֶׁר־רָאוּ עֵינֶיךָ וּפֶן־יָסוּרוּ מִלְּבָבְךָ כֹּל יְמֵי חַיֶּיךָ וְהוֹדַעְתָּם לְבָנֶיךָ וְלִבְנֵי בָנֶיךָ יוֹם אֲשֶׁר עָמַדְתָּ לִפְנֵי ה׳ אֱלֹהֶיךָ בְּחֹרֵב
>
> *Only beware and guard yourself carefully, lest you forget the things your eyes have seen and lest they stray from your heart all the days of your life. And you are to make them known to your children and to your children's children — the day you stood before* H*ASHEM*, *your God, at Sinai* (*Devarim* 4:9-10).

According to most authorities, remembering the Giving of the Torah at Sinai is not counted as one of the 613 mitzvos. *Ramban,* however, does count it as a mitzvah, citing the above verses. He writes that we are commanded never to forget the events at Sinai; they should be on our minds constantly and should never leave our hearts.

Ramban continues that it is absolutely essential that this event be remembered. Without the clarity of this happening in the minds of the people, there would be a great risk to the continuity and strength of the Torah and to the belief in its Divine origin. Although Moshe was accepted as a true prophet, another prophet may one day arise and claim that we should obey a new law, supporting his words with some sign or miracle. As the latter would also be a prophet, there would be no reason to listen to the prophecy of Moshe any more than this new prophecy. With the perpetuation of the events at Sinai, however, there is no longer any possibility of this happening. The Torah was not given as a prophecy to Moshe, who transmitted it to the people, but as a prophecy to the entire people as one; we ourselves experienced the Revelation, and no one can come along and contradict something to which we ourselves were witnesses. Thus is the continuity of the Torah assured.

As we have learned in earlier studies, *Rambam* (*Hilchos Yesodei HaTorah* 8:1) writes that the revelation at Sinai was the clearest and most irrefutable proof to the truth of the prophecy of Moshe. For although he performed many wonders, other explanations can always be found for these supernatural phenomena. But at the Revelation, we all saw and heard how Moshe received his orders from Hashem Himself. From then on, Moshe's prophecy was not subject to any shadow of a doubt.

Although *Rambam* does not include this mitzvah in his count of the mitzvos, he does consider it to be a primary foundation of the faith, and an obligation upon us to constantly recount the extraordinary events of that day. In a letter that he wrote to the persecuted Jewish community in Yemen, he makes this a centerpiece of their educational goals, basing his exhortations on the above verses. "We are obligated always to remember and never to forget the events of Mount Sinai. We are to transmit it to our children that they may be raised with this knowledge. It is proper, our brothers, that you speak of the Giving of the Torah in your communities and in your assemblies, of the surrounding events of greatness and splendor. For an entire nation to hear the word of Hashem and behold His glory with their own eyes is an event that is unmatched in the history of the world and will never be repeated. Such remembrances should serve to strengthen our faith so that it can never be shaken."

QUESTION OF THE DAY:

Is it possible to transgress this violation (לִפְנֵי עִוֵּר) with respect to a non-Jew?

For the answer, see page 118.

פרשת קדושים

TUESDAY

PARASHAS KEDOSHIM

A TORAH THOUGHT FOR THE DAY

וְאָהַבְתָּ לְרֵעֲךָ כָּמוֹךָ
And you shall love your fellow as yourself
(*Vayikra* 19:18).

The Torah commands us to love every Jew, regardless of his identity or to which community he belongs. It is also not enough to love him in your heart; your love must express itself in concrete ways. Among these are: One must pursue the best conditions for others, look out for their honor, and praise them and speak well of them whenever the opportunity arises (*Rambam, Hilchos Dei'os* 6:3). However, it should be noted that one must be careful to avoid speaking well of someone when it is likely to elicit a negative response (see *Sefer Chofetz Chaim* §9).

The *Chazon Ish* demonstrates that one is required by this mitzvah to love even the most severe transgressors of Torah law. The Gemara (*Pesachim* 75a) uses this verse to preclude using painful methods of execution for those who are found liable for capital punishment. Thus, it must be that even these offenders are included in the word רֵעֲךָ, *your fellow.*

R' Moshe Shternbuch (in his *Taam VeDaas*) notes that while the Gemara also says that it is permitted to hate one who transgresses Torah law, this refers only to a transgressor who has been rebuked and has refused to heed this rebuke. Nowadays, we no longer have anyone who is considered qualified enough to properly administer rebuke (see *Arachin* 16b). Therefore, it cannot be claimed about anyone that he transgressed after refusing rebuke, for the rebuke must be administered properly and, lacking a qualified person to give it, we cannot assume that it was. This prevents anyone in our generation from harboring hatred toward any Jew.

R' Shternbuch states further that another important aspect of this mitzvah can be learned from R' Akiva's comment on this verse: זֶה כְּלָל גָּדוֹל בַּתּוֹרָה, *This is a fundamental rule of the Torah.* This means that the fulfillment of this mitzvah must be the basis of one's fulfillment of the entire Torah. As a result of a deep love for all Jews, a person will scrupulously adhere to all the mitzvos governing interpersonal relationships (בֵּין אָדָם לַחֲבֵרוֹ): He will make sure that he is never the cause of another's physical, financial or spiritual harm, and will seek to help others in whatever way he can. This mitzvah can also serve as the impetus for one to fulfill the mitzvos that are בֵּין אָדָם לַמָּקוֹם, *between man and God.* When one sensitizes himself to feel an appreciation and love for every Jew, he will automatically love his Creator as well. For Hashem gave him life and continues to give him, on a constant basis, much more than any mortal can.

Thus, this mitzvah, performed correctly, can be the foundation of all the mitzvos.

Conversely, one who purports to love all Jews, while consistently downgrading the importance of the other mitzvos of the Torah, cannot be considered to be properly fulfilling even this mitzvah. For this mitzvah, if it is performed for the right reason and in the proper way, works to open up to a person all the mitzvos of the Torah.

MISHNAH OF THE DAY: ERUVIN 7:9

The previous Mishnah provided for a minimum quantity for an *eruv.* This Mishnah limits this requirement:

אָמַר רַבִּי יוֹסֵי — ***R' Yose said:*** **בַּמֶּה דְּבָרִים אֲמוּרִים** — ***Regarding what were these rules*** of measurements ***stated?*** **בִּתְחִילַּת עֵירוּב** — ***Regarding the inception of the eruv.***[1] **אֲבָל בִּשְׁיָרֵי עֵירוּב כָּל שֶׁהוּא** — ***However, in regard to the remnants of the eruv,***[2] ***any amount*** is sufficient, and the food need not be replenished for the upcoming Sabbaths.[3] **וְלֹא אָמְרוּ לְעָרֵב בַּחֲצֵירוֹת** — ***And they*** [the Sages] ***said that*** residents ***must make eruvin for chatzeiros*** even after they have joined in a *shituf* **אֶלָּא כְּדֵי שֶׁלֹּא לְשַׁכֵּחַ אֶת הַתִּינוֹקוֹת** — ***only so as not to cause the children*** of *chatzeiros* ***to forget*** the law of *eruvei chatzeiros.* Therefore, we may rule leniently in this case.[4]

NOTES

1. The *eruv* measurements stated above apply only when the *eruv* is initially made.

2. Once the *shituf* or *eruv* takes effect at the onset of the first Sabbath, it remains valid even if the food dwindles to below the required amount, as long as even a minute portion remains.

3. *R' Yehonasan.* R' Yose disputes the first opinion of our Mishnah (*Rashi*), which requires the food to be replenished each week (see above, Mishnah 7 note 2). The halachah follows R' Yose's opinion (*Orach Chaim* 368:4).

4. *Rashi.* When all the *chatzeiros* of a *mavoi* join in a *shituf,* there is actually no need for the residents of the individual *chatzeiros* to join in an *eruv,* since they are already considered joined as a result of the *shituf.* However, the Sages upheld the *eruv* requirement in order to educate the children as to its function. That is, if a *shituf* were relied upon in lieu of an *eruv,* the children of those *chatzeiros* in which the *shituf* was not kept might mistakenly conclude that carrying from one's house into the courtyard is permitted without benefit of any modifying procedure — i.e., either *eruv* or *shituf.* Therefore, although an *eruv* is required, a lenient ruling is appropriate in this case. Hence, the Sages upheld the validity of an *eruv* that had become diminished after its installation. According to this explanation, R' Yose's ruling is limited to *eruvei chatzeiros,* when all the *chatzeiros* have already joined in a *shituf.*

GEMS FROM THE GEMARA

The Gemara (71b-72a) dealt with the matter of whether we may rely on a *shituf* to serve in place of an *eruv* as well. For an *eruv* serves two functions: It permits carrying from separately owned houses into the common *chatzeir,* and it permits carrying from one *chatzeir* to another when the two join together in an *eruv.* This second function of *eruv* (merging *chatzeiros* together) and the function of *shituf* seem to be identical. Thus, there is a question whether a *shituf* may serve in place of the *eruv* as well.

Rashi there explains that according to the opinion that a *shituf* may serve in place of an *eruv* as well, the *shituf* may serve in lieu of an *eruv* to allow the residents to carry objects from one *chatzeir* to another through their common entrance. According to some authorities, *Rashi* holds that the *shituf* also satisfies the requirements of the *other* function of *eruv* — to allow carrying from each individual house into its *chatzeir* (*Ritva; Beis Yosef, Orach Chaim* §387).

According to this interpretation of *Rashi's* opinion, they must understand that R' Yose's lenient ruling here, which requires at least that a valid *eruv* be established initially, refers to the *shituf* itself, not to an *eruv* previously made by the residents of the *chatzeiros.* For many *poskim* maintain that the remnants of an *eruv* or *shituf* are inherently valid, because the minimum is required only to establish the *eruv* — not to continue it. They are consequently valid even if there is no *shituf* to back up the *eruv.*

Consequently, R' Yose's lenient ruling is not based on the existence of an auxiliary adjustment, but is an independent leniency. According to this interpretation, the conclusion of the Mishnah is a separate, unrelated statement. It is stated to clarify the necessity for making any *eruv* at all when the residents of the *chatzeir* have already been incorporated in a *shituf* (*Ohr Zarua* 2:184).

QUESTION OF THE DAY:

Hillel said to a potential convert, "What is hateful to you do not do to your friend." Why did he not simply say, "Love your neighbor as yourself"?

For the answer, see page 118.

A MUSSAR THOUGHT FOR THE DAY

We have seen above (see *A Torah Thought for the Day*) that we are enjoined to love our fellow as ourselves, to look out for his good, and to speak his praises. This may not present a difficulty when we are dealing with people whom we like and admire, or people who are kind to us. However, we are obligated to love every Jew, no matter his behavior toward us, or how much we find ourselves disliking him. How does one go about influencing his heart to love someone whom he does not like, or someone with whom he has had disagreements in the past?

The *Chofetz Chaim* (in *Shaar HaTevunah,* Ch. 6 of *Sefer Chofetz Chaim*) answers this question, using the following parable:

Reuven had disagreements with Shimon, and did not think well of him. One day, Yehudah, a truthful person and trusted friend of Reuven, approached Reuven and told him of something that he had seen with his own eyes. He was with Shimon when Shimon was approached by the *gadol hador,* the greatest sage in the generation — a sage known both for his Torah greatness and for his extraordinary perceptiveness. Said Yehudah, "How could you tell me about him that he is a low individual? The Rav spoke to Shimon with respect, and showed him great love and admiration. You must be sorely mistaken in your assessment of him!"

Reuven was taken aback. "You have certainly shaken my certainty. I guess it is possible that Shimon is indeed a good person, and my opinion of him was built on prejudice. On the other hand, it is also possible that he is a smooth-talking liar, and managed to fool even the *gadol hador.*"

A few days later Yehudah approached Reuven once again. "I was witness to an amazing thing. I heard from the great *Tannaim* (authors of the Mishnah) that they were told by Eliyahu HaNavi that Hashem Himself loves Shimon!"

Upon hearing these words, Reuven fell upon his face in shock. "Woe is me! I was sure that I was right and he was wrong, but I see how mistaken I was. Hashem, Who knows a person's essence, personally loves Shimon! I must have misread the situation, because of the way it affected me. Or Shimon has since truly regretted what he did and did not feel that he could approach me about it. Whatever the case, from now on I must start to love Shimon as Hashem does!"

TUESDAY

PARASHAS KEDOSHIM

The verse commanding us to love our fellow concludes: *I am HASHEM.* We are being told, "I am Hashem, and I love your fellow; you too can love him." Hashem does not look at the external, incidental qualities of a person, but at their very essence — a pure and holy Jewish soul. It is this essence that we must train ourselves to look at and appreciate, as Hashem Himself does.

HALACHAH OF THE DAY

Another of the thirty-nine forbidden labors of Shabbos is מְכַבֶּה, the act of *extinguishing* a fire. During the construction of the Mishkan, it was necessary for the artisans to melt various metals in order to create the vessels of the Mishkan. The melting of metals requires the application of very intense heat. In order to produce such high levels of heat, it was necessary to burn charcoal, which burns hotter than wood. The production of charcoal requires that flaming fire be extinguished.

The *melachah* of *extinguishing* may be defined as either the extinguishing or the diminishing of a fire. This can be accomplished in various ways, as we will explain below.

The act of extinguishing upon which this *melachah* is based, namely the extinguishing of a wood fire with the intent to produce charcoal, was performed in order to produce a required item in the only way that the item could be produced. For this reason, it is seen as an act that was done *for its own sake,* i.e., the act of *extinguishing* was necessary to produce something that could be created only through extinguishing. This stands in contrast to an act of extinguishing that is not done for *its own sake* — for the sake of a product of the extinguishing itself — but rather to rectify an undesirable situation, such as to prevent fire damage to one's property or to darken a room lit by a flame.

Since the source of the prohibited *melachah* is an act that was done for *its own sake,* the Biblical prohibition against *extinguishing* is violated only in such cases. In instances where extinguishing is performed without providing a direct positive benefit, there is no violation of Biblical law.

While an act of extinguishing a fire that provides no direct positive benefit is not Biblically prohibited, it is forbidden by Rabbinic decree. Accordingly, if one extinguishes a fire in order to conserve fuel, or in order to prevent his belongings from being burned, he is in violation of a Rabbinic decree.

The Rabbinic prohibition against extinguishing is treated more stringently than other Rabbinic decrees. This is because the act prohibited by Rabbinic decree is in essence identical to the act that is Biblically prohibited — they differ only in the intent of the transgressor. Consider the following: If one extinguishes a lit candle with the intent of charring the wick so that the candle will light easily on another occasion, he violates the Biblical prohibition against extinguishing. Since his act of extinguishing was done in order to produce a charred wick through the extinguishing of the flame, this is extinguishing done *for its own sake,* Biblically prohibited on Shabbos.

If, however, one extinguishes the lit candle because he no longer desires the light it provides, he violates only the Rabbinic prohibition against extinguishing. Thus we see that the same exact act — the extinguishing of the flame on the candle — may yield either a Biblical transgression or a Rabbinic one, depending solely upon the intent of the transgressor.

A CLOSER LOOK AT THE SIDDUR

In many versions of the *siddur,* the following sentence appears before מַה טֹּבוּ at the beginning of the morning prayers: הֲרֵינִי מְקַבֵּל עַל עַצְמִי מִצְוַת עֲשֵׂה שֶׁל וְאָהַבְתָּ לְרֵעֲךָ כָּמוֹךָ, *I hereby accept upon myself the positive commandment to love your fellow as yourself.* The source for this custom is in the writings of the *Arizal* (cited in *Magen Avraham* §46), where it states that the acceptance of this mitzvah is a prerequisite to prayer.

One explanation for this is found in the *Sefer Yeri'as Shlomo*: Almost all of our prayers are composed in the plural form because we are not supposed to pray for ourselves as individuals, but for all of Klal Yisrael. It is therefore imperative that before praying one make sure that he feels a love for every Jew. Without being infused with such a feeling, his intention while praying will naturally focus primarily on his own needs, not those of the nation as a whole. One who prays with only himself in mind is not praying in the proper way, as indicated by the plural nature of the texts of the prayers.

R' Shimshon Pincus explains another aspect of the connection that the fulfillment of this mitzvah has with our prayers. At the very foundation of the act of praying lies a certain set of beliefs. One must believe that Hashem runs the world and that one can throw his entire pack of problems, so to speak, onto Hashem. Furthermore, he must believe that

Hashem loves every Jew and that Hashem desires the well-being of every Jew, and that it is the wish of Hashem to shower everyone with blessings and to assist each person in all his endeavors.

A logical consequence of these assumptions is the following conclusion: If I am praying based on the belief that as a Jew, and as a child of Hashem, Hashem loves me and wishes to respond to my prayers, then He must also love every other Jew as well, for we are all His children and fit to receive His love (see above, *A Mussar Thought for the Day*). [And, "every Jew" includes one's neighbor, co-worker, etc.]

One who finds himself having difficulty loving every Jew must realize that he has a corresponding weakness in the articles of faith that serve as the basis for any prayer. After a person accepts upon himself this mitzvah and strengthens his heart in these beliefs — that all depends on the will of Hashem, and everything we have is a result of His direct loving-kindness — he can then stand before Hashem and begin to pray.

A TORAH THOUGHT FOR THE DAY

וְכִי־תָבֹאוּ אֶל־הָאָרֶץ וּנְטַעְתֶּם כָּל־עֵץ מַאֲכָל וַעֲרַלְתֶּם עָרְלָתוֹ אֶת־פִּרְיוֹ שָׁלֹשׁ שָׁנִים יִהְיֶה לָכֶם עֲרֵלִים לֹא יֵאָכֵל. וּבַשָּׁנָה הָרְבִיעִת יִהְיֶה כָּל פִּרְיוֹ קֹדֶשׁ הִלּוּלִים לַה׳. וּבַשָּׁנָה הַחֲמִישִׁת תֹּאכְלוּ אֶת־פִּרְיוֹ לְהוֹסִיף לָכֶם תְּבוּאָתוֹ אֲנִי ה׳ אֱלֹהֵיכֶם

When you shall come to the land and you shall plant any fruit tree, you shall treat its fruit as forbidden; for three years they shall be forbidden to you, they shall not be eaten. In the fourth year, all of its fruit shall be sanctified to laud HASHEM*. And in the fifth year you may eat its fruit — so that it will increase its crop for you — I am* HASHEM *your God* (*Vayikra* 19:23-25).

The Torah tells us that when we plant a fruit tree, the fruit of the first three years shall be *orlah* — which *Rashi* explains as meaning literally *blocked.* This fruit is blocked to us; we are forbidden to eat it or to use it in any way. [Also included in this Torah passage is the law of *revai,* sanctified fourth-year fruits, and the permit to eat fruits from the fifth year and onward, after these mitzvos have been carried out. See *A Closer Look at the Siddur.*]

Commenting on the great importance of the mitzvah of *orlah,* the Midrash (*Vayikra Rabbah* 25:2) contrasts the Jewish people's successful fulfillment of this mitzvah when they refrain from eating the fruits of a new tree for three years to Adam's inability to withstand the temptation to eat from the *Eitz HaDaas* in Gan Eden for even a few hours, which of course resulted in spiritual destruction for the world and eventual death for himself and all of humanity.

Panim Yafos explains the connection between our observing the mitzvah of *orlah* and Adam's failure to refrain from eating from the tree. The Torah tells us that on the third day of Creation, Hashem commanded the earth to give forth: עֵץ פְּרִי עֹשֶׂה פְּרִי לְמִינוֹ, *fruit trees yielding fruit* ***each after its kind*** (*Bereishis* 1:11), which *Rashi* explains as meaning that the taste of the tree would be identical to the taste of the fruit that it would produce. However, the earth disobeyed and, instead of growing trees yielding fruit ***each after its kind,*** it simply gave forth עֵץ עֹשֶׂה פְּרִי, *trees yielding fruit* (ibid. 1:12); the trees, however, did not — and do not — have any taste of their own. *Panim Yafos* points out that the earth's refusal to obey Hashem ultimately influenced all of Creation, for in proclaiming that Adam was created עָפָר מִן־הָאֲדָמָה, *dust from the earth* (ibid. 2:7), the Torah is telling us that man contains within himself the spiritual qualities of the raw materials from which he was formed. Thus, because the earth disobeyed Hashem, this susceptibility to sinning became ingrained in man as well. The inclusion of earth in man allows him the option — against the desires of his lofty *neshamah* — to disobey Hashem.

Panim Yafos explains that when Hashem told Adam: וּמִלְאוּ אֶת־הָאָרֶץ וְכִבְשֻׁהָ, *fill the earth and conquer it* (ibid. 1:28), He was in essence commanding him to make the correct decisions and allow his spiritual *neshamah* to emerge victorious in the conflict with his earthly body. The message to Adam was: Allow the spirituality within you to totally overcome — and *conquer* — your earthliness, by using your corporality as a tool to become closer to Hashem and achieve spirituality. Sadly, Adam did not live up to this mission, and, when he ate from the fruit of the *Eitz HaDaas,* he failed at the one opportunity he had been given to fulfill this task while still in Gan Eden. The result of his acquiescence to the earthly urges within him was that, instead of living the refined, almost automatically spiritual lifestyle that he enjoyed in Gan Eden, these mundane qualities would now define him. As punishment for his sin, Hashem sent Adam: לַעֲבֹד אֶת־הָאֲדָמָה אֲשֶׁר לֻקַּח מִשָּׁם, *to work the soil from which he was taken* (ibid. 3:23). Moreover, it was decreed that at the end of his life he would return to the earth: בְּזֵעַת אַפֶּיךָ תֹּאכַל לֶחֶם עַד שׁוּבְךָ אֶל־הָאֲדָמָה כִּי מִמֶּנָּה לֻקָּחְתָּ כִּי־עָפָר אַתָּה וְאֶל־עָפָר תָּשׁוּב, *By the sweat of your brow you shall eat bread, until you return to the ground from which you were taken, for you are dust and to dust you shall return* (ibid. v. 19). Since Adam had not withstood his challenge to rise above the earth within him, his punishment was that he would have to lead the corporeal existence that he had chosen.

As Adam's descendants, the Jewish people were given the Torah to allow us the opportunity of correcting Adam's error through living a life of mitzvos and bringing mankind back to the spiritually elevated existence of closeness to Hashem. This lifelong aim may be accomplished in two ways: in addition to spending our lives actively building our relationship with Hashem by performing mitzvos, the root of the problem that caused our distance from Hashem must also be rectified. *Panim Yafos* explains that since, as we mentioned, the only reason Adam was able to disobey Hashem's commandment was because of the influence of the earth from which he was created, a person, in order to become closer to Hashem, must break the hold that the earth — and the implications of total mundanity that it carries — has on him. The way that our *neshamah's* will to obey Hashem can be asserted over our urges for earthliness, explains *Panim Yafos,* is by our showing, even when actively working the ground itself, that the aims and satisfactions that these involvements bring are secondary to Hashem's commandments.

This proper order of priorities is evidenced by performing the mitzvah of *orlah,* where, even though a person has of course worked to plant and nurture a tree and is certainly permitted to enjoy the benefits of his long and hard labor, he nevertheless waits three years — which is the period needed to demonstrate qualitative ownership — before beginning to enjoy its fruits. In this way, a person firmly establishes that he is the one in control; while it is true that he is spending his days involved in farming, he is only *using* this land, instead of becoming *dominated* by it. This person has shown that he is not a mere "farmer" who maintains an orchard and whose entire objective in life is a better harvest. Rather, he is someone who is interested only in serving Hashem, and will even give up these hard-earned satisfactions should Hashem tell him to do so.

Refraining from eating fruits of *orlah* shows that a person has not become overcome by corporeality, for even when he is actively involved in using — and ultimately enjoying — the earth's qualities, he shows that he will obey Hashem and wait several years before enjoying the fruits of his labors. By performing the mitzvah of *orlah,* concludes *Panim Yafos,* we are able to achieve in the area where Adam did not, for even when we are involved in mundane areas of life, we totally subjugate our earthliness to our *neshamah's* lead in following Hashem's will. Furthermore, by using the earth itself as a way to perform mitzvos, we are fulfilling Hashem's command to Adam: וּמִלְאוּ אֶת־הָאָרֶץ וְכִבְשֻׁהָ, *fill the earth and conquer it,* for we are bringing out the inherent potential for *kedushah* in even the most mundane parts of Creation.

MISHNAH OF THE DAY: ERUVIN 7:10

This Mishnah discusses the foods with which one may make an *eruv* or *shituf*:[1]

בַּכֹּל מְעָרְבִין וּמִשְׁתַּתְּפִין — ***Any*** **food *may be used to make an eruv or a shituf*** חוּץ מִן הַמַּיִם וּמִן הַמֶּלַח — ***except water and salt.***[2] דִּבְרֵי רַבִּי

NOTES

1. In this Mishnah, the laws for an *eruv* and a *shituf* are not identical.

2. *Rashi* (to Gemara 26b) explains that an *eruv* effectively establishes a Sabbath residence because a person is considered to dwell where his food is kept. Since water and salt do not nourish, and therefore would not be eaten alone as a meal, they do not qualify as food for the purpose of an *eruv.* Alternatively, these substances are given freely without compensation and are therefore not considered sufficiently significant to be used as a medium of exchange for an *eruv* or a *shituf* (*Meiri*).

אֱלִיעֶזֶר — These are ***the words of R' Eliezer.*** רַבִּי יְהוֹשֻׁעַ אוֹמֵר — ***R' Yehoshua says:*** כִּכָּר הוּא עֵירוּב — Only **a** whole ***loaf*** of bread ***is*** valid as ***an eruv;***[3] אֲפִילוּ מַאֲפֵה סְאָה — ***even if*** a loaf ***is baked from a se'ah***[4] of flour, וְהוּא פְּרוּסָה אֵין מְעָרְבִין בָּהּ — but ***it is*** slightly ***broken, we may not make an eruv with it.***[5] כִּכָּר בְּאִיסָּר — However, ***a loaf*** the size ***of an issar,***[6] וְהוּא שָׁלֵם מְעָרְבִין בּוֹ — as long as ***it is whole, may be used for an eruv.***[7]

NOTES

3. R' Yehoshua is making two points: Only bread may be used for *eruvei chatzeiros,* and the bread must be a complete loaf (see *Gems from the Gemara*).

4. A *se'ah* equals the volume of 144 average-size chicken eggs. The Mishnah purposely mentions an exaggerated figure.

5. The Gemara explains why such a large loaf of bread is invalid, even if it is only slightly broken (see *Gems from the Gemara*).

6. A small silver coin (*Rashi* from *Kiddushin* 2a).

7. Even the smallest loaf may be used, provided that enough of them are contributed to meet the minimum requirement, outlined in the previous Mishnah (*Shulchan Aruch* 366:6). *Rashi* explains that if the total number of participants is less than eighteen, the *eruv* must contain enough of these small loaves to equal a dried fig for each resident.

GEMS FROM THE GEMARA

The Mishnah taught that an *eruv* may be made with all types of food except water and salt. The Gemara points out that this very ruling was already taught above. Why does our Mishnah repeat it?

The Gemara quotes Rabbah bar bar Chanah as answering that our Mishnah repeats this ruling to exclude the opinion of R' Yehoshua, who said that only a whole loaf may be used for *eruvei chatzeiros;* a broken loaf may not be used. Our Mishnah informs us that in R' Eliezer's view an *eruv* may be made with all manner of bread, even with a broken loaf.

The Gemara explains the reason for R' Yehoshua's ruling — ill will. I.e., the residents who contributed complete loaves might complain about those who contributed only broken loaves. Therefore, R' Yehoshua ruled that everyone must contribute a complete loaf. [The Sages were particularly concerned that an *eruvei chatzeiros* should not cause discord, because its primary function is to promote goodwill among the residents (see *Yerushalmi* cited by *Rif*).] And even should all the residents contribute broken loaves to the *eruv* (where one might suggest that since the contributions are more or less equal, no discord will develop), R' Yehoshua would not approve, for perhaps the situation will revert to its problematic state. If we permit the use of broken loaves in this case, it might become an accepted practice even when others donate complete loaves.

An exception to this rule is taught by *Maharam MiRotenberg* (cited in *Rosh*), who rules that if one of the residents donated his own bread on behalf of all the residents (see Gemara 79b), he may use even broken loaves for the *eruv*. Since there are no other contributors, this arrangement cannot develop into a precedent for unequal contributions.

The Gemara discusses the procedure for reattaching a disqualified broken loaf: According to Rav Chisda, if one joins the pieces with a splinter thrust inside and the loaf appears whole, we may make an *eruv* for him with it. [Although the loaf is actually broken, its use will not engender ill will, because its break is not apparent (*Mishnah Berurah* 366:40).]

The Gemara questions this explanation from a contradictory Baraisa that taught that we may not make an *eruv* with a reattached loaf of bread. The Gemara answers that the ruling of the Baraisa refers to a loaf whose break is noticeable; since the loaf does not appear whole, it is invalid for use as an *eruv*. This ruling of Rav Chisda, however, refers to a loaf whose break is not noticeable. Since the loaf appears whole, it is valid for use as an *eruv*.

A MUSSAR THOUGHT FOR THE DAY

After stating that the fruit that comes from a tree during the first three years after planting is *orlah,* literally *blocked,* the Torah tells us that the fruits of the fourth year are also not permitted for mundane use. Fourth-year fruits must be קֹדֶשׁ הִלּוּלִים לַה׳, *sanctified to laud HASHEM* (*Vayikra* 19:24), which according to *Toras Kohanim* (cited in *Rashi*) does not mean literal sacrifice on the Altar, but rather means that these fruits are imbued with a level of sanctity that does not permit us to sell them or to eat them as we do regular produce. Instead, they must be taken to Yerushalayim and eaten there in a state of purity. After these mitzvos have been performed during the first four years after planting, the Torah tells us that the fruit of this tree is now permitted for ordinary use.

In giving us this permission (ibid. v. 25) — וּבַשָּׁנָה הַחֲמִישִׁת תֹּאכְלוּ אֶת־פִּרְיוֹ, *And in the fifth year you may eat its fruit* — the Torah adds the promise לְהוֹסִיף לָכֶם תְּבוּאָתוֹ, *so that it will increase its crop for you,* and concludes אֲנִי ה׳ אֱלֹהֵיכֶם, *I am HASHEM, your God.*

Rashi, citing R' Akiva, explains that the assurance of *so that it will increase its crop for you* is mentioned together with the mitzvos of *orlah* and *neta revai,* (sanctified) fourth-year fruits, in order to help in the battle against a person's *yetzer hara,* evil inclination. Since it is of course extraordinarily difficult — after investing so much effort into planting, pruning, and tending to a tree — to refrain from eating or selling its fruit until four long years later (and, since *orlah* is forbidden in benefit, to see the fruits of the first three years go to waste), a person will almost certainly be tempted to ignore, disregard or otherwise "cut corners" when faced with these mitzvos. The Torah therefore reminds us that in the long run, a person who properly keeps these halachos will not lose, for we are told that our crop will in fact be increased for having done so. The Torah concludes that we may be assured that these blessings will in fact occur, for *I am HASHEM, your God;* I am certainly trustworthy to fulfill My promises.

R' Dovid Kviat offers a deeper insight into *Rashi's* explanation that the promise of *so that it will increase its crop for you* is written to forestall the *yetzer hara's* arguments. There is a Mishnah in *Pirkei Avos* (1:3) that tells us: אַל תִּהְיוּ כַּעֲבָדִים הַמְשַׁמְּשִׁין אֶת הָרַב עַל מְנָת לְקַבֵּל פְּרָס אֶלָּא הֱווּ כַּעֲבָדִים הַמְשַׁמְּשִׁין אֶת הָרַב שֶׁלֹּא עַל מְנָת לְקַבֵּל פְּרָס, *Be not like servants who serve their master for the sake of receiving a reward; instead be like servants who serve their master not for the sake of receiving a reward.* A person is supposed to fulfill the mitzvos because this is Hashem's will, not because of the great rewards that he is promised for doing so. While it is true that most — if not all — of us are far from this lofty level of performing a mitzvah only *lishmah* — for the singular purpose of fulfilling Hashem's commandments — it is nevertheless puzzling that the Torah mentions a reward for the mitzvah in the same passage where the mitzvah is commanded. If we are not meant to perform the mitzvah for the reward that it brings — and a pure servant of Hashem should not think of any reward when doing the mitzvah — why is the reward *so that it will increase its crop for you* told to us in the same breath as the mitzvos of *orlah* and *revai*?

R' Dovid Kviat explains that *Rashi* is in fact telling us the answer to this question. While it is true that the reward promised for a mitzvah is ideally not the *reason* we fulfill Hashem's will, nevertheless, even if one wishes to perform the mitzvah simply because Hashem desires him to do it, there still exists the possibility that the *yetzer hara* will attempt to dissuade him by using the argument that he cannot afford to keep this mitzvah. It is to prevent the *yetzer hara* from being able to marshal such an argument that the Torah promises blessing to those who observe the mitzvos of *orlah* and *revai,* not to identify the reason one should do so.

HALACHAH OF THE DAY

The following activities are all violations of the *melachah* of *extinguishing*: extinguishing a fire, decreasing the size of a fire, and removing the fuel from a fire.

All methods of *extinguishing* a fire are prohibited on Shabbos. These include extinguishing a fire by pouring liquid upon it, extinguishing a fire by either blowing or otherwise directing air pressure upon the flames, and smothering the flames by throwing something over them.

Even if one does not extinguish a flame completely, but instead merely decreases its size, he transgresses the *melachah* of *extinguishing.* Accordingly, one must exercise great care when moving a table with a lit oil lamp upon it (in cases where it is permitted to move such a table on Shabbos) not to move too quickly, lest the flame decrease in size due to the moving of its fuel.

One who removes the fuel from a fire causes the fire to go out more quickly. This too is a violation of the *melachah* of *extinguishing.* Therefore, one may not remove oil from a lit oil lamp, or cut off the bottom part of a lit candle on Shabbos.

If there is even the most remote possibility that a fire poses a threat to human life, one may extinguish it on Shabbos. Likewise, if necessary, one may use a phone or any other method necessary to summon the fire department to the scene of a fire in order to deal with it. Therefore, since a house fire almost always constitutes a danger to human life, as a general rule one may take whatever action may be necessary in order to extinguish such a fire.

As a general rule, *melachah* that is performed through indirect causation, or *grama,* is prohibited by Rabbinic law. There are, however, instances where such indirect actions are permissible.

The Mishnah teaches us that in order to prevent monetary loss, one may cause a fire to be extinguished by placing barrels of water in the path of the oncoming flames. Since the extinguishing of the flames will happen only as an indirect consequence of the person's actions (when the heat of the fire will cause the barrels to burst, releasing the water), and this course of action is being take in order to prevent the suffering of monetary loss, this form of extinguishing is permissible.

This ruling has many practical ramifications. For instance, if a tablecloth ignites, and its burning — while perhaps posing no danger to human life — will cause significant monetary loss, one may extinguish the flames in an indirect manner. We will discuss the practical application of this ruling further as we continue our study of this *melachah.*

A CLOSER LOOK AT THE SIDDUR

As we mentioned in *A Mussar Thought for the Day,* the fruit of a tree that grows during the first four years after planting may not be used for ordinary purposes; the first three years are *orlah* and are altogether forbidden in benefit, and the (sanctified) fourth-year fruits, *neta revai,* are imbued with *kedushah* that requires them to be eaten in Yerushalayim. The Midrash (*Shir HaShirim Rabbah* §7) includes these two mitzvos in its list of several examples of Hashem's praise of the Bnei Yisrael in *Shir HaShirim*: מַה־יָּפִית וּמַה־נָּעַמְתְּ אַהֲבָה בַּתַּעֲנוּגִים, *How beautiful and how pleasant are you, befitting the pleasures of spiritual love* (7:7). The Midrash explains that Hashem states to the Jewish nation: *How beautiful are you* in your care not to wear or plant forbidden *kilayim* mixtures, and *how pleasant are you* in fulfilling the mitzvah of *tzitzis. How beautiful are you* in adhering to the laws of *orlah,* and *how pleasant are you* in fulfilling the mitzvah of (sanctified) fourth-year fruits. *How beautiful are you* in fulfilling the mitzvah of *bris milah* (circumcision), *and how pleasant are you* in fulfilling the mitzvah of *pri'ah* (folding back the foreskin after making the *milah* incision to ensure that the circumcision remains visible and the foreskin will not grow back to its previous position).

The *Beis HaLevi* (*Parashas Lech Lecha*) explains that each of the three sets of mitzvos — *kilayim* and *tzitzis, orlah* and *neta revai,* and *milah* and *pri'ah* — highlighted in the Midrash are examples of the relationship between two areas of *avodas Hashem* that we mention during the *Pesukei D'Zimrah* of Shabbos and festivals: סוּר מֵרָע וַעֲשֵׂה־טוֹב, *Turn from evil and do good* (*Tehillim* 34:15). *Mesillas Yesharim* explains (Ch. 6) that in order to fully live a life of following Hashem, two disparate — even contradictory — perspectives must always be kept in mind. On the one hand, a person must constantly maintain an almost restraining vigilance on every step that he takes over the course of his life and refrain from undertaking any action that may lead to sin. However, at the same time that he is *turning from evil* by holding himself back from doing something because it may possibly violate Hashem's will, a person should realize that he cannot fully serve Hashem with an overall perspective of caution. Rather, he must also energetically *do good,* by taking whatever initiatives he can to actively carry out positive mitzvos and better develop the many areas of his relationship with Hashem.

On many occasions, these two perspectives are not connected to one another. For example, a person can act with great caution when it comes to the laws of kashrus, but act with zeal when wearing *tefillin.* However, the *Beis HaLevi* explains that many mitzvah areas require both of these attitudes if one is to achieve perfection. For after a person *turns from the evil* inherent in a certain prohibition, he is then able to build upon this quality in a positive way, and *do good* by fulfilling a positive mitzvah as well. For example, as we mentioned in *A Torah Thought for the Day,* the message of the prohibition of *orlah* is that even when involved in the highly mundane action of working the earth, a person must always remember that his *neshamah's* desire to perform mitzvos is the guiding force in his life. For three years, this message — that the *neshamah* directs man's more earthly characteristics — is firmly established by telling man to *stay away* from areas of earthliness. After this period, once a person has established the guidelines necessary to avoid becoming overcome by involvement in the earthly, material world, he is then able to use these qualities in a positive way: by eating earthly fruits in a manner — in a state of purity in Yerushalayim — that brings him closer to Hashem.

Beis HaLevi explains that the two other sets of mitzvos mentioned in the Midrash carry a similar message. The prohibition of *kilayim* tells us of prohibited mixtures that a Jew must refrain from planting or wearing. At the same time, however, he is commanded to wear *tzitzis* — which are also made from a mixture of wool and linen. In addition to *turning from evil* and generally treating combinations of these materials with caution, a person must *do good* when it comes to mixtures of *tzitzis.*

The same principle applies, concludes the *Beis HaLevi,* when performing a *bris milah,* for the Torah tells us that the human body is not complete until the foreskin is cut away. After *turning from evil* and removing this substance, the Torah commands us to *do good,* and actively make it clear on the body that the mitzvah of circumcision has been fulfilled by performing *pri'ah.* It is for this reason that the latter *berachah* recited at a *bris milah,* which contains the words וְצֶאֱצָאָיו חָתַם בְּאוֹת בְּרִית קֹדֶשׁ, *and You sealed his offspring with the sign of the holy covenant,* is recited only after performing *pri'ah,* for only after the *milah* incision has been made visible and permanent does this emblem allow the person to maintain an ongoing connection of *kedushah* with Hashem.

QUESTION OF THE DAY:

What do we learn from the Torah's use of the words וַעֲרַלְתֶּם, עָרְלָתוֹ, and עֲרֵלִים all in one verse?

For the answer, see page 118.

A TASTE OF LOMDUS

The Mishnah (*Orlah* 3:9) tells us that although the laws of *orlah* forbidding the use of a tree in its first three years also apply to trees grown outside of Eretz Yisrael, those grown in the Land have particular stringencies regarding *orlah* — such as the prohibition to benefit from a tree or fruit that is even doubtful *orlah* — that do not apply anywhere else.

Mishneh LaMelech (*Hilchos Maachalos Asuros* 10:11) rules that nowadays, although the laws of *orlah* must still be observed, the unique status of trees in Eretz Yisrael is due only to Rabbinic enactments. The reason for this leniency, *Mishneh LaMelech* explains, may be better understood by looking at other *mitzvos hateluyos ba'aretz,* agriculturally related mitzvos that apply only in Eretz Yisrael, such as the requirements to refrain from working the land during the *shemittah* year and to separate *terumah* and *maaser* from fruits that are grown there. The need to perform these special mitzvos in Eretz Yisrael is based on *kedushas haaretz* — the sanctity of the Land, which descended upon it when Yehoshua led the Jewish people into Eretz Yisrael and conquered and divided it among the twelve tribes. However, the *Rambam* (*Hilchos Terumos* 1:5) rules that this *kedushah* was not permanent. Since it was limited to the time when the Jewish nation would remain in the Land, *kedushas haaretz* — and the accompanying need to keep the unique mitzvos that it requires — was lost when the Jews were exiled to Babylon after the destruction of the first *Beis HaMikdash.* Similarly, explains *Mishneh LaMelech,* the *kedushah* with which Ezra, when he led the Jewish return from Bavel to rebuild the *Beis HaMikdash,* endowed Eretz Yisrael also did not last forever, and was lost with exile. Accordingly, *Mishneh LaMelech* (based on *Tosafos* to *Yevamos* 81a ד״ה מאי) concludes that nowadays, since Eretz Yisrael is not Biblically sanctified, it is only Rabbinic enactment that requires us to observe these unique agricultural laws. Thus, just as it is clear that the requirements of *terumah, maaser,* and *shemittah* do not carry Biblical weight, the same is true in regard to *orlah.* Accordingly, the leniencies that are appropriate to Rabbinic *orlah* — such as the permission to be lenient in cases where the *orlah* status of a tree is only doubtful — may be followed.

Malbushei Yom Tov (2:2) argues with *Mishneh LaMelech* and maintains that while it is true that the mitzvos of *terumos, maasros* and *shemittah* are only Rabbinically binding nowadays, the mitzvah of *orlah* nevertheless must still be observed on a Biblical level. A basic difference between these mitzvos, explains *Malbushei Yom Tov,* may be discerned by noting the time when Bnei Yisrael began to fulfill these respective obligations. The Gemara (*Kesubos* 25a, with *Rashi* ד״ה ולא נתחייבו) tells us that the mitzvos of *terumah, maaser* and *shemittah* did not become obligatory until after the 14-year period of conquering and apportioning Eretz Yisrael was completed. The prohibition of *orlah,* however, took effect as soon as the Jews entered Eretz Yisrael, as the Torah tells us (*Vayikra* 19:23): וְכִי־תָבֹאוּ אֶל־הָאָרֶץ, *When you shall come to the land* etc., *you shall treat its fruit as forbidden* (see *Yerushalmi Orlah* 1:2). Thus, since the *Rambam* (*Hilchos Terumos* 1:2) tells us that agricultural *kedushah* of Eretz Yisrael — and the need to observe the mitzvos of *terumah* and *maaser* — was a product of Yehoshua's dividing the land (for only when each family was assigned its portion could Eretz Yisrael truly be considered as the home of the Jewish nation), it is clear, states *Malbushei Yom Tov,* that a law that applied before this apportionment took place — such as *orlah* — cannot be dependent on this sanctity. The requirement to observe the law of *orlah, Malbushei Yom Tov* concludes, must be based on a different aspect of Eretz Yisrael's uniqueness (which *R' Aharon Kotler* identifies as Eretz Yisrael being the Land that was given to the *Avos*). Thus, just as this aspect was present — and *orlah* applied — during the 14-year period *before* the Jewish people finished conquering and apportioning the Land, there is no reason to think that the same should not prevail nowadays, even though the *kedushah* that comes from the Jewish nation living in Eretz Yisrael is, sadly, no longer present.

Kehillos Yaakov (*Zera'im* §26) offers a defense for *Mishneh LaMelech's* position that present-day *orlah* in Eretz Yisrael is only Rabbinically binding. Although it is true, he says, that *orlah* took effect before Yehoshua *completed* his conquest, the Jewish people had already *come to the land* for the purpose of settling it. Since the path to the goal of conquering Eretz Yisrael in order to sanctify it had begun, some of the mitzvos of Eretz Yisrael were already able to be observed. [It is for this reason, he explains, that the *Sifri* requires a Scriptural exegesis to tell us that *orlah* would not go into effect when a few Jewish spies *came in to the land* as advance scouts; since this action was in fact the beginning of Yehoshua's conquest, it would have been assumed — had the Torah not told us otherwise by stressing בְּבֹאֲכֶם, *when you come* (as a nation) (*Bamidbar* 15:18) — that *orlah* would begin.] Accordingly, concludes *Kehillos Yaakov,* since *orlah* was also based on the *kedushah* established

פרשת קדושים

WEDNESDAY

PARASHAS KEDOSHIM

by the Jewish conquest of Eretz Yisrael — for the beginning of the conquest was considered partial conquest — we may understand *Mishneh LaMelech's* ruling that nowadays, when the *kedushah* achieved by this conquest and settlement is no longer present, *orlah* — like *terumah, maaser,* and *shemittah* — is not Biblically required. Since, as we explained in regard to *terumah* and *maaser,* the sanctity of Eretz Yisrael achieved through conquest was lost when the Jewish people went into exile, all mitzvos related to this sanctity are no longer binding; accordingly, the Biblical mitzvah of *orlah* does not apply.

A TORAH THOUGHT FOR THE DAY

אֶת־שַׁבְּתֹתַי תִּשְׁמֹרוּ וּמִקְדָּשִׁי תִּירָאוּ אֲנִי ה׳
My Sabbaths you shall observe and My Sanctuary you shall revere — I am HASHEM (*Vayikra* 19:30).

From the juxtaposition of these two seemingly unrelated mitzvos, the Gemara (*Yevamos* 6a-b) learns three laws regarding the reverence to which we are obligated in regard to the Sanctuary:

(1) Although the building of the *Beis HaMikdash* is a positive commandment, we are not to desecrate the Shabbos to build it. We expound the statement of the verse: *and My Sanctuary you shall revere — I am* HASHEM, as teaching that the Sanctuary too must honor Hashem, by not being built through any violations of the Torah. The Sanctuary is meant to increase the honor of Hashem and to facilitate the keeping of the mitzvos. It is therefore improper that the Shabbos be violated in its construction.

(2) From the words *My Sanctuary you shall revere,* one might mistakenly think that the physical building of the Sanctuary should be treated with reverence, as if the Sanctuary itself had godlike qualities. The Torah thus juxtaposed the mitzvah of observing Shabbos with the mitzvah of revering the Sanctuary, to tell us that just as the day of Shabbos cannot be "served" — rather one must comport oneself in the proper way on the Sabbath in observance of its laws — so is the Sanctuary itself not to be revered or served. Rather, we are obligated to conduct ourselves in a way that shows reverence for the One Who commanded us regarding it. Practical ramifications of this obligation are the prohibition to walk on the Temple Mount carrying a walking stick or moneybelt, or when wearing shoes. It is also forbidden to use the area as a short-cut to another destination, and one may not sit while within the area of the Sanctuary.

(3) The mitzvah of Shabbos teaches us yet another law about the sanctity of the Sanctuary: Just as Shabbos observance is forever (for the Shabbos day never changes), so is the reverence for the Sanctuary forever. Even after the Temple building itself is destroyed, one must keep all the laws of reverence for the place where the Temple stood.

Chasam Sofer adds that there is another allusion that can be found within the wording of this verse. The words: אֶת־שַׁבְּתֹתַי תִּשְׁמֹרוּ, *My Sabbaths you shall "safeguard",* may be understood as commanding us to enact Rabbinic legislation to distance people from actually violating a Biblical Shabbos law. However, we know that the Sages did not extend

most Rabbinic enactments regarding the Sabbath to the service in the *Beis HaMikdash.* [The Kohanim were in any case very scrupulous regarding all the laws, both of the Temple service and of the observance of Shabbos.] This exception, too, is hinted at in this verse: *Safeguard My Sabbaths,* however, *My Sanctuary you shall revere;* the safeguards need not be applied to the Temple service.

MISHNAH OF THE DAY: ERUVIN 7:11

This Mishnah discusses the procedure and requirements for purchasing a share in an *eruv* or *shituf*:

נוֹתֵן אָדָם מָעָה לַחֶנְוָנִי וְלַנַּחְתּוֹם — ***A person may give a ma'ah***[1] ***to a grocer or baker***[2] כְּדֵי שֶׁיְּזַכֶּה לוֹ עֵירוּב — ***so that*** [the grocer or baker] ***can confer upon him ownership in*** the ***eruv*** (or *shituf*). דִּבְרֵי רַבִּי אֱלִיעֶזֶר — These are ***the words of R' Eliezer.*** וַחֲכָמִים אוֹמְרִים — ***But the Sages say:*** לֹא זָכוּ לוֹ מְעוֹתָיו — ***His money does not acquire*** a share of the *eruv* ***for him;***[3] וּמוֹדִים בִּשְׁאָר כָּל אָדָם — ***and*** the Sages

NOTES

1. A *ma'ah* is a small silver coin, worth one-sixth of a *dinar.*

2. The grocer lives in the *mavoi* and sells wine, which may be used for a *shituf,* and the baker lives in the *chatzeir* and sells loaves of bread, which may be used for an *eruv.* This person pays a grocer (or baker) in advance for foodstuffs to be contributed to the *shituf* (or *eruv*) on his behalf. Although he does not actually take possession of the items he has paid for, he can stipulate that when the *shituf* collection is made and the residents of the *mavoi* approach the grocer to buy food for the *shituf,* the grocer should give them a portion on his behalf (*Rashi*).

3. Monetary payment is not a valid method of acquiring ownership of מְטַלְטְלִים, *movable property;* rather, מְשִׁיכָה, *pulling or moving the object,* is required. Therefore, the food for which the person prepaid never legally belonged to him. Even if the grocer makes the *shituf* for the entire *mavoi* from his own food, and confers possession upon the other residents without requesting payment (using the method explained in the Gemara, 79b), each person still does not acquire ownership of his part; since the grocer accepted payment from this individual and desires to retain the payment, the grocer does not intend to give him a free share in the *shituf* (rather, he intends to sell it to him, and the sale never was consummated). Because this individual has no share in the *eruv,* it is invalid. However, if the merchant would specifically intend to give him a *free* share, it would be valid (*Rashi,* as explained by *Ritva* and *Tos. Yom Tov*).

Tosafos explain that the individual has demonstrated that he does not wish to accept a free portion in the *eruv,* but wants to acquire it by his payment. Since this does not happen, he is left with no part in the *eruv.* Consequently, even if the storekeeper specified that he was also conferring possession gratuitously on this individual, the *eruv* or *shituf* would be invalid.

concur that ***in*** regard to ***all other people*** (who are not merchants), to whom a resident gave money with which to acquire for him a portion of the *eruv,* **שֶׁזָּכוּ לוֹ מְעוֹתָיו** — ***that his money acquires for him ownership*** in a portion of the *eruv* food,[4] **שֶׁאֵין מְעָרְבִין לָאָדָם אֶלָּא מִדַּעְתּוֹ** — ***for we cannot make an eruv for a person without his consent.***[5]

אָמַר רַבִּי יְהוּדָה — ***R' Yehudah said:*** **בַּמֶּה דְּבָרִים אֲמוּרִים** — ***Regarding what were*** these ***words said?***[6] **בְּעֵירוּבֵי תְחוּמִין** — ***In regard to eruvei techumin.***[7] **אֲבָל בְּעֵירוּבֵי חֲצֵירוֹת** — ***But in regard to eruvei chatzeiros,*** **מְעָרְבִין לְדַעְתּוֹ וְשֶׁלֹּא לְדַעְתּוֹ** — ***we may make an eruv*** for him ***with his consent or without his consent,***[8] **לְפִי שֶׁזָּכִין לָאָדָם שֶׁלֹּא בְּפָנָיו** — ***because we may benefit a person in his absence,*** **וְאֵין חָבִין לָאָדָם שֶׁלֹּא בְּפָנָיו** — ***but we may not disadvantage*** a person ***except in his presence*** and with his consent.[9]

NOTES

4. Although the instruction is the same as in the case of the grocer — "Obtain for me possession in an *eruv*" — the intent is different. Since ordinary people do not sell loaves of bread, he intended merely to appoint the other person to act as his agent and gain entry for him into the *eruv,* the money being provided for the service rather than as payment for a loaf of bread. Indeed, had he given a *ma'ah* to the grocer and instructed him to make an *eruv* for him, the *eruv* would also be valid (*Rashi*).

5. This statement of the Mishnah explains the ruling concerning a grocer. When one gives a grocer a *ma'ah* and instructs him, "Acquire ownership for me in an *eruv,*" he means to buy ownership in an *eruv* loaf. One cannot infer from the language of the instruction that the grocer was appointed to act as an agent for the person. Therefore, if the grocer does act to confer ownership in the *eruv* upon the person, he is acting on his own. The Mishnah now explains that such an *eruv* is invalid because one cannot make an *eruv* for a person without his consent, i.e., without express instructions to act as his agent.

However, if the resident acquired a loaf from the merchant by actually taking possession of it, and then returned the loaf to the merchant for inclusion in the *eruv,* it is considered as though he appointed the merchant as his agent (*Rashi*).

6. That in order to acquire an *eruv* for another [i.e., by acting as his agent], one must obtain his prior consent.

7. Since the extension of his *techum* in one direction entails a corresponding contraction of his *techum* in the opposite direction, joining the *eruv* is not an unqualified benefit, inasmuch as one may prefer to retain his original *techum* (*Rashi*). Therefore, one may not act as an agent without specific appointment.

8. Participation in an *eruvei chatzeiros,* which allows one to carry into the *chatzeir,* is generally considered an unqualified benefit, and his approval need not be obtained. [The Gemara discusses exceptions to this rule.]

9. Our Mishnah states a principle that applies in all legal matters. An act may be performed for a person without his prior consent only if it is clearly advantageous to him, and his consent may be assumed.

GEMS FROM THE GEMARA

The Gemara questions the opinion of R' Eliezer in our Mishnah. For as explained earlier, payment for an object is not a valid means of acquiring movable objects (מִטַּלְטְלִין). Rather, the purchaser must move the objects into his domain, in a method of acquisition known as מְשִׁיכָה, *pulling.* If so, how could R' Eliezer maintain that one may acquire a share in the *eruv* simply with payment, when he did not pull the food into his possession?

Rav Nachman said in the name of Rabbah bar Abahu: R' Eliezer treated this matter like the case of "four seasons of the year." Just as a monetary payment completes the acquisition in that case, so it completes the acquisition of the *eruv* food. [R' Yochanan explains below that on the Biblical level, monetary payment *is* a valid method of acquisition. The Rabbis later invalidated it, for reasons to be explained below. In the case of the "four seasons" the Sages waived the necessity for taking physical possession on account of special circumstances. R' Eliezer rules that in the case of *eruv* the Rabbinic method was likewise waived, in order to facilitate the making of an *eruv* (*Rashi*).]

The Gemara cites the Mishnah (*Chullin* 83a) that discusses the case of "four seasons of the year." The Mishnah enumerates four days as the busiest days of the year for butchers. They are: the day before Shemini Atzeres, the day before Pesach, the day before Shavuos, and the day before Rosh Hashanah. At these four times, we compel the butcher to slaughter an animal against his will, if someone had paid for even a small amount of meat. Even if a bull is worth 1,000 *dinars* and the customer has paid for only 1 *dinar's* worth of meat before Yom Tov, we compel him to slaughter the animal to provide the meat, even if he does not have customers for the rest of the meat. The Mishnah adds that if the animal dies before being slaughtered, the customer loses his money.

The Gemara wonders why the customer suffers the loss, if he did not pull the animal into his possession, and payment alone is not a valid means of acquiring ownership. If so, why must he sustain a loss if the animal dies?! The Gemara explains in the name of R' Yochanan that at these four seasons of the year, the Sages reestablished their rulings on the basis of Biblical law.

The Gemara explains that R' Yochanan held that according to Biblical law, monetary payment acquires an object without the necessity of taking physical possession. [This law is derived from the laws of redemption of sanctified property, where monetary payment alone allows one to reacquire possession. *Rashi* reasons that if monetary payment can cause one to acquire ownership of sanctified property, it is certainly a valid method of acquiring ownership of non-sacred property.] But the Sages decreed that only pulling the object into one's possession acquires it, and not monetary payment, out of concern that the seller might say to the purchaser, "Your wheat (for which you have already paid) has burned in the attic." If the buyer acquires his purchase with mere payment, the seller will have no incentive to save it from a fire. Therefore, the Sages decreed that one must take physical possession of the goods in order to acquire ownership, so that the seller will safeguard the goods until their delivery.

Hence, just as the Sages restored the law of acquisition to its Biblical status during these four seasons, in order to expedite the purchase of meat for Yom Tov, so R' Eliezer ruled leniently in this matter in order to facilitate the making of an *eruv,* whose purpose is to enhance the enjoyment of the Sabbath.

A MUSSAR THOUGHT FOR THE DAY

By now we are familiar with the concept that all service of Hashem finds its source in one of two emotions within the heart — *ahavah* (love) and *yirah* (fear or awe). *Yirah* is ordinarily designated as the initial, lower level of service, while *ahavah* is identified as the higher level, and the ideal motivator for the service of Hashem. The sources do speak, however, of a type of *yirah* that is not the basic level of service but is an outgrowth of the highest levels of *ahavah.*

One source for this idea is to be found in the writings of the *Nesivos Shalom* (*R' Shalom Noach Berzovski,* the *Admor* of *Slonim*) on the verse cited in *A Torah Thought for the Day*: אֶת שַׁבְּתֹתַי תִּשְׁמֹרוּ וּמִקְדָּשִׁי תִּירָאוּ אֲנִי ה׳, *My Sabbaths you shall observe and My Sanctuary you shall revere — I am* H*ASHEM* (*Vayikra* 19:30).

He explains that both Shabbos and *Mikdash* (the Sanctuary) represent a dimension of love between Hashem and His nation, the former in time and the latter in space. On Shabbos, Hashem, as it were, invites every Jew to spend the day in His House, to live in the holiness of Hashem's embrace and bask in His radiance. The *Mikdash,* too, represents this loving relationship, as symbolized by the two *Cherubim* that faced each other in the Sanctuary's innermost chamber, the *kodesh hakodashim.*

It therefore seems puzzling that our relationship to the *Mikdash* is described as "reverence," akin to awe and fear. Similarly, *Sefer Yere'im* extrapolates from the juxtaposition of Shabbos and *Mikdash* in our verse that we are to approach Shabbos too with a sense of reverence. We may ask: Why so much reverence? What of the reciprocal love which so permeates the space of the *Mikdash* and the time of Shabbos?

It is here that we are introduced to the concept of *yirah machmas ahavah,* fear as a result of love. There is a form of fear of violating the will of Hashem that is an outgrowth, not an antecedent, of *ahavah.* When one has reached the level of *ahavas Hashem,* he can be overwhelmed by the depths of the love that Hashem feels for him. This can cause him to be seized with a great fear, lest anything happen to disturb or diminish that love.

This is the *yirah* that is expected of us in our relation to Shabbos and to *Mikdash.* Through the *ahavah* that is engendered by the sanctity of the Sabbath and the sanctity of the *Mikdash,* we are to experience the love of Hashem so greatly that it itself brings us to fear anything that could cause a diminution of that love.

HALACHAH OF THE DAY

We will now turn our attention to some common applications of the *melachah* of *extinguishing.*

Turning off an incandescent light bulb on Shabbos is a violation of the *melachah* of *extinguishing.* Since the bulb contains a filament that glows red-hot while lit, turning it off is akin to extinguishing a flame.

Although fluorescent bulbs do not contain such a filament, since they too have a metallic element that becomes hot while in use, the same ruling may apply to fluorescent bulbs.

As we mentioned previously, a fire that ignites in a house is usually deemed to be a threat to human life. As such, the fire may be put out in the most expeditious manner possible, without regard for the possibility of transgressing any *melachah.* However, if it is clear that the fire is small and cannot possibly spread and pose a threat to life, there are several methods that may be employed to extinguish it within the halachic guidelines that we have herein set forth.

One may pour liquid on the part of the burning item that has not yet ignited. By so doing, one will assure that when the fire reaches the wet area it will go out of its own accord. Since this is only an indirect act of extinguishing, it is permissible in such a case.

One may carry or otherwise move the burning item to a location where it may safely be left to burn itself out without doing further damage.

If burning candles are located in close proximity to a window, one must take care not to open the window if wind conditions outside will cause the candles to be extinguished. Even if the wind temporarily abates, one may not take advantage of the momentary respite to open the window. Since it is the nature of wind to ebb and flow, we know that the wind will pick up once again and blow the flame out. However, if a room is uncomfortably hot (or if there is some other pressing need to open the window), one may wait for the wind to abate for a moment and open the window at that time.

We mentioned previously the need to take care when carrying a table upon which there is a burning oil lamp. The concern in moving the lamp is that the motion of the table may result in the liquid fuel of the lamp moving away from the flame, causing the size of the flame to decrease, which is a violation of the *melachah* of *extinguishing.* This does not apply to a burning candle. Since the fuel source of a candle is solid, we are not concerned that the fuel will move away from the flame.

We must note that a table supporting a burning lamp is sometimes subject to the restrictions of *muktzeh* that apply to a "base for a forbidden item." In many instances, such a table may not be moved at all on Shabbos.

This concludes our discussion of the *melachah* of *extinguishing.*

A CLOSER LOOK AT THE SIDDUR

In the Friday night *Kiddush,* the Shabbos is referred to as תְּחִלָּה לְמִקְרָאֵי קֹדֶשׁ זֵכֶר לִיצִיאַת מִצְרָיִם, *The first of the festivals, a memorial to the Exodus from Egypt.* This seems difficult to understand. Shabbos commemorates the creation of the world; in what way is it a memorial to the Exodus? In our earlier studies, we cited *Tur* (*Orach Chaim* §271), who offers two explanations of this. In the first, he explains that the latter phrase does not qualify the Shabbos, but is a description of the festivals. The observance of Shabbos is written in the section of the Torah that sets out all the festivals, but before any of them are mentioned. Thus, the meaning of the above sentence is that Shabbos is the first of the festivals, which themselves — each in their own way — serve as a memorial to the Exodus.

In his second explanation, *Tur* cites *Ramban,* who explains that the

פרשת קדושים

THURSDAY

PARASHAS KEDOSHIM

phrase *a memorial to the Exodus from Egypt* does indeed describe the day of Shabbos. The Exodus, with all its accompanying miracles, was a clear demonstration that Hashem is all-powerful, and that, as the Author of all creation, He can manipulate it at will. Thus, Shabbos, which stands as a memorial to the creation of the world by Hashem, is also a memorial of that which was learned from the Exodus from Egypt.

In *Nesivos Shalom,* the *Admor* of *Slonim* points out that this dual nature of Shabbos, serving as a memorial to Creation and to the Exodus, is hinted at in the plural used in our verse — אֶת שַׁבְּתֹתַי תִּשְׁמֹרוּ, *My* ***Sabbaths*** *you shall observe.* These two aspects of Shabbos are reflected in the two ways in which Shabbos affects the world, and in the different ways in which each person can approach the holiness of Shabbos.

Ohr HaChaim writes (*Bereishis* 2:3) that the spiritual energy necessary for the continuation of the existence of the world is depleted at the end of each six-day cycle. It is only the effect of Shabbos that infuses a power of regeneration into the world for the next six days. This is the "creation" aspect of Shabbos. As for the aspect of Exodus, the spiritual light of Shabbos is likened to the redemption as compared to the weekdays that are shrouded in the darkness of exile.

One whose soul is able to resonate with the "creation" quality of Shabbos can, on this day, without repentance and without directly addressing his sins, transform himself into a new person and reach a new and higher plane of spiritual living. For one who cannot reach this level, there is also the "redemptive" quality of Shabbos. The mark of exile is the distance and separation between man and his Creator; on Shabbos, a person can return to Hashem, become closer to Him, and thus be elevated by the redemption that Shabbos brings to his soul.

QUESTION OF THE DAY:

What lesson can we learn from the comparison between the Sanctuary and the Sabbath?

For the answer, see page 118.

A TORAH THOUGHT FOR THE DAY

אִישׁ אִישׁ . . . אֲשֶׁר יִתֵּן מִזַּרְעוֹ לַמֹּלֶךְ מוֹת יוּמָת עַם הָאָרֶץ יִרְגְּמֻהוּ בָאָבֶן. וַאֲנִי אֶתֵּן אֶת־פָּנַי בָּאִישׁ הַהוּא וְהִכְרַתִּי אֹתוֹ . . . וְאִם הַעְלֵם יַעְלִימוּ עַם הָאָרֶץ אֶת־עֵינֵיהֶם מִן־הָאִישׁ הַהוּא בְּתִתּוֹ מִזַּרְעוֹ לַמֹּלֶךְ לְבִלְתִּי הָמִית אֹתוֹ. וְשַׂמְתִּי אֲנִי אֶת־פָּנַי בָּאִישׁ הַהוּא . . . וְהִכְרַתִּי אֹתוֹ וְאֵת כָּל־הַזֹּנִים אַחֲרָיו

[2] Any man . . . who shall give of his offspring to Molech, he shall surely die; the people of the land shall pelt him with stones. [3] And I shall concentrate My attention upon that man, and I shall cut him off. . . [4] If the people of the land ignore that man, when he gives of his offspring to Molech, not to kill him, [5] then — I shall concentrate My attention on that man . . . and I shall cut him off, and all who stray after him (*Vayikra* 20:2-5).

Tevuos Shor points out many apparent peculiarities in the verses quoted above. Among them: Why is the unique term עַם הָאָרֶץ, *people of the land,* used in reference to those who will punish this man? If the verse already contains the phrase: אִם הַעְלֵם יַעְלִימוּ עַם הָאָרֶץ אֶת־עֵינֵיהֶם, *If the people of the land ignore that man,* why is the phrase לְבִלְתִּי הָמִית אֹתוֹ, *not to kill him,* necessary? Also, the phrase לְבִלְתִּי הָמִית אֹתוֹ is grammatically irregular. The expected phrase would be וְלֹא יָמִיתוּ אֹתוֹ, *and they did not kill him.* In light of these difficulties, he suggests a novel way of reading these verses that not only answers these questions but also addresses another point of contention among the commentaries. While according to some commentaries the child that was given over to Molech was burned to death, others hold that the child was not harmed, but merely passed between two rows of fire in an idolatrous ritual (see *Ramban* to 18:21).

According to *Tevuos Shor,* both forms of worship are referred to in the above verses. Verses 2 and 3 refer to the worship in which the child actually loses his life in the process. In this reading, the verse would be translated thus: *Any man who shall give of his offspring to Molech in which he (the son) shall die* [לַמֹּלֶךְ מוֹת יוּמָת]. This is a crime so heinous that none would let it pass. The people of the land, those to whom civil society is important and who wish to see the land settled, would surely vent their outrage at such a person and punish him for his abominable crime. In a case where it was not witnessed and could not be prosecuted in a court, Hashem Himself will punish only the person who committed the crime (verse 3), not anyone else, for this is not the sort of practice that would ever find imitators.

Verses 4 and 5 refer to the second type of ritual, in which the child does not die. In this more "benign" form of worship, it is possible that the people will be more apathetic to the crime, and not pursue its punishment. We thus read (verse 4): *If the people of the land ignore that man, since he gave of his offspring to Molech, [but] did not kill him [the child]* [לְבִלְתִּי הָמִית אֹתוֹ]. The punishment for this service, which could conceivably gain a following, is addressed both to the perpetrator and to anyone who may be drawn to him (verse 5): *I shall concentrate My attention on that man . . . and I shall cut him off, and all who stray after him.*

MISHNAH OF THE DAY: ERUVIN 8:1

As we have learned earlier, a person is limited to traveling within 2,000 *amos* from the edge of his city, unless he makes an *eruvei techumin.* The *eruv* establishes a person's place of residence at its location, allowing the owner to travel *from that spot* another 2,000 *amos.* The Mishnah discusses how this may be done on a communal level: **כֵּיצַד מִשְׁתַּתְּפִין בִּתְחוּמִין** — ***How does one make a communal eruvei techumin?*** I.e., how does one set up an *eruv* so that anyone who wishes to establish his Sabbath dwelling at the spot where the *eruv* food was deposited can do so easily? **מֵנִיחַ אֶת הֶחָבִית וְאוֹמֵר הֲרֵי זֶה לְכָל בְּנֵי עִירִי** — ***One places a barrel*** of food at the *eruv* site[1] ***and declares, "Let this be for all the people of my town,"***[2] **לְכָל מִי שֶׁיֵּלֵךְ לְבֵית הָאֵבֶל אוֹ לְבֵית הַמִּשְׁתֶּה** — ***for whoever will go to a house of mourning or to a wedding banquet.***[3] **וְכָל שֶׁקִּיבֵּל עָלָיו מִבְּעוֹד יוֹם מוּתָּר** — ***Whoever accepted*** to have his Sabbath dwelling established at the site of the *eruv* ***while it was***

NOTES

1. The one making the *eruv* deposits at the spot designated for the *eruv* a container holding enough food to meet the *eruv* needs of all the participants (see next Mishnah).

2. If the food has been collected from each of the individuals concerned, the declaration is sufficient. But if the food belongs to the person making the *eruv,* he must also confer possession to the potential *eruv* participants by means of a formal act of acquisition.

3. The Gemara explains that this clause could have been interpreted as listing routine purposes for an *eruv;* most people, when they do utilize an *eruv,* do so for the purpose of fulfilling a mitzvah. But the Gemara concludes that in fact the declaration and the *eruv* are limited to those engaged in mitzvah-related activities; such an *eruv* may not be made for one who wishes to go beyond his personal *techum* for purely personal reasons.

פרשת קדושים

FRIDAY

PARASHAS KEDOSHIM

yet day is permitted, i.e., he may walk within the entire area contained in the borders of the *techum* established by the *eruv,* **מִשֶּׁתֶּחְשַׁךְ אָסוּר** — but if he accepted only ***after dark,*** so that the *eruv* gains its validity only after the onset of the Sabbath, ***he is prohibited;*** he must remain within the parameters of the *techum* as defined by his real dwelling, **שֶׁאֵין מְעָרְבִין מִשֶּׁתֶּחְשַׁךְ** — ***for one cannot make an eruv after dark.***[4]

NOTES

4. In order for an *eruv* to be valid, it must take effect at the beginning of the Sabbath.

GEMS FROM THE GEMARA

The Mishnah stated that whoever accepted to have his Sabbath dwelling established at the site of the *eruv* while it was yet day is permitted to do so. Accepting the *eruv* on the Sabbath day itself, however, is not valid, because an *eruv* must take effect before the Sabbath.

However, the following point must be addressed: In the case of the Mishnah the *eruv* has already taken effect before the Sabbath for anyone in the town who wishes to participate in it. Acceptance of the *eruv* by a particular individual is merely a retroactive clarification that one was included in the *eruv.* Now, there is a wide-ranging Tannaic controversy concerning the dynamics of retroactive clarification (known as "*bereirah*"): Specifically, does it take effect retroactive to the time when the action it clarifies was to take effect, or is the clarification effective only from the time it was actually made?

The Gemara assumes now that the ruling of the Mishnah — that the *eruv* must be accepted while it is still day — is based on a negation of the principle of retroactive clarification. That is, we may derive from the Mishnah that there is no retroactive clarification, for if the Mishnah accepts the principle of retroactive clarification, even if one accepted the *eruv* on the Sabbath, let it be clarified retroactively that the *eruv* was acceptable to him even before the Sabbath. Seemingly, the Mishnah, by disallowing the participation of those who did not accept the *eruv* before the Sabbath, proves that we do not accept the principle of retroactive clarification.

Rav Ashi explains that the Mishnah need not be viewed as negating the concept of retroactive clarification. Instead of interpreting the Mishnah as distinguishing between "acceptance of the *eruv*" before the beginning of the Sabbath and after it, one should interpret that the Mishnah teaches us

to differentiate between when the makers of the *eruv* "informed him of the existence of the *eruv*" and when they did not inform him. When the Mishnah says he accepted, it does not insist on actual acceptance; potential acceptance, which can occur when he has knowledge of the existence of the *eruv,* suffices. Once the person has knowledge of the *eruv* before the Sabbath, he may accept the *eruv* on the Sabbath itself. By applying the principle of clarification, his acceptance is retroactively extended to the pre-Sabbath time, and the *eruv* is validated for him. However, even if one accepts the principle of retroactive clarification, the clarification can be extended only to such time that the potential for actual clarification existed. Thus, a person's acceptance cannot be extended retroactively to a time before he had knowledge of the existence of the *eruv* (*Rashi*).

A MUSSAR THOUGHT FOR THE DAY

The Torah describes the effects of a person's sacrificing his son to Molech with the following words (*Vayikra* 20:3): לְמַעַן טַמֵּא אֶת־מִקְדָּשִׁי וּלְחַלֵּל אֶת־שֵׁם קָדְשִׁי, *in order to defile that which is sacred to Me, and to desecrate My holy Name. Rashi* explains that *that which is sacred* refers to the nation of Israel, who are sanctified and designated for Hashem. *Ramban,* in explaining the concept of defiling and causing impurity to the Jewish nation, draws a parallel between the terrible sin of sacrificing to Molech and the seemingly relatively minor infraction of eating without the proper blessing! We will attempt to elucidate this concept more fully while focusing on the severity of one who does not properly bless Hashem before eating, based on the explanation of *R' Yerucham Levovitz* in *Daas Torah.*

The world was created so that man would recognize his Creator, thank Him and praise Him for all His goodness. When a person receives blessing from Hashem, whether in the form of children, a plentiful crop, or even a slice of bread to eat, he must take this opportunity and recognize the One Who has given him this blessing and express his gratitude to Him. This expression of gratitude fulfills the purpose of Creation and is the reason for Hashem's bounty. It therefore has the effect of causing the continuation and increase of blessing from Hashem. Moreover, the continuation of blessing is not limited to the individual alone. When Hashem's Name is blessed by His people, the entire nation receives the benefits of increased sustenance and blessing from Him.

Conversely, one who enjoys the blessings of this world and does not use them to bring greater glory to Hashem does not make the connection between what he has received and the One Who gave it to him. This causes this connection to be broken for the entire nation as well, and the level of blessing will be diminished, for the purpose of the blessing has been frustrated. The very connection between Hashem and His people is interrupted because that connection has not been recognized.

When one takes the greatest blessing Hashem bestows upon him, his own children, and not only does not recognize the source of the blessing and praise Him for it, but actually destroys it to give glory to an idol, he has actively corrupted the source of blessings for the Jewish people as a whole. The Torah writes that it is the responsibility of the "people of the land" to bring him to justice, for it is they who suffer from his actions with the departure of Hashem's Presence from the land and the accompanying diminishment of blessing.

Partaking of the world's goodness without expressing recognition of its Source and praising the One Who gave it by reciting the proper *berachah* is a grave offense. While it is not a crime on the same level as giving one's child to Molech, it is of the same nature, and its effects are likewise to the detriment of the entire Jewish people.

HALACHAH OF THE DAY

The act of *kindling a fire,* מַבְעִיר, is another of the thirty-nine labors prohibited on Shabbos. As mentioned previously, all of the thirty-nine forbidden *melachos* have as their origin activities that were performed during the construction of the Mishkan. As part of the preparation of the various fabrics necessary for both the Mishkan and the vestments of the Kohanim, textiles needed to be dyed to the specifications given in the Torah. To this end, the artisans had to kindle fires in order to prepare the necessary dyes.

The definition of the *melachah* of *kindling* is both the creating as well as the enlarging of a fire. We will soon discuss the many activities that fit this halachic definition.

The Biblical prohibition of *kindling* applies to lighting a fire for any beneficial purpose, such as lighting a torch to illuminate a room. If one kindles a fire for no beneficial purpose, he transgresses only a Rabbinic prohibition.

פרשת קדושים

FRIDAY

PARASHAS KEDOSHIM

The activities restricted as part of the *melachah* of *kindling* may be categorized into two groups: creating a new fire, and enlarging or prolonging an existing fire. We will now give examples of activities from each category.

The first category is comprised of actions that create fire. While some actions obviously fall into this category, there are others that may seem less obvious.

Striking a match creates a new flame and is an obvious violation of *kindling.* It is likewise forbidden to strike sparks off a flint onto a pile of kindling, causing it to burst into flame. Another example of a forbidden act of creating fire is the setting of an object aflame by concentrating sunlight onto it with the aid of a magnifying glass.

Using one lit candle to light another one is also prohibited. Even though the fire already exists on the first candle, a new flame is being created on the second candle.

Heating a metal to the point where it becomes red hot is considered an act of creating fire. Thus, heating a piece of metal until it glows red is a violation of *kindling.* [We must note that metal is considered to have reached this point only if and when it is capable of igniting another object placed in contact with it.]

Accordingly, turning on an incandescent bulb, which contains a filament that glows red-hot when lit, is a violation of the *melachah* of *kindling.* [Although only incandescent bulbs use a red-hot filament, fluorescent bulbs too contain a piece of metal that heats up during use. This metal piece might even become red hot; therefore, turning on a fluorescent bulb could constitute a violation of *kindling.*] All of the above are examples of creating a new fire.

A CLOSER LOOK AT THE SIDDUR

The word בָּרוּךְ, traditionally translated as *blessed,* is the operative word in all our *berachos* (blessings) recited throughout the day. However, according to *Nefesh HaChaim,* it is not simply a praise, but a plea for continued and increased blessing. The literal translation of the word בָּרוּךְ is *addition* or *increase.* When we say: בָּרוּךְ אַתָּה ה׳ . . . בּוֹרֵא פְּרִי הָעֵץ, we are praying that Hashem, Who created the fruits of the tree and gave them to us, should continue to bestow upon us, and increase for us, this blessing. With this recognition of the Source of our good, we are consummating the very goal of Creation — that Hashem's creations should recognize Him and give praise to His Name (see above, *A Mussar Thought for the Day*).

R' Yerucham Levovitz explains that it is for this reason that every *berachah* is focused on the creation of the subject of the *berachah.* We do not say: *Who has given to us the fruit of the tree,* but *Who* **created** *the fruit of the tree,* for with our blessing we are identifying with Hashem's will in Creation — that His Name be praised.

Regarding the explanation of *Nefesh HaChaim* that all *berachos* are actually requests for further blessing, *R' Dessler* (in his *Michtav MeiEliyahu*) asks: Why should we not simply "bless" Hashem by recognizing that He is the Source of all good? Why must we include a request and plea for continued blessing? He answers that we are not using the praise as an opportunity to ask for blessing; we are using the plea as an expression of our praise.

Before one prays, he must feel that he is indeed missing that for which he is praying. The content of his request represents for him a real need. Would it not be a need for him, or if he feels that he can do without it, he would not pray for it. Additionally, one must be of the firm belief that his need cannot be filled in a "natural" way, but only through the help of Hashem. Were one to want for money, but feel that the wealthy are the only source of wealth, he would not turn to Hashem, but to the rich, to fill his need.

Thus, the act of standing before Hashem and asking that He continue to bless us is, in essence, the highest form of praise. We are declaring at once that we cannot survive without receiving continued help, and that the Source of all help and blessing is Hashem. Hence, when we say בָּרוּךְ, we are declaring Hashem's praise in the form of a plea for His continued giving.

QUESTION OF THE DAY:

Why is the idolatry of Molech worse than other idolatry?

For the answer, see page 118.

פרשת קדושים

SHABBOS

PARASHAS KEDOSHIM

A TORAH THOUGHT FOR THE DAY

וִהְיִיתֶם לִי קְדֹשִׁים כִּי קָדוֹשׁ אֲנִי ה׳
וָאַבְדִּל אֶתְכֶם מִן־הָעַמִּים לִהְיוֹת לִי

You shall be holy for Me, for I HASHEM, *am holy; and I have separated you from the peoples to be Mine* (*Vayikra* 20:26).

From the words לִהְיוֹת לִי, *to be Mine,* R' Elazar ben Azaryah learns an important lesson regarding the proper approach to the mitzvos of the Torah. "How do we know that a person should not say, 'I am disgusted by pork; I detest wearing *kilayim* (forbidden mixture of wool and linen)'? The Torah says: *I have separated you from the peoples to be Mine;* your separation should be for My sake alone. One should rather say, 'I would like to eat pork and wear *kilayim,* but I refrain due to the command of my Father in Heaven.' In this way one's refraining from sin is done in a manner of bearing the yoke of the Kingdom of Hashem" (*Rashi*).

This lesson seems to contradict the basic assumption that people have in judging the merits of individuals. Imagine that you had to judge which of the following two people is on a higher spiritual level. One person never experiences an inclination to harm his fellow and is naturally sensitive to the needs of others, always striving to help whomever he can. His basic nature is one that propels him to the constructive and the good, abhorring any destructive behavior. The second person is identical to the first in his actions. He helps others and does not harm them etc., but this is only accomplished after waging many battles with his instincts. By nature he is lazy and spiteful, and expends great effort to control his actions so that they should not be reflective of his nature.

Is there anyone who would say that the second person is a greater saint than the first? That we should strive to be like the second person and not the first? Surely the first person is on a higher spiritual level! How then do we understand the instructions of *Chazal* that we should endeavor to desire sin?

Rambam, in *Shemoneh Perakim* (§6), explains that both of these approaches are correct; however, each one is addressed to a different type of mitzvah.

A person is indeed considered to have a degenerate nature if he desires to steal and to murder. *Chazal* never advised nurturing such inclinations. These are Torah laws that are self-understood to be wrong, both for society and for the moral standing of the individual. With these mitzvos, it is the more refined soul who finds his nature in consonance with the demands of the Torah.

It is only the mitzvos that are beyond human reason about which *Chazal* say that one should keep them only due to the command of Hashem. Because they do not have an intrinsically understandable moral value, they should be kept only for the sake of Hashem and not for any personal preference. Thus, the examples chosen by *Rashi* are the eating of pork and the wearing of *shaatnez* — both *chukim,* decrees of Hashem without reasons that we can clearly understand. In those instances, says *Rashi,* one can indeed say that were it not for the command of Hashem, he would indeed desire the items.

MISHNAH OF THE DAY: ERUVIN 8:2

This Mishnah discusses how much food must be used to establish the communal *eruvei techumin* described in the previous Mishnah: **כַּמָּה הוּא שִׁיעוּרוֹ** — ***What is its*** [the *eruvei techumin's*] ***quantity?*** **מְזוֹן שְׁתֵּי סְעוּדוֹת לְכָל אֶחָד וְאֶחָד** — ***Food for two meals***[1] ***for each and every person*** who wishes to participate in the *eruv.* **מְזוֹנוֹ לְחוֹל וְלֹא לַשַּׁבָּת** — The quantity is determined by ***his food for the weekday*** meals, ***and not*** by his food ***for the Sabbath.*** **דִּבְרֵי רַבִּי מֵאִיר** — These are ***the words of R' Meir.***[2] **רַבִּי יְהוּדָה אוֹמֵר** — ***R' Yehudah says:*** **לַשַּׁבָּת וְלֹא לְחוֹל** — The quantity is determined by his food ***for the Sabbath*** meals, ***but not*** by his food ***for the weekday.*** **וְזֶה וָזֶה מִתְכַּוְּונִים לְהָקֵל** — ***And both intend to rule leniently;*** each of these Tannaim insists that the *eruv* quantity be determined by the meal that is smaller. They differ, however, as to which meals are smaller, weekday meals or Sabbath meals.[3]

NOTES

1. An *eruvei techumin* may be made with any type of food (see Mishnah 3:1). The minimum quantity required for an *eruv* does not refer to the equivalent of two meals. Rather, it refers only to the quantity of the specific food used for the *eruv* that one normally consumes in two meals (Gemara 29a-b).

2. The amount a person eats at a Sabbath meal differs from that which he eats at a weekday meal, as explained further in the next note.

3. R' Meir insists that a person eats more at the Sabbath meals because of the tastiness of the food. R' Yehudah, however, maintains that a person eats less at each Sabbath meal, in order to preserve an appetite for the third Sabbath meal (*Rashi*). [As expounded by the Gemara (30b), the *eruv* quantity is determined in two ways: (1) the amount of food eaten at a meal by the person making the *eruv* (if he eats less than the average person); (2) the amount of food eaten at a meal by an average person (if the person making the *eruv* eats more than the average person). *Rashi* seems to assume that the dispute between R' Meir and R' Yehudah concerns both modes of determination, and that they reject the norms fixed by R' Shimon and R' Yochanan.]

The Mishnah now records the views of various Tannaim on the required quantity for a standard *eruvei techumin* when bread is used as the *eruv* food:

רַבִּי יוֹחָנָן בֶּן בְּרוֹקָה אוֹמֵר — ***R' Yochanan ben Berokah says:*** מִכִּכָּר בְּפוּנְדְּיוֹן מֵאַרְבַּע סְאִין בְּסֶלַע — The quantity of bread necessary for an *eruv* is ***a loaf that is*** purchased ***for a pundyon when four se'ah*** of grain ***are*** purchased ***for a sela.***[4] רַבִּי שִׁמְעוֹן אוֹמֵר — ***R' Shimon says:*** שְׁתֵּי יָדוֹת לְכִכָּר מִשָּׁלֹשׁ לְקַב — The quantity of bread necessary for an *eruv* is ***two parts*** [i.e., thirds] ***of a loaf of which there are three to a kav.***[5] חֶצְיָיהּ לַבַּיִת הַמְנוּגָּע — ***Half of it***[6] [the loaf discussed above] ***is*** equivalent to the minimum amount of food necessary ***for a house afflicted with tzaraas,***[7] וַחֲצִי חֶצְיָהּ לִפְסוֹל אֶת הַגְּוִיָּה — ***and half of half of it***

NOTES

4. Initially, R' Yochanan is understood as referring to a loaf that has the volume of half a *kav* (12 egg-volumes). The calculation is as follows:

The relationship between the monetary units mentioned here is: 1 *sela* = 4 *dinars,* 1 *dinar* = 6 *ma'ahs,* 1 *ma'ah* = 2 *pundyons.* There are thus 48 *pundyons* in a *sela.*

The relationship between the volume measures mentioned here is: 1 *se'ah* = 6 *kavs,* 1 *kav* = 4 *rovas* (*rova* means *quarter;* thus, a *rova* here is a quarter- *kav*), 1 *rova* = 6 *beitzahs* (a *beitzah* is an average chicken egg).

Consequently, since a *pundyon* is 1/48 of a *sela* (2 x 6 x 4 = 48), a loaf purchased for a *pundyon* when four *se'ah* (24 *kav*) are a *sela* has a volume of 1/2 *kav.* The Gemara, however, modifies this calculation; see *Gems from the Gemara.*

5. The loaf that is used to establish the criterion is 1/3 of a *kav.* Since 2/3 of the loaf contains the measure — enough for two meals — required for an *eruv,* the entire loaf — 1/3 *kav* — suffices for three meals. Thus, according to R' Shimon the quantity of bread necessary for one meal is 1/9 *kav,* while R' Yochanan, as he is initially understood, requires more than double that amount — 1/4 *kav* per meal (*Rashi*).

6. Both R' Shimon and R' Yochanan use a loaf to establish the measure of an *eruv.* They disagree only regarding the size of the loaf used to establish the standard. The Mishnah now states that the loaf that serves as the standard for the *eruv* measure also serves as the standard for the *peras,* half-loaf, which is the minimum amount of food necessary for a house afflicted with *tzaraas* (see next note). [Since the loaf used by R' Shimon is 1/3 *kav,* the half-loaf discussed is 1/6 of a *kav,* or 4 *beitzahs* (a *kav* contains 24 *beitzahs,* as explained above). According to R' Yochanan, as he is initially understood, the loaf is 1/2 of a *kav,* and the half-loaf discussed is 1/4 of a *kav,* or 6 *beitzahs.*] Although R' Shimon defines a meal as 1/3 of a loaf for the law of *eruv,* this is a leniency that pertains only to *eruv.* Regarding *tzaraas,* which is a Biblical law, a relative stringency is called for, and so a larger minimum is necessary.

The half-loaf discussed here is the פְּרַס, *peras,* referred to often in the Talmud, and is so called because it is a פְּרוּסָה (*perusah*), *a broken loaf* (*Rashi*).

7. A house that has been pronounced by the Kohen to be afflicted with *tzaraas* is *tamei.* One of the aspects of this *tumah* is that anyone who enters the house is rendered *tamei.* There are two levels of this *tumah*: If the person exits the house immediately after entering, only he, but not his clothing, is *tamei.* If, however, he

[one-quarter of the loaf] ***is*** equivalent to the minimum amount of food necessary ***to render the body pasul.***[8]

NOTES

tarries in the house for as much time as is necessary to eat a minimal meal, even his clothing is *tamei* (see *Vayikra* 14:46-47). The Mishnah states that half of the loaf that serves as the standard for the *eruv* quantity is sufficient for a minimal meal, as it is defined in the context of a house afflicted with *tzaraas* (*Rashi*).

8. [The term *pasul* is used to indicate a low level of *tumah*, at which the person himself is *tamei* and may not eat *terumah* or *kodashim*, but does not necessarily transmit his *tumah* even to food.]

According to Biblical law, food that has become *tamei* cannot ordinarily render a person coming in contact with it *tamei*. However, the Sages promulgated a decree that one who eats *tamei* food equivalent to 1/4 of the standard loaf discussed here is himself rendered *pasul*, and may not eat *terumah* or *kodashim* (*Rashi*).

GEMS FROM THE GEMARA

The Mishnah taught a dispute between R' Yochanan ben Berokah and R' Shimon concerning the size of the two meals required for an *eruv techumin* (see note 5 to Mishnah). The Gemara quotes a Baraisa that teaches that "R' Yochanan's and R' Shimon's views are close to being identical." How can that be, the Gemara asks, the quantities required by R' Yochanan and R' Shimon are not even similar! R' Yochanan's measure is based on a criterion of *four* meals to a *kav*, while R' Shimon's quantity is based on a criterion of *nine* meals to a *kav*!

The Gemara attempts to resolve the inconsistency based on a statement of R' Chisda that one must deduct *one-third* of the one- *pundyon* cost of the loaf for the grocer's profit, so that only 2/3 of a *pundyon* figures in the calculation. The calculation according to R' Shimon is based on the price of 4 *se'ah* for a *sela* of grain. Based on this price, one can purchase 1/2 *kav* of grain for a *pundyon*, but surely a grocer cannot sell a 1/2 *kav*-loaf of bread for the same *pundyon*! Rather, one must assume that the grocer adds a 50 percent markup to the cost of the grain itself in order to cover the cost of labor involved in producing the loaf and to see a profit. According to this computation, the grain in a loaf purchased for a *pundyon* cost the grocer 2/3 of a *pundyon*, and contains not 1/2 of a *kav* of wheat, but 1/3 a *kav*; thus a meal is 1/6 of a *kav* (*Rashi*). The size of a loaf bought from a grocer for a *pundyon* is therefore diminished in size by one-third.

The Gemara is dissatisfied with the proposed solution, because although the gap between R' Yochanan and R' Shimon has been narrowed on the basis of R' Chisda's statement, still, according to R' Shimon, there are *nine* meals in a *kav,* while according to R' Yochanan there are only *six* meals in a *kav.* This is far from being "close to identical"!

The Gemara modifies its solution, resolving the difficulty based on another statement of R' Chisda: One must deduct *one-half* of the payment for the grocer's profit. Thus, only half of the *pundyon* paid for the loaf figures in the calculation. Accordingly, when one purchases a loaf for one *pundyon,* he can assume that it contains 1/2 a *pundyon* worth of grain (which works out to 1/4 of a *kav*). According to this calculation, a meal consists of 1/8 of a *kav* (half the loaf). If so, R' Shimon holds that there are nine meals in a *kav,* while according to R' Yochanan, there are only eight meals in a *kav.* This is why the Baraisa says: Their views are "close to being identical."

The Gemara subsequently studies the contradictory statements of Rav Chisda: In one statement he asserts that the grocer's profit is one-third of the total price, while in another he claims that it is one-half! The Gemara resolves this by saying that the grocer is given only one-third of the total price as profit in a situation where the buyer paid for the wood used to bake the loaf. But the grocer is given half the total price in a situation where the buyer did not pay for the wood and the grocer had to supply it.

A MUSSAR THOUGHT FOR THE DAY

In *A Torah Thought for the Day* we discussed the injunction of *Chazal* that one should not separate oneself from that which is forbidden due to personal taste, but only for the sake of Hashem. *R' Yitzchak Issac Sher* points out that the mitzvos mentioned as examples are those about which the Torah writes that they are to serve as a demarcation between the Jewish people and the nations of the world. He explains that it is this distinction that *Chazal* are addressing.

Each nation has its own distinct culture. It is the sum total of the likes and dislikes, habits and aversions that the nation inherited from its ancestors and its history. These are expressed in its diet, its dress, and its customs. The Jewish nation, too, has a "culture," "habits," and "customs" in which they engage that make them distinct as a nation. These are the mitzvos of the Torah pertaining to diet, dress, etc., that serve to separate us from the other nations. *Chazal* warn us that we are not to relate to these mitzvos as the other nations do to their culture. We do not hold onto them for the purpose of national identity. On the contrary, we must say, "I would like to eat what they do, and wear what they do, but my Father in heaven has decreed, and I must obey." These laws must never be an issue of nationalism, built on societal factors, but simply the expression of our obeying the commandments of the Torah.

In *Havdalah* we say: הַמַּבְדִּיל ... בֵּין אוֹר לְחֹשֶׁךְ בֵּין יִשְׂרָאֵל לָעַמִּים, *Who has distinguished between light and darkness, between Israel and the nations. Beis HaLevi* points out that the distinction between light and darkness is inviolable; no matter what is done, one cannot mix the two or bring one into the boundary of the other. So too is the separation between the Jewish people and the nations. If the Jews try to blur this distinction, the nations themselves will come to remind them of it, and reinstate the distinction. [*R' Chaim* of *Volozhin* used to say: If the Jews do not make *"Kiddush"* (sanctify themselves to separate themselves from the nations), then the nations will make *"Havdalah"* (separation); they will enforce the distinction through persecution.]

R' Elchanan Wasserman remarked that this rule is proportional — in the exact measure that the Jewish people attempt to behave like the nations, in that same measure will the nations repel them and persecute them. While some people say, "It is hard to be a Jew," history has shown that it is exponentially harder to be a non-Jew. It is an easily observed phenomenon in Jewish history that the very places where the Jews made the most progress in erasing a sense of their distinction, there they suffered the most persecution. It is the fate of the Jewish people to either keep separate from the nations, or to be reminded of this responsibility by the very nations with whom they have assimilated.

HALACHAH OF THE DAY

The second category of activities restricted by the *melachah* of *kindling* is the enlarging or prolonging of an existing fire on Shabbos. Thus, one may not enlarge a fire by fanning it, as is done with a bellows. Likewise, one may not lift a burning wick so that more of it is exposed, because this, too, enlarges the flame.

Prolonging the duration of a fire's burn is also prohibited under the *melachah* of *kindling.* Thus, one may not add oil to a burning oil lamp, for by doing so he causes the fire to burn for a longer period of time.

We will now discuss practical applications of the *melachah* of *kindling.*

Depressing the accelerator pedal of a car causes fuel to be introduced into the combustion chambers of the engine, where it is then ignited. Thus, driving a car is a continuous transgression of the *melachah* of *kindling.*

It is prohibited to make a bulb burn more brightly by raising a rheostat, or dimmer, to a higher setting. By raising the setting one enlarges the fire.

One may not sterilize a needle by placing it in a fire and making it red hot.

One must take care when moving a table with a burning oil lamp on it. If one shakes the lamp, he may cause the oil to move closer to or further away from the flame, which would violate the *melachos* of *kindling* and *extinguishing* respectively.

Because of the possible relationships that exist between the *melachah* of *kindling* and the use of electricity, it is appropriate at this time for us to discuss the use of electrical appliances on Shabbos.

We mentioned earlier that heating the filament in an incandescent bulb until it is red hot is considered to be kindling a fire. Many electrical appliances, however, do not have filaments that are heated to such a degree. The use of such appliances on Shabbos is the subject of much debate among the later halachic authorities. Although all authorities agree that it is forbidden to turn on electrical appliances on Shabbos, they disagree as to the *melachah* being transgressed, and whether it is a Biblical or Rabbinic prohibition being violated.

This dispute has many ramifications. There are instances where one is permitted to ask a non-Jew to perform an activity for him, provided that the activity is prohibited only by Rabbinic law. If turning on an electrical appliance is forbidden only by Rabbinic law, it would be permissible in these instances to ask a non-Jew to turn on the appliance. If, however, it is forbidden by Biblical law, this would not be permissible.

Tomorrow we will discuss the various *melachos* that may come into play when analyzing the question of electricity from the standpoint of halachah.

QUESTION OF THE DAY:

According to this verse (20:26) what condition must we fulfill to earn Hashem's protection?

For the answer, see page 118.

A CLOSER LOOK AT THE SIDDUR

We continue our discussion of the Friday night *zemiros.*

One of the more well-known *zemiros* is *Tzur MiShelo,* an early *zemer* of unknown authorship. Usually sung toward the end of the meal, it begins by noting that we have eaten the food of Hashem and that we must bless Him in thanks, according to the commandment of the Torah (*Devarim* 8:10) that bids us recite *Bircas HaMazon.* The next three stanzas of the *zemer* (not counting the chorus/refrain) parallel the first three blessings of *Bircas HaMazon,* while the final stanza is a prayer for the rebuilding of the *Beis HaMikdash* and the restoration of Jerusalem.

Some commentaries note that there does not seem to be a stanza paralleling the fourth blessing of *Bircas HaMazon* in this *zemer,* and conclude that it is possible that the *zemer* was composed during the early Tannaic period, and predates the Sages' establishment of that blessing. Others maintain that in fact the final stanza is meant to represent the fourth blessing of *Bircas HaMazon.* They explain that the final blessing of *Bircas HaMazon* was instituted by the academy of Rabban Gamliel in Yavneh as an expression of gratitude that the bodies of those killed in the Roman massacre at Beitar were eventually able to be buried properly (*see Berachos* 48b). Since the reason for the institution of that blessing was an outgrowth of the Temple's destruction, it is appropriate that the stanza speaks of the rebuilding of the Temple.

The end of the final stanza states: הָרַחֲמָן הַנִּקְדָּשׁ יִתְבָּרַךְ וְיִתְעַלֶּה עַל כּוֹס יַיִן מָלֵא כְּבִרְכַּת ה׳, *May the Merciful and Sanctified One be blessed and exalted, over a full cup of wine, as befits the blessing of* H*ASHEM.* This is a reference both to the cup of wine over which *Bircas HaMazon* is usually recited, and to the metaphorical cup of overflowing blessing that we hope to merit with the redemption and the rebuilding of Jerusalem.

[It is noteworthy that *Haamek She'eilah* (§130) cites *R' Chaim Volozhin* as objecting to the singing of this *zemer,* because it so closely resembles *Bircas HaMazon* that one would discharge his Biblical obligation of *Bircas HaMazon* by singing it. However, most authorities are not concerned for this (possibly because those singing the *zemer* either do not realize the parallel, or have no such intent).]

ANSWERS TO QUESTIONS OF THE DAY

Sunday:

It was stated to a group because the Torah seeks to instill *kedushah* in one who gets along with others (*Chasam Sofer*).

Monday:

One who assists a non-Jew in transgressing one of the Seven Noahide Laws also violates this transgression.

Tuesday:

Hillel knew that it is easier to accept upon oneself not to hate another, than it is to accept that one must love another (*Chidushei HaRim*).

Wednesday:

We learn that *orlah* may not be eaten, that it is forbidden for benefit, and that one cannot even use it for fuel (*Pesachim* 22b).

Thursday:

The Gemara tells us that just as we must not fear the Sabbath, but He Who commanded us concerning it, so too we must not be in awe of the *Beis HaMikdash,* but of He Who commanded us regarding it.

Friday:

Using fire to go against Hashem's ways is especially abhorrent because Hashem is considered an אֵשׁ אוֹכְלָה, *an all-consuming fire* (*Alshich*).

Shabbos:

Rabbeinu Bachya says that the Jews must separate themselves from the nations and then Hashem will protect them.

פרשת אמור
Parashas Emor

פרשת
אמור

SUNDAY

PARASHAS
EMOR

A TORAH THOUGHT FOR THE DAY

אֱמֹר אֶל־הַכֹּהֲנִים בְּנֵי אַהֲרֹן וְאָמַרְתָּ
אֲלֵהֶם לְנֶפֶשׁ לֹא־יִטַּמָּא בְּעַמָּיו

Say to the Kohanim, the sons of Aharon, and tell them: Each of you shall not become impure to a [dead] person among his people (*Vayikra* 21:1).

The root word אמר is repeated in this verse: *"Say"* (אֱמֹר) *to the Kohanim and "tell"* (אָמַרְתָּ) *them. Rashi,* quoting *Chazal,* explains that the Torah is hinting with this repetition that it is the responsibility of adults to ensure that minors do not violate the laws of impurity.

According to *Ramban,* this added clause included in the general laws of the Kohanim is of the same type as those written with regard to other prohibitions, where it is learned that we are not to directly assist a minor in doing something forbidden. For example, with regard to the prohibition against eating insects, the Gemara (*Yevamos* 114a) applies the methods of exegesis to read the words לֹא תֹאכְלוּם, *do not eat them* (*Vayikra* 11:42), to convey the command לֹא תַאֲכִילוּם, *do not feed them.* At the same time, if a minor obtains forbidden food, we are not obligated to take it away from him. *Ramban* explains that the laws regarding minors that are spelled out in the above verse and in others are representative of all the laws of the Torah in which we are cautioned not to directly assist minors in violating them, but need not intervene if they act on their own initiative.

However, *Tur,* in his commentary on the Torah, differs with *Ramban.* He explains that when the Torah indicates that we are not to actually feed minors forbidden foods, it may be inferred that we do not have to prevent them from doing so on their own. Here, however, the Torah did not phrase the words as an injunction that we are not to bring them to the violation. Rather, by using a repeated phrase, it widened the general prohibition that applies to adults. Therefore, in the case of these prohibitions, even if a minor wanted to become impure on his own, we would be obligated to prevent him from doing so. The holiness of the Kehunah demands that a more stringent approach be taken in the way in which its laws relate to minors. [See *Yoreh Deah* 373:1 for further discussion. It should be noted that the halachah regarding the responsibility that adults have regarding a minor's adherence to Torah prohibitions involves many other variables, such as the age of the child in question and what responsibilities devolve upon the parent, a stranger, or the court.]

Ohr HaChaim presents another explanation for the double imperative to Moshe. He writes that it is not only a Kohen who is warned not to cause himself impurity; anyone, even a non-Kohen, may not cause impurity to a Kohen (see *Rambam, Hilchos Aveil* 3:5). Both groups are being addressed in the commandment to keep the Kohanim holy: *Say to the Kohanim, the sons of Aharon;* and also *tell them,* i.e., impart the same message to the people of Israel — neither the Kohanim nor the people should in any way cause impurity to a Kohen.

MISHNAH OF THE DAY: ERUVIN 8:3

The Mishnayos at the end of the previous chapter and the beginning of this one discussed the procedure for making an *eruv* or *shituf,* and other related topics. The rest of this chapter will discuss various laws of *eruv,* particularly the ramifications of failing to make an *eruv*:

אַנְשֵׁי חָצֵר וְאַנְשֵׁי מַרְפֶּסֶת — We discuss ***the residents of a chatzeir and the residents of a gallery***[1] שֶׁשָּׁכְחוּ וְלֹא עֵירְבוּ — ***who forgot to make an eruv,***[2] so that carrying between the *chatzeir* and the gallery is prohibited. The question now is, which nearby areas belong to the *chatzeir* and which to the gallery? כֹּל שֶׁגָּבוֹהַּ עֲשָׂרָה טְפָחִים לַמִּרְפֶּסֶת — ***Whichever*** area ***is ten tefachim high*** above the floor of the *chatzeir* belongs

NOTES

1. The people whose apartments are at ground level and open directly into the *chatzeir* are called "residents of the *chatzeir.*" Others have apartments that are situated above ground level, and open to a gallery (or porch). At the end of the gallery, there is a stairway that descends to the *chatzeir.* These people are here called "residents of the gallery" (*Rashi*).

2. The residents of the *chatzeir* made an *eruv* among themselves, as did the residents of the gallery, but the two groups did not make a mutual *eruv.* Consequently, each of these areas is permitted for carrying, but carrying from one area to the other is prohibited. Because the gallery is elevated 10 *tefachim* above the *chatzeir,* but is connected to the *chatzeir* by means of a stairway, the two areas are similar to two *chatzeiros* that are separated by a partition, but open into one another. Hence, the residents have the option of making a mutual *eruv* to permit carrying from one area to the other, or to make separate *eruvin* to permit carrying only within each area (see Mishnah 7:2). Although the staircase that connects the gallery to the *chatzeir* is viewed as a portal between the two areas, it still retains the aspect of a partition, so that the two areas are considered separated from each other, but accessible by means of a portal (*Rashi*).

פרשת אמור

SUNDAY

PARASHAS EMOR

to the gallery,[3] פָּחוֹת מִכַּאן לֶחָצֵר — but whichever area is elevated ***less than this*** belongs ***to the chatzeir.***[4]

The guiding principle here is that an area shared by two other areas is considered to be the province of the area to which it is more accessible, even if they are not contiguous. The Mishnah cites an example of the above ruling:

חוּלְיַית הַבּוֹר וְהַסֶּלַע — ***The embankment of a pit***[5] ***or a rock*** **גְּבוֹהִים עֲשָׂרָה טְפָחִים לַמִּרְפֶּסֶת** — that are ***ten tefachim high*** above the floor of the *chatzeir* belong ***to the gallery,*** **פָּחוֹת מִכַּאן לֶחָצֵר** — but if they are elevated ***less than this,*** they belong ***to the chatzeir.***

The Mishnah qualifies its rule that a 10-*tefach* high pillar, pit, embankment or rock belongs to the gallery:

בַּמֶּה דְּבָרִים אֲמוּרִים בִּסְמוּכָה — ***Regarding which*** case ***were these*** words ***said? Regarding*** an area ***that is close*** to the gallery. **אֲבָל בְּמוּפְלֶגֶת אֲפִילוּ גָּבוֹהַּ עֲשָׂרָה טְפָחִים לֶחָצֵר** — ***But regarding*** an area ***that is distanced*** from the gallery, ***even*** if it is ***ten tefachim high,*** it belongs also ***to the chatzeir.***[6] **וְאֵיזוֹ הִיא סְמוּכָה** — ***And what is*** considered ***close?*** **כֹּל שֶׁאֵינָהּ רְחוֹקָה אַרְבָּעָה טְפָחִים** — ***Whatever is not four tefachim away.***

NOTES

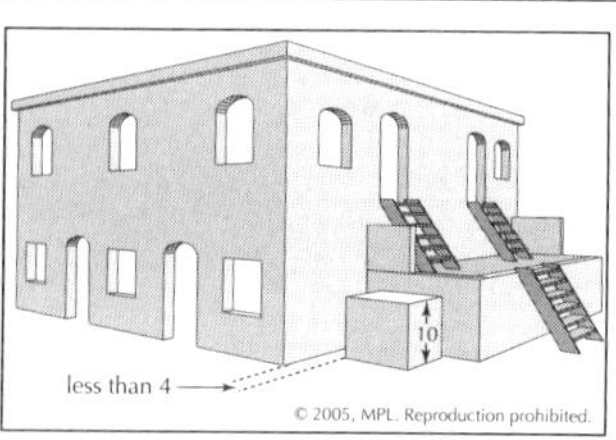

3. If within the *chatzeir* there is a mound or pillar 10 *tefachim* high that is close to the gallery, it is considered part of the gallery area. Carrying is permitted between the mound and the gallery, but not between the mound and the *chatzeir* (*Rashi*). See diagram.

4. This may be understood in one of two ways. It may mean either: (1) that the pillar area belongs *exclusively* to the residents of the *chatzeir* and is available for their use; as a result, it is off limits to the residents of the gallery; or, (2) that the pillar area belongs to the residents of the *chatzeir also,* in addition to its association with the gallery. As a result, the area is prohibited for use to the residents of both the *chatzeir* and the gallery, since it is an area whose "residents," i.e., those who have access to it, have not united in an *eruv.*

5. The earth from a pit that was piled up around it to serve as a fence.

6. In this case, there is only one interpretation — the pillar area belongs to the residents of the *chatzeir also,* in addition to its association with the gallery. See *Gems from the Gemara.*

QUESTION OF THE DAY:

Are the daughters of Kohanim allowed to contaminate themselves with corpse-tumah?

For the answer, see page 176.

GEMS FROM THE GEMARA

The principle that underlies the rulings of the Mishnah is that an area near two other areas is considered to be the province of the area to which it is more accessible. The Gemara discusses a number of situations and demonstrates how this principle applies in each case:

(1) Where a given area is readily accessible to the residents of two neighboring *chatzeiros,* each through a portal, carrying between the given area and either of the two *chatzeiros* is forbidden, as it is equally in the province of both *chatzeiros.* Similarly, when a given area is *not* readily accessible to either of two neighboring *chatzeiros,* it is equally in the province of both *chatzeiros,* because neither of them can claim greater accessibility to it. An example would be if the area is at least 10 *tefachim* high, so that use of the area from both *chatzeiros* is possible only by means of throwing with an upward motion. Or, the area is at least 10 *tefachim* below the area for which it is providing use, so that use of the area from both *chatzeiros* is possible only by means of lowering with a downward motion. In both cases, carrying between the middle area and any of the two *chatzeiros* is forbidden.

(2) When a given area is more readily accessible to one of two neighboring *chatzeiros,* the area belongs to the *chatzeir* that has access with the least effort. For example, two *chatzeiros* are near but separate from each other, one elevated above the other. Between them lies a mound whose top is 10 *tefachim* higher than the ground level of one *chatzeir,* but less than 10 *tefachim* higher than the floor of the other *chatzeir.* This area is readily accessible to the residents of one *chatzeir,* but to the other *chatzeir* it is accessible only by means of throwing objects onto the area in an upward motion. Or, two *chatzeiros* are elevated one above the other, and in the area between them lies a mound whose top is 10 *tefachim* below the ground level of one *chatzeir,* but less than 10 *tefachim* higher than the floor of the other *chatzeir.* This area is accessible to the residents of the second *chatzeir* through a portal but to the first *chatzeir* only by means of lowering objects downward to the area. In both cases, the area belongs to the *chatzeir* that has access with the least effort.

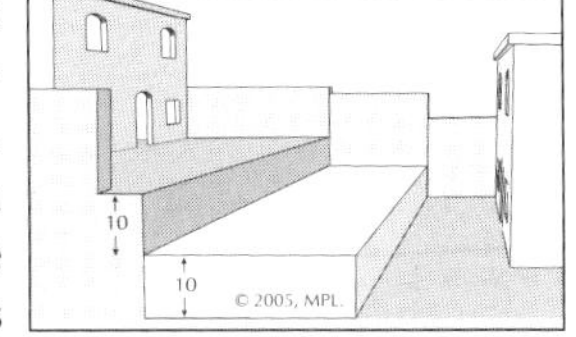

(3) Finally, the Gemara presents a case in which there is disagreement where the middle area belongs: if a given area is

accessible to the residents of one *chatzeir* only by means of lowering objects to the area, and to the other *chatzeir* only by means of throwing objects to the area with an upward motion. This would be the case if the mound is situated 10 *tefachim* lower than one *chatzeir,* and 10 *tefachim* higher than the other. See diagram on previous page. To which *chatzeir* does this area belong?

[The basis for the query is as follows: Are throwing and lowering considered equal, inasmuch as both are classified as difficult, so that this case is analogous to cases where access to both *chatzeiros* is equally difficult? If so, the area under discussion would be prohibited to both *chatzeiros.* Or is lowering considered to be easy vis-a-vis throwing, and therefore this case would be considered one where the higher *chatzeir* has easier access. If so, the area under discussion would be permitted to the higher *chatzeir,* and prohibited to the lower *chatzeir* that has access only by means of throwing upward (*Rashi*).]

Rav holds that in such a case, the residents of both *chatzeiros* are prohibited to carry to and from the given area, for the area belongs to both. But Shmuel holds that we award the given area to the *chatzeir* that has access by means of lowering, for its access is deemed more convenient. Thus, the residents of the upper *chatzeir* may carry to and from the area, but the residents of the lower *chatzeir* may not.

Nevertheless, in the Mishnah's concluding case (where the pillar is 10 *tefachim* high but more than 4 *tefachim* away from the wall of the house), use of the area is difficult for residents of both the *chatzeir* and the gallery. The Gemara assumes that such an area belongs to both the *chatzeir* and the gallery (i.e., "*also* to the *chatzeir*"), even according to Shmuel who would normally award the pillar to the gallery (that has access through lowering) over the *chatzeir* (that has access through throwing). Since the gallery residents must traverse the vertical distance of 4 *tefachim* from the gallery and must also lower objects onto the pillar, their access is deemed no more convenient than that of the *chatzeir* residents, who have use only through throwing in an upward motion (*Rashi*).

A MUSSAR THOUGHT FOR THE DAY

We have seen above how the various commentators explained the repetitious phrase found at the beginning of *Parashas Emor* [אֱמֹר, וְאָמַרְתָּ] to impart halachic teachings (see *A Torah Thought for the Day*). The same phrase is treated in the Aggadic (homiletic) portion of

Torah as well, where we find *Midrash Rabbah* (26:5) making the following comment: "The angels, who do not have a *yetzer hara* (evil inclination), suffice with one 'telling' to do the will of Hashem, as the verse says: *with the 'saying' of the decree to the holy ones* (*Daniel* 4:14). For humans, who do have a *yetzer hara,* would that two 'sayings' would suffice for them! — as the verse says: אֱמֹר אֶל הַכֹּהֲנִים וְאָמַרְתָּ אֲלֵיהֶם."

The *Dubno Maggid* notes that the Midrash does not say that man needs to be commanded numerous times; rather, it states that two times should (hopefully) be sufficient. This implies that there is a significant difference between the first time one is commanded, and the second. An explanation is in order. Why should one more exhortation make such a difference? Once man must contend with his *yetzer hara,* why is two times so much better than one?

The *Dubno Maggid* answers with a parable. When one is warned by a doctor to avoid certain foods that are harmful to him, the patient may or may not heed that warning. In the case that he does not, and he indeed becomes sick from those foods, although he has ignored the warning once, he is now much more inclined to heed the doctor's warning. The second warning, given after the effects of his disobedience were felt, is of a totally different nature than the first.

So too, when a person does not heed the mitzvos of the Torah and then suffers the consequences through Divine punishment, the second warning carries much more weight. The Midrash means that while angels suffice with one time, and their compliance is ensured, people need two instances of exhortation — one before they sin, and, if necessary, one after they have sinned and tasted the bitter fruits of their deeds. The message of the second time is: "Did I not tell you that it is not worth it to sin? Now that you know firsthand the folly of abandoning the Torah, return to full observance and heed all the mitzvos from now on."

The *Dubno Maggid* adds that this message is built into the grammatical structure of the word וְאָמַרְתָּ (*and you shall say*). In Hebrew, a *vav* at the beginning of a verb can serve to switch the tense from past to future, or vice versa. Thus, אָמַרְתָּ (without the *vav*) means *you said,* in the past tense; וְאָמַרְתָּ means *and you shall say.* The reason the Torah employs this grammatical device here instead of simply using a direct form of the future tense (תֹּאמַר) is to convey the above concept. וְאָמַרְתָּ refers to the second warning, that which pertains to the time after the sin. The Torah is saying: Take the message that you have already heard (אָמַרְתָּ) and switch it so that it applies to your future (וְאָמַרְתָּ); that is, heed the Torah's commandments from now on.

HALACHAH OF THE DAY

We will now discuss the various prohibitions that one may possibly violate when turning on an electrical appliance.

The Sages instituted a prohibition against creating a new entity on Shabbos. This prohibition is known as מוֹלִיד, *molid.* For example, one may not crush ice on Shabbos in order to transform it into water. Several authorities rule that switching on an electrical appliance is a transgression of this Rabbinic prohibition. They reason that the introduction of an electric current into an appliance creates something new — a functioning appliance.

Other authorities present a different rationale for including turning on an appliance in the prohibition of *molid.* They reason that since the completion of an electrical circuit generates sparks, the generation of the sparks that are a new entity constitutes a violation of *molid.*

Another of the thirty-nine labors forbidden on Shabbos is the *melachah* of *makeh b'patish,* or *striking the [final] blow.* Under this *melachah,* which we will cover shortly, one is prohibited to perform the final act in finishing a product and making it useful. For example, if one purchases a brand new pair of shoes that has never had laces inserted into them before, he may not insert a set of laces into them on Shabbos. Since the shoes are not considered usable without laces, the insertion of the laces represents the final step in the process of making the shoes usable, and is thus prohibited on Shabbos.

Some authorities feel that since an electrical appliance is useless without the introduction of electricity, turning on the appliance and introducing the electric current represents the final step of creating a usable appliance, and is therefore prohibited.

The *Chazon Ish,* in his famous ruling, states that the completion and closing of an electrical circuit is prohibited because it represents an act of *building,* as well as an act of assembling the parts of a utensil, which is also prohibited under the *melachah* of *building.* Concurrent with this ruling, he also states that the act of turning *off* an electrical appliance is prohibited because it is an act of *demolishing.*

The Chazon Ish mentions as another possibility the fact that if the electric current passing through a wire raises the temperature of the wire above the level of *yad soledes bo* (110 degrees Fahrenheit), turning on the current would be prohibited under the *melachah* of *cooking.*

Finally, there is yet one more possible violation of *melachah* involving the completion of an electrical circuit. Initiating a new circuit may have the effect of causing the power station supplying the electricity to burn more fuel. If this is an inevitable outcome of turning on the circuit, it would fall under the *melachah* of *kindling a fire.*

Once again we must stress that regardless of which *melachah* one violates by turning on an electrical appliance on Shabbos, all authorities prohibit this activity.

A CLOSER LOOK AT THE SIDDUR

The struggle with the *yetzer hara* (evil inclination) takes on different forms, depending on whether one has previously fallen prey to the sin with which he is being tempted, or if he has sinned and is now trying to extricate himself from the sin's clutches (see above, *A Mussar Thought for the Day*). According to many commentaries, this is reflected in the words of the הַשְׁכִּיבֵנוּ blessing recited before the *Shemoneh Esrei* of the evening prayers: וְהָסֵר שָׂטָן מִלְּפָנֵינוּ וּמֵאַחֲרֵינוּ, *remove spiritual impediment from before us and from behind us.*

R' Menachem Katz explains: A person who has never sinned is not likely to suddenly commit a major Torah violation. The *yetzer hara* works on such a person by getting him to violate what seems like only minor infractions. After each violation, the *yetzer* works to convince him that the next step is also not a severe violation, but only a further minor infraction. In this manner a person can be brought, God forbid, to commit the most severe of sins.

It may happen that after a while a person suddenly realizes that he has strayed very far from the proper path. He may feel that he wants to return to the way he was prior to all these "minor" infractions, and to repent. At this point the *yetzer* changes tactics completely. Instead of working on minimizing the sins in his eyes, it looks to convince the person that the sins that he has already committed are so great that they represent an insurmountable obstacle to true repentance. There is no longer any hope, says the *yetzer hara,* for a person like you, who has reached the point of committing such terrible sins, to ever repent.

We therefore pray: הָסֵר שָׂטָן מִלְּפָנֵינוּ, *Remove spiritual impediment from before us;* do not allow the *yetzer hara* to seduce us into sin when we are still innocent. But if we do fall, we pray that Hashem also remove the impediments מֵאַחֲרֵינוּ, *from behind us,* i.e., those arguments with which the *yetzer* assails us when the sin is already in our past.

The *Dubno Maggid* explains this prayer as referring to the dual role of the *Satan.* He presents the following illustration. When a person is invited to a banquet, a messenger is sent from the host to escort the guest to the right place. In this case, the messenger walks before the guest to guide him. In contrast, when a criminal is being sent to prison, the officer walks behind him to make sure that he does not try to run away.

Chazal teach that the angel who comes to us in the guise of the *yetzer hara* to persuade us to sin is the very same angel that is sent to exact retribution for the sin; this time he comes as the Angel of Death. We ask Hashem to save us from experiencing any of these situations. Remove him from before us, when, like a servant leading a guest to the banquet, he is convincing us to enjoy the fruits of sin. And remove him from behind us, when, like an officer of the law, he comes to deliver the punishment for the sins that he has caused us to commit.

A TORAH THOUGHT FOR THE DAY

וְלֹא תְחַלְּלוּ אֶת־שֵׁם קָדְשִׁי וְנִקְדַּשְׁתִּי
בְּתוֹךְ בְּנֵי יִשְׂרָאֵל אֲנִי ה׳ מְקַדִּשְׁכֶם

You shall not desecrate My holy Name; rather,
I shall be sanctified among the Children of Israel;
I am HASHEM *Who sanctifies you* (*Vayikra* 22:32).

From the words *I shall be sanctified among the Children of Israel,* we learn the obligation for one to give up his life so as not to desecrate the Name of Hashem. *Rashi,* citing the story of Chananyah, Mishael and Azaryah (who were cast into a furnace by Nevuchadnezzar when they refused to worship idols — see below), adds a caveat to this obligation. When giving up one's life, it must be done without the expectation that a lifesaving miracle will occur. One who does rely on a miracle will not merit having one performed for him. One must be prepared to actually die for the honor of Hashem.

R' Dovid Kviat (in *Succas Dovid*) illuminates *Rashi's* lesson by drawing our attention to a Midrash that describes the full story of Chananyah, Mishael and Azaryah.

Nevuchadnezzar had set up an effigy of himself, to which his subjects were commanded, on pain of death, to pay homage. Picking three members of the Jewish people as their representatives, he commanded that Chananyah, Mishael and Azaryah be present at a ceremony where homage to the king would be given. Since it was more of a demonstration of submission to the monarch than real idol worship, they were not sure what their obligation was, and therefore went to the prophet Yechezkel for guidance. He told them that they should hide until the storm passes. At that point, they expressed their desire to go anyway, to show the world that the Jewish people do not bow down to anything that resembles an idol, thus sanctifying the Name of Hashem. They asked Yechezkel: Would Hashem save them from death? He answered in the Name of Hashem that He would not. They then decided that they would go anyway, and that they were prepared to die. Only after they left did Hashem tell Yechezkel that He would indeed save them.

This story seems perplexing. First of all, why did these *tzaddikim* first offer to sanctify Hashem's Name only if they would be saved? Did they not know that one must be prepared to give up one's life completely? Furthermore, why did Hashem first seem to mislead them?

R' Kviat explains that their primary goal was that the nations see that this statue had no power whatsoever, and that Hashem is stronger than

פרשת אמור

MONDAY

PARASHAS EMOR

both the effigy and the king whom it represents. This message would have been most clear if the statue would have been defied in a show of loyalty to Hashem, and those who defied it would clearly be saved by Hashem. In this way, all would see that He is the only real power. They had desired that Hashem would save them so that His honor would be increased. However, Hashem told Yechezkel that it could not work that way. For one can never merit a miracle without having first completely abandoned any hope for one's own life. Only one who defies his own nature to that extent — by being ready to give up his life — can be rewarded by Hashem bending the nature of the world for him. They were therefore told that they would not be saved. However, once they decided to go ahead and actually die, they were eligible to have a miracle occur, both to save their lives and to fulfill their wishes to give the greatest possible glory to Hashem.

Rashi therefore shows from this story that even with the noblest of intentions, one who relies on a miracle when sanctifying Hashem cannot be granted that miracle, while one who gives up all thoughts of his own life may indeed merit miraculous intervention.

MISHNAH OF THE DAY: ERUVIN 8:4

An *eruvei chatzeiros* joins all the residents of a *chatzeir* in a symbolic partnership in a single dwelling. The *eruv* bread must therefore be placed in one of the dwellings of that *chatzeir.* A *shitufei mevo'os,* on the other hand, joins the residents of all the *chatzeiros* of the *mavoi* into a symbolic partnership. The *shituf* food may therefore be placed in a *chatzeir.*[1] This Mishnah outlines the type of building in which an *eruv* may be placed:

הַנּוֹתֵן אֶת עֵירוּבוֹ בְּבֵית שַׁעַר אַכְסַדְרָה וּמִרְפֶּסֶת — If ***one places his eruv in a gatehouse,***[2] ***a portico,***[3] ***or a gallery,***[4] **אֵינוֹ עֵירוּב** — ***it is not a***

NOTES

1. Or in a house that is in the *chatzeir* (*Rashi; Tosafos,* however, disagree). The *shitufei mevo'os* may not be placed in the *mavoi,* because it is not a secure area.

2. A small, roofed structure at the entrance of a *chatzeir,* through which people pass as they enter and exit the *chatzeir;* a sort of vestibule to the *chatzeir.* In the case being discussed, the *eruv* was placed here instead of in one of the houses in the *chatzeir.*

3. A roof supported by columns, but lacking side walls (see *Rashi* to 90b).

4. A porch situated above ground level, onto which apartments open.

valid *eruv;*[5] וְהַדָּר שָׁם — *and one who lives there* [in one of these] אֵינוֹ אוֹסֵר עָלָיו — *does not restrict the other* residents of the *chatzeir* from carrying.[6]
בֵּית הַתֶּבֶן וּבֵית הַבָּקָר וּבֵית הָעֵצִים וּבֵית הָאוֹצָרוֹת — If the *eruv* was placed *in a straw shed, barn, woodshed or storehouse* in the *chatzeir,* הֲרֵי זֶה עֵירוּב — *this is a* valid *eruv;*[7] וְהַדָּר שָׁם אוֹסֵר עָלָיו — *and one who lives there* [in one of these buildings] *restricts the other* residents from carrying if he did not contribute to the *eruv.*[8]
רַבִּי יְהוּדָה אוֹמֵר — *R' Yehudah says:* אִם יֵשׁ שָׁם תְּפִיסַת יָד שֶׁל בַּעַל הַבַּיִת — *If the owner retains a holding there,* i.e., he retains the right to store some of his belongings in his tenants' quarters,[9] אֵינוֹ אוֹסֵר עָלָיו — *he does not restrict the other* residents, because the entire *chatzeir* is considered the domain of the owner, and the tenants are viewed as his guests.[10]

NOTES

5. An *eruvei chatzeiros* must be deposited in one of the dwellings of the *chatzeir,* thus symbolizing the designation of that house as the common dwelling of all the residents of that *chatzeir.* A portico and gallery are not considered dwellings, because they are not enclosed by walls. A gatehouse, although it has walls, is not considered a dwelling because the residents of the *chatzeir* are constantly passing through it on their way into and out of the *chatzeir* (*R' Yehonasan; Meiri*).

6. Since these areas are not viewed as dwellings, someone staying there does not restrict. Thus, he need not contribute to the *eruv* (*Rashi*).

7. These are considered fit for dwelling (as the next ruling of the Mishnah makes clear); the *eruv* may therefore be kept in them even if they are currently empty (*Tosafos*).

8. If the owner loaned (or leased) one of these structures to someone to live in, that person restricts the other residents of the *chatzeir* from carrying into the *chatzeir* and he must therefore contribute to the *eruv* (*Rashi*).

9. This section of the Mishnah refers to any tenant (not just to one who lives in a shed, etc.). A tenant does not restrict his landlord if the latter retains the right to keep his belongings in the tenant's domain. Since the landlord did not totally remove his presence from the residence, the tenant is considered as though he were living with the landlord as a guest, and consequently does not restrict by his failure to contribute to the *eruv* (*Rashi;* see, however, next note).

10. Some say that the tenant in this situation is not considered a guest in all respects. Rather, his situation is analogous to that of the father who lives in the same *chatzeir* with grown sons whom he supports (see Mishnah 6:7). Thus, the Mishnah's ruling that the tenant does not restrict refers solely to a case where the landlord and tenant are the only residents of the *chatzeir;* no *eruv* is required in this case. However, if there are other people living in the *chatzeir* as well, and the landlord is contributing to an *eruv,* the tenant must also contribute, and restricts if he did not (*R' Yehonasan; Rama* 370:2).

GEMS FROM THE GEMARA

The Gemara discusses R' Yehudah's ruling regarding a homeowner who allowed someone else to use his property but retained the right to keep belongings there, offering an example of the type of belongings meant. Rabbah bar bar Chanah said that this would include even the peg of a plow [i.e., even something that is not of great significance (*R' Yehonasan*)]. Even if the homeowner retained the right to keep only a single tool in the house, he is viewed as living there, and his tenant-guest does not restrict the right to carry in the *chatzeir.* [Earlier (85b), the Gemara had defined R' Yehudah's ruling as applying to homes that were loaned to guests. This implied that R' Yehudah was discussing an instance where the homeowner had left significant items of furniture in the apartment. Rabbah bar bar Chanah thus teaches us that even if a single tool is placed in the home, this is sufficient for us to consider the homeowner as a resident for *eruv* purposes (*Geon Yaakov* based on *Ritva*).]

Rav Nachman qualifies this ruling based on the following Baraisa: If the item that the homeowner is keeping in the house is something that may be moved on the Sabbath (i.e., it is not *muktzeh,* an item which may not be moved on the Sabbath), the tenant of the house restricts the *chatzeir,* as if that item had not been in the house. [Since the tenant could remove it from the house during the Sabbath, the owner is not viewed as having a residence there (*Rashi*). *Tur* and *Shulchan Aruch* (370:2), however, understand this to mean that the owner might decide to remove it on the Sabbath (cf. *Korban Nesanel* §4). This qualification is not disputed by Rabbah bar bar Chanah. The Mishnah in Shabbos (123b) lists a יְתַד מַחֲרֵישָׁה, *peg of a plow,* as an article that may not be moved on the Sabbath for any reason.]

But if the item is something that may not be moved on the Sabbath because it is *muktzeh* [or even items that are not *muktzeh,* but are heavy and would therefore not be moved on the Sabbath (*Shulchan Aruch* 370:2; see *Mishnah Berurah* there §8)], the tenant does not restrict.

The Gemara brings a support for this ruling from a Baraisa that taught that if the owner has *tevel* (untithed produce, which a Jew is forbidden to eat) or metal bars in the apartment, or anything that may not be moved on the Sabbath, the tenant does not restrict the *chatzeir.* [Since the tithing of produce on the Sabbath is Rabbinically prohibited, this food cannot be consumed on this Sabbath. It therefore has the status of מוּקְצֶה מֵחֲמַת גופו, i.e., things that are unusable and therefore may not be moved. Since these metal bars have not been fashioned into utensils, they too have no use on the Sabbath and are *muktzeh.*]

A MUSSAR THOUGHT FOR THE DAY

In a letter to his son, dated Thursday, *Parashas Noach,* 5706 (1946), *R' Eliyahu Eliezer Dessler* reflects on the fate of the town of his youth, Kelm. To appreciate the full meaning and intensity of this letter it must be read in the original and in full (it is printed in *Michtav MeiEliyahu* vol. 3, p. 346). Here we present some excerpts of the letter, diminished by omission and translation:

"There was a great yeshivah in Kelm, the Beis HaTalmud, filled with unassuming modest scholars, but who were in fact the great men of their generation. I remember how on Simchas Torah nights, the great men of this yeshivah would leave the building and go through the town, in the main streets, dancing with such joy and intensity: *Ashreinu, mah tov chelkeinu — How fortunate are we! How good is our portion! . . .*

"Forty years passed, and again the streets filled with people. This time, however, it was a different occasion. The people of the town — men, women and children — are being beaten, chased and pushed to the killing fields outside of town.

"And the men of the yeshivah, these holy and sublime *tzadikkim,* were among them. They were not wailing at their fate or crying for their loved ones. For again they were caught up in fervor, dancing and singing: *Ashreinu! Mah tov chelkeinu!* How fortunate are we that we are Jews; how good is our lot that we merited to die for our *Yiddishkeit.* And so they danced, with ever growing fervor, with a tenacity bred of holiness, until they reached the edge of the city. There did they yield their souls to their Master, with devotion, amid a deep bond formed through the joy of the mitzvah.

"Many have questioned: What benefit could possibly have come from these deaths? If they had had any choice, if they would have chosen death out of loyalty to the Torah, then their deaths would have at least served as a great *kiddush Hashem.* However, that was not their fate. They were killed indiscriminately; as long as they were Jewish, no differentiation was made between believer and apostate, sinner and saint.

"They, however, understood. They knew that here they were not being called to sanctify the Name of Hashem before the nations, or to make a public show of devotion. No, here the test was infinitely harder than that. It was a challenge of sanctifying the Name of Hashem in one's heart. Who would have the strength to accept the misfortune that was befalling them, and with joy — a joy of blessed devotion to Hashem? Who would be able to turn his heart, completely and without any reservation

whatever, to Hashem? Indeed, this is a higher accomplishment; it is the service required of us in the days of Mashiach.

"And, in our own feeble generation, our great men reached this exalted level. They withstood this most awesome of tests and cleaved to the *Shechinah* in purity and in truth."

HALACHAH OF THE DAY

We will now discuss some practical applications regarding the use of electrical appliances on Shabbos.

[It is important to note that many of the facts pertinent to the permissibility of using appliances on Shabbos are ever-changing, due to the constant changes manufacturers make to their product lines. Furthermore, the steady advances in technology present new challenges, as manufacturers add new functions and features to their products. Our intent here is to present some of the basic questions that come into play when analyzing these issues from the standpoint of halachah, as a means of applying the concepts we have discussed to daily life. These discussions should not be relied upon for practical application. Rather, all questions should be presented to a competent halachic authority, to ensure up-to-date, accurate halachic decisions.]

It is a matter of dispute among the *poskim* whether it is permissible for one to open the door of a refrigerator on Shabbos. On a most basic level, opening the door of a refrigerator allows warm air to enter, thus raising the temperature inside the refrigerator. This, in turn, registers in the thermostat, and eventually causes the cooling apparatus to start functioning. While at times the unit does not start running until some time has elapsed after the door has been opened, if the temperature in the refrigerator was already high when the door was opened, the unit would begin running immediately.

Based on these facts, there are *poskim* who prohibit opening the door of a refrigerator because this action will eventually cause the appliance to begin operating. Many of these *poskim* rule that it is forbidden to open the door *only* while the unit is off, since by opening it one causes it to turn on. However, if the unit is already on, they permit opening the door. In this case, the act of opening the door does not cause anything to turn on; it merely causes the unit to run for a longer period than it would otherwise.

Other *poskim* rule that it is permissible to open the door of a refrigerator even when it is not running. They reason that since the unit generally does not begin running until some time after the door is opened, its running is not regarded as a direct consequence of the person's action. Rather, it is an *indirect* consequence (a גְּרָמָא) and is therefore permitted.

According to these latter *poskim,* although there are times when the motor will begin running immediately after the door is opened, it is not the person's intention to turn on the motor. This action thus gains the status of a דָּבָר שֶׁאֵינוֹ מִתְכַּוֵּן, *an unintended consequence.* As we have discussed several times previously, such an act is prohibited only when the result is a פְּסִיק רֵישֵׁיהּ, *an inevitable consequence,* of the person's action. Since, in our case, opening the door of the refrigerator does not always result in the unit turning on immediately, these *poskim* permit this activity on Shabbos.

A CLOSER LOOK AT THE SIDDUR

Just as one is not to rely on a miracle to save one's life (see above, *A Torah Thought for the Day*), so too it is not proper to pray that Hashem perform a miracle for him. One who does has prayed a תְּפִלַּת שָׁוְא, *futile prayer* (see *Berachos* 54a). The *Bechor Shor* (cited in *Shaarei Teshuvah, Orach Chaim* 187:2) questions this statement by stating that there are certain prayers found in our *siddurim* in which we do explicitly ask Hashem to perform miracles for us. One example is the prayer that is added in *Bircas HaMazon* if one forgot to recite the *Al HaNissim* for Chanukah or Purim. It begins: הָרַחֲמָן הוּא יַעֲשֶׂה לָנוּ נִסִּים וְנִפְלָאוֹת כַּאֲשֶׁר עָשָׂה לַאֲבוֹתֵינוּ . . ., *The compassionate One! May He perform for us miracles and wonders as He performed for our forefathers . . .* Another example is found in the prayer that some recite during *Bircas Kohanim* (the Priestly Blessing), which includes the request: וְתַעֲשֶׂה עִמִּי נִפְלָאוֹת וְנִסִּים, *may You perform wonders and miracles with me.* How are we to understand these prayers in light of the above rule?

The *Bechor Shor* offers two answers. The first is that there is a difference between a miracle that is completely out of the realm of the natural, for which we may not pray, and a phenomenon, which, while miraculous, does not defy natural law. An example of the latter is the military victory of the Chashmonaim over the Syrian-Greeks. Stones did not fall from the sky and the sun did not stop in its path. However, it was

surely miraculous for a small band of men to triumph against the great Syrian-Greek armies. It is for these types of miracles that we are praying, to be performed for us in our day.

The second answer is that it is only for an individual — whom we cannot assume is worthy to have a miracle performed for him — that we may not pray for Hashem to perform a miracle. However, it is permitted to pray for a miracle on behalf of the whole nation. Thus, all the prayers in which we ask for miracles and wonders to be performed should be recited in the plural. [According to this answer, the prayer is not תַּעֲשֶׂה עִמִּי, *perform for me,* but rather תַּעֲשֶׂה עִמָּנוּ, *perform for us.*] In the הָרַחֲמָן mentioned above as well, we are praying only for miracles to be performed for the benefit of the Jewish people as a whole.

R' Dovid Cohen (in his *Yemei Chanukah*) uses this answer to explain a Midrash describing the beginning of the military campaign of the Chashmonaim. We have learned that one is not to sanctify the Name of Hashem relying on miracles. However, the Midrash quotes Matisyahu as proclaiming before a battle: "I am confident that Hashem will perform miracles and wonders." How could Matisyahu risk his life for Hashem while relying on a miracle? R' Kohein answers that Matisyahu was not confident that he personally would emerge alive, but that the overall war would not be lost. For just as one may pray for a miracle for the nation as a whole, so may one fight and risk his life, with the confidence that the cause of the Jewish people will triumph, even if only through the intervention of a miracle.

QUESTION OF THE DAY:

Is a non-Jew required to give up his life rather than transgress one of the three cardinal sins?

For the answer, see page 176.

A TORAH THOUGHT FOR THE DAY

דַּבֵּר אֶל־בְּנֵי יִשְׂרָאֵל וְאָמַרְתָּ אֲלֵהֶם מוֹעֲדֵי ה׳
אֲשֶׁר־תִּקְרְאוּ אֹתָם מִקְרָאֵי קֹדֶשׁ אֵלֶּה הֵם מוֹעֲדָי

Speak to the Children of Israel and say to them: The appointed times of HASHEM, that you are to designate as holy convocations; these are My appointed times (*Vayikra* 23:2).

After introducing the chapter of the festivals with this verse, the Torah proceeds to speak about the Sabbath in the next verse. *Rashi* explains that the Torah speaks of the Sabbath when listing the festivals in order to teach us that one who desecrates the festivals is viewed as one who has desecrated the Sabbath, while one who observes the festivals is viewed as one who has observed the Sabbath.

This correlation needs explanation. What difference does it make that one who desecrates the festivals is viewed as if he desecrated the Sabbath as well?

R' Moshe Feinstein (in *Darash Moshe*) explains that the lessons of the Sabbath and the festivals are complementary. The observance of the Sabbath demonstrates our *emunah* in the fact that Hashem created the world in six days and rested on the seventh. And the observance of the festivals demonstrates our belief that Hashem Himself continues the management of the world, and changes nature as He wills to benefit His nation. We celebrate Pesach to commemorate the fact that Hashem took us out of Egypt with wonders and miracles to make us His nation; we celebrate Succos to commemorate that He provided us with Clouds of Glory to shelter us in the Wilderness; and we celebrate Shavuos to commemorate the fact that Hashem gave us the Torah and mitzvos so that we would pursue the proper path. The Torah places the observance of the Sabbath next to the observance of the festivals to teach us that belief in one of these truths without the other is insufficient. If one believes that Hashem created the world, but thinks that control of the world is delegated to "nature" or angels or other Heavenly forces, it is as if he does not accept Hashem as the Creator. For if he does not believe that Hashem runs the world, then he has no reason to keep observing the Torah and mitzvos. Such an attitude will eventually cause a person to fall into the ways of idolatry, as occurred in the generation of Enosh.

Similarly, if a person believes that Hashem runs the world, but believes that it was created by other forces, or that it came into being

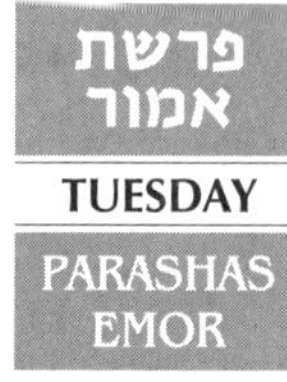

somehow many millions of years ago, his belief in Hashem's control will also not endure. Thus, the Torah places these two injunctions together, to teach that they must be two parts of a whole; one must believe both that Hashem created the world and that everything that occurs is under His management.

MISHNAH OF THE DAY: ERUVIN 8:5

This Mishnah deals with the question of whether an absentee resident must contribute to an *eruvei chatzeiros*:

הַמַּנִּיחַ בֵּיתוֹ וְהָלַךְ לִשְׁבּוֹת בְּעִיר אַחֶרֶת — ***One who left his house and went to spend the Sabbath in another town,*** **אֶחָד נָכְרִי וְאֶחָד יִשְׂרָאֵל** — ***whether he is an idolater*** who did not rent out his rights,[1] ***or a Jew*** who did not join in the *eruv,* **הֲרֵי זֶה אוֹסֵר** — ***he restricts*** those remaining in the *chatzeir* from carrying, because he is considered a member of the *chatzeir* despite his absence; **דִּבְרֵי רַבִּי מֵאִיר** — these are ***the words of R' Meir.***[2] **רַבִּי יְהוּדָה אוֹמֵר** — ***R' Yehudah says:*** **אֵינוֹ אוֹסֵר** — ***He does not restrict.*** Only those actually residing in the *chatzeir* on the Sabbath need participate in the *eruv.*[3] **רַבִּי יוֹסֵי אוֹמֵר** — ***R' Yose says:*** **נָכְרִי אוֹסֵר** — ***An idolater*** who went to another town ***restricts,*** **יִשְׂרָאֵל אֵינוֹ אוֹסֵר** — ***but a Jew does not restrict,*** **שֶׁאֵין דֶּרֶךְ יִשְׂרָאֵל לָבֹא בַּשַּׁבָּת** — ***for it is unusual for a Jew to return on the Sabbath.***[4] **רַבִּי שִׁמְעוֹן אוֹמֵר** — ***R' Shimon says:*** **אֲפִילּוּ הִנִּיחַ בֵּיתוֹ וְהָלַךְ לִשְׁבּוֹת אֵצֶל בִּתּוֹ בְּאוֹתָהּ הָעִיר** — ***Even [a Jew] who left his house and went to spend***

NOTES

1. An idolater restricts a *chatzeir* unless the residents rent his rights from him, as we learned above, 6:1.

2. The Gemara (62b) demonstrates that (according to R' Meir) an absentee idolater restricts only when there is reason to assume that he will return on that Sabbath (e.g., he is in a nearby town), but a Jew restricts even where he cannot return (e.g., if the town to which he went is beyond the *techum*).

R' Meir holds that an absentee Jew restricts (even where he cannot return that day) because דִּירָה בְּלֹא בְּעָלִים שְׁמָהּ דִּירָה, *a residence without owners* [present on the Sabbath] *is considered a residence;* i.e., his house is treated like any other house in the *chatzeir* even though he is not home (*Rashi*).

3. R' Yehudah holds that a residence whose owner is away is not legally defined as a "residence" [דִּירָה בְּלֹא בְּעָלִים לֹא שְׁמָהּ דִּירָה] (*Rashi*).

4. R' Yose concurs with R' Yehudah that the residence of an absent person is not reckoned a proper residence, and it therefore cannot restrict. However, when the absentee is an idolater, one must take into consideration the likelihood that he will return to his home on the Sabbath, and thereby restrict (*Rashi*).

the Sabbath with his daughter, whose house is ***in that*** same ***city,***[5] אֵינוֹ אוֹסֵר — ***does not restrict,*** שֶׁכְּבָר הִסִּיעַ מִלִּבּוֹ — ***for he has already dismissed from his mind*** any thought of returning.[6]

NOTES

5. To this point, the Tannaim mentioned in this Mishnah discussed only the case of a Jew who had left town for the Sabbath, implying that if he were in a different part of the town, he would restrict the *chatzeir,* since he could conceivably return on the Sabbath.

6. Literally: from his heart. R' Shimon is the most lenient. He concurs with R' Yehudah and R' Yose that the residence of an absent person is not reckoned a proper residence and does not restrict. He extends this principle even to where it is permissible for the resident to return on the Sabbath, but it is unlikely that he will. R' Shimon argues that even in such an instance he does not restrict.

GEMS FROM THE GEMARA

Rashi here explains that R' Meir's reason for ruling that an absentee Jew restricts (even where he cannot return that day) is because he holds that דִּירָה בְּלֹא בְּעָלִים שְׁמָהּ דִּירָה, *a residence without owners* [present on the Sabbath] *is considered a residence;* i.e., his house is treated like any other house in the *chatzeir* even though he is not home.

This seems to contradict the Gemara's conclusion (see *Gems from the Gemara* to Mishnah 6:1) that in essence R' Meir accepts the view that it is not treated as a residence [דִּירָה בְּלֹא בְּעָלִים לֹא שְׁמָהּ דִּירָה], but that the Rabbis decreed a restriction on the house of an absentee Jew to avoid confusion (*Tos. R' Akiva Eiger* in *Mishnayos;* see *Sfas Emes* for a discussion of *Rashi's* view).

Now, if the idolater has gone to another town, there is no reason to assume that he will return on the Sabbath, and even R' Meir will agree that the idolater does not restrict. On the other hand, if we are aware of the idolater's intention to return on the Sabbath, then even R' Yehudah agrees that he restricts. They disagree only when the idolater's intentions are unknown. R' Meir holds that since he is able to return, he restricts. R' Yehudah maintains that since we do not know for certain that he will return, we need not assume that he will, and so he does not restrict (*Turei Zahav* 371:1). Others understand that they disagree even when the idolater's intention to return is known. Only the idolater's actual presence restricts; his intended presence does not (*Chazon Ish, Orach Chaim* 82:24, based on *Rashi* to 62b).

The Gemara quotes Rav as saying that the halachah follows the opinion of R' Shimon — any residence without a resident owner is not reckoned a proper residence, and does not restrict even where it is permissible for the resident to return on the Sabbath but it is unlikely that he will. R' Shimon's view regarding an absentee idolater is not known. Thus, Rav's ruling remains ambiguous with regard to one of the cases of our Mishnah. *Rambam* (*Hil. Eruvin* 4:13) rules in accordance with R' Yose that as long as it is possible for him to return, he restricts. *Rosh* and *Rashba* rule with R' Yehudah that he does not restrict. *Shulchan Aruch* (391:1) cites both rulings; *Rama* accepts the latter, more lenient view.

The Gemara adds, however, that R' Shimon stated his ruling specifically for one who visits his daughter, but not for one who went to visit his son. For if one quarrels with his son-in-law, he may stay in his house [as a daughter would not allow her father to leave on the Sabbath, even under such circumstances (*Rabbeinu Chananel*)]; but one who quarrels with a daughter-in-law will leave. Thus, it is possible that someone visiting his married son may indeed return home on the Sabbath, if his daughter-in-law should quarrel with him. Consequently, he does not entirely dismiss the possibility of returning home, and he thus restricts the *chatzeir* residents.

A MUSSAR THOUGHT FOR THE DAY

In *A Torah Thought for the Day* we learned that the Torah speaks of the Sabbath in the passage of the festivals to teach us that the lessons of the two are complementary. There is another lesson to be learned from this placement. The festivals, which each occur but once yearly, are typically greeted with a great deal of enthusiasm and anticipation. The special preparations that are undertaken serve to bring us into the spirit of the Yom Tov that is to come, and we greet each one with vigor. The Sabbath, however, which comes without fail every seven days, can become like a familiar houseguest, whose arrival does not occasion much of a reaction.

The Torah wishes to teach us that this should not be the case. The Sabbath is a special, Divine gift, given to us so we can elevate ourselves above the physicality of the days of the workweek. Indeed, the fact that it comes every week is part of its special nature: Who among us has not wondered how the non-Jews can survive without the Sabbath! We must strive to treat the Sabbath with the same delight and anticipation that we do any of the festivals.

It is all too easy to fall into the trap of regarding the Sabbath simply as a day of rest, and to use it only as a chance to catch one's breath before heading back into the grind of the following week. The folly of this approach, too, is highlighted by the location of the Sabbath among the festivals. Nobody makes the mistake of looking at Pesach or Succos as times of rest! These festivals are clearly identified as times to celebrate the closeness and special care that Hashem has demonstrated toward His people. So too with the Sabbath. A non-Jew is forbidden to observe the Sabbath; the Torah describes the Sabbath as: בֵּינִי וּבֵין בְּנֵי יִשְׂרָאֵל אוֹת הִוא לְעֹלָם, *between Me and the Children of Israel it is a sign forever* (*Shemos* 31:17). Each Sabbath refreshes anew the special bond that Hashem has with His people, and affords every Jew the chance to turn away from the weekday world and bask in the radiance of the *Shechinah.* Thus, every Sabbath *is* a festival; but rather than commemorating a single event, it serves to strengthen and nurture the connection between the Jews and their Father in Heaven.

HALACHAH OF THE DAY

Yesterday, we discussed the question of opening a refrigerator door on Shabbos. A similar question arises in regard to the opening of the door to an oven. Opening the door allows cool air to enter the oven, which triggers the thermostat, which in turn ignites the fire in the oven. There are those *poskim* who rule that opening the oven door is prohibited as long as the oven is turned on. Other *poskim* compare the question of opening an oven to that of opening a refrigerator, and permit opening the oven door when the flame is already on, but prohibit it when the flame is off. Still others permit opening the door at all times. Once again we must stress that a competent halachic authority should be consulted for practical application of these concepts.

We will now discuss the question of using a telephone on Shabbos.

Using a telephone involves four basic actions, each of which is prohibited on Shabbos. These actions are: lifting the receiver, dialing, speaking, and returning the receiver to its cradle. Let us analyze each of these steps from the perspective of halachah:

When lifting the receiver, one completes an electrical circuit that activates the phone. As we have explained, according to the *Chazon Ish,* completing an electrical circuit violates the Biblical prohibition of *building.* According to other *poskim,* it is a violation of the Rabbinic

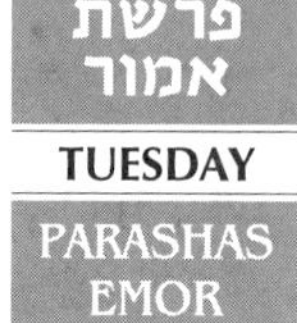

prohibition of *molid.* Furthermore, in many phone systems, lifting the handset causes an electric light to turn on; as we have discussed, this may constitute a violation of the *melachah* of *kindling.*

Dialing a phone number initiates an electrical connection between the telephone being dialed and the one receiving the phone call. As discussed in regard to lifting the receiver, this is a violation of *building* and/or *molid.* In addition, it is a violation of the Rabbinic prohibition of הַשְׁמָעַת קוֹל, *creating sound,* because by dialing one causes the receiving phone to ring.

Some authorities rule that speaking on a telephone violates the Rabbinic prohibition of *creating sound,* since the telephone causes a reproduction of one's voice to be heard elsewhere.

According to the Chazon Ish, who rules that lifting a handset and completing an electrical circuit is a violation of *building,* it follows that returning the phone to its base and interrupting the circuit is prohibited as a violation of *demolishing.*

A CLOSER LOOK AT THE SIDDUR

This week, we continue to discuss the second of the Six Remembrances, which bids us to remember daily the Giving of the Torah at Mount Sinai, by reciting the verses:

> רַק הִשָּׁמֶר לְךָ וּשְׁמֹר נַפְשְׁךָ מְאֹד פֶּן־תִּשְׁכַּח אֶת־הַדְּבָרִים אֲשֶׁר רָאוּ עֵינֶיךָ וּפֶן־יָסוּרוּ מִלְּבָבְךָ כֹּל יְמֵי חַיֶּיךָ וְהוֹדַעְתָּם לְבָנֶיךָ וְלִבְנֵי בָנֶיךָ יוֹם אֲשֶׁר עָמַדְתָּ לִפְנֵי ה׳ אֱלֹהֶיךָ בְּחֹרֵב
>
> *Only beware and guard yourself carefully, lest you forget the things your eyes have seen and lest they stray from your heart all the days of your life. And you are to make them known to your children and to your children's children — the day you stood before* H*ASHEM*, *your God, at Sinai* (*Devarim* 4:9-10).

There is a reciprocal relationship between remembering the Giving of the Torah and actual Torah study. *Ramban* mentions that through learning with one's children and grandchildren, one accomplishes the goal of speaking to them of the revelation at Sinai. The *Ohev Yisrael* writes that when a person begins to learn, he should set before his eyes the scene of the Giving of the Torah in all its awesome splendor. In this way he will learn with the proper awe and fear, just as when the Torah was given. Thus, learning the Torah fosters the remembering of the events of its giving.

Just as learning Torah may be equivalent to remembering the Giving of the Torah, the remembering of the Giving of the Torah is one of the most potent motivators for adhering to and studying the Torah. The *Chofetz Chaim* (in his *Chomas HaDas,* Ch. 12) expounds on this idea at length:

It is important to consider the meaning of the fact that Hashem in His glory, accompanied by many thousands of ministering angels, lowered Himself, as it were, to earth so as to bestow upon the Jewish people this gift. If a great and powerful king were to take his entourage and make a special trip to a town to give the townspeople a royal message, would every word not be measured and guarded? Would the very fact of the king's journey not be enough to demonstrate to all that it must be a most important subject of which the king had spoken? In the same way we must consider the revelation of Hashem at Sinai.

Upon realizing this, one will feel the great obligation every person has to study and fulfill each detail of the Torah. When a person ignores his obligation to the Torah, he is likened to one who received a special, expensive medal from the king, but refuses to wear it. To ignore the fine gift of a king is tantamount to rebellion. So too, when a person takes the Torah, given as a gift to the Jewish people, and whose worth is more precious than pearls, and does not deign to give it any attention, he shows that he does not believe it to be a thing of real value.

Chazal relate: "Every single day a Heavenly voice emanates from Mount Chorev (Sinai), proclaiming and saying: 'Woe to them, to the people, because of [their] insult to the Torah!' " The Chofetz Chaim explains this metaphorically. The Heavenly voice emanating from Mount Horeb is the strong message that is awakened by the memory of what happened on that mountain. Hashem Himself descended to speak with us, to share with us His Torah, yet we are delinquent in our responsibilities toward it. This is the voice that proclaims, "Woe to them, to the people, because of their insult to the Torah!"

Chavakuk declared (2:4): צַדִּיק בֶּאֱמוּנָתוֹ יִחְיֶה, *A righteous man shall live by his faith.* The faith of which he speaks is the faith in the Torah itself. Once that faith is secure, once we firmly believe and remember the Giving of the Torah, the rest will come on its own, in time.

QUESTION OF THE DAY:

What halachah do we learn from the fact that the festivals are called מִקְרָאֵי קֹדֶשׁ?

For the answer, see page 176.

A TORAH THOUGHT FOR THE DAY

שֵׁשֶׁת יָמִים תֵּעָשֶׂה מְלָאכָה וּבַיּוֹם הַשְּׁבִיעִי
שַׁבַּת שַׁבָּתוֹן מִקְרָא־קֹדֶשׁ כָּל־מְלָאכָה לֹא תַעֲשׂוּ

For six days labor may be done, and the seventh day is a day of complete rest, a holy convocation; you shall not do any work (*Vayikra* 23:3).

An interesting observation is pointed out in the Responsa of *Mayim Chaim.* The mitzvah of Shabbos is written in the Torah five times. Each time, it is introduced with the statement that on six days labor is permitted. Three of these times the word is written in passive form — תֵּעָשֶׂה מְלָאכָה, *labor may be done* — while the other two times it is written in the active form — תַּעֲבֹד, *you shall work.* In addition, in each of the three times that it is written in the passive form (*Shemos* 31:15, 35:2, and our verse), the day of Shabbos is described as שַׁבַּת שַׁבָּתוֹן (translated above as *a day of complete rest*), while the other two times (*Shemos* 20:9-10 and *Devarim* 5:13-14), it is simply described as שַׁבָּת. What is the meaning of these differences, and how are they connected?

Mayim Chaim explains that when the Jewish people are at their ideal state and the nation as a whole is considered completely righteous, they are blessed with being completely free of all economic obligations. Their planting and reaping are done by others, while they involve themselves in work of a more spiritual nature. Other times, when they are at a less than ideal state, they themselves must labor to produce their bread, leaving only limited time for Torah study (see *Berachos* 35b and *Tosafos* there ד״ה כאן).

The phrase תֵּעָשֶׂה מְלָאכָה, *labor may be done,* indicates that the people are not themselves laboring in the fields; rather, the labor is being done for them. This is the Jewish people at their most exalted level, when the entire week is spent as if it were Shabbos, free of mundane labor and involved in that which is sacred. When the entire week is "Shabbos," then Shabbos itself becomes a day of even higher spirituality, a Shabbos after a week of Shabbasos. This level is described in the Torah with the words שַׁבַּת שַׁבָּתוֹן, meaning a *double Sabbath* or *a Sabbath of Sabbaths.*

However, when the level of the Jewish nation is such that during the week they themselves must work, described in the Torah as שֵׁשֶׁת יָמִים תַּעֲבֹד, *six days you shall work,* then Shabbos itself is not on that double level of intensity, and it is called, simply, שַׁבָּת.

Apiryon offers a different explanation of the passive term תֵּעָשֶׂה. One who works with the feeling that the level of his sustenance is strictly confined to the amount of effort that he himself puts in, is bound to have a difficult time with a commandment to abstain from work for one day a week. How will he turn a profit when he must stop working for one day each week?

The Torah's message to this person is that he must change his attitude to the relationship between income and labor. A person cannot take sole credit for his income, nor sole responsibility for his losses. His every success is decreed from Above; his efforts are a mere token input, so that Hashem can send him his livelihood. He must look at his work as if it is done by others and not by himself. This is the meaning of the passive תֵּעָשֶׂה מְלָאכָה, *labor may be done.*

When a person looks at his labor in this way, he will happily fulfill the rest of the verse: *the seventh day is a day of complete rest.*

MISHNAH OF THE DAY: ERUVIN 8:6

The remainder of this chapter discusses the necessary procedures for drawing or disposing of water in a *chatzeir.* This Mishnah discusses a cistern that is located between two adjoining *chatzeiros* that are separated by a proper partition. Each *chatzeir* has its own *eruv,* but the two have not joined in a common *eruv.* Consequently, the residents of one *chatzeir* cannot carry from the other *chatzeir* to their own:

בּוֹר שֶׁבֵּין שְׁתֵּי חֲצֵירוֹת — If ***a cistern is between two chatzeiros,*** partially in one and partially in the other,[1] **אֵין מְמַלְּאִין מִמֶּנּוּ בְּשַׁבָּת** — ***one may not draw water from it on the Sabbath***[2] **אֶלָּא אִם עָשׂוּ לוֹ מְחִיצָה גָּבוֹהַּ**

NOTES

1. I.e., the wall between the two *chatzeiros* passes over the top of the cistern. See diagram.

2. Drawing water from this cistern is, in effect, drawing water from the neighboring *chatzeir* (*Rashi*). The Gemara explains that the cistern is governed by the principle of עֲרִיבֵי מַיָּא, *the waters are mixed;* i.e., the water cannot be said to be fixed in either courtyard.

Although even without an *eruv* it is permitted to carry from one *chatzeir* to another items that were present in the *chatzeir* when the Sabbath began (Mishnah 9:1), this cistern presents a twofold problem: (a) The bucket brought from the house of one *chatzeir* is in effect being lowered into the other *chatzeir.* [Accordingly, this is prohibited only if the bucket used was in a house at the beginning of the Sabbath; however, using a bucket from the *chatzeir* would be permitted (*Rama* 376:1).] (b) The water is

עֲשָׂרָה טְפָחִים — *unless they made for it a partition ten tefachim high,* בֵּין מִלְמַעְלָה בֵּין מִלְמַטָּה בֵּין מִתּוֹךְ אוֹגְנוֹ — *either above* the water level, *or down below,*[3] *or within its lip.*[4] רַבָּן שִׁמְעוֹן בֶּן גַּמְלִיאֵל אוֹמֵר — *Rabban Shimon ben Gamliel says:* בֵּית שַׁמַּאי אוֹמְרִים — *Beis Shammai say*: The partition must be placed מִלְמַטָּה — *down below;*[5] וּבֵית הִלֵּל אוֹמְרִים — *but Beis Hillel say* that the partition may also be placed מִלְמַעְלָה — *above.*[6] אָמַר רַבִּי יְהוּדָה — *R' Yehudah said:* לֹא תְהֵא מְחִיצָה גְּדוֹלָה מִן הַכּוֹתֶל שֶׁבֵּינֵיהֶם — *A partition*

NOTES

considered to have been drawn from one *chatzeir* and carried into a house in the other *chatzeir.* [Accordingly, even if the bucket had begun the Sabbath in the *chatzeir,* it would still be prohibited to carry the water drawn from the cistern into a house (*Magen Avraham* 376:4).]

Chazon Ish (103:6) adds that the cistern is essentially an area separate from both *chatzeiros* (since it is more than 10 *tefachim* deep, as emerges from the Mishnah below). However, since both *chatzeiros* have equal access to it, carrying from it to a house in either *chatzeir* would be forbidden in the absence of an *eruv* joining the two *chatzeiros.* Accordingly, a proper partition is required to divide the cistern into sections unique to each *chatzeir.*

3. The partition may be placed either just above the surface of the water or just below.

4. The water level generally does not reach the rim of the cistern, often being considerably below it. The partition may be placed anywhere within these walls of the cistern, even at a distance above the surface of the water, as long as it is below the rim of the cistern.

This is a special leniency instituted by the Sages for water. It enables us to view the partitions as descending beyond their actual end [גוד אַחִית] to divide the water. As long as the partition is located inside the cistern, so that it appears to divide the water, it is valid (*Rashi*). Although the water is not physically divided by this partition, the Sages were lenient for the sake of allowing the drawing of water, and permitted it as long as there is a clear division in the water (*Ritva*).

5. The Gemara gives two interpretations for the opinions of Beis Shammai and Beis Hillel. We will follow that of Rav Yehudah, the interpretation adopted by most of the commentators. Rav Yehudah explains the terms "above" and "below" as being in reference to the water of the cistern. Beis Shammai thus hold that the partition need be "down below," meaning below the surface of the water; the partition must be situated on the floor of the cistern.

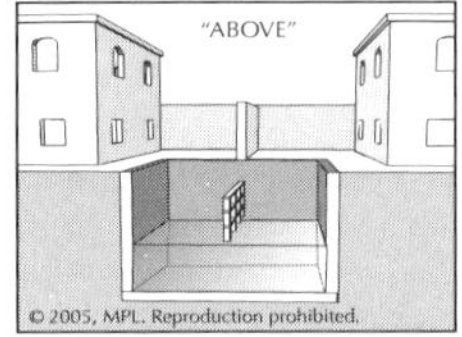

6. Beis Hillel hold that the partition may be even "above," meaning above the surface of the water; the partition may be totally above the water, but must be near its surface. See diagram.

The Gemara concludes that according to Rav Yehudah, Beis Shammai require an actual division of the water, accomplished with a complete partition that reaches the floor of the cistern. Conversely, Beis Hillel require only a symbolic partition of 10 *tefachim* (*Rashi*).

should not be more effective ***than the wall that is*** already ***between [the chatzeiros].***[7]

NOTES

7. R' Yehudah maintains that the wall separating the *chatzeiros,* which passes over the cistern, is itself sufficient to legally divide the water, even though it does not actually enter the cistern's cavity (*Rashi*).

GEMS FROM THE GEMARA

Our Mishnah taught that according to R' Yehudah, a separate partition should not be needed in the first place; the wall that is already between the *chatzeiros* should be able to divide the waters of the cistern over which it passes. Clearly, R' Yehudah holds that a hanging partition, i.e., one not reaching the ground, is valid to serve as a halachic divider. The Gemara cites a similar ruling by R' Yose.

The Mishnah in *Succah* discusses the construction of *succah* walls. If one constructs the walls from the top down, beginning near the *s'chach* and working downward, then, if the bottom of the wall is 3 or more *tefachim* above the ground, the *succah* is invalid, because suspended partitions are not valid. Since there is a space of 3 *tefachim* between the bottom of the walls and the ground, small goats can slip underneath. This nullifies the partition. However, if the walls reached to within 3 *tefachim* of the ground, the principle of *lavud* would apply, allowing us to view the walls as actually reaching the ground. But R' Yose said that such *succah* walls are valid, as long as they measure 10 *tefachim* tall, even if they do not reach the ground.

We see from this that R' Yose permits a suspended partition, just as R' Yehudah in our Mishnah.

However, the Gemara rejects R' Yochanan's assertion that the opinions of R' Yehudah and R' Yose are interrelated. First, R' Yehudah might not necessarily hold like R' Yose. For perhaps R' Yehudah validates a suspended partition only in regard to *eruvei chatzeiros,* which is of Rabbinic origin. However, for a *succah,* which is of Biblical origin, he might not validate a suspended partition. In general, laws involving Rabbinic prohibitions are treated more leniently. Therefore, R' Yehudah's lenient ruling in our Mishnah is not indicative of a similar leniency in regard to laws of Biblical origin.

Furthermore, R' Yose might not necessarily hold like R' Yehudah. For perhaps R' Yose validated a suspended partition only in regard to a

mitzvah such as *succah,* whose prohibition only has the force of a positive commandment. [A man is prohibited from eating a meal outside of a *succah* during the Succos holiday. This is derived by implication from the positive commandment requiring one to eat in a *succah* (*Vayikra* 23:42): בַּסֻּכֹּת תֵּשְׁבוּ שִׁבְעַת יָמִים, *You shall dwell in succos for seven days.* Such a transgression is not punishable by the courts, and is therefore considered less stringent than a regular prohibition, whose transgression is punishable by the courts.]

However, in regard to the Sabbath, whose prohibition is punishable by stoning, he did not explicitly validate suspended partitions, and such a partition may be treated more stringently. [While the actual comparative value of these mitzvos is not known, a comparison of the severity of the punishment for their transgression is an indication of the severity with which each particular mitzvah is viewed (see *Rambam* to *Avos* 2:1). Thus, if we find a leniency regarding the laws of *succah,* whose transgression is not punishable by the courts, we cannot assume that the same leniency would be allowed regarding the laws of the Sabbath.]

[Although the case of our Mishnah involves only a Rabbinic prohibition, as the Gemara mentioned above, its rules are modeled after the corresponding Biblical prohibition. Thus, even R' Yose might invalidate suspended partitions for *eruvei chatzeiros,* since a transgression of the Biblical prohibition against carrying is punishable by death (*Rashi*).]

A MUSSAR THOUGHT FOR THE DAY

One of the most easily distorted mitzvos of Shabbos is that of *oneg Shabbos,* literally, *the delight, or pleasure, of Shabbos.* This mitzvah obligates a person to engage in physical pleasures on Shabbos, to wear fine clothes, and to partake of delicious food.

Shelah warns that this mitzvah is not fulfilled by spending the day catering to one's own appetites and enjoyments. *Chazal* speak of the reward of one who *delights the Shabbos* (מְעַנֵּג אֶת הַשַּׁבָּת). That is, he makes Shabbos a day of delight, not that he brings pleasure to himself on Shabbos. One should approach this mitzvah as if he were a person who is not used to spending money on luxuries and is not accustomed to indulging in pleasures, but who must make an exception in honor of an important guest.

Shelah goes on to severely censure those who spend Shabbos overeating and then sleeping off their meals, leaving their bodies lethargic and their brains dull. This type of behavior is not a fulfillment of any mitzvah at all. Such a person has merely wasted food and caused harm to himself physically and spiritually. [Indeed, *Abudraham* notes that the primary reason for the mitzvah to eat an extra meal on Shabbos is to avoid overeating on Shabbos, for knowing that there is another meal later in the day will stop people from eating too much in the first meal of the day.]

Shelah goes on to sketch the picture of a Shabbos well spent. The Shabbos table should be set with food that is high-quality and tasty. One is to eat it in good spirits and drink enough wine to lighten his mood. However, one should not eat until he is full, nor should he drink himself into a stupor. After the meal he may rest for a short time, but then he should arise and spend his time in Torah study to the extent of his abilities.

The Shabbos *Minchah* should then be prayed properly, followed by the third meal of Shabbos. At the meal, one should converse in matters of Torah and the meal should be concluded after a fitting amount of time. After reciting *Bircas HaMazon* on a cup of wine, he should return to the synagogue to either learn or pray, according to the time.

Beis HaLevi points out that there are two types of mitzvos. In one, the person is required to abstain from or shun that which the world offers. On Shabbos, however, we commemorate Hashem's creation of the world and all that is in it. Therefore, the mitzvah of *oneg Shabbos* is to embrace that which the world offers and to derive pleasure from it. However, it must be done in a way that takes the enjoyment a person has and elevates it, thereby proclaiming the Name of Hashem on even one's physical pleasure.

HALACHAH OF THE DAY

Yesterday, we discussed the halachic ramifications of using a telephone on Shabbos.

In cases of emergency, where someone is in danger and time is of the essence (e.g., an accident has occurred), if help must be summoned by phone, one should use the telephone in the usual manner. [In such cases one should not attempt to use the phone in an unusual way in an attempt to mitigate any violation of the Shabbos. Since people are in danger, doing anything that might contribute to a delay in the arrival of assistance is *forbidden.*]

If an emergency occurs and time is *not* of the essence, one should try to get a non-Jew to place the phone call. If this is not possible, one should use the telephone in an unusual manner in order to minimize the prohibitions involved in its use.

The following are some methods that may be employed when it is necessary to make use of a phone in an unusual manner. When removing the receiver from the cradle, one should lift the receiver by either knocking it off or lifting it in the crook of his arm. When dialing, one should dial with one's knuckle or with a utensil, instead of using one's fingers. Since there is no halachically "unusual" way to actually talk on the phone, one may speak in the normal manner. If one must replace the receiver on the hook (for instance, so as to be able to receive a call back from a doctor), it too should be done in an unusual manner, such as with one's mouth. However, since we are talking about a case where there is an emergency, if one cannot use the phone in an unusual manner, he should place the call in the usual manner.

In the event that a telephone must be used on Shabbos for a חוֹלֶה שֶׁאֵין בּוֹ סַכָּנָה, *a patient who is ill but whose life is not in danger,* one should try to get a non-Jew to make the telephone call. If one cannot find a non-Jew, he may place the call himself. However, since this is an instance where there is no danger involved, it *must* be done in an unusual manner. See examples described above for a description of how one may place a phone call in an unusual manner.

A CLOSER LOOK AT THE SIDDUR

In the *Mussaf* prayers on Shabbos, three aspects of the mitzvah of Shabbos are described, each with its own form of reward: מְעַנְּגֶיהָ לְעוֹלָם כָּבוֹד יִנְחָלוּ, טוֹעֲמֶיהָ חַיִּים זָכוּ, וְגַם הָאוֹהֲבִים דְּבָרֶיהָ גְּדֻלָּה בָּחָרוּ, *Those who make it a day of delight will inherit eternal honor, those who savor it will merit life, and even those who love its words have chosen greatness.* We may ask: How does each reward mentioned here fit its corresponding aspect of the mitzvah?

To explain, *R' Zundel Kroizer* (in his *Siddur, Ohr HaChamah*) cites the explanation of the *Vilna Gaon* on the first part of this three-part phrase.

Above (see *A Mussar Thought for the Day*), we noted that *Chazal* speak of those who are מְעַנֵּג אֶת הַשַּׁבָּת, make Shabbos a day of delight, rather than merely giving *themselves* delights on Shabbos. Here too, the

phrase highlights מְעַנְּגֶיהָ, *those who make "it" delightful,* where their goal is only to provide honor for Shabbos. Their reward is parallel to their actions. They endeavor to use their own enjoyment selflessly, only for the honor of Shabbos; in return, כָּבוֹד יִנְחָלוּ, *"they" inherit eternal honor.*

Using the explanation of the Gaon as a springboard, R' Zundel goes on to explain the rest of this prayer. One would think that one who honors Shabbos by partaking of its physical pleasures would receive a reward involving physical matters — wealth and possessions. However, the *siddur* teaches that his reward is not limited to the physical; he also inherits *eternal honor,* a reward in the World to Come.

The next phrase is the other side of this coin. טוֹעֲמֶיהָ can be understood to refer to those who delve into the reasons (טְעָמִים) behind the many and varied laws of Shabbos. Their honor of Shabbos is in the spiritual realm, learning the Torah associated with Shabbos. One may suppose that the reward for such action would likewise be only in the spiritual realm. We therefore say: חַיִּים זָכוּ, *they merit life,* not only eternal life (as in *eternal honor*) but also a physical life of blessings here in this world.

The natural outgrowth of delving into the Torah of Shabbos and exerting efforts in understanding its laws is that one becomes naturally more careful regarding the execution of those laws. This care to keep all the laws of Shabbos is borne of a love for the Shabbos, which is nurtured by the study of its commandments. These people are referred to in the next phrase of our prayer as הָאוֹהֲבִים דְּבָרֶיהָ, *those who love its words,* and we say that גְּדֻלָּה בָּחָרוּ, *they have chosen greatness,* for they have magnified the value of their learning and have given themselves the status not only of one who learns, but of one who learns in order to fulfill what he has learned. They receive reward even for the learning itself equal to one who has actually fulfilled all the laws, because of their great love for Hashem and His beloved day, Shabbos.

QUESTION OF THE DAY:

What else can we learn from the fact that the Torah places the Sabbath and the festivals together?

For the answer, see page 176.

פרשת אמור

THURSDAY

PARASHAS EMOR

A TORAH THOUGHT FOR THE DAY

בַּחֹדֶשׁ הַשְּׁבִיעִי בְּאֶחָד לַחֹדֶשׁ יִהְיֶה לָכֶם
שַׁבָּתוֹן זִכְרוֹן תְּרוּעָה מִקְרָא קֹדֶשׁ

In the seventh month, on the first of the month, there shall be a rest day for you; a remembrance with shofar blasts, a holy convocation (*Vayikra* 23:24).

What is the "remembrance" associated with the mitzvah of hearing the *shofar*? *Rashi* explains that this is an allusion to the Scriptural verses of *Zichronos* (remembrances) and of *Shofaros* (*shofar* blasts) that are recited on Rosh Hashanah in conjunction with the *shofar* blasts. They are alluded to with this word, because they serve to bring to Hashem the remembrance of Israel (the verses of remembrance) and the merit of the *Akeidah* (binding) of Yitzchak who was substituted for a ram (this is accomplished through recital of the verses of *shofar* blasts, as the *shofar* horn comes from a ram).

Ramban explains that the term *remembrance with shofar blasts* is used to highlight for us the significance of this festival. The other festivals mentioned in this section are all accompanied by a reason for the occasion. Here, the Torah explains that Rosh Hashanah is a day on which it is necessary to be remembered before Hashem for good and that this remembrance is accomplished through the *shofar* blasts. Since we know that Rosh Hashanah is followed by Yom Kippur (the Day of Atonement) ten days later, we may surmise that the remembrance of this day is due to the judgment that Hashem begins on it. We understand that on this day every person passes before Hashem for Heavenly judgment, followed ten days later by a day of atonement for one's sins.

The Gemara (*Rosh Hashanah* 29b) finds in the wording of this verse an allusion to the Rabbinic prohibition against blowing the *shofar* on Shabbos. The Gemara asks: Why is it that one verse describes Rosh Hashanah as *a rest day, a remembrance with shofar blasts* [which indicates that the *shofar* is not actually sounded, but only remembered through the recitation of the verses], while another verse says: יוֹם תְּרוּעָה יִהְיֶה לָכֶם, *a day of shofar blasts it shall be for you* (*Bamidbar* 29:1) [meaning actual *shofar* blasts]? The Gemara explains that there is no contradiction: Here (in *Vayikra*), the Torah is speaking of a Rosh Hashanah that occurs on Shabbos, when the *shofar* is not blown; there (in *Bamidbar*), the Torah is referring to a Rosh Hashanah that occurs on a weekday, when the *shofar* is blown. [The Gemara goes on to clarify that this prohibition is not a Biblical one; it is actually Rabbinic in origin. The Sages feared that if people were obligated to hear the *shofar* on Shabbos, a person might inadvertently carry a *shofar* in the public domain (a forbidden labor on Shabbos) to an expert, to learn how to blow it. They therefore forbade the blowing of the *shofar* on a Rosh Hashanah that occurs on Shabbos. The wording of the verses merely alludes to the later Rabbinic decree.]

Kli Yakar points out that this hint can be read into the previous words of this verse as well. For the words בַּחֹדֶשׁ הַשְּׁבִיעִי בְּאֶחָד לַחֹדֶשׁ יִהְיֶה לָכֶם שַׁבָּתוֹן זִכְרוֹן תְּרוּעָה מִקְרָא קֹדֶשׁ can be rendered thus: When the first of the seventh month falls out for you on Shabbos (שַׁבָּתוֹן), then it is to be a day of only remembrance of *shofar* blasts (זִכְרוֹן תְּרוּעָה), for the *shofar* itself may not be blown.

MISHNAH OF THE DAY: ERUVIN 8:7

The Mishnah presents another case in which it is not permitted to draw water without corrective partitions:

אַמַּת הַמַּיִם שֶׁהִיא עוֹבֶרֶת בְּחָצֵר — If ***a water canal passes through a chatzeir,*** אֵין מְמַלְּאִין הֵימֶנָּה בַּשַּׁבָּת — ***one may not draw*** water ***from it on the Sabbath,***[1] אֶלָּא אִם כֵּן עָשׂוּ לָהּ מְחִיצָה גָּבוֹהַּ עֲשָׂרָה טְפָחִים — ***unless they erected a partition ten tefachim high for it*** within the canal,[2] בַּכְּנִיסָה וּבַיְצִיאָה — ***at*** its ***entrance*** to the *chatzeir* ***and at*** its ***exit from it.***[3] רַבִּי יְהוּדָה אוֹמֵר — ***R' Yehudah says:*** כּוֹתֶל שֶׁעַל גַּבָּהּ תִּידּוֹן מִשּׁוּם מְחִיצָה —

NOTES

1. The canal is at least 10 *tefachim* deep and 4 *tefachim* wide, giving it the dimensions of an independent *reshus* (domain). Since it flows from the river, which is a *karmelis* (see Shabbos 6a), it too is considered a *karmelis* (*Rashi; R' Yehonasan*), even where it passes through the *chatzeir,* which is a *reshus hayachid.* Water may therefore not be drawn from it into the *chatzeir.* However, if the canal is smaller in either of these dimensions, it is subsidiary to the *chatzeir* and acquires the status of a *reshus hayachid* (*Rashi*).

2. Although a suspended partition is valid over water (see previous Mishnah), it must be evident that the partition was erected for the water. Therefore, the *chatzeir* wall passing over the canal is not effective (according to the first Tanna) and a special partition must be erected. Because the use of a hanging partition is a special dispensation granted by the Sages, its validity is made subject to special restrictions, namely that it clearly enclose the waterway by being within its banks (*Rashi*).

3. Since the segment of the canal within the *chatzeir* is partitioned off from the river, it appears to be self-contained in the *chatzeir* (*Rashi*). It is therefore considered a *reshus hayachid* like the rest of the *chatzeir* (*Mishnah Berurah* 356:3).

The** chatzeir **wall** that passes **over [the canal]** at each end **may be considered a partition.[4]

R' Yehudah cites an incident as support for his position:

אָמַר רַבִּי יְהוּדָה — ***R' Yehudah said:*** מַעֲשֶׂה בְּאַמָּה שֶׁל אָבֵל — ***It happened with the canal of Aveil,***[5] which flowed through the *chatzeiros* of the town, שֶׁהָיוּ מְמַלְאִין מִמֶּנָּה עַל פִּי זְקֵנִים בְּשַׁבָּת — ***that they would draw** water **from it on the Sabbath, by authority of the elders.*** Although this canal had no special partitions constructed within it, they relied on the suspended partitions of the *chatzeir* walls that passed over the canal. אָמְרוּ לוֹ — ***They answered him:*** מִפְּנֵי שֶׁלֹּא הָיָה בָּהּ כְּשִׁיעוּר — That incident is no proof, ***because [the canal] did not have the** minimum **dimensions.***[6] However, a regular canal is a *karmelis,* and the *chatzeir* walls do not permit it.

NOTES

4. R' Yehudah maintains that a special partition is not necessary. The water in the *chatzeir* is already separated from the water outside it by the wall suspended over the canal's banks. R' Yehudah is consistent with his view in the previous Mishnah that a suspended partition is valid even if it is not erected specifically for the water.

5. Aveil was the name of the town where this incident occurred.

6. As explained above (note 1), the canal is a *karmelis* only if it is 10 *tefachim* high and 4 *tefachim* wide. If it lacks either of these dimensions, it is subsidiary to the *chatzeir,* and thus a *reshus hayachid.*

GEMS FROM THE GEMARA

The Gemara cites a Baraisa that discusses other particulars of the law regarding drawing water from a canal: In the Baraisa, a canal passed through a *chatzeir* or *mavoi* lined by houses along its banks. Residents

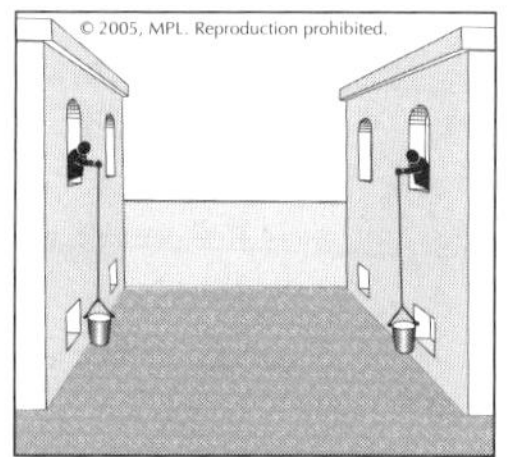

of these houses would draw water from the canal via windows overlooking the canal. See diagram. The Baraisa teaches that "if it is less than 3 *tefachim* wide," one may lower a bucket from a window and draw water from it; but if it is 3 or more *tefachim* wide, one may not lower a bucket and draw water from it.

The Gemara explains this Baraisa: Which area's width is being referred to? If you say the water canal itself, according to this explanation, a *karmelis* may even be 3 *tefachim* wide. Therefore, if it is 3 *tefachim* wide, one may not draw from it to his house, which is a *reshus hayachid.* But Rav Dimi said in the name of R' Yochanan that a *karmelis* cannot be less than 4 *tefachim* wide!

In its primary explanation of the Baraisa's ruling, the Gemara says that the canal does have the minimum measurements of a *karmelis* — 10 *tefachim* deep and 4 *tefachim* wide. But the width measurements refer to the banks of the canal, and the issue is to pass the bucket and water between the canal, which is a *karmelis,* and the house, which is a *reshus hayachid,* by placing the bucket on the bank before completing the exchange. Since the banks are a *mekom petur,* exempt area, this is permitted, because transferring between a *mekom petur* and any other area (e.g., a *reshus hayachid* or *karmelis*) is permitted. Accordingly, it is permitted to lower a bucket from the window to the bank of the canal (which constitutes a transfer from a *reshus hayachid* to a *mekom petur*), and then to raise the bucket from the bank and drop it into the canal (a transfer from a *mekom petur* to a *karmelis*). The reverse would then be permitted as well. The canal bank, by virtue of its *mekom petur* status, would thus serve as an exchange point between the house and the canal.

The Gemara notes that Rav Dimi elsewhere reported in the name of R' Yochanan that it is Rabbinically prohibited to transfer items from the *reshus harabim* to the *reshus hayachid* or vice versa via this *mekom petur,* so that people should not come to transfer objects from one domain to the other without any intermediate steps. This ruling would seem to refute this explanation of the Baraisa, which permits transferring water between two otherwise prohibited areas (the canal, a *karmelis,* and the house, a *reshus hayachid*) via a *mekom petur* (the bank).

The Gemara answers that this last ruling of Rav Dimi refers to an exchange between a *reshus harabim* and a *reshus hayachid,* where a direct transfer would violate a Biblical prohibition. Therefore, it is Rabbinically prohibited to transfer items even by way of a *mekom petur.* However, here in the case of the Baraisa, the exchange is between a *karmelis* and a *reshus hayachid.* Since even a direct transfer between the two would not violate any Biblical prohibition, a two-step transfer via a *mekom petur* is permitted.

QUESTION OF THE DAY:

Why does the Midrash refer to the חֹדֶשׁ הַשְּׁבִיעִי, the seventh month, as the חֹדֶשׁ הַשְּׁבוּעָה, the month of the oath?

For the answer, see page 176.

A MUSSAR THOUGHT FOR THE DAY

Although the Sages forbade the blowing of the *shofar* on Rosh Hashanah that falls on Shabbos (see above, *A Torah Thought for the Day*), it would seem that there is an inherent danger in omitting this mitzvah from our Rosh Hashanah service, even on Shabbos. The Gemara (*Rosh Hashanah* 16b) declares that any year in which the *shofar* is not blown on Rosh Hashanah will yield misfortune by year's end, the reason for the omission notwithstanding. For this is not a punishment for a sin, but a natural effect of not having the protection of the *shofar*. It is comparable to one who is ill who must suffer the effects of neglecting to take his medication, whatever the reason for that neglect. This being the case, shall we then expect that every year in which Rosh Hashanah falls on Shabbos will be one of misfortune, God forbid?

Meshech Chochmah addresses this question, and in so doing illuminates for us the true meaning of our service on Rosh Hashanah, whether it falls on a weekday or on Shabbos. Indeed, it is a lesson as to how a Jew must serve Hashem all year round.

Yes, it is a fact that going without the *shofar* blasts on Rosh Hashanah is dangerous. It leaves the Heavenly accuser of the Jewish people free to call attention to their sins without the defense of the *shofar*. Knowing this, the Jewish people have given up this protection for the sake of Shabbos. Let the Accuser accuse, let the decrees be handed down, let suffering and misfortune be our lot — but let not the Name of Hashem be desecrated even once with the transgression of His Shabbos laws! This is more important to us than everything, even our very survival.

And in this declaration of willingness to give up everything for Hashem lies our protection. For the merit of the *shofar* itself is based on this *mesiras nefesh*. We blow the horn of a ram to elicit the merit of the *Akeidah* of Yitzchak, who was prepared to die for Hashem, but was later substituted for a ram. What we are doing is bringing up his merit and that of his children, the Jewish people, who have inherited this quality. The Jewish people suffer abuse and indignation of every type for carrying the Name of Hashem. They "bind" their personal desires and goals on the Altar of their great love for Hashem and His Torah. This is the protection that the *shofar* provides and is its response to the Accuser in Heaven.

Therefore, the very surrender of our protection of the *shofar* is our *shofar* on Shabbos. Our declaration that we are prepared to risk everything for the sake of Hashem highlights the very quality that the blowing of the *shofar* does in other years. It proclaims our spiritual "*akeidah*" and serves to protect us and bring our remembrance before Hashem for a year of blessing.

HALACHAH OF THE DAY

Today we will discuss other practical applications relating to use of electrical appliances on Shabbos.

One may not turn on a microphone on Shabbos, due to the various violations inherent in using electricity, as discussed above. Furthermore, a microphone may not be used on Shabbos (even in a synagogue, to enable people to better hear the services) even if it was switched on before Shabbos. The *poskim* give various reasons for this ruling. Among these are that the use of the microphone creates the flow of additional electric current, and also that its use violates the Rabbinic decree against use of instruments that create sound.

One may leave an intercom on before Shabbos in order to monitor the welfare of a child. However, one may not speak into the intercom with intent that his voice be projected via the intercom.

One may wear a hearing aid on Shabbos, provided that it was turned on before Shabbos. Some *poskim* advise placing a piece of tape over the volume-control knob of the hearing aid, to prevent one from inadvertently raising the volume on Shabbos. Other *poskim* rule that this is unnecessary.

Some *poskim* rule that one should refrain from speaking directly into the ear of a person who is wearing a hearing aid on Shabbos. However, in case of need, it is permissible. Other *poskim* maintain that there is no reason to avoid speaking directly into the hearing aid. They rule that it is permissible under all circumstances. One may rely on these *poskim.*

It is forbidden to cause automatic doors to open or close on Shabbos.

If one must use automatic doors on Shabbos (e.g., to stay with a sick person in a hospital), he should try to enter between two non-Jews who are walking through the automatic doors. In this way, he is neither opening nor closing the doors. If he simply walks behind one non-Jew, when he walks away from the door he will be activating the closing device that causes the door to automatically close. If there are no non-Jews entering, one should walk through the doors in an unusual manner, such as by walking backwards. This is permitted because visiting the sick is regarded as a vital necessity.

It is forbidden to ring a doorbell on Shabbos. In the event that one mistakenly rang an electric doorbell, he is permitted to remove his finger from the button.

A CLOSER LOOK AT THE SIDDUR

Remembrance (זִכָּרוֹן) is a recurring theme in the prayers of Rosh Hashanah. Indeed, we refer to Rosh Hashanah as יוֹם הַזִּכָּרוֹן, the *Day of Remembrance.* While the description in the *siddur* for the day is יוֹם תְּרוּעָה, *a day of sounding the shofar,* on Shabbos, when the *shofar* is not sounded (see above, *A Torah Thought for the Day*), it is described as יוֹם זִכְרוֹן תְּרוּעָה, *a day of recalling the sounding of the shofar.* And again, in the *Mussaf* prayer we say about Rosh Hashanah: זֶה הַיּוֹם תְּחִלַּת מַעֲשֶׂיךָ זִכָּרוֹן לְיוֹם רִאשׁוֹן, *This day is the anniversary of the start of Your handiwork, a remembrance of the first day.*

Although *Parashas Emor* is far from Rosh Hashanah, an insight into the word זִכָּרוֹן by *R' Shimon Schwab* (in his *Maayan Beis HaSho'eivah*) provides a message that is relevant for us throughout the year.

There is a significant difference between the words זֵכֶר and זִכָּרוֹן. The word זֵכֶר refers to a commemoration of a past event, as in זֵכֶר לְמַעֲשֵׂה בְרֵאשִׁית, *a commemoration for the days of Creation.* The word זִכָּרוֹן connotes a reminder of something in the past for its practical application to the future.

To illustrate, R' Schwab points out that *Rambam* (*Hilchos Teshuvah* 3:4), when he notes that the message of the *shofar* is for us to shake ourselves from the slumber of our ways, adds the following, from the Gemara in *Kiddushin* (40b): "Therefore, throughout the year a person must view himself as being perfectly balanced between righteousness and wickedness, and the whole world as being perfectly balanced as well. This will cause him to feel that with one sin, he can bring upon himself and upon the entire world destruction; on the other hand, with one merit he can bring for himself and for the whole world salvation."

R' Schwab asks: Why is *Rambam,* in the middle of discussing the way we are to act during the Days of Awe, speaking about how a person must behave throughout the year? The answer is that the objective of the sound of the *shofar* is to act as a זִכָּרוֹן — not merely a remembrance of things past or present, but a reminder for the future. The effects of the *shofar* blasts are meant to last throughout the year, constantly reminding us of the importance of our actions and their far-reaching effects. It is therefore fitting for *Rambam* to include an admonition for the whole year in his description of the message of the *shofar.*

Thus, Rosh Hashanah itself, the יוֹם זִכָּרוֹן, is a day that must serve as a reminder for us throughout the year. Until the last day of the year, we must remember the day of Rosh Hashanah, the זִכָּרוֹן לְיוֹם רִאשׁוֹן, *remembrance of the first day [beginning of Creation]* and adjust our actions accordingly.

A TORAH THOUGHT FOR THE DAY

אַךְ בֶּעָשׂוֹר לַחֹדֶשׁ הַשְּׁבִיעִי הַזֶּה יוֹם הַכִּפֻּרִים הוּא מִקְרָא־קֹדֶשׁ יִהְיֶה לָכֶם וְעִנִּיתֶם אֶת־נַפְשֹׁתֵיכֶם

But on the tenth day of this month it is the Day of Atonement; there shall be a holy convocation for you, and you shall afflict yourselves (*Vayikra* 23:27).

The Mishnah (*Yoma* 8:1) explains that the commandment to *afflict ourselves* on Yom Kippur prohibits us from performing five types of activities on this holy day: eating and drinking, wearing leather shoes, bathing, anointing, and engaging in marital relations. The commentaries offer several explanations as to how the need to abstain from these physical pleasures is essential to Yom Kippur's essence as the day of final judgment when we are given the opportunity for doing *teshuvah* and achieving closeness with Hashem.

Rambam (*Moreh Nevuchim* 3:43) explains that the reason the Torah ordained Yom Kippur as a day when almost all types of physical activities are prohibited is because it is the day on which Hashem is especially open, as it were, to accepting our *teshuvah.* Thus, since the entire day must be utilized in our doing whatever we can to become closer to Him through thoughts and actions of repentance, and to realize the great gift that He has allowed us, it is inappropriate for a person to have any other focus during this time that will distract him from this goal. To encourage us to use the day to its fullest, the Torah does not permit us to engage in physical activities such as labor or physical pleasures. Every moment of this lofty day must be spent only on the spiritual pursuit of *teshuvah.*

Pirkei D'Rabbi Eliezer (§46), cited in *Ramban* (*Vayikra* 16:8), offers a different reason as to why we totally abstain from physical pleasures on Yom Kippur: we do so in order to act like Heavenly angels. When we properly observe Yom Kippur, the *Satan* exclaims to Hashem, "Master of the World! You have a nation on earth that are like ministering angels! Just as angels do not wear shoes, the Jewish people are barefoot on Yom Kippur. Just as angels do not eat or drink, the Jewish people do not eat or drink on Yom Kippur. Just as angels do not bend their knees, the Jewish people spend the entire day of Yom Kippur standing. Just as angels have peace among themselves, the Jewish people on Yom Kippur are a nation without argument."

Binyan Av points out that our desire to appear as angels on the Day of Judgment may be better understood by noting *Sefer HaChinuch's* explanation of the *inuyim,* afflictions, of Yom Kippur (*mitzvah* 313). *Sefer*

HaChinuch explains that besides actively distracting a person from wholeheartedly doing *teshuvah,* involvement in physical matters — even those actions such as eating or drinking, which of course must be performed to survive — subtly changes who the person is. It cannot be said, at the moment when a person is eating, that he is someone who is fully engaged in spiritual growth. While it is of course true that Hashem created man with a body as well as a *neshamah,* and the need for physical involvements is an integral part of a human being, it is nevertheless inappropriate for a servant to be involved in selfish mundane activities at the very time that he comes before his master to be judged.

This is especially important, *Sefer HaChinuch* points out, because of the principle: אֵין דָּנִין אֶת הָאָדָם אֶלָּא לְפִי מַעֲשָׂיו שֶׁל אוֹתָהּ שָׁעָה, *a person is judged only according to his actions at the present time* (*Rosh Hashanah* 16b). Thus, although a person is usually driven by his body's needs and desires, on Yom Kippur we are given the opportunity to undergo Hashem's judgment without the encumbrances of these mundane parts of our life. Moreover, our standing in judgment while free of physical involvements shows that these mundane actions, while they may need to be performed over the course of ordinary life, do not truly define who we are. When Hashem is judging us — or asking us to define the values that we hold as important — we are showing Him that becoming closer to Him through prayer and *teshuvah* is the only thing on our minds. The other, mundane parts of our lives are merely tasks that must be carried out. When, under the scrutiny of judgment, a person demonstrates that he is able to rise above his physical nature and spend a day focused on nothing but spirituality, he shows that, in essence, he is someone who is truly worthy of becoming closer to Hashem, and thus merits receiving Hashem's forgiveness on the Day of Judgment.

This, concludes *Binyan Av,* is the purpose of our acting as angels on Yom Kippur. By doing so while under the scrutiny of judgment, we show Hashem that although we are of course human, our true aspiration is to live the life of angels, whose entire existence is devoted exclusively to selfless service of Hashem.

QUESTION OF THE DAY:

Can a person who earns the punishment of* וְהַאֲבַדְתִּי אֶת־הַנֶּפֶשׁ הַהִוא *(23:30) be saved?

For the answer, see page 176.

MISHNAH OF THE DAY: ERUVIN 8:8

The Mishnah discusses another case of water being drawn from a body of water on the Sabbath:

גְּזוּזְטְרָא שֶׁהִיא לְמַעְלָה מִן הַמַּיִם — If ***a balcony*** protrudes ***over*** a body of ***water,*** **אֵין מְמַלְאִין הֵימֶנָּה בְּשַׁבָּת** — ***one may not draw*** water ***from it on the Sabbath,***[1] **אֶלָּא אִם כֵּן עָשׂוּ לָהּ מְחִיצָה גְּבוֹהָה עֲשָׂרָה טְפָחִים** — ***unless they made for it a partition ten tefachim high,***[2] **בֵּין מִלְמַעְלָה בֵּין מִלְמַטָּה** — ***either above or below*** the balcony.[3]

וְכֵן שְׁתֵּי גְזוּזְטְרָאוֹת זוֹ לְמַעְלָה מִזּוֹ — ***Similarly,***[4] ***two balconies, one above the other,*** which protrude over the water: **עָשׂוּ לָעֶלְיוֹנָה** — ***If they constructed*** a partition ***for the upper*** balcony **וְלֹא עָשׂוּ לַתַּחְתּוֹנָה** — ***but they did not construct*** a partition ***for the lower one,***[5] **שְׁתֵּיהֶן אֲסוּרוֹת עַד שֶׁיְּעָרְבוּ** — ***both*** balconies ***are prohibited*** to draw water through the upper balcony's hole, ***until they join in an eruv.***[6]

NOTES

1. Because this is a transfer from a *karmelis* (the body of water) to a *reshus hayachid* (the balcony). Although the balcony is not surrounded by partitions, it is still considered a *reshus hayachid* because a door or window of the house opens to it, rendering it a חוֹרֵי רְשׁוּת הַיָּחִיד, *crevice of the reshus hayachid,* which is classified as a *reshus hayachid* (*Shulchan Aruch Orach Chaim* 355:1; see *Tosafos* to 86b ד״ה גזוזטרא for alternative explanations).

2. The partitions are erected around the perimeter of the balcony (which is 4 *tefachim* by 4 *tefachim*), or around a hole of 4 by 4 *tefachim* in the balcony's floor (partitions are valid only if they surround an area of 4 by 4 *tefachim*).

These hanging partitions legally extend downward because of the principle of *gud achis,* so that the water directly underneath the balcony is also considered surrounded by halachic partitions attached to the balcony, and thus a *reshus hayachid.* Consequently, water may be drawn to the balcony (*Rashi*).

3. The partitions may be erected above the balcony or be attached to the underside of the balcony (*Rashi*). *Tosafos* explain that although the previous Mishnayos all required the partitions to be close to the water, in this instance even partitions above the balcony are permitted because they were clearly erected for the water.

4. The similarity of this case to the previous one is that it also deals with balconies that protrude over water. However, this discussion is actually totally independent of the previous one and the issues dealt with bear no relation to the previous ruling. *Rashi* therefore deletes the word וְכֵן, *similarly,* from the Mishnah's text.

5. The upper balcony made a partition so that it should be able to draw water. However, the people of the lower balcony also draw water, through the hole of the upper balcony, to their balcony.

6. Certainly, residents of the house that opens to the lower balcony may not draw water directly from their balcony. Their balcony retains its *reshus hayachid* status

NOTES

(even when it does not have partitions), while the water underneath is a *karmelis.* Thus, when water is drawn, it is transferred from a *karmelis* to a *reshus hayachid* (*Rashi*). Although the upper balcony has partitions, since the residents of both houses have access to it, it requires an *eruv* with the lower one and is prohibited without one.

This discussion is not necessarily limited to two balconies one directly above the other. As long as the balconies are not separated by a lateral distance of 4 *tefachim,* this ruling applies (*Rashi*).

GEMS FROM THE GEMARA

The Mishnah said that two balconies one above the other must join in an *eruv* to permit drawing water from the upper balcony. The Gemara explains in the name of Rav that the balconies must join in an *eruv* when they are within 4 lateral *tefachim.* But when they are distanced, the upper balcony, which has partitions, is permitted to draw water even if no *eruv* has been made. [Since the lower balcony's residents can use the upper balcony only by throwing to it across 4 *tefachim* of lateral distance, their usage of that balcony is difficult. Such usage does not prohibit the residents of the upper balcony from carrying, in accordance with Rav's opinion (*Rashi*).] Rav, in this explanation, follows his own reasoning, stated elsewhere, that a person does not restrict his friend from carrying in his area by way of "throwing through the air." That is, if his only access to the other person's domain is by throwing, this difficult type of usage does not obligate his friend to join with him in an *eruv.*

The Gemara further defines the case of the Mishnah. Rav Sheishess said that the Mishnah is dealing with a case in which the residents of both houses contributed toward its construction. Therefore, the upper balcony is legally usable by both, and an *eruv* is required.

The Gemara asks that if so, even if the residents of the lower balcony erected partitions for the lower balcony, an *eruv* should still be required for the upper one, since they are partners in the upper balcony. However, our Mishnah did not require an *eruv* for the upper balcony in such a case. [The Mishnah limited its ruling to a case where the residents of the house opening to the lower balcony did not make partitions for it, implying that had they done so, no *eruv* would be required for the upper balcony.]

The Gemara answers that by erecting partitions for the lower balcony, whose only purpose is to permit them to draw water from their balcony on the Sabbath, the residents of the house opening to the lower balcony have shown their intent not to use the upper balcony during the Sabbath. They are saying, in effect, to the upper balcony: "I have no desire to be with you." Therefore, the residents of the house opening to the upper balcony have sole dominion over their balcony, and an *eruv* is not required.

A MUSSAR THOUGHT FOR THE DAY

In addition to the reasons for the Yom Kippur afflictions that we mentioned in *A Torah Thought for the Day,* we may understand a different perspective of the *inuyim* from the text of *Tefillah Zakkah,* the pre-Yom Kippur prayer. In this poignant *tefillah,* we proclaim to Hashem that the discomfort we suffer from the five *inuyim* on Yom Kippur should atone for the different sins that, over the year, we have unfortunately committed with our senses or body parts. Abstaining from food and drink, *Tefillah Zakkah* explains, atones for our possibly having consumed forbidden foods; refraining from wearing comfortable shoes on our feet is an act of *teshuvah* for the many times that our feet ran to commit sin. A day without the bodily pleasures of washing and anointing corrects our having derived forbidden pleasures over the course of the year; and forgoing marital relations atones for sins that we may have committed in this area. *Yesod VeShoresh HaAvodah* likens a person who undergoes the afflictions of Yom Kippur but does not perform *teshuvah* to *toveil v'sheretz b'yado* — a person who immerses in a mikveh while grasping an impure rodent — who clearly remains contaminated. Although *Viduy,* confession, must be recited for every misdeed we have done, and strong feelings of *teshuvah* — or the resolve to change — are vital, it is clear that an inherent part of the forgiveness that Yom Kippur brings is achieved through the *inuyim.*

Shevet MiYehudah adds another dimension to explain how the *inuyim* serve to atone for our *aveiros.* Hashem, in His great mercy, considers the suffering we undergo on this day as taking the place of the great punishment that we may deserve for our sins. For example, a person who committed a sin for which he must be punished with hunger "fulfills" this sentence with the pain he feels while fasting; physical discomforts of not washing or wearing shoes free a person from a far greater punishment of undergoing affliction throughout the year. With this in mind, *Shevet MiYehudah* explains that we may now understand why the

פרשת אמור

FRIDAY

PARASHAS EMOR

commandment of afflicting ourselves on Yom Kippur is phrased: וְעִנִּיתֶם אֶת־נַפְשֹׁתֵיכֶם, (literally) *you shall afflict your souls,* even though a more apt description of the *inuyim* would be the *physical* discomfort that they bring. In referring to the afflictions as *afflictions of the soul,* the Torah is telling us that although it is true that these discomforts are primarily physical, they are also a minuscule part of a punishment — such as hunger or pain — that, if it would be meted out in full, would torment the person's soul, or entire life. Thus, Hashem applies here the merciful principle of מִקְצַת נֶפֶשׁ כְּכָל הַנֶּפֶשׁ, *punishing a minor part of the soul is nevertheless considered punishment of the soul* (see *Koheles Rabbah* 7:25 and *Mesillas Yesharim* Ch. 4), and allows the discomforts that we undergo on Yom Kippur to replace the greater punishments that we may deserve.

Yesod VeShoresh HaAvodah (11:10) points out that once a person realizes the great value of the *inuyim,* his entire perspective on Yom Kippur will be changed. Instead of seeing it as a day of burden, restriction and unpleasantness, he will view it as a day to which he actually looks forward, for he understands that every moment of discomfort brings added dimensions of forgiveness. [For another great benefit that *Yesod VeShoresh HaAvodah* finds in the *inuyim,* see *A Closer Look at the Siddur.*]

HALACHAH OF THE DAY

Pursuant to our continuing discussion of Shabbos issues pertinent to the use of electricity, we will now turn our attention to some of the problems presented by various security apparatus and their use.

In today's security-conscious world, we often encounter sophisticated devices intended to protect people and their properties. One such device, the motion sensor, raises Shabbos issues not only for its owners, but even for guests and the unwitting passersby. A motion sensor works by sending out a signal that is reflected off an object or person that comes into its range. Such sensors placed in homes as part of a home security system are typically linked to a central panel, which treats activation of the sensor as a sign of illegal entry and activates an alarm. While the central control panel can usually be disarmed before Shabbos, the individual sensors still operate. These sensors often contain LEDs (Light Emitting Diodes) that light up when they sense movement within their effective range. The activation of the light naturally presents a halachic difficulty on Shabbos.

Motion sensors set up outside homes are often used to activate a security floodlight upon sensing movement on the grounds. Sometimes, depending on the placement of the sensor, this floodlight can be activated even by people strolling by on the public sidewalk in front of the house.

In order to avoid all halachic issues and any possibility of transgression, one should preferably deactivate all such sensors before Shabbos. In the case of home security systems, one should deactivate the individual motion sensors before Shabbos. This will prevent the LED light from being turned on when people pass the sensor. It will also prevent the central controller from being activated.

However, there are *poskim* who rule that one is permitted to walk by a sensor that activates a light, provided that activating the light is not his intention. Therefore, if one disarms an alarm system but forgets to deactivate the individual sensors, he may rely upon these *poskim.* In the case of an exterior motion-activated light, if one is walking outside and cannot avoid (or even if it is inconvenient to avoid) walking in an area covered by a sensor, he may rely on the *poskim* who permit activating the light unintentionally.

The above discussion relates to the question of surveillance cameras as well. Many public buildings, such as hospitals and hotels, have surveillance cameras mounted for security reasons. These pose a potential problem on Shabbos, since a person walking by such a camera initiates electrical activity in the camera. In case of need, one may rely on the *poskim* who permit walking by a motion sensor on Shabbos.

If one has surveillance cameras inside or outside of his home in areas where people generally walk, the cameras should be deactivated before Shabbos. If one forgets to deactivate them he should avoid walking within their range. If this is impossible or inconvenient, one may rely on the permit mentioned above.

A CLOSER LOOK AT THE SIDDUR

Before reciting *Bircas HaMazon* after a meal on weekdays, many have the custom to recite Psalm 137, עַל נַהֲרוֹת בָּבֶל, to recall the Destruction of the *Beis HaMikdash.* However, this sort of remembrance is inappropriate on the Sabbath and on festivals, when the joy of the holiday is not to be marred. Thus, instead we recite Psalm 126, שִׁיר הַמַּעֲלוֹת, which speaks of the joy that will accompany the ultimate redemption (*Shelah*).

[The discussion of the joy that will attend the redemption can also cause us to remember that today we are in exile; however, this is acceptable, as the destruction is not directly mentioned.]

Let us examine the שִׁיר הַמַּעֲלוֹת prayer more closely. There are actually fifteen consecutive psalms (Chs. 120-135) that begin with the words שִׁיר הַמַּעֲלוֹת (or, in the case of the first of the series, שִׁיר לַמַּעֲלוֹת), which literally means: *A Song of Ascents.* These "ascents" correspond to the fifteen steps that led up to the inner courtyard of the *Beis HaMikdash.* When the water libation was offered in the *Beis HaMikdash* on Succos, the Leviim would stand on the steps singing these psalms, as the libation was brought into the courtyard.

The psalm begins by describing the time בְּשׁוּב ה׳ אֶת־שִׁיבַת צִיּוֹן, *when HASHEM will return the captive [people] of Zion. Meiri* states that the word אֶת in this verse can be understood to mean *with,* and is therefore saying: Hashem, Who is in exile along with His nation, will Himself return with the captives. The verse continues, stating: הָיִינוּ כְּחֹלְמִים, *we will be as dreamers.* This refers either to the fact that the splendor of the redemption will seem to be a dream come true (*Sforno*), or that the oppression of the previous exile will fade like a bad dream (*Radak*).

The psalm continues: אָז יִמָּלֵא שְׂחוֹק פִּינוּ וּלְשׁוֹנֵנוּ רִנָּה, *Then our mouth will be filled with laughter, and our tongue with glad song.* It is noteworthy that the word *mouth* in this verse is written in the singular. *Ibn Ezra* states that this is because every Jew will personally be filled with joy over the redemption. Moreover, each mouth will be *filled* with laughter; the joy of the redemption will be total, unadulterated by any tinge of sorrow. Similarly, our tongue will be *filled* with glad song. It will no longer be necessary for us to use our tongue to pray for salvation, and it will be free to concentrate exclusively on thanking Hashem for our redemption.

We will continue our discussion of this psalm next week.

A TASTE OF LOMDUS

The Mishnah (*Yoma* 8:1) tells us that the obligation to afflict ourselves on Yom Kippur prevents us from performing five different actions — eating and drinking, wearing leather shoes, bathing, anointing, and engaging in marital relations. [Incidentally, eating and drinking are prohibited also because of the negative commandment understood from: כִּי כָל־הַנֶּפֶשׁ אֲשֶׁר לֹא־תְעֻנֶּה בְּעֶצֶם הַיּוֹם הַזֶּה וְנִכְרְתָה מֵעַמֶּיהָ, *For any soul who will not be afflicted on this very day will be cut off from its people* (*Vayikra* 23:29). *Rambam* (*Sefer HaMitzvos, Lo Saaseh* 196) explains that the mention of the punishment of *kares* makes it clear that a negative commandment is being instructed. Thus, a person who wrongfully eats or drinks on Yom Kippur transgresses two separate prohibitions.] Although all commentaries agree that all five types of *inuyim* (afflictions) must be observed on Yom Kippur, some opinions — such as *Ran* and *Rambam* — rule that all these afflictions are Biblical obligations, while others — *Tosafos* and *Rosh* — explain that the Biblical commandment of וְעִנִּיתֶם אֶת־נַפְשֹׁתֵיכֶם, *you shall afflict yourselves,* precludes only eating and drinking. The other four *inuyim* — wearing leather shoes, bathing, anointing, and engaging in marital relations — are prohibited only by Rabbinic law. [*Mishnah Berurah* 611:3 rules that practically, it is appropriate to treat all five *inuyim* as Torah law.]

One of the reasons brought to prove that the four latter prohibitions are only Rabbinic in nature is the Mishnah's (*Yoma* 8:1) statement that a king and a newlywed bride, because of their exceptional need to always look presentable, are permitted to wash their faces on Yom Kippur; Torah law would not make this distinction between people. [Nowadays, *Chayei Adam* (cited in *Mishnah Berurah* 613:26) rules that, since we spend the entire day of Yom Kippur in the synagogue engaged in prayer, this leniency does not apply.] If the prohibition against washing is Torah based, as *Ran* and *Rambam* maintain, how could the Sages permit something that is forbidden by Torah law?

Although he ultimately brings other conclusive proofs demonstrating that the four *inuyim* are only Rabbinic, *Tosafos Yeshanim* offers an answer to defend *Ran* and *Rambam's* opinion and to show that although these restrictions may be Torah based, nevertheless, the Sages still permitted a king and a bride to wash their faces. The Biblical obligation of *you shall afflict yourselves,* explains *Tosafos Yeshanim,* forbids only washing (or anointing) the entire body. However, everyone — even those who maintain that washing is forbidden by Torah law — agree that washing only part of the body is not included in this Torah ordinance, and is only Rabbinically forbidden. Thus, the Sages who prohibit us to wash even part of our body on Yom Kippur did not include a king or bride in this decree.

Ohr Gadol (in his *Hagahos* to *Mishnayos Yoma*) asks a question on *Tosafos Yeshanim's* explanation that the Sages are able to permit a king or bride to wash their faces on Yom Kippur because washing the entire body is only Rabbinically forbidden. We know that although the *shiur*

(measurement) of forbidden foods that must be consumed in order to be liable to punishment is a *kezayis* (an olive's volume), the Gemara (*Yoma* 73b) tells us that eating *chatzi shiur,* half of the [forbidden] measurement, is also prohibited. If this is the case, since the face — or any limb — is of course part of the body, why do we not apply the principle of *chatzi shiur* to say that just as it is Biblically forbidden to wash the full body, washing any individual part is also included in this Torah prohibition? How are the Sages able to allow a king or bride to transgress the *chatzi shiur* extension of the Torah prohibition of bathing?

R' Chaim Shmulevitz (*Sefer Zikaron* p. 204; see also *Emek Berachah* p. 127) answers the *Ohr Gadol's* question by explaining that although it is true that the extension of *chatzi shiur* does not allow a person to do even a small part of something that the Torah prohibits — such as eating half a *kezayis* of nonkosher food — this rule applies only when the smaller substance is qualitatively similar to the larger one. Since half a *kezayis* of forbidden food is still forbidden food, it is included in the Torah's prohibition of consuming any amount of this substance. However, the difference between bathing the entire body and washing one limb is far greater than the simple question of how much of the person is being washed with water. Inherently, the enjoyment that comes from bathing the entire body is incomparably greater than the enjoyment that comes from washing one limb. With this in mind, explains R' Chaim, we may understand that when *Tosafos Yeshanim* tells us that the Torah-level obligation to *afflict ourselves* on Yom Kippur refers only to bathing the entire body, he is not describing the number of limbs that must be washed in order to be punished for violating this prohibition, in which case the extension of *chatzi shiur* would indeed tell us that a lesser amount would be forbidden as well. Rather, *Tosafos Yeshanim* is describing the level of enjoyment that the Torah, by telling us to *afflict ourselves,* is commanding us to refrain from experiencing on Yom Kippur. Lesser enjoyment — experienced by washing only part of the body — does not bring this feeling of contentment, and is thus, on a Torah level, not forbidden by the extension of *chatzi shiur* that prohibits a smaller version of the whole. Accordingly, concludes *Tosafos Yeshanim,* since lesser forms of enjoyment are prohibited only because of Rabbinic law, the Sages enjoy the option of not including a king or bride in their decree of refraining from these lesser levels of pleasure.

A TORAH THOUGHT FOR THE DAY

וּלְקַחְתֶּם לָכֶם בַּיּוֹם הָרִאשׁוֹן פְּרִי עֵץ הָדָר
כַּפֹּת תְּמָרִים וַעֲנַף עֵץ־עָבֹת וְעַרְבֵי־נָחַל
וּשְׂמַחְתֶּם לִפְנֵי ה׳ אֱלֹהֵיכֶם שִׁבְעַת יָמִים

You shall take for yourselves on the first day the fruit of a citron tree (esrog), the branches of date palms (lulav), twigs of a plaited tree (hadas), and brook willows (aravah); and you shall rejoice before HASHEM, your God, for seven days (*Vayikra* 23:40).

The rejoicing *before HASHEM* mentioned in this verse was fulfilled during the Intermediate Days of the festival with actual celebrations held in the complex of the *Beis HaMikdash. Rambam* describes the celebrations in detail: The festivities would start from after the bringing of the afternoon *tamid*-offering and last until morning. Musical instruments were played and songs of praise were sung to Hashem.

Although it is a mitzvah that there be great celebration, only a select group were chosen to actively participate. These were the great men of the nation, the heads of the yeshivos, the pious ones and the elders. They would dance, clap and jump in holy ecstasy, while the rest of the nation, men on the lower floor and women on the balcony, would come to watch and to listen (see *Rambam, Hilchos Lulav* 8:12-14).

What is the reason for the great joy on the festival of Succos? *Sefer HaChinuch* (*mitzvah* 324) writes that Succos falls at the end of the agricultural cycle. In this season, the produce of the harvests and the fruits of the orchards were gathered into the houses and the storehouses. This is a universal time of gladness, for a person naturally rejoices in gathering in the fruits of his labors and being able to provide for himself and his family for the coming year. The festival is therefore called חַג הָאָסִיף, the *Festival of the Harvest* (*Shemos* 34:22).

However, there is a great risk in these celebrations, for the nature of man is that such unbridled joy brings out his base nature and causes him to forget his fear of God. Therefore, Hashem commanded us to make this time of year into a festival dedicated to Him, so that we may take this joy and channel it in the proper direction — by giving thanks and honor to the Name of Hashem. The Four Species that we take are plants that gladden those who see them. We are thus reminded to direct our joy to God.

On a deeper level, the joy of the festival of Succos is a result of the atonement that was attained on the Yom Kippur that has just passed. There is no greater joy than being freed from the shackles of sin and cleansed of the impurity that sin brings in its wake. However, *R' Yerucham Levovitz* states, this joy is only proportional to the amount of anguish and remorse that the sins had previously caused a person. As *Rabbeinu Yonah* writes regarding the joy one has with the atonement of *Yom Kippur*: תִּהְיֶה לוֹ לְעֵדָה עַל דַּאֲגָתוֹ לְאַשְׁמָתוֹ, וִיגוֹנוֹתָיו לַעֲוֹנוֹתָיו, *it is a demonstration of his anguish for his guilt and his pain for his sins.* Only who has experienced remorse for his failings in the depths of his soul merits to celebrate the festival of Succos in the heights of joy.

MISHNAH OF THE DAY: ERUVIN 8:9

The previous Mishnayos discussed drawing water on the Sabbath. The Mishnah now discusses disposing of waste water on the Sabbath:

חָצֵר שֶׁהִיא פְּחוּתָה מֵאַרְבַּע אַמּוֹת — If ***a chatzeir is less than four amos*** by four *amos* in area, **אֵין שׁוֹפְכִין בְּתוֹכָהּ מַיִם בַּשַּׁבָּת** — ***one may not pour*** waste ***water into it on the Sabbath,***[1] **אֶלָּא אִם כֵּן עָשׂוּ לָהּ עוּקָה** — ***unless they made a cesspool for it*** **מַחֲזֶקֶת סָאתַיִם מִן הַנֶּקֶב וּלְמַטָּה** — ***that can contain two se'ah*** of water ***below the*** overflow ***hole.***[2] **בֵּין מִבַּחוּץ בֵּין מִבִּפְנִים** — This cesspool may be situated ***either*** just ***outside*** the *chatzeir* in the *reshus harabim* ***or inside*** it; **אֶלָּא שֶׁמִּבַּחוּץ צָרִיךְ לִקְמוֹר** — ***except that*** if it is situated ***outside, he must cover***

NOTES

1. In Mishnaic times it was customary to pour dirty water into the courtyard, and from there it would flow into the street. Since in doing so one transfers the water from a *reshus hayachid* (the enclosed *chatzeir*) to a *reshus harabim* (the street), it is prohibited to pour the water into the *chatzeir* unless one can reasonably expect the water to be absorbed by the ground of the *chatzeir.*

A typical household used to pour two *se'ah* of water from their homes on one day. This amount of water can be readily absorbed by an area equivalent to 4 square *amos* without making it muddy.

2. This refers to the hole in the cesspool's wall that is used to discharge overflow sewage into the *reshus harabim.* The Mishnah informs us that the hole must be situated high enough in the cesspool for the area below it to contain 2 *beis se'ah,* and thus hold the entire volume of water usually poured out on the Sabbath. Otherwise, the waste water poured into it would flow out into the *reshus harabim* before it had a chance to be absorbed, which would make it forbidden to pour water into the cesspool (*Rashi; R' Yehonasan*).

it,[3] מִבִּפְנִים אֵין צָרִיךְ לְקַמּוֹר — whereas, if it is situated ***inside, he need not cover*** it.

NOTES

3. In order for it to be permissible to pour water into a pool outside the *chatzeir,* the pool must qualify as a *mekom petur* [or a *reshus hayachid;* in general, however, the cesspool would not be deep enough — 10 *tefachim* — to qualify as a *reshus hayachid*]. Thus, it must be less than 4 *tefachim* wide, and at least 3 *tefachim* deep. If debris were to accumulate at the bottom of the cesspool, so that it was no longer 3 *tefachim* deep, its status would change to that of the *reshus harabim* surrounding it. If this occurred, one would no longer be permitted to pour water from the *chatzeir* into it. People, however, might not be aware of the change in status and would continue pouring in water. Therefore, the Rabbis required that the cesspool be kept covered to prevent the accumulation of debris (*Rashi,* as explained by *Beis Meir, Orach Chaim* 357).

Rama (*Darkei Moshe, Orach Chaim* 357) suggests that the need for a covering is not related to the laws of the Sabbath, but to the legal obligation to safeguard against people stumbling into the pit. *Rambam* (*Hil. Shabbos* 15:16, as understood by *Beis Yosef, Orach Chaim* 357) explains that this is necessary so that people will not accuse others of carrying sewage into the *reshus harabim* and discarding it there.

GEMS FROM THE GEMARA

The previous Mishnah permitted drawing water from a balcony containing hanging partitions. Rabbah bar Rav Huna said that only drawing water is permitted, but pouring out sewage through a hole in the balcony is prohibited, because it will be carried beyond the area immediately below the balcony's partitions. This constitutes a transfer from a *reshus hayachid* (the balcony) to a *karmelis* (the water outside of the area enclosed by the balcony's partitions).

The Gemara questioned this ruling from our Mishnah, which permits the disposal of liquid waste in a *chatzeir* that is smaller than 4 *amos* only if a cesspool is dug that can contain 2 *se'ah* of liquid. The Baraisa permits pouring waste into the cesspool even after it is full. Apparently, we are not concerned about the incidental runoff of liquid into another domain. Why, then, should we not permit pouring out waste water through a balcony into the river below?

The Gemara answers that the waters of the cesspool generally become absorbed in the ground before flowing out to the *reshus harabim.* Therefore, one does not intend for them to leave the *chatzeir.* [And even if the sewage does overflow the cesspool and run out of the *chatzeir,* it was his intention for it to be absorbed in its place, and this transfer to the neighboring *reshus harabim* is unintended. Since even if he intended for the sewage to run out of his *chatzeir* it is not a blatant violation, because he is pouring into a *reshus hayachid,* it is permitted where he does not intend it to happen (*Rashi*).] However, waters poured from the balcony are never absorbed in their place. Therefore, he knows that the sewage will certainly flow beyond the partitions, and it is prohibited.

The Gemara presents another version of the previous discussion, according to which pouring out sewage through a hole in the balcony to a river running below is *also permitted.* [Although he knows that the sewage dropping into the river below will flow beyond the area of his partitions, he has no particular interest in this happening. Therefore, since the area in which it first falls is within his partitions, it is permitted. However, when it comes to pouring out sewage in a *chatzeir* of less than 4 *amos,* the next Mishnah requires that he dig a cesspool to absorb the sewage. Otherwise, he intends for it to run off out of the *chatzeir,* so as not to dirty it (*Rashi*).]

And although you might have thought to distinguish between these cases, Rabbah bar Rav Huna informs us that it is permitted even in this case of the balcony, though it is certain that the sewage will flow beyond the partitioned area.

A MUSSAR THOUGHT FOR THE DAY

In delineating the laws of rejoicing on Succos, *Rambam* (*Hil. Lulav* 8:15) finds the opportunity to elaborate on the importance of the joy that must accompany the performance of all mitzvos: "The joy that a person must have upon fulfilling a mitzvah and in the love of Hashem is a significant undertaking and service of Hashem. One who holds back from feeling such joy is worthy of punishment. One whose feeling of self-importance and whose desire to maintain his position of prominence and honor keep him from displaying such joy where it is called for, is a sinner and a fool. Conversely, one who disregards his personal honor and dismisses his own pride in order to show excitement and elation for a mitzvah, he is a great man and truly honored."

In his *sefer Alei Shur, R' Shlomo Wolbe* records a series of *mussar vaadim* (meetings) in which the subject of the joy in doing mitzvos is discussed. Following are excerpts from the second *vaad*:

"A reasonable person, who is able to realistically assess his situation, can without much difficulty reach a level of happiness with his lot. The happiness that is required in doing mitzvos, however, is another matter. *Rambam* calls this 'a great undertaking.' *Kuzari* too speaks of the self-preparation and the focusing of one's mind that is necessary before one is able to perform a mitzvah with joy. One is obligated to feel a happiness with the mitzvah itself, out of a sense of love for the One Who commanded us to do it, and from a recognition of the great privilege it is to be able to perform a mitzvah.

"The *Arizal* (*Rav Yitzchak Luria*) once confided to one of his followers that he attained his great levels of spirituality only due to the joy with which he performed every mitzvah. Obviously, we are very far from the level of the *Arizal.* How are we to begin to reach the point where we can perform mitzvos, on our own level, with joy?

"For each person there is one mitzvah, whether it be learning Gemara, praying, the mitzvos of Shabbos or of kindness, with which he feels a special connection or appreciation. The place to begin is with that mitzvah. Do not rush into the mitzvah. Take a moment before beginning it to consider that you are about to do a mitzvah that was commanded to you by Hashem, and through which you will have a connection to Him. The *Chazon Ish* (*R' Avraham Yeshayah Karelitz*) once remarked that one who puts *tzitzis* on his garment in the proper way as required by halachah will be filled with an overwhelming joy for the privilege of being attached to Hashem.

"To reach a genuine feeling of closeness to Hashem through the performance of mitzvos is not something that comes easily. We must remember that there is great benefit to be had even from the exercise of attempting to reach the goal of performing a mitzvah with joy. The work ahead is difficult; with determination and endurance, and with the help of God, we will see success."

HALACHAH OF THE DAY

Today we will continue our discussion of various electronic apparatus, and how they should be dealt with to avoid any transgression of *melachah* on Shabbos.

If one's home is wired with a burglar alarm, it must be disabled before Shabbos. If one forgot to disable it before Shabbos, he may not disable it on Shabbos, nor may he open the door, as that will activate the alarm. However, one is allowed to instruct a non-Jew to disable the alarm. Likewise, if one accidentally set off the alarm on Shabbos, he may not turn it off, but he may instruct a non Jew to do so.

Even when an alarm system is disabled, opening a door often causes various lights and indicators to flash on the alarm's keypad. If this is the case, one must completely deactivate the alarm system before Shabbos. If one forgets to do so and wishes to open the door of the house on Shabbos, there are two methods that may be employed in order to facilitate entering the home. One may ask a non-Jew to open the door, or, alternately, one may instruct a child, who is unaware that he is causing a light to go on, to open the door.

In cases of great need where neither of these two options are practicable, one may instruct an adult to open the door, provided that he is not aware that his action is causing a light to operate.

It is common for people to use timers, or "Shabbos clocks," in order to activate and/or deactivate their lights on Shabbos. At times, people making use of such devices realize on Shabbos that the timer has been improperly set, or that their schedule has changed and will no longer be served by the timing that was entered into the device prior to Shabbos. In the case of electronic timers (namely, the digital non-mechanical variety), it is obvious that the programming may not be changed on Shabbos. Adjusting such devices would be no different than using any other electronic device on Shabbos. However, there are also mechanical devices whose programming may be adjusted through changing the position of the dial, or the removal and replacement of varying types of pins or clips. The question therefore arises: May these devices be adjusted on Shabbos?

We will discuss this question tomorrow, as we continue our discussion of the *melachah* of *kindling.*

A CLOSER LOOK AT THE SIDDUR

Of all the psalms recited during the prayers, regarding only one of them does the halachah say that one should say it with song. This is the Psalm of *Mizmor LeSodah* (*Tehillim* 100:1-5; see *Shulchan Aruch, Orach Chaim* 51:9). In this psalm we sing the following verse: עִבְדוּ אֶת־ה' בְּשִׂמְחָה בֹּאוּ לְפָנָיו בִּרְנָנָה, *Serve Hashem with gladness, come before Him with joyous song.*

What is this service of Hashem about which the Psalmist declares that it must be done with gladness? *R' Shamshon Raphael Hirsch* explains that it does not refer to praying or learning, but to the service of *living*

for Hashem. It is a great and all-encompassing service to fill every action of one's life, especially the mundane, with the spirit of the Divine, by doing everything for the sake of Heaven. It is a truly happy person whose entire life is permeated with the ways of Hashem and whose sole focus in all his endeavors is His service.

One who lives in this way can *come before Him;* he can go to the House of Hashem, the place dedicated to the service of Hashem, *with joyous song.* However, a person who fills his life with the material and the base, and then comes to the House of Hashem for the requisite few minutes at the end of his self-directed day, cannot come with joy, for his visit is not an event that is pleasing to Hashem.

R' Yehudah Elbaz (in his *Shevus Yehudah*) offers another explanation of this verse and the subsequent ones in this psalm. The primary reward that one earns for doing mitzvos is for the joy that one has in their execution. No one can claim reward for the actual service of the mitzvah itself, for every person, by virtue of having been created by Hashem, is like an indentured servant of Hashem who is required to do His bidding without the privilege of remuneration. Only the joy with which he serves cannot be required, and it is for this joy that he is rewarded.

If you *serve HASHEM with gladness* you have earned great reward for your fulfillment of the mitzvos. Then, when the time comes for you to *come before* Hashem in judgment, it will be with *joyous song* and you will receive your recompense.

Why is the reward only for the joy? This is addressed in the next verse: דְּעוּ כִּי־ה׳ הוּא אֱלֹהִים הוּא עָשָׂנוּ וְלוֹ אֲנַחְנוּ, *Know that HASHEM, He is God;* He has made everything and He is All-powerful. *It is He Who has made us and we are His;* we are obligated to serve Him because He is our Creator, and we are all His. Thus, we are not due any reward for heeding His commands. Our entire reward comes from the way in which we serve Him: עִבְדוּ אֶת־ה׳ בְּשִׂמְחָה, *Serve HASHEM with gladness*!

QUESTION OF THE DAY:

Why, when we take the Four Species, do we make the berachah on the lulav?

For the answer, see page 176.

ANSWERS TO QUESTIONS OF THE DAY

Sunday:

Yes. The prohibition applies only to the *sons* of Aharon.

Monday:

Tosafos (*Sanhedrin* 74b) states that he is not.

Tuesday:

We learn that one must make *Kiddush* on Yom Tov (*Mechilta*).

Wednesday:

Toras Kohanim states that in Heaven, equally severe punishment is meted out for transgressing the festivals and for transgressing the Sabbath.

Thursday:

It is called "the month of the oath" because it was in this month (according to this Midrash) that Hashem swore to Avraham that He would be merciful to his children because he had consented to bring Yitzchak to the *Akeidah.*

Friday:

HaKesav VeHaKabbalah states that the ultimate redemption will bring back even the אוֹבְדִים, *lost ones.* This includes even such sinners.

Shabbos:

The *berachah* is recited on the *lulav* because it is the tallest of the *minim.*

פרשת בהר

Parashas Behar

פרשת בהר

SUNDAY

PARASHAS BEHAR

A TORAH THOUGHT FOR THE DAY

כִּי תָבֹאוּ אֶל־הָאָרֶץ אֲשֶׁר אֲנִי נֹתֵן לָכֶם וְשָׁבְתָה
הָאָרֶץ שַׁבָּת לַה'. שֵׁשׁ שָׁנִים תִּזְרַע שָׂדֶךָ וְשֵׁשׁ שָׁנִים
תִּזְמֹר כַּרְמֶךָ וְאָסַפְתָּ אֶת־תְּבוּאָתָהּ.
וּבַשָּׁנָה הַשְּׁבִיעִת שַׁבַּת שַׁבָּתוֹן יִהְיֶה לָאָרֶץ

When you come into the land that I give you,
the land shall observe a Sabbath rest for HASHEM.
For six years you shall sow your field and
for six years you shall prune your vineyard;
and you shall gather its crop. But the seventh year
shall be a complete rest for the land (*Vayikra* 25:2-4).

The observance of the mitzvah of *shemittah* (the Sabbatical year), in which the land is left fallow for a complete year, is surely a great testament to the depths of the *bitachon* (trust) that the Jewish nation has in Hashem. In a primarily agricultural economy, the abandonment of all lands over the course of a year left each individual farmer, and indeed the country as a whole, without any visible source of support. Through this mitzvah, the Jews learned to integrate the lesson that Hashem, Who clearly orchestrated their conquest of the land (*When you come into the land "that I give you,"* v. 2 above), continues to orchestrate their success, both militarily and economically.

Kli Yakar points out, however, that it was not only the one year out of each seven that was unusual. With a careful reading of the verses, he demonstrates that the Torah actually tells us that all seven years — the entire agricultural cycle in Eretz Yisrael — would proceed differently than was customary at the time.

The prevalent custom in those times was to plant fields in a three-year cycle of planting the field for two years and then leaving it fallow for one. If the land were not allowed to rest one year out of three, it would inevitably become devoid of nutrients and too weak to produce an adequate crop the next year.

In contrast to this, the Torah commands that the fields are *not* to be left fallow over the first six years of the *shemittah* cycle: שֵׁשׁ שָׁנִים תִּזְרַע שָׂדֶךָ, *For six years you shall sow your field.* But even with such an unrelenting planting schedule, the Torah assures: וְאָסַפְתָּ אֶת־תְּבוּאָתָהּ, *and you shall gather its crop,* i.e., the earth will continue to produce as if it had had the benefit of the fallow years.

In addition, instead of a meager yield, which would be expected in the sixth year of consecutive planting, the Torah promises that the sixth year will yield the highest quality crop of all the six years. Regarding the sixth year, the verse declares: וְעָשָׂת אֶת־הַתְּבוּאָה לִשְׁלֹשׁ הַשָּׁנִים, *it will yield "the" crop for three years* (v. 21). This indicates that the same crop, i.e., the same amount of harvest, would suffice for three years.

By living continuously with such a clearly miraculous agricultural cycle, the Jewish people are constantly reminded that they cannot take credit for their economic successes. The miracles of the six years would attest to Hashem's central role in providing for the sustenance of the people. And the practice of the seventh year, when they would completely abandon all physical efforts toward their sustenance, would reinforce this lesson and allow it to be internalized.

MISHNAH OF THE DAY: ERUVIN 8:10

The previous Mishnah discussed under what circumstances waste water may be poured into a *chatzeir* when the water will run from there into the *reshus harabim.* The following Mishnah continues discussing this topic:

רַבִּי אֱלִיעֶזֶר בֶּן יַעֲקֹב אוֹמֵר — *R' Eliezer ben Yaakov says:* בִּיב שֶׁהוּא קָמוּר אַרְבַּע אַמּוֹת בִּרְשׁוּת הָרַבִּים — If ***a drainage conduit*** running from a *chatzeir* through the *reshus harabim* ***is covered for*** its first ***four amos in the reshus harabim,***[1] שׁוֹפְכִים לְתוֹכוֹ מַיִם בְּשַׁבָּת — ***they may pour*** waste ***water into it on the Sabbath.***[2] וַחֲכָמִים אוֹמְרִים — ***But the Sages say:*** אֲפִילוּ גַּג אוֹ חָצֵר מֵאָה אַמָּה — ***Even*** if the conduit runs alongside ***a roof or chatzeir that is one hundred amos*** long before reaching the *reshus harabim,* לֹא יִשְׁפּוֹךְ עַל פִּי הַבִּיב — ***one may not***

NOTES

1. This means that the conduit used to drain water from a *chatzeir* into the *reshus harabim* is covered for the first 4 *amos* of its length after it emerges into the *reshus harabim* (*Rashi*).

2. The covered portion of the conduit must be 4 *amos* by 4 *amos* in area [or 16 square *amos*] (*Rashi* as explained by *Tosafos*). An earthen conduit that has this area is capable of absorbing the 2 *se'ah* of water that a person uses daily. Therefore, the conduit will usually be empty before the Sabbath, and none of the sewage will flow beyond the covered area on the Sabbath. Even if, on occasion, there is some water in the conduit before the Sabbath, and as a result the sewage poured out on the Sabbath flows into the *reshus harabim,* it is an unintended transfer. Since no Biblical infraction would occur even if he intended this to happen — because he is not pouring directly into the *reshus harabim* — it is permitted in this case (*Rashi*).

pour directly *into the opening of the conduit.*[3] אֲבָל שׁוֹפֵךְ מִגַּג לְגַג — *However, he pours* water *from roof to roof,* וְהַמַּיִם יוֹרְדִין לַבִּיב — *and the water will* then *descend to the conduit.*[4]

The previous Mishnah taught that one may pour water into a *chatzeir* if it is 4 *amos* square. The Mishnah now explains what areas may be measured together to equal the 4 *amos* square that is necessary:

הֶחָצֵר וְהָאַכְסַדְרָה מִצְטָרְפִין לְאַרְבַּע אַמּוֹת — *A chatzeir and* an adjoining *portico combine to* the total of *four amos.*[5]

NOTES

3. Although the conduit travels a sufficient distance in the *chatzeir* to absorb 2 *se'ah* of water, since he pours directly into the conduit and the water exits to the *reshus harabim* with some intensity, he might be accused of disposing of the water right next to the *reshus harabim,* and specifically intending to discharge it from his *chatzeir* (*Rashi*).

Although the area of the conduit is sufficient to absorb the usual amount of water — 2 *se'ah* — the Sages prohibit pouring water into such a conduit. They disagree with the view expressed in Mishnah 9, according to which water may be poured into any courtyard that has an area of 16 square *amos.* [That view reflects the opinion of R' Eliezer ben Yaakov, and is disputed by the Sages here (based on the view of R' Zeira in the Gemara 88a).] In their opinion, only if the courtyard (or ditch) measures 4 *amos* (or more) *in both dimensions* may water be poured into it. If it does not measure 4 *amos* in one dimension, it is prohibited even if it has a total area of 16 square *amos* (e.g., it is 8 by 2 *amos*). See *Gems from the Gemara.*

4. The water will then not exit the *chatzeir* with such intensity, and the previous concern does not apply. [In Talmudic times, the roofs were basically flat and coated with a thick plaster. A comprehensive system of drainage grooves was built into the plaster to cause the rainwater to run off. Therefore, when one would pour water onto the roof, it would flow into the drainage system of the roof.]

5. The Mishnah explains that two adjoining areas, although differing in their functions, may be measured together so that their combined areas equal 4 *amos.*

GEMS FROM THE GEMARA

As noted above, the Sages and R' Eliezer ben Yaakov disagree as to whether it is permitted to pour water into any courtyard having an area of 16 square *amos.* According to the Sages, only if the courtyard (or ditch) measures 4 *amos* (or more) in both dimensions may water be poured into it. If it is smaller than 4 *amos* in either dimension, it is prohibited even if it has a total area of 16 square *amos* (e.g., it is 8 by 2 *amos*). R' Eliezer ben Yaakov maintains that pouring water is permitted there. The Gemara explains that the disagreement between the Sages and R' Eliezer centers on the reason for the dispensation to pour out water in a courtyard.

As explained in the previous Mishnah, causing the water to flow out from the courtyard to the public domain is only Rabbinically prohibited (as long as one does not pour directly into the private domain), and the Rabbis permitted it whenever no intent to have it go into the public domain is evident. R' Eliezer ben Yaakov is of the opinion that this requirement is met whenever the 2-*se'ah* measure of water is generally absorbed by the ground of the courtyard. He therefore permits water to be poured out in any courtyard or conduit having a total area equivalent to 16 square *amos,* even though it measures less than 4 *amos* on one side.

The Sages, however, consider this insufficient, and require yet another condition — that it appear as though the person pouring out the water has an interest in its remaining in the courtyard. Since the courtyards of those days were of earth, it was common to spread water over them to keep the dust down, and a person pouring out water into his courtyard would appear to be doing it for this purpose. However, this would only be done in a courtyard measuring at least 4 *amos* square. A courtyard less than 4 *amos* in width was too narrow [and too constricted in its use] for the proprietor to bother with spreading water over it. For this reason, one may not pour out water in such a courtyard according to the Sages, although it has an area of 16 square *amos* and is thus able to absorb the water. Similarly, a conduit, even if it measures 4 *amos* in width, is not accorded this dispensation because no one is concerned with the level of dust in it.

A MUSSAR THOUGHT FOR THE DAY

In a *mussar* lecture on *Parashas Behar, R' Chaim Shmulevitz* discussed the proper approach to *bitachon.*

According to some authorities, the highest level of *bitachon* is for one to completely abandon all natural efforts to satisfy his physical needs. The source for this approach is that which *Chazal* relate about the generation of the prophet Yirmiyah. When he chastised the people that they were not learning Torah, they told him that they did not have time to learn, since they were busy earning a livelihood. In response, Yirmiyah retrieved a jar of manna that was stored in the Holy of Holies in the Temple and showed it to them. "See how your forefathers survived

without any effort on their part at all. As long as you learn Torah all your needs will be provided for by Hashem!" (See *Rashi* to *Shemos* 16:32.)

There is, however, one caveat to this approach. For a person to merit support from Heaven, he must have complete and total faith in Hashem. The *Alshich* once declared that one who spends his time learning, and has faith in Hashem, will be completely provided for. Of all those who heard him and attempted to live this way, only one was successful — the town wagon driver. He was a simple man, who, through an amazing twist of events, received a chest of gold coins. When the more learned disciples of the *Alshich* asked him why they did not merit such Divine intervention, he replied that only the simple wagon driver had truly believed.

Other authorities hold that even one who lives with complete faith must also arrange some natural source of income for himself. However, one must still remember that it is not his job or business that brings about his sustenance. Work must be done only in order that the curse of Adam — בְּזֵעַת אַפֶּיךָ תֹּאכַל לֶחֶם, *by the sweat of your brow shall you eat bread* — be fulfilled. Once a person has already exerted himself, the "bread" is given to him directly from Hashem.

In fact, in a way, one who works for a living has a distinct advantage in achieving proper *bitachon,* over one who does not, for the former is constantly taught through personal experience that success is not the result of his own efforts. One invests time, energy, and money into one venture, only to find that the bulk of his income is coming from another enterprise entirely, one that he did not expect to be successful.

This is the meaning of the astounding statement of *Chazal* (*Yalkut Shimoni, Tehillim* 881): גָּדוֹל הַנֶּהֱנֶה מִיגִיעַ כַּפָּיו יוֹתֵר מִירֵא שָׁמָיִם, *One who benefits from his own labor is greater than a God-fearing individual.* One who does not work for a living may always harbor thoughts that if he would only put in the effort, he would earn a decent living. One who does work, however, is under no such pretensions. He sees clearly the hand of Hashem that provides sustenance in no relation to the amount or direction of his investment.

QUESTION OF THE DAY:

Why is the command not to plant during shemittah written in the singular, while the command not to plant during Yovel is written in the plural?

For the answer, see page 236.

HALACHAH OF THE DAY

Yesterday, we began discussing the question of whether it is permissible to adjust "Shabbos clocks" on Shabbos.

According to the view of *R' Moshe Feinstein,* it is forbidden under any circumstances to adjust a timer on Shabbos. Depending on the desired outcome of the adjustment, this would at times be a violation of a Biblical prohibition, and in other cases it would involve a Rabbinic prohibition.

Thus, one who wishes an appliance or light to be turned on or off at a time other than the one scheduled, whether earlier or later, may not adjust the timer to achieve that effect. In other words, if the timer is set to go on at 9:00 a.m. and one wants it to go on at 8:00 a.m., he may neither move the dial one hour ahead, nor may he remove the pin and reposition it at the 8:00 setting. Likewise, if the timer is scheduled to go off at 10:00 p.m. and one wishes to keep the lights on until 11:00 p.m., he may not move the timer back, nor reposition the pins in order to keep the lights on for an additional hour.

Not only is one forbidden to cause a light or appliance to turn off or on at a different time from the one originally scheduled, one also may not simply cancel a scheduled action, causing the appliance to remain in its current state. This is due to the fact that the timer may not be handled at all, under the prohibition of *muktzeh.*

The *poskim* debate whether it is permissible to use an elevator on Shabbos, if one will not press any buttons, assuming that a non-Jew will press the buttons. One who finds it necessary to use an elevator on Shabbos should consult a competent halachic authority.

If an electric blanket is turned on before Shabbos, it may be used on Shabbos. Some *poskim* suggest covering the switch with a piece of tape before Shabbos, so that one will not inadvertently change the setting on Shabbos.

This concludes our discussion of electronic appliances and their use on Shabbos. We will now turn our attention to acts that are forbidden by Rabbinic decree in order to protect against violation of *kindling* on Shabbos.

The following activities are prohibited by Rabbinic decree on Shabbos: washing of one's body in hot water and reading alone by the light of an oil lamp. Tomorrow we will begin to elaborate on each of these activities.

A CLOSER LOOK AT THE SIDDUR

The first of the five "*Halleluyah*" chapters (*Tehillim* Ch. 146), which are recited daily in the *Pesukei D'Zimrah* section of the *Shacharis* prayers, deals primarily with the concept of *bitachon.* We are enjoined to abandon any reliance on human beings, even the nobles among them: אַל־תִּבְטְחוּ בִנְדִיבִים בְּבֶן־אָדָם שֶׁאֵין לוֹ תְשׁוּעָה, *Do not rely on nobles, nor on a human being, for he holds no salvation* (v. 3), for a mortal being cannot be depended on in the long run: תֵּצֵא רוּחוֹ יָשֻׁב לְאַדְמָתוֹ בַּיּוֹם הַהוּא אָבְדוּ עֶשְׁתֹּנֹתָיו, *When his spirit departs, he returns to the earth; on that day his plans all perish* (v. 4). Conversely, אַשְׁרֵי שֶׁאֵל יַעֲקֹב בְּעֶזְרוֹ שִׂבְרוֹ עַל־ה׳ אֱלֹהָיו, *Praiseworthy is one whose help is Yaakov's God, whose hope is in* HASHEM, *his God* (v. 5). Hashem is eternal and all-powerful, and there is nothing beyond His control: עֹשֶׂה שָׁמַיִם וָאָרֶץ אֶת־הַיָּם וְאֶת־כָּל־אֲשֶׁר־בָּם, *He is the Maker of heaven and earth, the sea and all that is in them* (v. 6).

Verse 5 in this chapter (cited above), אַשְׁרֵי, *Praiseworthy is one. . . ,* seems repetitive. Is one *whose help is Yaakov's God,* not the same as one *whose hope is in* HASHEM, *his God*? *R' Tzvi Pesach Frank* explains that the verse is not being redundant, but is to be read as one continuous statement. Who is truly praiseworthy? One who, even while the *God of Yaakov is his help,* i.e., he is experiencing success in all his endeavors, continues to place *his hope in* HASHEM, *his God;* he does not claim credit for his accomplishments and does not attribute his successes to his own talents.

The *Satmar Rav, R' Yoel Teitelbaum,* explains the verse differently. According to his approach, the verse is referring to two distinct areas of *bitachon.* He explains that true *bitachon,* where one trusts completely in Hashem in every aspect of his life — and this is not merely an idea that one has learned, but a deep-seated belief that informs his approach to life — is not within the ability of a human being to reach on his own. A person must do whatever he can to foster this feeling and outlook within himself, and then, as with all of one's endeavors, one must have *bitachon* that Hashem will grant him the ability to reach the level of true *bitachon*!

In this way, we can understand an apparently redundant verse in *Yirmiyah* (17:7), which praises the person of complete faith. בָּרוּךְ הַגֶּבֶר אֲשֶׁר יִבְטַח בַּה׳ וְהָיָה ה׳ מִבְטַחוֹ, *Blessed is the man who trusts in* HASHEM, *and* HASHEM *is his trust.* The Satmar Rav explains that the end of the verse is not merely paraphrasing the beginning, but is adding that besides trusting in Hashem in all of his other endeavors, one also places his trust in Hashem in the achievement of this very *bitachon.*

The Satmar Rav explains our verse in this vein as well. אַשְׁרֵי שֶׁאֵל יַעֲקֹב בְּעֶזְרוֹ, *Praiseworthy is one whose help is Yaakov's God,* i.e., he trusts in Hashem to help him in every aspect of his life, including that of achieving the quality of trust; שִׂבְרוֹ עַל־ה׳ אֱלֹהָיו, and for *his hope* and trust in Hashem, he also relies *on HASHEM, his God.*

פרשת בהר

MONDAY

PARASHAS BEHAR

A TORAH THOUGHT FOR THE DAY

וַעֲשִׂיתֶם אֶת־חֻקֹּתַי וְאֶת־מִשְׁפָּטַי תִּשְׁמְרוּ
וַעֲשִׂיתֶם אֹתָם וִישַׁבְתֶּם עַל־הָאָרֶץ לָבֶטַח

And you shall perform My decrees, and observe My ordinances and perform them; then you shall dwell securely in the land (*Vayikra* 25:18).

Ramban explains that the *decrees* (חֻקֹּתַי) mentioned in this verse are the laws of *shemittah* and *Yovel* discussed previously, and the *ordinances* (מִשְׁפָּטַי) are the laws of fraud and returning of slaves, which are more easily understood. However, the last part of the verse — וִישַׁבְתֶּם עַל־הָאָרֶץ לָבֶטַח, *then you shall dwell securely in the land* — is explained by *Rashi* to refer specifically to the laws of *shemittah,* for as a result of the sin of not keeping *shemittah,* the Jews will be exiled from the land. This is echoed by the Mishnah in *Avos* (5:11) that states: גָּלוּת בָּאָה לָעוֹלָם עַל עוֹבְדֵי עֲבוֹדָה זָרָה וְעַל גִּלּוּי עֲרָיוֹת וְעַל שְׁפִיכוּת דָּמִים וְעַל שְׁמִטַּת הָאָרֶץ, *Exile comes to the world on account of idolatry, immorality, murder, and not keeping the laws of shemittah.*

The question may be asked: Why does failing to observe *shemittah* carry the penalty of exile? *Maharam Schik* (to *Avos* ibid.) explains that the lesson of *shemittah* is that Hashem is the true owner of the land and the One responsible for its production. When a person truly believes that Hashem controls the production of the land, and that He can cause it to bring forth the plentiful pre-*shemittah* crop that will sustain those who abstain from planting during *shemittah,* he will not find it difficult to fulfill the mitzvah. However, if a person believes that it is he who is in charge, it will be difficult for him to sit back and refrain from working the land. The punishment for such people is ejection from the land that they deem to be their own. This demonstrates that Hashem is the true owner of the land.

Beis Shaul offers another explanation. He cites the Gemara in *Gittin* (57b) that remarks upon the miraculous ability of Eretz Yisrael to expand to fit as many inhabitants as necessary. This phenomenon is also noted in the statement of the Mishnah in *Avos* (5:7): וְלֹא אָמַר אָדָם לַחֲבֵרוֹ צַר לִי הַמָּקוֹם שֶׁאָלִין בִּירוּשָׁלַיִם, *No man ever said to his fellow, "There is no place for me to remain overnight in Jerusalem."* *Beis Shaul* likens this ability of the land to accommodate its residents to a garment made for a young child: The garment is made with a hem, which is let down as the child grows. He explains that this special quality of the land is linked to the Jewish people's fulfillment of the mitzvah of *shemittah.* When the

Jews treat Eretz Yisrael with the deference that it is due, the land welcomes them in turn. However, if they treat it with disdain, it shrivels and becomes inhospitable. Eventually, the inhabitants cannot sustain themselves therein, and the result is exile.

MISHNAH OF THE DAY: ERUVIN 8:11

The Mishnah describes one last case that deals with pouring water into a *chatzeir*:

וְכֵן — ***Similarly,***[1] שְׁתֵּי דְיוֹטָאוֹת זוֹ כְּנֶגֶד זוֹ — if ***two upper stories are opposite each other,*** with a *chatzeir* of less than 4 *amos* below, so that it is necessary to make a cesspool to permit pouring water into the *chatzeir,* מִקְצָתָן עָשׂוּ עוּקָה — and ***some of them*** [the residents of one] ***made a cesspool*** in the *chatzeir* to contain their water, וּמִקְצָתָן לֹא עָשׂוּ עוּקָה — ***and some of them*** [the residents of the other] ***did not make a cesspool;*** אֶת שֶׁעָשׂוּ עוּקָה מוּתָּרִין — the residents of ***[the story] that made a cesspool are permitted*** to pour their water into the *chatzeir,*[2] אֶת שֶׁלֹּא עָשׂוּ עוּקָה אֲסוּרִין — but the residents of ***[the story] that did not make a cesspool are forbidden*** to pour their water into the *chatzeir.*[3]

NOTES

1. According to our interpretation of the Mishnah, which follows *Rashi,* the word וְכֵן, *similarly,* is out of place, because what follows is not similar to the previous case. Therefore, we must assume that this word was not present in *Rashi's* version. However, *Meiri* and *R' Yehonasan* offer an alternative explanation that is compatible with the printed version; see there.

2. The pit they made is effective in removing the prohibition to pour out the water, as stated above, Mishnah 9.

As explained below, even the residents who made the cesspool may not pour the water directly into the *chatzeir;* they may pour water only on the floor of their balcony, so that it will run off into the cesspool below (see *Gems from the Gemara*).

3. The Sages prohibited those who did not make a pit from even pouring water onto the balcony and allowing it to fall into the *chatzeir* (see *Gems from the Gemara*).

QUESTION OF THE DAY:

What is the difference between the blessing of* וִישַׁבְתֶּם עַל־הָאָרֶץ לָבֶטַח *(in Behar, 25:18) and* וִישַׁבְתֶּם לָבֶטַח בְּאַרְצְכֶם *(in Bechukosai, 26:5)?

For the answer, see page 236.

GEMS FROM THE GEMARA

The Mishnah taught that if two upper stories are opposite each other over a small *chatzeir* and the residents of only one of the balconies made a cesspool, only those residents may pour water into the *chatzeir.* The Gemara quotes Rava as saying that even if the residents of both stories joined in an *eruv,* so that they may carry into the *chatzeir,* nevertheless those who did not make a cesspool may not pour their sewage into their neighbors' cesspool on the Sabbath. Although those residents may carry their wastes down to the *chatzeir,* Rava still prohibits them from pouring the wastes into the *chatzeir.*

Abaye challenged this ruling by asking why those residents who did not make a cesspool, but have joined with the other residents in an *eruv,* are prohibited from pouring water into the *chatzeir.* For even if the 4 *se'ah* of water ordinarily used by the two households exceeds the cesspool's capacity of 2 *se'ah,* it was taught in a Baraisa that we are not concerned about unintentional overflow!

The Gemara accepts Abaye's objection and suggests that Rava was misquoted, and he must have said: The Mishnah's ruling prohibiting those residents who did not make a cesspool from pouring water into the *chatzeir* is limited to a case where they did not join in an *eruv* with the residents who did make the cesspool. Since they may not carry into the *chatzeir,* they may not pour water into the *chatzeir* either. [However, the residents who did make the cesspool may pour water into the *chatzeir* even though they, too, may not carry into the *chatzeir* in the absence of an *eruv.* This is because the Mishnah here does not refer to pouring directly into the *chatzeir* (which is forbidden to all in the absence of an *eruv*), but rather to indirect pouring. That is, they may pour water on the floor of their balcony, and it will run off into the cesspool below. Although deliberate runoff is not permitted into the *reshus harabim,* it is permitted into an unjoined *chatzeir.*]

But if they joined in an *eruv,* they are both permitted to pour water into the *chatzeir,* since they may carry into the *chatzeir.*

Now, since even the residents who made the cesspool are permitted to pour their wastes into the *chatzeir* only indirectly (as explained above), why is the same leniency not available also to those who did not join in making the cesspool?

Rav Ashi explains that the residents who did not join in an *eruv* may not pour water into their neighbors' cesspool, even indirectly, as this is prohibited by Rabbinic decree, lest they go to take water out to the cesspool and pour the water there. That is, since the residents of the second balcony are distant from their neighbors' cesspool, the method of indirect transfer described above (see note 2) will significantly muddy their area of the *chatzeir.* Therefore, they might unwittingly descend to pour their water directly into the cesspool (*Tosafos*). Since this would violate the prohibition against carrying into an unjoined *chatzeir,* they are prohibited from even indirect transfer. Those residents who did, however, participate in the making of the cesspool, probably put it in a place where it is readily accessible from their balcony. Therefore we are not concerned that they will descend into the *chatzeir* with their wastes (*Rashba*).

A MUSSAR THOUGHT FOR THE DAY

In *A Torah Thought for the Day* we cited the Mishnah in *Avos* that lists four causes for exile: idolatry, immorality, murder, and neglect of the laws of *shemittah.* The inclusion of neglect of *shemittah* in this list seems somewhat perplexing. Idolatry, immorality and murder are the three cardinal sins, and a Jew is required to give up his life to avoid transgressing them. *Shemittah,* on the other hand, does not carry such a requirement. Moreover, idolatry, murder and many violations of immorality all carry the death penalty; *shemittah* does not. Why is *shemittah* grouped together with these severe sins?

An explanation is offered in the name of *Rav Shmuel Rosenberg* of Unsdorf, based on a statement in the preface to *Chovos HaLevovos* that explains that the reason the *yetzer hara* (evil inclination) in a person is often so much stronger than his *yetzer tov* (good inclination) is because the *yetzer hara* is so much better nourished. The food of the *yetzer hara* is the earthly pleasures, including eating and drinking, that a person pursues during his life, while the food of the *yetzer tov* is the Torah and mitzvos that he performs. As a person must eat to survive, he perforce supplies the *yetzer hara* with constant nourishment, while the *yetzer tov* is often undernourished.

However, notes R' Shmuel, there is a way to ensure that the physical food does not serve to strengthen the *yetzer hara* — by scrupulously adhering to the laws of *shemittah.* For just as Shabbos is the soul of the week, *shemittah* is the soul of the seven-year cycle; keeping its laws imbues all of the produce with the sanctity that prevents it from nourishing the *yetzer hara.* But if those laws are not kept, then the *yetzer hara*

will grow ever stronger, and the person can be led further and further down the path of sin, powerless to resist, until he is susceptible to falling prey even to the lure of cardinal sins. Thus, it is correct to list transgression of the *shemittah* laws along with those sins, for if a person *does* succumb to such sins, it is quite possible that it was neglect of the *shemittah* laws that started him down the slippery slide to transgressing them.

HALACHAH OF THE DAY

The Sages enacted a prohibition against washing one's body with hot water on Shabbos. The reasoning behind this decree was as follows: While, in theory, it would seem to be permissible for one to heat water prior to the onset of Shabbos and to use this water in order to wash on Shabbos, the Sages were concerned that unscrupulous bathhouse attendants would heat water on Shabbos for washing and claim that the water had been heated before Shabbos. By doing so, the attendants would violate two *melachos,* the *melachah* of *kindling* by starting a fire, as well as the *melachah* of *cooking* through the heating of the water. In order to prevent this desecration of Shabbos from taking place, the Sages forbade one to wash himself in hot water on Shabbos — even by using water that was heated before Shabbos.

The decree of the Sages prohibits one from washing his entire body, or even a majority of his body, on Shabbos. Furthermore, the prohibition applies regardless of whether one washes his entire body at once, or one limb at a time. It also applies to any type of washing, whether showering, bathing in a tub, or washing oneself with hot water from a utensil. With regard to this prohibition, "hot water" is defined as water that is above body temperature, or greater than 98.6 degrees Fahrenheit. Pertaining to this prohibition, water below body temperature is considered to be cold water.

One is permitted to wash less than 50 percent of his body in hot water, provided that the water was heated before Shabbos.

Water that was set up to be heated before Shabbos, even if it first became hot on Shabbos, is considered to have been heated before Shabbos, and may therefore be used for washing on Shabbos. For instance, if an urn was filled with water before Shabbos and the water became heated on Shabbos, one may still use that hot water to wash himself on Shabbos. Likewise, if one left the hot water tap running before Shabbos, one may wash his hands with this water on Shabbos. This is permitted because in these cases the actions that caused the heating of the water were performed before Shabbos.

However, if one performed an action that caused heating of water on Shabbos, even if it is one that does not violate any prohibition, the water that was heated as a result of his action may not be used for washing on Shabbos. For example, if one placed water next to a *blech* on Shabbos (in a place where the water could not possibly reach the temperature of 160 degrees), and the water became lukewarm as a result, even though this does not entail a transgression of the *melachah* of *cooking,* the water may not be used for washing even a single limb on Shabbos.

A CLOSER LOOK AT THE SIDDUR

Today we will begin to discuss the third of the Six Remembrances, the actions of Amalek, which we are bidden to remember daily by reciting the verse (*Devarim* 25:17-18):

> זָכוֹר אֵת אֲשֶׁר־עָשָׂה לְךָ עֲמָלֵק בַּדֶּרֶךְ בְּצֵאתְכֶם מִמִּצְרָיִם. אֲשֶׁר קָרְךָ בַּדֶּרֶךְ וַיְזַנֵּב בְּךָ כָּל־הַנֶּחֱשָׁלִים אַחֲרֶיךָ וְאַתָּה עָיֵף וְיָגֵעַ וְלֹא יָרֵא אֱלֹהִים
> *Remember what Amalek did to you on the way as you were leaving Egypt, that he happened upon you on the way, and he struck those of you who were hindmost, all the weaklings at your rear, when you were faint and exhausted, and he did not fear God.*

These verses describe the attack that was launched by the Amalekites upon the Jews after they left Egypt. It is a positive commandment to always remember their ambush and their evil deeds.

Rambam (in *Sefer HaMitzvos* 189) explains that this remembrance is not required merely to commemorate a historical episode that took place many years ago. Rather, we are bidden to always remember Amalek's pernicious deeds in order to inspire hatred of them at all times, and to constantly rile up the masses to loathe and despise them.

Rambam seems to view this hatred as a catalyst to fulfillment of the next related commandment — to erase the memory of Amalek — that is stated in the next verse: תִּמְחֶה אֶת־זֵכֶר עֲמָלֵק מִתַּחַת הַשָּׁמָיִם, *you shall erase the memory of Amalek from beneath the heavens.* Reading about the deeds of Amalek should awaken a visceral and emotional reaction, a refreshed feeling of hatred toward them.

One might ask: Why was Amalek singled out from among all the nations in the world that have oppressed and harmed the Jews?

The answer lies in three words of the *Rambam*: בְּהַקְדִּימוֹ לְהָרַע לָנוּ, *they made a preemptive strike to harm us.*

This is explained in the *Sefer HaChinuch* [603] as follows: While other nations attacked the Jewish people, some with great and devastating effect, there was always a reason for doing so, be it revenge, or jealousy, or to capture land, etc. However, at this point in history, when the Jewish nation was in its infancy, newly formed without a home or a place to go, they nevertheless cast a spell of fear on all the surrounding peoples. Amalek decided to attack them for one reason only — to undermine and minimize the status of the nation that had recently been recognized throughout the world as Hashem's chosen people, as stated in the verse: עַד־יַעֲבֹר עַמְּךָ ה׳, *Until Your people passes through,* H*ASHEM* (*Shemos* 15:16). For this grave assault on Hashem, their fate is dictated by Hashem — total extinction — to remind us that evil for the sake of evil, with no other motive, has no future.

A TORAH THOUGHT FOR THE DAY

וְכִי תֹאמְרוּ מַה־נֹּאכַל בַּשָּׁנָה הַשְּׁבִיעִת הֵן
לֹא נִזְרָע וְלֹא נֶאֱסֹף אֶת־תְּבוּאָתֵנוּ.
וְצִוִּיתִי אֶת־בִּרְכָתִי לָכֶם בַּשָּׁנָה הַשִּׁשִּׁית
וְעָשָׂת אֶת־הַתְּבוּאָה לִשְׁלֹשׁ הַשָּׁנִים

If you will say: What will we eat in the seventh year?
— behold! we will not sow and not gather in our crops!
I shall ordain My blessings for you in the sixth year,
and it will yield a crop sufficient for the three-year period
(*Vayikra* 25:20-21).

Many commentaries find the implication of the above verses difficult. In either case — whether they ask the question, "What shall we eat?" or not — a triple crop is necessary in order for them to survive the *shemittah.* Is the special blessing of a triple crop bestowed upon them only if they make such a request?

Sforno explains that the ideal way for the people to approach the coming *shemittah* year is without any questions at all. They are to have full trust in Hashem that He will provide for all their needs. When the people are on this level then the crop is blessed, not with a triple quantity, but a triple *quality.* In the parlance of *Chazal,* אוֹכֵל קִמְעָא וְהוּא מִתְבָּרֵךְ בְּמֵעָיו, *one eats a bit and it becomes blessed in his innards.* The harvest will be of such quality that even a small amount will provide a great deal of nourishment.

This super-quality harvest, however, is insufficient when the people are not at an optimal level of *bitachon.* Since it *appears* to be the same as the regular harvest, they will not see the blessing and will worry throughout the year about the next year. The Torah therefore writes that if the people do ask questions, then *I shall ordain My blessings for you,* i.e., the blessing will have to take the form of a plentiful harvest, so that the people can see with their own eyes that Hashem has provided for their needs. [However, this lack of *bitachon* comes at a cost. The tripled quantity of produce will require three times as much work to process and store, work that the person with true *bitachon* will not have to do.]

It once occurred that a man invested his entire fortune in a business venture. In the event that the venture failed, he stood to lose everything and be cast into abject poverty. Because of the risks involved, he approached the *Netziv* (*R' Naftali Tzvi Yehudah Berlin*) to ask him to pray for success. The *Netziv* responded by encouraging the man to place his trust in Hashem, and then he will surely merit His assistance. "Rebbi," answered the man, "I know that it is good to have *bitachon,* but I can't

פרשת בהר
TUESDAY
PARASHAS BEHAR

seem to stop worrying." The *Netziv* replied by quoting our verse: "The Torah repeats the doubts of the people, expressed in their query, *'What will we eat in the seventh year?'* It seems, however, that the seventh year was not the right time for this question. Each year is provided for by the harvest of the previous year. During the sixth year of the *shemittah* cycle, it was permitted to work the land as usual. Thus, the seventh year is provided for by the produce of the sixth. Why then would they spend the seventh year worrying, when their storehouses are full from the harvest of the sixth?"

The *Netziv* explained: A rich man, who is accustomed to having his every need fulfilled at all times, will have a very difficult time achieving *bitachon.* The moment there is a question about his future, even if at the time all his needs are provided for, he will inevitably worry. So too, the people who had been accustomed to having storehouses filled for the future, even while having enough for the present year, worried about the next one.

"Your job," concluded the *Netziv,* "is to strengthen yourself in your faith in Hashem, and He will provide!"

MISHNAH OF THE DAY: ERUVIN 9:1

The law of *eruvei chatzeiros* prohibits carrying objects from one private domain to another if the residents of the two areas have not joined in an *eruv.* This Mishnah proceeds to clarify what constitutes "another" domain in regard to this law:

כָּל גַּגּוֹת הָעִיר רְשׁוּת אַחַת — ***All*** adjoining ***roofs***[1] ***of the town are one domain,*** even though the houses below are owned and occupied by different people. That is, carrying from one roof to the other is permitted, even if the residents below did not join in an *eruv,*[2] **וּבִלְבַד שֶׁלֹּא יְהֵא גַּג גָּבוֹהַּ עֲשָׂרָה אוֹ נָמוּךְ עֲשָׂרָה** — ***provided that one roof is not ten***

NOTES

1. The Mishnah refers to adjoining roofs. As regards transferring an object between non-adjoining roofs, see *Orach Chaim* 353:1.

2. [The houses below are considered separate domains because they are constantly used by their owners as private areas. This exclusivity Rabbinically marks them off as separate domains, and an *eruv* is necessary to permit carrying between them.] Although the roofs are also used as private areas, they are not used regularly. Thus, their level of exclusiveness is not significant enough to render them separate domains. Therefore, objects that began the Sabbath on one roof may be transferred to another roof even without the benefit of an *eruv* (*Rashi*).

tefachim ***higher or lower*** than the other roof. But if there is a 10-*tefach* height difference between the roofs, carrying between them is forbidden, according to this Tanna.[3] דִּבְרֵי רַבִּי מֵאִיר — These are ***the words of R' Meir.*** וַחֲכָמִים אוֹמְרִים — ***But the Sages say:*** כָּל אֶחָד וְאֶחָד רְשׁוּת בִּפְנֵי עַצְמוֹ — ***Each*** roof ***is a domain unto itself.*** Therefore, if the residents below did not join in an *eruv,* carrying from one roof to another is forbidden.[4] רַבִּי שִׁמְעוֹן אוֹמֵר — ***R' Shimon says:*** אֶחָד גַּגּוֹת וְאֶחָד חֲצֵירוֹת וְאֶחָד קַרְפֵּיפוֹת — Adjoining ***roofs, chatzeiros, and karpafs***[5] רְשׁוּת אַחַת הֵן לְכֵלִים שֶׁשָּׁבְתוּ לְתוֹכָן — ***are one domain in regard to utensils that began the Sabbath in*** one of ***[these areas],***[6] וְלֹא לְכֵלִים שֶׁשָּׁבְתוּ בְּתוֹךְ הַבַּיִת — ***but not in regard to utensils that began the Sabbath in the house.*** That is, even if a utensil that began the Sabbath in the house was lawfully brought out to an outdoor enclosure, it may not be transferred to another outdoor enclosure.[7]

NOTES

3. R' Meir holds that there is a general prohibition against placing objects down on a 10-*tefach* high, 4-*tefach* wide post in a *reshus hayachid.* Even though both the surrounding area from which the object is taken and the post onto which it is being placed are *reshus hayachid,* R' Meir prohibits this, because such a situation could be confused with a post of such dimensions located in a *reshus harabim,* where a similar transfer is Biblically prohibited.

4. Unlike R' Meir, the Sages consider roofs to be separate domains, just like the houses below them.

5. [A *karpaf* is an enclosed area not designated for residential purposes.] The Mishnah here refers exclusively to *karpafs* that do not exceed 2 *beis se'ah* (*Rashi*).

6. I.e., any object that was in an outdoor enclosure when the Sabbath began may be freely moved throughout these contiguous areas, even if the areas are owned by different people who have not joined in a common *eruv.*

These three areas, because they are not regularly used as private areas, are all considered one domain with regard to the laws of *eruvei chatzeiros,* according to R' Shimon; thus, one may carry between the three areas even without an *eruv* (*Rashi*). R' Shimon agrees with R' Meir's basic premise that the separation of domains in regard to the laws of *eruv* is limited to houses only (as they are constantly in use). However, he disagrees with R' Meir on two points: (a) He permits objects to be transferred from one roof to another regardless of the difference in their heights, and (b) he permits objects to be transferred even between roofs, *chatzeiros* and *karpafs* (*Rav*).

7. This is because the utensil retains the status of the domain in which it began the Sabbath. Therefore, although one now wishes to transfer the utensil from *chatzeir* to *chatzeir,* for example, it is as if he were transferring it from the house in which it began the Sabbath to the second *chatzeir,* which is forbidden in the absence of an *eruv.*

For example, if a person brought a chair from his house into his *chatzeir* on the Sabbath, he may not move that chair to his friend's *chatzeir* unless the two have joined in an *eruv.*

GEMS FROM THE GEMARA

The Mishnah taught that according to the Sages, each roof is a domain unto itself, and one may not carry from one person's roof to another's roof unless the two are merged through an *eruv.* This implies that carrying on each roof remains permitted. But to what extent?

The Gemara cites a dispute between Rav and Shmuel in this matter. Rav says that according to the Sages, we may carry on either roof only within 4 *amos.* Since each roof is entirely open to the other one and they do not share an *eruv,* carrying on each roof is prohibited as in a *karmelis,* where carrying is permitted only within the restricted area of 4 *amos* by 4 *amos.* [Each roof is entirely open to an area that is "forbidden to it" (נִפְרַץ בִּמְלוֹאוֹ לְמָקוֹם הָאָסוּר), i.e., to an area to which the transfer of objects is forbidden. As a result, it is forbidden to carry even within the confines of each area (*Rashi*).] But Shmuel says that, according to the Sages, it is permitted to carry on the entire roof. Only carrying from roof to roof is prohibited.

The Gemara explains the basis of this dispute. When there is a space between the two buildings, so that a person standing on the roof and looking directly down can see the walls below that separate the two buildings, Rav and Shmuel would both agree that these walls are viewed as a valid separation between the roofs, and carrying on each roof area is unreservedly permitted. [The Sinaitic rule of *gud asik* (extend and raise up) allows us to view the walls of the house as extending upwards and partitioning the roof surfaces. Thus, the roofs are not legally considered open to each other (*Rashi*).]

Rav and Shmuel do argue, however, in a case where the two buildings are attached. In this case, Rav permits carrying on either roof only within 4 *amos,* because he does not apply the rule of "extend and raise up the partition" to a covered wall (i.e., a wall that cannot be seen). But Shmuel says that it is permitted to carry on the entire roof, because he applies the rule of "extend and raise up the partition" even to covered walls, and these walls serve to partition the area above. Thus, in the present case, since the two buildings are separated by walls, carrying on each roof is permitted.

The Gemara cites our Mishnah as apparently supporting Shmuel's position. For the Mishnah quotes the Sages as saying that each roof "is a domain unto itself," implying that although carrying between the roofs is prohibited, each roof in itself is an entirely permitted area. This fits well with the view of Shmuel, but presents a difficulty to Rav, who prohibits carrying on each roof beyond 4 *amos.* The Gemara reconciles the Mishnah with Rav's opinion by saying that the Mishnah could mean that each roof is a separate domain and carrying within 4 *amos* is permitted, whereas carrying from roof to roof is forbidden even within 4 *amos.*

A MUSSAR THOUGHT FOR THE DAY

A person is required to balance the approach toward his livelihood — part prayer and *bitachon* in Hashem, and part physical efforts to bring in an income (see *A Mussar Thought for the Day,* Sunday). Indeed, this balance must be struck in relation to all of a person's endeavors. We learn this from Yaakov Avinu, who prepared himself for the meeting with his murderous brother Eisav by praying as well as by preparing for warfare.

R' Yerucham Levovitz maintains that the more difficult part of this approach, by far, is the involvement in the natural world, for one must be ever vigilant not to fall into the trap of thinking that it his own efforts that bring about the results. When one's involvement consists only of praying for sustenance, there is no risk of his thinking that he was responsible. However, when working and receiving his sustenance from his work, one can forget that he is merely fulfilling the will of Hashem by working, and that the results are entirely dependent on Hashem.

This concept is illustrated beautifully by the following Midrash:

"There were four kings whose requests of Hashem differed from one another. Dovid HaMelech declared, 'I shall pursue my enemies and seize them.' Hashem responded, 'I shall grant it.' Asa declared, 'I do not have the strength to actually seize them; I will pursue them, and You, Hashem, will do the rest.' Hashem responded, 'I shall grant it.' Yehoshafat declared, 'I have no strength to pursue my enemies. I will sing (pray) to Hashem, and You, Hashem, will do the rest.' Hashem responded, 'I shall grant it.' Finally, Chizkiyahu declared, 'I do not even have the strength to sing to Hashem; I will sleep on my bed, and You, Hashem, will do the rest.' Hashem answered, 'I shall grant it.' "

What is the meaning of this Midrash? Clearly, the various kings were not referring to physical strength (surely pursuing the enemy and praying are not feats that demand might!). It is equally implausible to suggest that the later kings had more *bitachon* than the earlier ones, for Dovid HaMelech is repeatedly cited as the most righteous of the kings.

The true meaning of the Midrash becomes clear in light of the above lesson.

The last of the kings mentioned, Chizkiyahu, had the lowest relative level of inherent *bitachon* in Hashem. He feared that if he participated at all in the war, even if only by praying for victory, he would not be able to rise above the feeling, on some level, that he played a part in bringing it about. He therefore declared that he would not do anything, but would rely wholly on Hashem; when victory would be achieved, he would therefore be able to attribute it to its true source. Each preceding king was greater in his level of *bitachon.* They were each able to participate a little bit more in the war, and still wholeheartedly attribute the victory to Hashem. However, none were as great as David, who, in his consummate *bitachon,* could complete the entire victory himself and still have a full appreciation that he was no more than a vehicle of Hashem's actions.

HALACHAH OF THE DAY

We will now continue our discussion of the Rabbinic prohibitions involving *kindling.*

Yesterday, we spoke of the Sages' decree against washing on Shabbos. There are, however, certain cases where one is permitted to wash even his entire body in hot water on Shabbos.

The Sages permitted one to bathe even his entire body in hot water on Shabbos in cases where it is necessary in order to alleviate discomfort. For instance, if one has chicken pox or a rash that causes discomfort, it is permissible to bathe in hot water. However, as noted previously, this may be done only with water that was heated before Shabbos. One must consult a competent halachic authority with regard to the use of medicine in a bath on Shabbos.

It is permissible for a חוֹלֶה שֶׁאֵין בּוֹ סַכָּנָה, *a sick person whose life is not in mortal danger,* to wash his entire body with hot water on Shabbos. This is because the prohibition against washing in water heated before Shabbos is Rabbinic in origin, and the Sages did not apply their decrees to a sick person. Additionally, one may instruct a non-Jew to turn on the hot water tap, or to boil water, for this purpose.

If a child becomes dirty on Shabbos, it is permissible to wash the child's body with hot water. Once again, the water must have been heated before Shabbos.

TUESDAY

PARASHAS BEHAR

If a child has a rash or other skin disorder that causes him discomfort, the child is a חוֹלֶה שֶׁאֵין בּוֹ סַכָּנָה and may be washed with hot water on Shabbos. Additionally, in such cases one may instruct a non-Jew to perform even *melachos* that are otherwise Biblically forbidden on Shabbos. Accordingly, a non-Jew may be asked to place water on a flame, or to turn on the hot water tap, in order to provide the child with hot water for washing. A Jew, however, may perform only Rabbinically forbidden *melachos* for a *choleh she'ein bo sakanah.* If possible, any *melachah* for the ill person done by a Jew should be performed with a *shinui,* i.e., in an unusual manner.

Even in cases where bathing is permitted on Shabbos, it is necessary for one to take care not to transgress any other *melachos* that may come into play when bathing. One may not wash using a bar of soap, due to the possible violation of the *melachos* of *smoothing* and *scraping.*

We will continue this discussion tomorrow.

A CLOSER LOOK AT THE SIDDUR

We have learned (above, *A Torah Thought for the Day*) that Hashem's blessing of sustenance takes two forms: one is the delivering of the food to those who need it, and the other is the blessing in the food itself, that it should have an additional power of nourishment (אוֹכֵל קִמְעָא וּמִתְבָּרֵךְ בְּמֵעָיו). These two aspects of Hashem's blessing are reflected in our prayer for sustenance in the *Year of Prosperity* (בִּרְכַּת הַשָּׁנִים) blessing in the *Shemoneh Esrei.*

We say: וְתֵן בְּרָכָה עַל פְּנֵי הָאֲדָמָה, *give blessing on the face of the earth* [in the winter: טַל וּמָטָר לִבְרָכָה, *give dew and rain for a blessing*], וְשַׂבְּעֵנוּ מִטּוּבָהּ, *and satisfy us from its bounty.* The *Vilna Gaon* explains that the first part of the request is that the food of the earth grow in abundance, while the second part is a prayer that the food have the power to satisfy and sustain.

Another, homiletic, explanation of the phrase, וְשַׂבְּעֵנוּ, *and satisfy us,* is offered by the Gaon. The nature of physical desire is that it is never satiated: *one who has one hundred, desires two hundred.* We ask that we not fall prey to this when receiving our physical nourishment, that we may fill our needs and then be satisfied.

The version of this *berachah* according to the Gaon (and *Arizal*) is, as quoted above, וְשַׂבְּעֵנוּ מִטּוּבָהּ, *and satisfy us from "its" bounty.* The

TUESDAY

PARASHAS BEHAR

pronoun refers to the land (Eretz Yisrael) mentioned in the phrase immediately prior. The focus of our prayer, for those living both inside and outside of Eretz Yisrael, is always the harvest and produce of Eretz Yisrael. *Iyun Tefillah* explains that according to *Chazal,* when Hashem blesses the lands of the earth, He primarily sends his blessings through Eretz Yisrael; therefore, the prayer for Eretz Yisrael is in effect a prayer for blessing for all the lands of the earth.

However, according to many authorities (*Rosh, Ohr Zarua, Magen Avraham, Elyah Rabbah*) the proper version is וְשַׂבְּעֵנוּ מִטּוּבֶךָ, *and satisfy us from "Your" bounty,* since it is Hashem Who blesses the food and gives it the power to satisfy (*Ateres Zekeinim*).

An interesting compromise between these versions is found in the *Ateres Zekeinim.* He writes that when one is in a city, he should say מִטּוּבָהּ and when he is on the road, מִטּוּבֶךָ. *R' Elyah Lopian* explains this unusual formulation based on the difference in meaning between the words. When a person is in the city, his sustenance comes from the food found in the city. He therefore says, "Satisfy us from its (the land's) bounty," referring to the stores of food in the city. However, when traveling, a person usually has a very limited supply of food. Then, his prayer is that the small amount of food that he has should last him until he arrives at his destination. He is in essence asking for the blessing of אוֹכֵל קִמְעָא וּמִתְבָּרֵךְ בְּמֵעָיו, *eating a bit, and having the food blessed in his stomach.* This, as noted above, is the special blessing that comes, not as a result of the bounty of the land, but from Hashem Himself. A traveler therefore says, *Satisfy us from "Your" bounty.*

QUESTION OF THE DAY:

Why does the open miracle of a bumper crop every sixth year not prove to all that Hashem controls the world?

For the answer, see page 236.

A TORAH THOUGHT FOR THE DAY

וְכִי־יָמוּךְ אָחִיךָ וּמָטָה יָדוֹ עִמָּךְ
וְהֶחֱזַקְתָּ בּוֹ גֵּר וְתוֹשָׁב וָחַי עִמָּךְ

If your brother becomes impoverished and his means falter in your proximity, you shall strengthen him — proselyte or resident — so that he can live with you (*Vayikra* 25:35).

This verse is the source of the great mitzvah to help a fellow Jew financially in his time of need. The Midrash comments on this verse: A person who gives a small amount of money to the poor is repaid by Hashem with a small amount. The Midrash asks: Is this fair recompense? In the hands of a poor person, even a small amount of money could mean the difference between a loaf of bread and going hungry. In extreme circumstances, a few pennies could save a man's life. Why, then, does the giver receive only a small amount in return? The Midrash answers that when Hashem repays the small amount in return, it is indeed given when the person is at the end of his strength, when his soul is just about to leave his body. At that point Hashem gives him the few hours of life that he had given to the poor in the form of a few coins.

The *Dubno Maggid* is troubled by this Midrash. Is there no better way to repay a kind act than through such unfortunate circumstances? He answers that in fact this form of repayment is a great kindness from Hashem, Who gives a person his reward at the time that it means the most to him. Even in a case where the money he gave made the difference between life and death to the poor person, how much time did he buy the poor man? At most, the loaf of bread lasted him a day or so. A simple repayment would involve giving the benefactor a few hours of life. However, when Hashem returns these few hours of life to a person, He calculates it in such a way as to give him the maximum benefit.

Often, a doctor will tell the family of a deathly sick person that if the patient makes it through the night, or the next few hours, then there is hope. The doctor understands that the condition from which the patient suffers usually lasts only a given amount of time, after which it weakens and passes. The only question is, does the patient have the strength to survive the few hours while the illness runs its course? If he does, he is on the road to recovery; if not, the illness will claim him in its last hours.

If there is any time that a person would want a few hours of life, it is in such a situation, when those few hours could mean the difference between succumbing to the illness or recovering.

When Hashem wishes to repay one who has given a poor person a few hours, He waits for a time when those few hours will mean the most. Although the giver has received only a few hours in return for the few hours that he gave, it is calculated by Hashem to give him much more than just those few hours; for him, it is a new lease on life.

MISHNAH OF THE DAY: ERUVIN 9:2 (I)

The following Mishnah discusses the laws that apply to a place that is: נִפְרַץ בִּמְלֹאו לְמָקוֹם הָאָסוּר לוֹ, *open entirely to an area that is prohibited to it*:[1]

גַּג גָּדוֹל סָמוּךְ לְקָטָן — ***If a large roof is adjacent to a small one,*** and there is no partition along their common border nor an *eruv* to join them,[2] הַגָּדוֹל מוּתָּר — carrying between ***the large*** roof and the house below ***is permitted,*** because the large roof is partitioned on four sides.[3] וְהַקָּטָן אָסוּר — ***But*** carrying between ***the small*** roof and the house below ***is prohibited,*** because the small roof is completely open to the large one, which is a place forbidden to it.[4]

NOTES

1. There is a rule stating that if an area in which carrying should be permitted is entirely open along one of its sides to an area that is prohibited to it (i.e., to an area into which one may not carry), one may not carry in the first area either.

2. See diagram. The principle of *gud asik* [see above, *Gems from the Gemara,* Tuesday] allows us to extend upward the walls surrounding the exposed perimeters of the roofs, but not the wall that divides the buildings below.

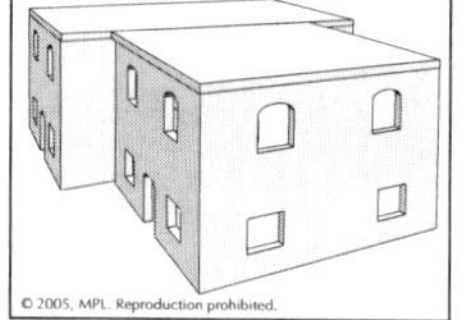

Thus, both roofs are legally partitioned on their three outer sides. And the large roof is partitioned even on the fourth side by sideposts, but the small roof is not. The smaller roof is not wider than 10 *amos;* therefore the gap between the large roof's sideposts is viewed as a mere entrance in its partition.

3. The large roof is like a *chatzeir* that has an entrance to another *chatzeir* but is not entirely open to it. In such cases, the *chatzeir* can remain separate from its neighbor, and carrying is permitted between it and its houses (if the houses are owned by a single individual, or by different owners who have joined in an *eruv*).

4. The imaginary *gud asik* sideposts partition only the large roof, but not the small one. Therefore, the small roof is completely open to the large one, with which it shares no *eruv*. This prohibits carrying between the small roof and the house below.

In using the terms "permitted" and "prohibited," the Mishnah here might refer only to carrying between the roof and the house below. However, the permissibility of carrying objects that began the Sabbath on the roof, on the small roof itself or

Thus, the Mishnah has taught that the sideposts flanking the small roof constitute a one-way wall that partitions the large roof, but not the small one. The Mishnah now presents a similar case:

חָצֵר גְּדוֹלָה שֶׁנִּפְרְצָה לִקְטַנָּה — ***A large chatzeir that was breached into a small one,***[5] **גְּדוֹלָה מוּתֶּרֶת** — carrying between ***the large chatzeir*** and its homes ***is permitted.*** **וּקְטַנָּה אֲסוּרָה מִפְּנֵי שֶׁהִיא כְּפִתְחָהּ שֶׁל גְּדוֹלָה** — ***But*** carrying between ***the small chatzeir*** and its homes ***is prohibited, because [the small chatzeir]*** that is completely open to the large one ***is like the entrance of the large chatzeir,*** and is not considered an independent area.[6]

We will continue the presentation of this Mishnah tomorrow.

NOTES

between the small roof and the large one, is subject to the Tannaic dispute in the previous Mishnah — whether all roofs are one domain or separate ones in regard to objects that began the Sabbath in one of them.

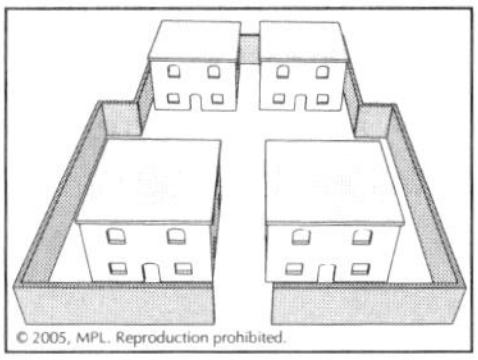

5. See diagram. In this case, the wall separating a narrow *chatzeir* from a wider one collapsed, so that nothing now separates the two. On either side of the narrow *chatzeir,* however, the intervening wall remains intact.

6. See *Gems from the Gemara* for ramifications of the small *chatzeir's* designation as "the entrance of the large one."

GEMS FROM THE GEMARA

The Mishnah refers to a small *chatzeir* as being "the entrance of the large one." The Gemara derives from this Mishnah that the domain of the residents of the large *chatzeir* extends into the small *chatzeir,* rendering it part of the large *chatzeir;* but the domain of the residents of the small *chatzeir* does not extend into the large *chatzeir* to render it part of the small one. The Gemara gives a number of practical applications of this principle:

(1) The Torah (see *Devarim* 22:9) prohibits the mixed planting of grapes and grain or greens. Such mixed planting is called כִּלְאֵי הַכֶּרֶם, *kilei hakerem* [mixtures of the vineyard]. Now, ordinarily, it is permitted to plant these other species at a distance of 4 *amos* or more from the vines in a vineyard. Furthermore, the law of *kilei hakerem* does not apply to different species planted on opposite sides of a legal partition, even if the species are physically in close proximity to each other.

The Gemara here infers from the Mishnah that if vines were planted in the large *chatzeir,* it is forbidden to plant grain or greens *anywhere* in the small *chatzeir* — even at a distance of 4 *amos* from the vines that are in the large one. For the *entire* small *chatzeir* is viewed as the entrance of the large one; thus, any plantings in the small *chatzeir* would be viewed as being in the domain of the large *chatzeir,* which would result in a state of *kilei hakerem* (*Rashi*). And the growth of these plantings in the proximity of the vines prohibits the plantings for all benefit, as the Torah forbids deriving benefit from the grapes or plantings of *kilei hakerem.*

But the grapevines in the large *chatzeir* are permitted, since they are from their standpoint separated by a wall from the small *chatzeir* (and its greens) and not subject to its influence. [The opening in the sideposts of the large *chatzeir* is viewed as a mere entrance in a partition that spans the entire area (*Rashi*).]

(2) To effect divorce, the husband must deposit a bill of divorce [*get*] into his wife's hand, or into her property — provided (according to our Gemara) that she is then present in that property. Accordingly, the Gemara discusses the case of a husband who wishes to divorce his wife by placing the *get* in one of two adjoining *chatzeiros* owned by his wife while she is present in the other:

If the wife is in the large *chatzeir* and her husband places the bill of divorce in the small *chatzeir,* she is divorced. Since the small *chatzeir* is like an annex of the large *chatzeir,* when the wife stands in the large *chatzeir,* her domain and presence extend to the small *chatzeir* as well. The *get* is thus viewed as placed in the presence of the wife, who stands in the large *chatzeir,* and therefore, a *get* placed there is in her presence and valid. However, if the wife is in the small *chatzeir* and her husband places the bill of divorce in the large *chatzeir,* she is not divorced, since the domain of the wife's present location does not extend to the place where the *get* is placed. Therefore, a *get* placed there is not in her presence and is invalid.

(3) A third application involves establishing a quorum of ten for prayer and other procedures. A Baraisa taught that if nine people are in the large *chatzeir* and one person is in the small *chatzeir,* they combine to form a quorum, since the individual in the small *chatzeir* is in the domain of the majority who are in the large *chatzeir.* But if nine people are in the small *chatzeir* and one person is in the large *chatzeir,* they do not combine to form a quorum, since the majority of nine people do not have a tenth in their presence.

(4) A fourth application involves the prohibition against reciting *Krias Shema* (or other sacred words) in the presence of excrement: If there is excrement in the large *chatzeir,* it is forbidden to recite the *Shema* in the small *chatzeir,* since one who recites *Shema* in the small *chatzeir* does so in the annex of the large *chatzeir* and thus in the presence of its excrement. However, if there is excrement in the small *chatzeir,* it is permitted to recite *Shema* in the large *chatzeir,* since the one reciting *Shema* in the large *chatzeir* finds a wall intervening between himself and the excrement, and the status of the small *chatzeir* can in no way adversely affect activities in the large one.

A MUSSAR THOUGHT FOR THE DAY

Those who, by the kindness of Hashem, are not familiar with the circumstances of poverty and its many hardships and degradations, can at times be lacking in the proper level of sensitivity that must be displayed to the poor. The *Chofetz Chaim,* in his *sefer Ahavas Chesed* (2:10), describes an imaginary scenario to demonstrate the great care that must be taken in dealing with the poor:

A man departs the world and his soul ascends to Heaven to face judgment on his life's deeds. There, he is given a *Sefer Torah;* then the questions, asking him about each mitzvah separately, begin. When they reach the mitzvah — וְכִי־יָמוּךְ אָחִיךָ ... וְהֶחֱזַקְתָּ בּוֹ ... וָחַי עִמָּךְ, *If your brother becomes impoverished . . . you shall strengthen him . . . so that he can live with you* (*Vayikra* 25:35) — he is asked: "Did you observe this mitzvah as well?" And when he answers that he surely did, they will remind him of an incident, which when it occurred many years earlier, was to his mind insignificant.

"You were sitting at home one night, comfortable and content, when a poor man from your town approached you with a request for a loan and offered collateral. Your response was quick and to the point: 'I cannot lend the money now!' He left your house and the incident left your mind.

"But what for you was merely a brief conversation was to that man a part of a much longer episode. You only saw him during the few moments when he approached you. You did not see the months of self-deliberation, and the discussions with his wife, trying to decide if he should lower his pride and ask for a loan, something he was trying with all his heart to avoid. When he did decide that it was necessary, he spent time trying to choose a collateral that would find favor in your eyes, something that would not be too cheap, but that he could afford to live without until the loan was paid off.

"And then he deliberated on the opportune time to approach you, when you would be in a good mood and inclined to receive him. And did you notice that he came to you only at night because he was too embarrassed to be seen approaching you during the day?

"After he left your house empty-handed, you promptly forgot about him. But he had to go home and face an expectant family, waiting for some relief from their difficult situation. He had to deal with their disappointment and cries, and with the subsequent results of simply not being able to feed his family. The results of your callous lack of mercy was the total dissolution of his home; a man who was once a respected homeowner was turned by your cruelty into a wandering beggar.

"As your actions were bereft of mercy, you do not qualify for a plea of mercy from this court. And now stand and accept judgment for your actions and their disastrous effects!"

The Chofetz Chaim concludes by writing that one who does develop within himself the quality of always having mercy on others will be graced with mercy from Above.

HALACHAH OF THE DAY

As we mentioned yesterday, even in cases where the Sages permitted washing on Shabbos, it is necessary to exercise care not to transgress any other Shabbos prohibitions while doing so.

Another *melachah* applicable to bathing is that of סְחִיטָה, *squeezing.* One may not use a sponge or washcloth when bathing or washing because as a result of the washing, it is inevitable that some water will be squeezed out of them.

One should also take care when drying wet hair not to squeeze out any water that may have become trapped between the hairs.

The decree of the Sages prohibiting washing was not applied to washing in cold water. However, the *poskim* cite a custom established a few hundred years ago that forbids one to wash his entire body with cold water on Shabbos. Indeed, the *poskim* write that one who violates this custom is liable to severe punishment.

Some *poskim* differentiate between bathing and showering with respect to this custom. These *poskim* permit one who is suffering from the heat to take a cold shower in order to cool down. However, bathing in cold water is forbidden even in such cases.

Due to the above-mentioned custom, swimming — whether done in a pool or a lake or a river — is forbidden on Shabbos even if the water is cold. Swimming in a river or lake on Shabbos not only violates this custom, it may involve the violation of other *melachos* as well.

The second decree enacted by the Sages in order to protect against inadvertent transgression of *kindling* on Shabbos is the prohibition against reading by the light of an oil lamp.

The reasoning behind this decree is as follows: It is common for the light of an oil lamp to fluctuate in its brightness. This is often caused by the oil drawing away from the wick while it is burning, resulting in a temporary dimming of the lamp's light. In order to correct this problem, one would typically tilt the lamp in order to bring the wick back into close contact with the fuel. The Sages feared that one who is distracted by his reading may inadvertently adjust the lamp in such a way on Shabbos, resulting in a violation of the *melachah* of *kindling.* They therefore forbade a person to read from the light of an oil lamp on Shabbos.

This prohibition applies to all types of oil lamps, regardless of the type of oil being used. It does not apply to candles, because candles generally burn with a steady flame and do not require adjusting. For the same reason, the prohibition does not apply to electric lights.

Since nowadays almost all homes are equipped with electric lighting, this prohibition is not commonly applicable. However, one must remember in instances where the lights may not be on — such as during a blackout — that it is forbidden to read by the light of an oil lamp.

There are times when it is permissible to read by the light of an oil lamp. If the person who is reading is being watched by another Jew, he may read by the light of the lamp since the other person will surely prevent him from adjusting the lamp. Additionally, if two people are reading together from the same *sefer,* they may read by the light of the oil lamp. Once again, we assume that they will remind each other not to adjust the lamp on Shabbos. It is important to note that this is true only if they are reading from the same *sefer.* If they are using two different *sefarim,* however, this is forbidden, because one may reach to adjust the lamp without the knowledge of the other.

This concludes our discussion of the *melachah* of *kindling.*

A CLOSER LOOK AT THE SIDDUR

There is an ancient custom to give a bit of money to *tzedakah* (charity) before praying (see *Bava Basra* 10a). The saintly *Arizal* chose to do it at one particular point in the middle of *Pesukei D'Zimrah.* It was after saying the words וְאַתָּה מוֹשֵׁל בַּכֹּל, *and You (HASHEM) rule over everything,* in *Vayevarech Dovid* (*Mishnah Berurah* 51:19). What is the connection between prayer and the giving of charity, and why is the time when one recites these words the most appropriate time to do it? These questions were the topic of a lecture about prayer given by *R' Shimshon Pincus* (subsequently printed in *Nefesh Shimshon* on the *siddur*).

He explained that two qualities of a prayer are examined before it is accepted. The prayer itself must be said with the proper devotion, and the one who offers the prayer must be worthy. The prayers of the "righteous" are accepted; those of the wicked are not. A person gives *tzedakah* so that he can be considered righteous for the purposes of this prayer. A person can go through all the Morning Blessings, *Korbanos,* and *Pesukei D'Zimrah,* enunciating each word carefully and thinking about its sublime meaning, but for all his fervor and intensity, as long as he did not translate this sublimity into concrete action, he is still not worthy of being called a *tzaddik.* He may declare that to Hashem alone is ascribed: הַגְּדֻלָּה וְהַגְּבוּרָה וְהַתִּפְאֶרֶת וְהַנֵּצַח וְהַהוֹד כִּי כֹל בַּשָּׁמַיִם וּבָאָרֶץ, *the greatness, the strength, the splendor, the triumph, and the glory, even everything in heaven and earth.* He may declare loudly that אַתָּה מוֹשֵׁל בַּכֹּל, *You (HASHEM) rule over everything,* but without action to that effect, he has not yet declared that he himself is a part of that rule.

Giving a few pennies to *tzedakah* does not a *tzaddik* create. But it can serve to give real expression to the elevated feelings that accompany his songs and praises, without which those feelings have no real value.

R' Pincus offers another insight into this custom. In the *Vayevarech Dovid* prayer, we ascribe many exalted qualities to Hashem. However, with many of these, we do not state that they pertain directly to our world. Yes, Hashem's greatness and splendor illuminate the heavens, but do they make a difference here on earth? It is only when we declare that אַתָּה מוֹשֵׁל בַּכֹּל, *You rule over everything,* that the earth is included in the scope of Hashem's power. Heaven and earth are thus bridged in giving honor to Hashem.

There is nothing that so symbolically bridges heaven and earth as the action of giving money for *tzedakah.* Money is the engine that drives the physicality of this world. Spirituality, Torah, cannot be bought with money. But anything that is crass and crude is moved and controlled by it. The natural effect of an abundance of money is the denial of Hashem (see *Mishlei* 30:9).

On the other hand, there is one place in this world where Hashem promises to reside, with those suffering misfortune: מָרוֹם וְקָדוֹשׁ אֶשְׁכּוֹן וְאֶת־דַּכָּא וּשְׁפַל־רוּחַ, *I abide in exaltedness and holiness but I am with the despondent and lowly of spirit* (*Yeshayah* 57:15).

While proclaiming Hashem's connection with this world and thereby bridging the separate worlds of the spiritual and the physical, we take the embodiment of the physical — money — and give it to the indigent, who serves as the resting place of the *Shechinah* (Divine Presence). Our words and our actions are then reflective of one another, bringing together these two spheres.

QUESTION OF THE DAY:

Why is lending money to another person called giving him life?

For the answer, see page 236.

פרשת בהר

THURSDAY

PARASHAS BEHAR

A TORAH THOUGHT FOR THE DAY

אַל־תִּקַּח מֵאִתּוֹ נֶשֶׁךְ וְתַרְבִּית
וְיָרֵאתָ מֵאֱלֹהֶיךָ וְחֵי אָחִיךָ עִמָּךְ

Do not take from him interest and increase; and you shall fear your God — and let your brother live with you (*Vayikra* 25:36).

The Torah does not permit us to lend money with רִבִּית (*ribbis*), *interest,* to another Jew, or to borrow money from another Jew and repay it with interest. The particular severity of the prohibition of *ribbis* may be seen in *Rambam's* ruling (*Hilchos Malveh V'Loveh* 4:2) that Torah law is violated in the very agreement to pay interest on a loan, even if the additional money is never actually paid. Moreover, continues *Rambam,* the borrower and lender are not the only people who are liable for their involvement with *ribbis. Anyone* who is involved with a *ribbis* transaction — including witnesses, guarantors, the scribe who drew up the document used to attest to the loan, and the agent who put the lender and borrower together — is liable for his violation of Torah law. In this mitzvah, the Torah is sending us a very clear message — that *ribbis* is to have no place in our lives. [See *A Mussar Thought for the Day* for a deeper message that can be gleaned from the prohibition of *ribbis.*]

The Gemara in *Bava Metzia* (62a, 65b) tells us that aside from these prohibitions that do not allow us to accept *ribbis,* the Torah commands the lender to refund interest money that has already — wrongly — been taken. This obligation is understood from the commandment of אַל־תִּקַּח מֵאִתּוֹ נֶשֶׁךְ וְתַרְבִּית . . . וְחֵי אָחִיךָ עִמָּךְ, *Do not take from him interest and increase . . . and* ***let your brother live with you;*** after you have wrongfully taken interest and increase, the Torah is telling us, you are commanded to *let your brother live with you,* by refunding this money and easing him of the burden that the extra debt has put upon him. [This mitzvah is designed to correct the damage that the debt of *ribbis* has caused. See *A Closer Look at the Siddur.*]

The commentaries differ as to the nature of the obligation that the Torah is imposing when commanding a lender to actively *let your brother live with you* and return interest to the borrower. Some opinions, such as that of *Rambam* in *Sefer HaMitzvos* (as explained by *Megillas Esther* there), explain that the need to return this money is in essence no different from a robber's obligation to return a stolen item. Since it is forbidden to charge interest, this money was taken illegally; the Torah never recognized the transaction. Accordingly, the interest money — like all stolen goods — in truth never belonged to the lender, and as such, like anything that belongs to somebody else, it must be returned to its rightful owner — the borrower who wrongly paid it. It is for this reason, explains *Megillas Esther,* that *Rambam* does not enumerate the obligation to refund *ribbis* as a separate commandment in the list of the 613 mitzvos; it is included in the general mitzvah of returning stolen property.

Others, such as *Ramban* (*Hasagah* 17 *to Sefer HaMitzvos*) and *Ritva* (cited in *Shitah Mekubetzes*) disagree. These authorities maintain that although it is certainly forbidden by the Torah to charge interest, and any agreement to pay interest is not legally binding, the money, once paid, is inherently different from other forms of illegal gain, for, unlike stolen goods, it was given willingly. Thus, the interest money now fully belongs to the lender who received it. The Torah, in commanding וְחֵי אָחִיךָ עִמָּךְ, *and let your brother live with you,* and stating that this money must be refunded to the borrower who wrongly paid it, is assigning a new obligation — one that is not based on any nullification of the original payment — on the lender to recompense the borrower for his loss.

Ohr Same'ach (*Hilchos Malveh V'Loveh* 4:5) points out that a difference in halachah could result from this argument if the lender would betroth a woman with an object that was taken as interest. Since the money or object used for *kiddushin* (betrothal) must belong to the groom, *Ramban* and *Ritva* would maintain that although, in line with the obligation of *and let your brother live with you,* the lender of course owes the borrower the amount of money that he received as interest, this obligation does not cancel the transaction; the actual item that was received is his. Thus, if he gives it to a woman in betrothal, the *kiddushin* is valid. *Rambam* would disagree, for since this object taken as interest is in essence stolen goods, it does not belong to the lender. Therefore, he is unable to use it for *kiddushin,* as the Torah specifically dictates that the object used for betrothal must belong to him.

QUESTION OF THE DAY:

What is another aspect of the "life" involved in lending money without interest?

For the answer, see page 236.

MISHNAH OF THE DAY: ERUVIN 9:2 (II)

The first half of this Mishnah discussed a case where a *chatzeir's* wall was breached, leaving it open to a neighboring smaller *chatzeir.* This Mishnah discusses a case where a *chatzeir's* wall was breached, leaving it open to the public domain:

חָצֵר שֶׁנִּפְרְצָה לִרְשׁוּת הָרַבִּים — If ***a chatzeir was breached into a reshus harabim,*** i.e., the wall that partitioned it along the *reshus harabim* collapsed entirely,[1] הַמַּכְנִיס מִתּוֹכָהּ לִרְשׁוּת הַיָּחִיד — ***one who carries*** an object ***from within [this breached chatzeir] to a reshus hayachid,*** אוֹ מֵרְשׁוּת הַיָּחִיד לְתוֹכָהּ — ***or from a reshus hayachid to it*** חַיָּיב — ***is liable,***[2] for the breached *chatzeir* is now considered a Biblical *reshus harabim.*[3] דִּבְרֵי רַבִּי אֱלִיעֶזֶר — These are ***the words of R' Eliezer.*** וַחֲכָמִים אוֹמְרִים — ***But the Sages say:*** מִתּוֹכָהּ לִרְשׁוּת הָרַבִּים — One who carries an object ***from within [this breached chatzeir] to a reshus harabim*** אוֹ מֵרְשׁוּת הָרַבִּים לְתוֹכָהּ — ***or from a reshus harabim to it*** פָּטוּר — ***is exempt,***[4] מִפְּנֵי שֶׁהִיא כְּכַרְמְלִית — ***because*** this breached *chatzeir* ***is like a karmelis,*** and not a Biblical *reshus harabim.*[5],[6]

NOTES

1. Thus, the *chatzeir* is enclosed on three sides, and entirely open to the *reshus harabim* on the fourth side.

2. To bring a *chatas*-offering for unintentionally violating the Biblical labor of *transferring* an object between a *reshus harabim* and a *reshus hayachid.* If done intentionally, he incurs the Divinely imposed premature death of *kares,* or capital punishment (if he transgresses in the presence of witnesses after being warned about the forbidden nature of the act and the capital penalty that is incurred).

3. Understood simply, R' Eliezer would seem to hold that the entire breached *chatzeir* is like a *reshus harabim.* See *Gems from the Gemara.*

4. The word פָּטוּר, *exempt,* used in regard to the laws of the Sabbath almost always means that no Biblical offense has been violated, but the action is nevertheless Rabbinically proscribed (see *Shabbos* 3a).

5. One would have expected the Sages to illustrate their disagreement with R' Eliezer using the same case used by R' Eliezer. Thus, since R' Eliezer ruled that one is liable for carrying between the breached *chatzeir* and a *reshus hayachid,* the Sages should have countered that one who carries between the breached *chatzeir* and a *reshus hayachid* is exempt. Why did the Sages change the case under discussion and speak instead of carrying between the breached *chatzeir* and a *reshus harabim*?

Tosafos Rid (for other considerations — see following note) emends the Mishnah's text to read even in the ruling of the Sages "from within [this *chatzeir*] to a *reshus hayachid.*" Accordingly, it corresponds to R' Eliezer's case.

6. The Mishnah apparently states that an area surrounded by walls on three sides but open on the fourth is classified as a *karmelis,* and even Biblically is not considered

NOTES

either a private or a public domain. This contradicts what most authorities understand to be the meaning of the Gemara on 12b that three enclosing walls are sufficient, Biblically speaking, to render an area a *reshus hayachid.* [It is because of this difficulty that *Tosafos Rid* emends the Mishnah's citation of the Sages' view to read "from within [this *chatzeir*] to a *reshus hayachid* . . . is exempt, because it is like a *karmelis.*" That is, the breached *chatzeir* is treated Rabbinically as a *karmelis,* but on a Biblical level remains a *reshus hayachid.*]

Tosafos (93b ד״ה חייב) suggest that the Sages refer to a case in which all the walls of the *chatzeir* collapsed, leaving it unenclosed even on a Biblical level. The Sages hold that this area, although devoid of partitions, does not become part of the *reshus harabim,* because it remains private property and the public does not have the legal right to use it. It is rather a *karmelis,* and one who carries there from the *reshus harabim* [or from a *reshus hayachid*] is exempt.

GEMS FROM THE GEMARA

The Gemara examines R' Eliezer's opinion: According to R' Eliezer, does the *chatzeir* become a *reshus harabim* because it was breached to a *reshus harabim*? [But the *chatzeir* is still privately owned, and its owner has the right to restrict the public from using it. Such an area cannot be a *reshus harabim*! (*Ritva; Meiri*).]

The Gemara replies that R' Eliezer is consistent with another opinion of his elsewhere. For R' Eliezer ruled that if the public regularly travels through a private field (when there was previously a publicly owned path going through that field, but its precise location became lost), the owner may not fence it off, and that road becomes like public property. In our Mishnah, R' Eliezer refers to a related case, in which the original site of the *chatzeir's* collapsed wall is no longer discernible, and the public uses an area that, according to the *chatzeir's* owner, was the original site of the *chatzeir's* wall. This claim is disputed by the public, who claim that the *chatzeir's* wall originally stood closer to the remaining *chatzeir.* See diagram.

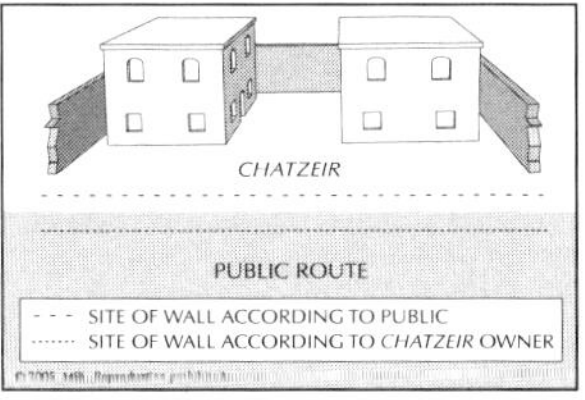

In this case as well, R' Eliezer would rule that the public's use of the disputed area has legal force in deciding the dispute in favor of the public (see *Rashi, Ritva*). The Sages, however, dispute R' Eliezer's ruling that public use decides the dispute (*Ritva*). [Thus, they rule that since the status of the disputed area is questionable, it therefore cannot be considered a *reshus harabim.*]

פרשת בהר

THURSDAY

PARASHAS BEHAR

In an alternative explanation, R' Eliezer and the Sages argue about the status of the sides of a *reshus harabim,* i.e., an area adjacent to the street that the public uses in times of heavy traffic for overflow crowds. R' Eliezer holds that the sides of a *reshus harabim* have the status of a *reshus harabim* even if privately owned, whereas the Sages hold that the privately owned sides of a *reshus harabim* do not have the status of a *reshus harabim.*

The Gemara asks: If their dispute is about the sides of a *reshus harabim,* let them argue about an ordinary case of the sides of a *reshus harabim.* Why does the Mishnah present their argument in the case of a *chatzeir* whose wall had fallen down?

The Gemara answers that if they had argued about an ordinary case of the sides of a *reshus harabim,* we might have said that the Sages maintain that the sides of a *reshus harabim* have the status of a *karmelis* only where there are obstructions in the sides of the *reshus harabim* that make it unsuitable for traffic. [Ordinarily, pegs or boulders were placed at the sides of a *reshus harabim* to prevent wagons from passing too close to the walls on the side and damaging them. The space between these obstructions and the side walls is what is generally referred to as "the sides of the *reshus harabim.*" Had the dispute involved this case, one could have argued that the Sages do not consider the sides a *reshus harabim* because public access to that area is hindered by the obstructions (*Rashi*).]

But where there are no barriers, such as in our Mishnah's case of a collapsed wall, I would say that the Sages concede to R' Eliezer that the sides attain the status of a *reshus harabim.* Therefore, our Mishnah, by using the case of a collapsed wall, comes to inform us that they argue about a case where the sides of the *reshus harabim* have no barriers.

A MUSSAR THOUGHT FOR THE DAY

We explained in *A Torah Thought for the Day* that *Ramban* understands the mitzvah to refund money that was taken as *ribbis* to be inherently different than the need to return stolen goods. The difference between these two areas, explains *Ramban,* is that a stolen object that was taken from a person against his will still belongs to the original owner, and thus must be returned to him. Money given as *ribbis,* however, is different, for although the Torah does not want this transaction to occur, the borrower nevertheless willingly paid the extra money. The commandment of returning to a person *his* item that has been taken from him no longer applies, for since the debt was paid willingly, keeping this money is not theft; this money no longer legally belongs to the borrower. Thus, concludes *Ramban,* in commanding וְחֵי אָחִיךָ עִמָּךְ, *and let your brother live with you,* the Torah is imposing a new obligation upon the lender — to refund this money to the person who wrongfully paid it.

Ramban continues his insight into the difference between theft and *ribbis* in his Torah commentary (*Devarim* 23:20-21), where he explains that these two prohibitions are based on totally different reasons, and are giving us entirely different messages. Unlike the prohibitions of theft or robbery, where the reasons behind them are obvious — man would not be able to live in places where lawlessness prevailed (see *Ramban* to *Bereishis* 6:13), and society would establish these laws on its own even had the Torah not specifically told us that theft is wrong — there is nothing inherently wrong in lending money with interest when both the lender and borrower agree on these terms at the outset. Rather, *Ramban* explains, the problem with a loan that includes *ribbis* is that it is not within the spirit of compassion that the Jewish people are meant to feel toward each other. Although accepting *ribbis,* when examined from the strictly legal point of view, may be acceptable, this is not how a Jew should act when his brother needs a loan. The directive of וְאָהַבְתָּ לְרֵעֲךָ כָּמוֹךָ, *you shall love your fellow as yourself* (*Vayikra* 19:18), requires us to set aside the possibility of profit so our fellow Jew will not suffer.

Understanding that the prohibition against *ribbis* is based on the level of *chesed* that people are expected to perform for one another allows us to understand why the Torah promises great reward — לְמַעַן יְבָרֶכְךָ ה׳ אֱלֹהֶיךָ בְּכֹל מִשְׁלַח יָדֶךָ, *so that HASHEM, your God, will bless you in your every undertaking* (*Devarim* 23:21) — for properly fulfilling this mitzvah. *Ramban* points out that we do not find promises of great blessing for someone who refrains from robbery or theft. However, since the mitzvah to lend money without *ribbis* is based on the desire to do *chesed* that will be a natural result of the extraordinary love that must be present between all Jews, and since this relationship results in our acting in an elevated way to our fellow Jews — even beyond the letter of the strict legal code — Hashem promises that we will be richly blessed for doing so.

Ramban concludes that the prohibition of *ribbis* as a mitzvah of *chesed* explains why we are permitted to lend or borrow money from a non-Jew with interest. Since, as we explained, it is not inherently wrong to lend money with interest, but is merely not the way that members of a close family act toward each other, we have no obligation to act in this manner

to someone who is not a member of this close-knit group.

In the verse written concerning the return of collected interest, the Torah refers to the borrower as אָחִיךָ, *your brother.* With this, the Torah tells us to look at the other person as you would at *your brother.* This closeness will engender the realization that the interest never should have been taken, and the lender will proceed to return it.

HALACHAH OF THE DAY

Next in the list of the thirty-nine labors forbidden on Shabbos is the *melachah* of מַכֶּה בְּפַטִּישׁ, *makeh b'patish.* While this is literally defined as *one who strikes with a hammer,* it specifically refers to the final blow that a craftsman would strike with his hammer in order to smooth out any rough edges remaining on a utensil under construction. After all the other labors that have been involved in the construction of the item have been performed, this is the final blow that completes and perfects the finished product. From the perspective of halachah, this constitutes a significant act that is considered a *melachah* in its own right.

During our discussions of this *melachah,* we will refer to it as the *melachah* of *finishing.*

As we have stated in regard to all the forbidden *melachos,* this *melachah* is based on an activity that took place in the Mishkan. All the utensils that were built for use in the Mishkan required some sort of "finishing touch" that was done to them at the completion of their construction.

The *melachah* of *finishing* encompasses any act that either marks the *completion* of an article, *perfects* the article, or is the final act that *makes the article usable.* Even if the act itself seems somewhat minor, its significance lies not in the scope or difficulty of the task, but rather in the fact that it constitutes the completion of the article.

By way of illustration: The Gemara (*Makkos* 3b) teaches: *If one makes a neck opening [in a garment] on Shabbos, he is liable to bring a chatas-offering. Rashi* explains that the Gemara speaks of a new garment whose manufacture has been completed with the exception of the creation of a neck opening. It is through the creation of this opening that the garment becomes usable and complete. It therefore follows that by making this opening, one violates the *melachah* of *finishing.*

Before we begin to explore the details of this *melachah,* let us attempt to clarify its parameters. Since it is the nature of this *melachah* that one may violate it by doing an act that would otherwise be classified as being part of a different *melachah,* there is a basic question that arises when trying to classify activities that may constitute violations of *finishing.* For example, when someone builds a table, he violates the *melachah* of *building.* When the table is complete except for the attachment of the fourth and final leg, which *melachah* does he violate by attaching the leg? The act of attaching the leg is an act of *building,* and as such, he should violate that *melachah.* Yet, it would also seem to be an act of *finishing,* since it is this act that completes and makes the table usable.

We will discuss this question further tomorrow.

A CLOSER LOOK AT THE SIDDUR

Although a person who lends money with *ribbis* violates a very severe Torah prohibition, the Gemara (*Bava Metzia* 62a) tells us that the punishment of *malkos,* lashes, is not administered for his doing so. As we explained in *A Torah Thought for the Day,* the lender is specifically required to return the *ribbis* money to the borrower. Thus, like in every instance of לָאו שֶׁנִּתַּק לַעֲשֵׂה, *a negative commandment that may be remedied by performing a specified positive commandment, malkos* are not administered for taking *ribbis. Rashi* (to *Makkos* 4b ד״ה שאין) explains that the Torah teaches that the fulfillment of the positive precept is the remedy it requires to atone for the violation of the prohibition. In this case, since the damage that was done by taking *ribbis* is fully repaired by fulfilling the positive commandment of returning the money, no further punishment — such as lashes — is necessary.

A broader message that may be understood from this law is that Hashem, in His great kindness, allows man other ways to atone for sin besides the need to undergo painful punishment. We ask Hashem to grant us this kindness as part of the prayers recited prior to the bedtime *Shema,* when we say: יְהִי רָצוֹן מִלְּפָנֶיךָ ה׳ אֱלֹהַי וֵאלֹהֵי אֲבוֹתַי שֶׁלֹּא אֶחֱטָא עוֹד וּמַה שֶּׁחָטָאתִי לְפָנֶיךָ מְחוֹק בְּרַחֲמֶיךָ הָרַבִּים **אֲבָל לֹא עַל יְדֵי יִסּוּרִים וָחֳלָיִים רָעִים**, *May it be Your will,* HASHEM, *my God and the God of my fathers, that I may sin no more. Whatever sins I have done before You, may You blot out in Your abundant mercies,* ***but not through suffering or bad illnesses.*** [This prayer is also found in the *Ne'ilah Shemoneh Esrei* of Yom Kippur, and is based on Rava and Rav Hamnuna Zuti's formula, mentioned in *Berachos* 17a.]

To better understand this *tefillah, Mishnas Moshe* cites a parable told

by the Baal Shem Tov that explains how Hashem blots out our sins through *His abundant mercy* instead of employing *suffering or bad illnesses.* There was once, explained the Baal Shem Tov, an arrogant commoner who publicly insulted the king. When they heard of this blasphemy, the royal guardsmen wanted to mete out severe and immediate punishment to this ill-bred person in order to maintain the king's honor. The king, however, told them to do the person no harm, and instead, the king would personally deal with him. The king instructed that the illiterate peasant be educated at the finest academies until he was fully conversant in royal etiquette. After the man completed this education, the king instructed that he join the king's court and be given royal duties. He excelled at these jobs and was gradually promoted until he became a high-ranking officer. One day, as he was carrying out important affairs of state, he was struck by the full extent of the king's grandeur and power, as well as the great kindness that this mighty monarch had bestowed upon him. Only then, concluded the Baal Shem Tov, did the peasant-turned-nobleman realize the full gravity of his crime. Had he been punished as soon as he had insulted the king many years earlier, he would no doubt have suffered tremendously. However, he would never have understood the full weight of what he did wrong. It was only after many years of being educated in, and witnessing, royal kindness that he was truly able to appreciate the glory of the king against whom he had sinned, and ask forgiveness for his crime.

The same is true, explains the Baal Shem Tov, when we disobey Hashem. Although we no doubt deserve terrible punishment, we ask Hashem not to punish us but instead to grant us great good. This way, after many years of feeling a tremendous debt of *hakaras hatov* (gratitude) for the unearned goodness from which we benefited, we will feel the weight of our sin of ignoring our all-powerful and benevolent King. Then, we will come to the realization that we must return to Him in *teshuvah.*

A TASTE OF LOMDUS

We mentioned in *A Torah Thought for the Day* that *Rambam* and *Ramban* differ as to why a person must return money that was accepted as interest to the borrower who wrongly paid it. *Rambam* explains that since the transaction was illegal, the money still belongs to the borrower and, as is the case with all stolen property, it must be refunded. *Ramban* argues (see *A Mussar Thought for the Day*) that *ribbis,* since it was given willingly, is different from theft, and must be returned only by virtue of a special Torah directive.

Machaneh Ephraim (*Dinei Ribbis* §2) rules like *Rambam* — the instruction to return interest is because the money still belongs to the borrower and was never legally given to the lender — and he explains this ruling in line with a Gemara in *Bava Kamma* (112a). The Gemara there states that although all agree that the children of a lender who collected interest and died before refunding the money are not obligated to return the extra money to the borrower, a dispute exists as to why they are exempt from this responsibility. The Gemara states that Rami bar Chama explains that in regard to stolen goods, the law is that use of a stolen item becomes permitted with two criteria: (a) *yi'ush* — the owner gives up hope of recovering his property and (b) *shinui reshus* — the property changes hands from the robber to another person. In regard to condition (b), an heir is like a buyer in the sense that he is considered to be a separate legal entity from the person whom he inherited. Thus, if a person steals something and dies after the owner had given up hope of ever getting it back, the two conditions needed to allow the use of a stolen item have been fulfilled, and there is no longer any reason why it must be returned to the original owner. Rava, although agreeing that the children need not return the money paid as *ribbis,* argues with Rami bar Chama's assumption that an heir is a separate legal entity from the person whom he is inheriting. Rather, Rava explains that the reason an heir need not return money that was taken as interest is implicit in the Torah's instruction: אַל־תִּקַּח מֵאִתּוֹ נֶשֶׁךְ וְתַרְבִּית . . . וְחֵי אָחִיךָ עִמָּךְ, *Do not take from him interest and increase . . . and let your brother live with you.* Just as the first half of the verse is directed at the lender himself, the mitzvah of returning interest, taught in the second half of the verse, is also directed at the person who actually lent the money. Thus, the Torah does not obligate the children of a person who took interest to return this money to the borrower.

It would appear at first glance, says *Machaneh Ephraim,* that the argument between Rami bar Chama and Rava is based on the above mentioned dispute between *Rambam* and *Ramban* as to the nature of the commandment to return interest. Rami bar Chama appears to understand that the need to return interest money is related to the general obligation to return stolen goods. Rava, however, rules that the heirs are allowed to continue to use the money that was given as interest, although in his view they would have to return stolen property. The need to return interest, it appears from Rava, has nothing to do with the lender's lack of legal ownership of this money.

However, explains *Machaneh Ephraim,* this is not necessarily so, and both opinions in the Gemara can in fact maintain, as does *Rambam,* that the lender never becomes the owner of the interest money, and the need to return the money to the borrower is the same as the need to return any illicit gain. The verse that Rava uses as a source proving that only the lender himself — and not an heir — must return interest money, points out *Machaneh Ephraim,* does not tell us the *nature* of this obligation, only *who* is obligated in it. The Torah, when stating the directive — *Do not take from him interest and increase . . . and let your brother live with you* — to the lender, is telling the heirs that they are not obligated in this mitzvah as well. Thus, it is very possible that Rava agrees in principle with Rami bar Chama, who maintains that the lender's obligation to pay back interest is based on the need to return stolen goods, and argues only as to whether an heir is a separate legal entity like a buyer. However, says Rava, the Torah, in the explicit statement: *Do not take from him interest and increase . . . and let your brother live with you* is specifically telling us that there is one difference between the need to return interest and the need to return other forms of illegal gain — the only person directed to return interest is the lender himself.

A TORAH THOUGHT FOR THE DAY

פרשת בהר

FRIDAY

PARASHAS BEHAR

וְחִשַּׁב עִם־קֹנֵהוּ מִשְּׁנַת הִמָּכְרוֹ לוֹ עַד שְׁנַת הַיֹּבֵל
וְהָיָה כֶּסֶף מִמְכָּרוֹ בְּמִסְפַּר שָׁנִים כִּימֵי שָׂכִיר יִהְיֶה עִמּוֹ

He shall make a reckoning with the purchaser from the year he was sold to him until the Jubilee Year; the money of his purchase shall be divided by the number of years, he shall be regarded with him like the years of a laborer (*Vayikra* 25:50).

The subject of our verse is a Jew who, due to financial hardship, has sold himself into slavery to a non-Jew. There is an obligation to redeem him by compensating his master financially for his service. The exact method of reimbursement is calculated as follows.

Any sale of a Jew is limited; when the *Yovel* (Jubilee Year) arrives, he automatically becomes free. The owner in effect has bought the services of the slave only for the amount of years from the time of the sale until *Yovel.* The dollar amount of the original sale is thus divided by the number of years of servitude, with the result representing the value of one year of service, just as if he would have been a hired laborer. To use *Rashi's* example, if there were twenty years remaining to the *Yovel,* and the slave was sold for 20 *maneh,* then each year's service is worth 1 *maneh.* If he is redeemed after five years, 15 *maneh* must be paid to the owner and the slave is free.

The *Chofetz Chaim* uses these calculations as an answer to those who have difficulty believing that the final redemption is at hand. They claim that it is improbable that the earlier generations, with their superior stature and greater merit, did not succeed in bringing Mashiach, and that our generation will be able to bring him. The Chofetz Chaim points to these verses in the Torah to illustrate that in our circumstance, no more than a few merits may do the job.

The two cases, that of the Jew sold into labor to a non-Jew, and that of the Jewish people in exile among the nations, are perfectly analogous. Just as a large debt was created right at the beginning of the sale in the former case, so was there a large debt of atonement for our sins, which began to be repaid right at the outset of the exile. Just as freeing a slave in the beginning of his term of service would require the most amount of money, as it is the furthest from *Yovel,* so too, achieving redemption for the Jewish people in the beginning of the exile would have called for a tremendous amount of merit, an amount that the nation did not possess at the time.

פרשת בהר

FRIDAY

PARASHAS BEHAR

In the case of the slave, as the years progress, less money is needed for his redemption. So too, as the years of exile draw to a close, much fewer merits are necessary to bring about an early redemption. It may very well be in our power to bring about this small amount of merit.

And even if, God forbid, our merits do not suffice, the exile contains an equivalent to the *Yovel* of the slave, a time that was set at the beginning of the exile at which point the redemption must occur.

Therefore, at this late stage of the exile, even if there would be no special merits to hasten the appointed time, we may hope and expect that that time is at hand and we will soon be redeemed.

MISHNAH OF THE DAY: ERUVIN 9:3

This next Mishnah discusses another case in which the wall of a *chatzeir* was breached:

חָצֵר שֶׁנִּפְרְצָה לִרְשׁוּת הָרַבִּים מִשְּׁתֵּי רוּחוֹתֶיהָ — A ***chatzeir that was breached to the reshus harabim*** on the Sabbath ***on two of its sides,***[1] so that it is no longer enclosed in the manner usually necessary to permit carrying there, וְכֵן בַּיִת שֶׁנִּפְרַץ מִשְּׁתֵּי רוּחוֹתָיו — ***and similarly, a house that was breached*** on the Sabbath ***on two of its sides*** so that it is no longer enclosed in the manner usually necessary to permit carrying there, וְכֵן מָבוֹי שֶׁנִּטְּלוּ קוֹרוֹתָיו אוֹ לְחָיָיו — ***and similarly, a mavoi whose korah or lechi was removed*** on the Sabbath, מוּתָּרִים בְּאוֹתוֹ שַׁבָּת — ***[all these] are permitted,*** i.e., carrying in them is permitted, ***for*** the remainder of ***that Sabbath*** as before the breach occurred, וַאֲסוּרִים לֶעָתִיד לָבֹא — ***but are prohibited,*** i.e., carrying in them is prohibited, on the Sabbath ***in the future*** until repairs are made.[2] דִּבְרֵי רַבִּי יְהוּדָה — These are ***the words of R' Yehudah.***[3]

NOTES

1. As above, the *chatzeir* wall was breached on the side facing the *reshus harabim,* so that it is no longer a valid partition (see *Gems from the Gemara* for a discussion of the exact nature of the breach being discussed here). Simply understood, if the breach discussed here is less than 10 *amos* wide, it should be considered an entrance and not invalidate the enclosure. See *Gems from the Gemara* for why the enclosure is invalidated.

2. Had the *lechi* or *korah* been removed before the Sabbath, the *mavoi* would have the status of a *karmelis.*

3. The prohibition to carry in the breached enclosure is Rabbinic in origin (though losing the status of a *reshus hayachid,* the area has not become a *reshus harabim*). Therefore, R' Yehudah applies the principle that the permitted status that prevailed at

רַבִּי יוֹסֵי אוֹמֵר — *R' Yose says:* אִם מוּתָּרִין לְאוֹתוֹ שַׁבָּת מוּתָּרִין לֶעָתִיד לָבֹא — ***If they are permitted*** to carry ***on that Sabbath, they are permitted*** to carry ***in the future*** as well, וְאִם אֲסוּרִין לֶעָתִיד לָבֹא אֲסוּרִין לְאוֹתוֹ שַׁבָּת — ***and if they are prohibited*** from carrying in ***the future, they are*** also ***prohibited on that Sabbath.*** R' Yose holds that the law for this Sabbath must be consistent with the law for future Sabbaths. Since carrying in the breached area certainly cannot be permitted on the next Sabbath, it also cannot be permitted for the duration of the Sabbath on which the breach occurred.[4]

NOTES

the onset of the Sabbath (before the breach occurred) remains in force for that entire Sabbath day.

4. R' Yose rejects the application — to this circumstance — of the principle that the halachic status prevailing at the onset of the Sabbath remains for the rest of that Sabbath.

GEMS FROM THE GEMARA

The Mishnah implies that a single breach in a *chatzeir* wall does not invalidate a partition, while a two-sided breach does. The Gemara first seeks to define the type of breach meant by the Mishnah. For if the Mishnah refers to a breach of 10 *amos* or less, why is it that only a breach from one side does not negate the enclosure (because one says that it is an entrance), but a similar breach of 10 *amos* or less occurring on two sides does negate the enclosure? That breach as well should be deemed a mere entrance, and the enclosure should not be negated!

The Gemara quotes Rav as saying that the Mishnah, when it said "breached on two sides," refers to a case where the wall was breached in its corner. Such a breach cannot be viewed as an entrance even if it does not exceed 10 *amos,* because people do not usually construct entrances in corners. It is therefore viewed as a breach that invalidates the partition.

Now, the Mishnah then discussed the case of a *house* that was breached on two sides. The Gemara asks: A breach on only one side of the house does not invalidate the enclosure, for we say that פִּי תִקְרָה יוֹרֵד וְסוֹתֵם, *the edge of the roof extends downward and seals* the breach. [This is a Sinaitic law of partitions, which allows us to construe the edge of a beam as descending to the floor and forming a valid partition.] If so, when breaches occur on two sides, we should also say that the enclosure remains intact because "the edge of the roof extends downward and seals" the breach. Why does the Mishnah rule that a two-sided breach invalidates the partition?

The Gemara answers in the name of Rav again: The Mishnah refers to a case in which the house was breached in the corner (so that we cannot view this two-sided breach as an entrance, even though it does not exceed 10 *amos*), and the house's roof is at an angle (so that we cannot say that "the edge of the roof extends downward and seals" the breach). See diagram. The principle of "the edge of the roof (or beam) descends and seals the breach" [פִּי תִקְרָה] does not apply to a beam or roof that is slanted, since the edge is not then perpendicular to the ground in a manner that its extension would result in a partition (*Rashi*).

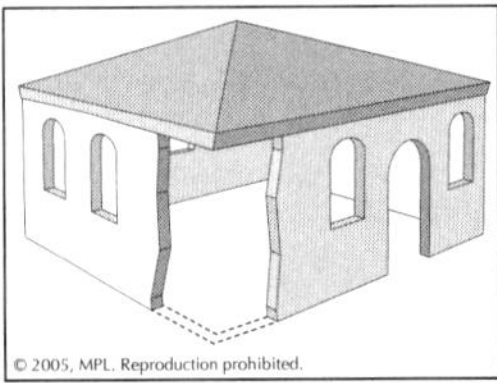

Thus, similar to his explanation of the Mishnah's first case of a breached *chatzeir,* Rav explains the Mishnah's case of a house breached on two sides as referring to a breach of 10 *amos* or less in the corner. Since the breach is in the corner, it cannot be viewed as a mere entrance even though it does not exceed 10 *amos.* And since the house's roof is slanted, we also cannot apply the principle of *pi tikrah* to close the breach.

A MUSSAR THOUGHT FOR THE DAY

How great is the obligation to anticipate the coming of Mashiach! Even the great Torah scholars are called to task for not anticipating his arrival enough. *Chazal* say that Hashem tells the righteous, "It is not proper that you loved My Torah but not my Kingdom." *Chazal* also relate that Hashem declared that when a generation appears that truly looks forward to the redemption, they will be immediately redeemed. Indeed, the question צִפִּיתָ לִישׁוּעָה, *Have you anticipated the redemption?,* is asked of a person at the time of his judgment in Heaven.

The *Chofetz Chaim* wrote a work with this title — צִפִּיתָ לִישׁוּעָה — devoted entirely to this subject. He cites the above statements from *Chazal,* among others, and answers any arguments against the belief that Mashiach's arrival can be expected at any time.

One argument dealt with in the *sefer* proceeds as follows: The Torah describes the generation that will be worthy of Hashem's salvation: וְשַׁבְתָּ עַד־ה׳ אֱלֹהֶיךָ וְשָׁמַעְתָּ בְקֹלוֹ . . . אַתָּה וּבָנֶיךָ בְּכָל־לְבָבְךָ וּבְכָל־נַפְשֶׁךָ. וְשָׁב ה׳ אֱלֹהֶיךָ אֶת־שְׁבוּתְךָ וְרִחֲמֶךָ וְשָׁב וְקִבֶּצְךָ, *And you will return to Hashem, your God, and listen to His voice . . . you and your children, with all your heart and with all your soul. Then Hashem, your God, will bring back your captivity and have mercy upon you, and He will gather you in* (*Devarim* 30:2,3). From the verse it seems that only a national repentance and religious revival will cause the redemption to arrive. As anyone can see, the nation as a whole hardly answers to this description. How then can we expect that the redemption will be a reality for us?

On the surface, this argument appears to be a valid one. However, the verses quoted do not constitute the entire picture. The Gemara (*Sanhedrin* 97a), describing the times in which Mashiach will come, gives a bleak description of a generation that has completely lost its spiritual bearings and possesses not even a modicum of respect for the Torah. Among the details given there is that insolence will be on the rise and those who keep the Torah will be despised. How can this picture be reconciled with the description from *Devarim*?

The answer, explains the Chofetz Chaim, is that both descriptions are a part of the larger picture, a picture that can indeed be applied to our generations. The people of the period preceding the coming of Mashiach will be comprised of two camps. One of these will be those who have lost the connection to all that is holy. Not only will this group reject the Torah, they will create difficulty for those who keep it. In the other camp will be those who tenaciously, and in the face of every difficulty, carry on the Torah way of life. Without the support of their brethren, and headlong against the spirit of the times, these people continue to cling to Torah and mitzvos, and raise their children to do likewise.

Those who keep the Torah in the face of every opposition can truly be described as serving Hashem בְּכָל־לְבָבְךָ וּבְכָל־נַפְשֶׁךָ, *with all your heart and with all your soul.* Even if they will be the minority, the power of their determination causes their merit to outweigh the negativity produced by those who abdicate their commitment.

And just as we witness, in our time, this phenomenon of determined servants of Hashem, who are described as "listening to His voice," אַתָּה וּבָנֶיךָ, *you and your children,* so shall we witness the reward of their devotion — וְשָׁב ה׳ אֱלֹהֶיךָ אֶת־שְׁבוּתְךָ וְרִחֲמֶךָ וְשָׁב וְקִבֶּצְךָ, *Then Hashem, your God, will bring back your captivity and have mercy upon you, and He will gather you in.*

פרשת בהר

FRIDAY

PARASHAS BEHAR

HALACHAH OF THE DAY

Yesterday, we asked: If a single action, for example the affixing of the final leg of a table, seems to be a violation of both a basic *melachah,* such as *building,* as well as an act of *finishing* that could be considered a violation of מַכֶּה בְּפַטִּישׁ, what is the halachah? Is this act indeed a violation of both *melachos*? Or is there perhaps a guiding principle that would differentiate between an act of *building* and an act of *finishing*?

The answer to this question is a dispute among the *Rishonim.* Some rule that such an act does indeed violate both *melachos.* Others disagree and rule that if an act can be classified both as a part of the actual *building* of a utensil, as well as the *finishing* touch to the utensil, it is considered a violation of the *melachah* of *building,* and is not seen as a violation of מַכֶּה בְּפַטִּישׁ.

This latter group of *Rishonim* reasons that the construction of a utensil is seen by halachah as consisting of two distinct stages. The first stage consists of the actual construction of the item. The second stage consists of the *final touches* that finish off, or perfect, the item whose basic construction is already complete. If we once again use the example of the table, the first stage would include all acts necessary to transform the raw materials into a functional table — including the attachment of all the table's legs. For this reason, according to these *Rishonim,* attaching the final leg of the table is a violation of *building.* Only an act that *follows* the actual construction and provides a *final finishing touch* can be considered a violation of מַכֶּה בְּפַטִּישׁ. Giving the table a final sanding in order to smooth out any imperfections on its surface is an activity that is performed after the construction has been completed; this would be a violation of מַכֶּה בְּפַטִּישׁ.

Another illustration of the same concept would be the person who writes the last letter in a *Sefer Torah.* According to the opinion of the first group of *Rishonim* mentioned above, this person would violate both the prohibition of *writing* and that of מַכֶּה בְּפַטִּישׁ, since the *Sefer* is now a kosher, usable Torah. By contrast, the second group of *Rishonim* would say that he is only in violation of the prohibition of *writing,* since the writing is a part of the actual creation of the *Sefer Torah* and, as such, cannot be seen as a "finishing touch."

QUESTION OF THE DAY:

Why is the word דדו in the phrase בֶּן־דדו יִגְאָלֶנּוּ spelled deficiently (דדו instead of דודו)?

For the answer, see page 236.

A CLOSER LOOK AT THE SIDDUR

Although the themes of redemption from exile and the salvation of Hashem are mentioned in our prayers countless times, there is one prayer that uses the actual verses cited above in *A Torah Thought for the Day,* to convey our plea for redemption. A brief introduction is necessary to explain the halachic and Midrashic background for this prayer, after which we will quote it with minimal explanation. The prayer itself is deeply moving and needs no elaboration.

A Jew who is sold to another Jew has a term of enslavement of six years, after which it is incumbent upon the master to free him. The only way that this term can be lengthened is if the slave himself declares that he loves his master and does not wish to leave. In this case, pursuant to a court ceremony, he becomes indentured until *Yovel* (the Jubilee Year) (*Shemos* 21:1-7).

In contrast, a Jew who is sold to a non-Jew does not leave after six years. His term of servitude is always until *Yovel.* However, because of the risk to the religious commitment of a person in the constant employ of a non-Jew, his relatives are required to attempt to redeem him, as the verse states: אֶחָד מֵאֶחָיו יִגְאָלֶנּוּ. אוֹ דֹדוֹ אוֹ בֶן־דֹּדוֹ יִגְאָלֶנּוּ, *One of his brothers shall redeem him, either his uncle or his cousin shall redeem him.* If they do not, then every Jew must try to redeem him. In the absence of this, he is to redeem himself with any money that he can possibly earn, אוֹ־הִשִּׂיגָה יָדוֹ וְנִגְאָל, *or if his own means become sufficient, he shall be redeemed* (*Vayikra* 25:48-49).

The Midrash interprets these verses homiletically to refer to the Jewish people in exile. אֶחָד מֵאֶחָיו יִגְאָלֶנּוּ, *One of his brothers shall redeem him,* refers to Mashiach, who will be a mortal Jew. דֹדוֹ, literally *his beloved,* refers to Hashem, the beloved of the Jewish people. The redemption can happen either through their own merit: אוֹ־הִשִּׂיגָה יָדוֹ, *his own means become sufficient,* or if they do not suffice, at the final time set for the redemption, represented by *Yovel* (Midrash cited by *Rabbeinu Bachya, Daas Zekeinim;* see also above, *A Torah Thought for the Day*).

In light of the above, we can fully appreciate the poetry of the *Selichos* recited on the fourth day prior to Rosh Hashanah, as we beg with one voice for national salvation:

לֹא אִישׁ אֵל וִיכַזֵּב אֲשֶׁר יַחֲלִיף עִנְיָנִים — *God is not a man to deceive or change his mind.* וְגָזַרְתָּ שֵׁשׁ שָׁנִים אֲשֶׁר לַעֲבָדִים נִקְנִים — *You decreed six years [of servitude] for those bought as slaves* (referring to the laws of the slave of a Jew), וְכַמָּה שֵׁשׁ חָלְפוּ לִי — *but,* cries the Jewish nation, my bondage is

פרשת בהר

FRIDAY

PARASHAS BEHAR

lasting much longer; *many times six years have gone by me [without redemption].* And if one will suggest that I am to be regarded as a slave who loves his master and wants to stay longer, וְלֹא אָהַבְתִּי אֲדוֹנִים — *but I did not love these masters;* my "masters" in exile were not good to me.

Maybe one will claim that I should be treated as one sold to a non-Jew, who does not leave after six years: וְאִם נִמְכַּרְתִּי לְעֵקֶר וְלֹא אֶגָּאֵל בַּשָּׁנִים — *And if I have been sold to idolatry, so that I am not redeemed by [the passing of six] years* — in that case, I submit that I be treated according to the law of the Torah and, בִּקְרוֹבִים דִּין עֵקֶר — *the law [passes] to my kin [to redeem me],* וְאַתָּה קְרוֹבִי וְגוֹאֲלִי — *and You [HASHEM] are my Kinsman and Redeemer!* Thus, ה׳ בֹּקֶר תִּשְׁמַע קוֹלִי — *HASHEM, at dawn hear my voice!*

A TORAH THOUGHT FOR THE DAY

כִּי־לִי בְנֵי־יִשְׂרָאֵל עֲבָדִים עֲבָדַי הֵם אֲשֶׁר־הוֹצֵאתִי אוֹתָם מֵאֶרֶץ מִצְרָיִם אֲנִי ה׳ אֱלֹהֵיכֶם

For the Children of Israel are servants to Me, they are My servants whom I have taken out of the land of Egypt — I am HASHEM, *your God* (*Vayikra* 25:55).

Many commentaries take note of the fact that a double usage seems to be employed in this verse: לִי בְנֵי־יִשְׂרָאֵל עֲבָדִים עֲבָדַי הֵם, *the Children of Israel are servants to Me, they are My servants.* A simpler and more direct construction would have been, *For the Children of Israel are My servants, whom I have taken out of the land of Egypt . . .*

R' Zalman Sorotzkin (in his *Oznayim LaTorah*) explains that the verse actually contains two separate messages, each with its own intended audience. We will first explain the two ideas being communicated, and then show how they are communicated in our verse.

The first message pertains to the law found in the preceding verse. There, the Torah writes that even if a Jew in bondage to a non-Jew is not redeemed by his relatives, he is to go free by *Yovel* (the Jubilee Year). The reason for this is that all the Children of Israel are servants of Hashem, and it is not fitting that a servant of Hashem should be eternally enslaved by a human master. Hashem's "claim" on the loyalties of the Jewish people dates back to the time when He freed them from bondage in Egypt. Thus, Hashem says, as it were, to any would-be master: "My contract precedes yours."

The second message pertains to the law spelled out in the preceding verses, that it is the responsibility of every Jew to see that a Jew enslaved by a non-Jew is redeemed as soon as possible, since a Jew whose master is not bound by the laws of the Torah is liable to be lost to his religion. Here too, the reason for redeeming the Jewish slave is because every Jew is a servant of Hashem, who must behave in a way that shows that Hashem is his God.

These two ideas are presented in the above verse. The first part of the verse: לִי בְנֵי יִשְׂרָאֵל עֲבָדִים, *the Children of Israel are servants to Me,* is addressed to the non-Jew, and is warning him that he may not keep a Jewish slave past *Yovel.* The reason is written at the beginning of the second half of the verse: אֲשֶׁר הוֹצֵאתִי אוֹתָם מֵאֶרֶץ מִצְרָיִם, *whom I have taken out of the land of Egypt;* My claim precedes yours. The second message is addressed to his fellow Jews: עֲבָדַי הֵם, *they are My servants,* and should be redeemed as soon as possible. The reason is explained at the end of the verse: אֲנִי ה' אֱלֹהֵיכֶם, *I am HASHEM, Your God,* i.e., it is to ensure that the slave retain his faith in God.

This reading of the verse is supported by the sudden change from the third person to the first person when referring to the Children of Israel. אֲשֶׁר הוֹצֵאתִי אוֹתָם מֵאֶרֶץ מִצְרָיִם, *whom I have taken out of the land of Egypt,* refers to the Jewish people in the third person; אֲנִי ה' אֱלֹהֵיכֶם, *I am HASHEM, your God,* is in the first person. According to the above interpretation, the reason for the change is clear. The first phrase is addressed to the non-Jew, telling him that the Jew must be freed by *Yovel;* thus, the Jewish nation is referred to as "they." In the second phrase, the Jewish people themselves are being addressed. Therefore, the first-person form is used, as Hashem says to the Jews, "*I am HASHEM, your God.*"

MISHNAH OF THE DAY: ERUVIN 9:4

The Mishnah offers another example of the usage of the principle of "*pi tikrah*" (introduced in the previous Mishnah):

הַבּוֹנֶה עֲלִיָּיה עַל גַּבֵּי שְׁנֵי בָתִּים — ***If one builds a second story over two houses*** that are on opposite sides of a *reshus harabim,*[1] וְכֵן גְּשָׁרִים הַמְפוּלָּשִׁים — ***and similarly,*** if there are ***bridges*** under which ***[a road] passes,***[2] מְטַלְטְלִין תַּחְתֵּיהֶן בַּשַּׁבָּת — ***we may carry beneath them on the Sabbath.*** דִּבְרֵי רַבִּי יְהוּדָה — These are ***the words of R' Yehudah.*** וַחֲכָמִים אוֹסְרִין — ***But the Sages forbid*** carrying.

Another case where R' Yehudah expresses a lenient opinion: וְעוֹד אָמַר רַבִּי יְהוּדָה — ***And moreover, R' Yehudah said:*** מְעָרְבִין לְמָבוֹי הַמְפוּלָּשׁ — ***We may make an eruv for an open mavoi.***[3] וַחֲכָמִים אוֹסְרִין — ***But the Sages prohibit*** this.[4]

NOTES

1. This second story forms an overpass across the *reshus harabim,* which as a result is flanked by walls and covered by a roof.

2. Literally: *bridges that are intersected* [by roads passing underneath]. In this case as well, the road is flanked by walls and covered by a roof.

3. I.e., we may make a *shitufei mevo'os* for an open *mavoi* (*R' Yehonasan*), since it has two walls (*Rashi*). R' Yehudah requires no third partition (but only an additional *lechi* or *korah* at each opening to structurally adjust it and permit carrying within on the basis of the *shitufei mevo'os*).

4. The Sages hold that a third partition is necessary before a *lechi* or *korah* can complete the adjustment and pave the way for a *shitufei mevo'os* to permit carrying in the *mavoi.*

GEMS FROM THE GEMARA

The Gemara discusses R' Yehudah's rationale for permitting one to carry under the second-story building or bridge that runs over the *reshus harabim.* Now, R' Yehudah's permit is certainly based on the premise that the street in question has been rendered a Biblical *reshus hayachid.* The question is: What has happened to the street to render it such, according to his view? Is it the mere presence of two walls, which are Biblically sufficient to enclose an area and render it a *reshus hayachid*? Or is it also the fact that the edges of the overpass descend and partition the two open sides, resulting in a total of *four* valid partitions? Rabbah explained that it is the presence of the overpass, which descends and partitions, that creates the *reshus hayachid,* and not the mere presence of two walls.

Abaye challenged Rabbah's understanding of R' Yehudah from the following Baraisa: In the first part of the Baraisa, R' Yehudah rules that it is permitted to carry in a *reshus harabim* under an overpass, since that area has two walls (the sides of the overpass) and a roof above. The Baraisa then continues: Moreover, R' Yehudah says [that even when there is no roof overhead to allow for פִּי תִקְרָה, *the edge of the roof extends downward and seals . . .* and thus], if someone has two houses on two opposite sides of a *reshus harabim,* he may construct a *lechi* here at the end of one of the houses, and a *lechi* here at the end of the other house, or a *korah* here and a *korah* here, i.e., at each end of the house, and he may then carry in the street that is between. We see, then, that the essential factor in creating a Biblical *reshus hayachid* according to R' Yehudah is the two walls, and not the principle of *pi tikrah*!

Rabbah answered Abaye that R' Yehudah's permit to carry under the overpass *is* in fact due in part to the principle of *pi tikrah.* Now, it is true that R' Yehudah considers a two-wall enclosure a Biblical *reshus hayachid* even in cases where there is no roof overhead. But when there is no roof overhead, R' Yehudah will not permit carrying on a Rabbinic level unless a *lechi* or *korah* is placed at the open sides to adjust the area. His ruling in the first part of our Mishnah — going so far as to permit carrying under the overpass without any further adjustments — is because the open sides are considered closed by the principle of *pi tikrah* (see *Geon Yaakov* and *Sfas Emes*).

Rav Ashi then said that the language of our Mishnah also supports Rabbah's explanation that R' Yehudah's permit to carry under the overpass is due in part to the principle of *pi tikrah.* For the Mishnah states: "And moreover, R' Yehudah said: We may make an *eruv* for an open

mavoi." Now, if R' Yehudah permits one to carry under the overpass (the Mishnah's first case) because he holds "the edge of the roof extends downward and seals" the openings, as Rabbah asserts, this is why the Mishnah states "and moreover," introducing a new case in which there is no roof overhead and R' Yehudah still permits carrying. For the expression "moreover" implies that the new case illustrates a new principle not indicated in the first case. This must be the principle that an enclosure of two walls suffices on a Biblical level (according to R' Yehudah).

But if you say that the reason for R' Yehudah's first permit (to carry under the overpass) is that he holds that two partitions are Biblically sufficient to enclose an area and render it a *reshus hayachid,* why would the Mishnah introduce the second case with the expression "and moreover"? The Mishnah is merely illustrating for the second time the principle that two walls Biblically enclose an area according to R' Yehudah!

A MUSSAR THOUGHT FOR THE DAY

Above (see, *A Torah Thought for the Day*), we discussed one explanation for the repetition in the verse: כִּי־לִי בְנֵי יִשְׂרָאֵל עֲבָדִים עֲבָדַי הֵם, *For the Children of Israel are servants to Me, they are My servants* (*Vayikra* 25:55). *Sfas Emes* presents another explanation. With these words, he says, the Torah is qualifying the type of servants that the Children of Israel should strive to be. They are not just servants, but they are "My" servants, i.e., their intention is to serve Me and not for their own benefit. The same idea is formulated in the Mishnah in (*Avos* 1:3) in the following words: אַל תִּהְיוּ כַּעֲבָדִים הַמְשַׁמְּשִׁין אֶת הָרַב עַל מְנַת לְקַבֵּל פְּרָס אֶלָּא הֱווּ כַּעֲבָדִים הַמְשַׁמְּשִׁין אֶת הָרַב שֶׁלֹּא עַל מְנָת לְקַבֵּל פְּרָס, *Be not like servants who serve their master for the sake of receiving a reward; instead be like servants who serve their master not for the sake of receiving a reward.*

Regarding the wording of this Mishnah, *R' Yehoshua Heller* (author of *Chosen Yehoshua*) asks: Why does the Mishnah not simply say, "Do not serve Hashem for the sake of a reward"? What is learned from the comparison to this or that type of servant?

Rav Heller explains that the Mishnah could not have precluded all service of Hashem for the sake of reward, because it is in fact permitted to do mitzvos with their reward in mind. The Gemara says (*Bava Basra* 10b) that one who gives charity so that his son will recover from an illness is considered completely righteous. The main lesson of the Mishnah is that one should not be like a servant whose entire motivation for serving his master is *only* the calculation of his own reward.

When a servant serves his master for the reward alone, then each service that he renders will have to first pass the test of "What is in it for me?" If a certain service must be done, but carries a smaller payment than a less necessary one, this servant will focus his energies only on the one that affords him the greatest profit. Not so the servant for whom his master's needs are the initial motivation of his service. While he may also anticipate reward for his service, the reward is not the sole criterion for his action. He will pursue those things for which his master has the greatest needs, and worry about his own reward only in a secondary manner.

So too, in our service of Hashem we are to do what it is that Hashem desires done, and not make our sole focus the relative reward for mitzvos. For example, there is no mitzvah that is greater than Torah study. Were one to measure the reward for Torah study against that of any other mitzvah, the reward for Torah study would certainly be greater. However, there are times when a person is required to stop learning so that he can fulfill a mitzvah that cannot be fulfilled by another person. Were one's sole criterion his reward, he would simply continue his learning and ignore the other mitzvos. We are told in this Mishnah, however, to imitate the servant whose primary motivation for service is the needs of his master, and to pursue the reward for the mitzvos only as a secondary goal.

HALACHAH OF THE DAY

It is possible for one to violate the *melachah* of *finishing* with or without the use of tools or other utensils.

There are various types of activities that may involve acts of *finishing,* and may therefore be restricted by halachah. For the sake of clarity, we will divide these acts into several categories, and then discuss the details of each. The five categories we will discuss are:

(1) Making an article usable.
(2) Perfecting or improving a usable article.
(3) Creating or assembling a utensil.
(4) Repairing or reassembling a broken utensil.
(5) Making a new opening in a container.

The first category of activities mentioned above is that of making an article usable. As we mentioned earlier, the Gemara states that one who

makes a neck opening in a garment on Shabbos is liable to bring a *chatas*-offering. This is because by making the opening, he has made the garment usable, a violation of *finishing.* The Talmud also cites as an example one who makes a hole in a chicken coop that has no other windows. Such a coop requires a small opening to be made near its top, to allow fumes generated by the chicken's droppings to escape, so as not to harm the chickens. The Talmud cites the opinion of Shmuel that one who makes this hole on Shabbos has violated the *melachah* of *finishing,* as this is the final act needed to make the chicken coop usable.

A more practical example of this would be the case of a new book that has some pages that were never cut through completely. Since the book cannot be properly read while the pages are still attached, cutting them makes the book fully usable, and is thus forbidden under the *melachah* of *finishing.* [This refers specifically to pages that were never cut, not to pages that became stuck together after the pages were cut.]

The second category of activities mentioned above is that of perfecting or improving a usable article. The example cited by the Gemara is that of someone who engraves an image in a utensil. This refers to a utensil that has been crafted to the point where it is fully functional, but it is of the type that is customarily beautified with engravings, and would not be sold without being engraved. Thus, the engraving is the finishing touch, and adding this embellishment is considered an act of *finishing.* However, adding an embellishment to a utensil that does not require the embellishment to be considered complete is not a violation of *finishing.*

Improving the functionality of an article is also included in the prohibition against *finishing.* If an article is fully usable, but one nonetheless improves it so that it functions better, that too is an act of *finishing.* For example, oiling the hinges of a squeaky door is considered an act of *finishing,* since eliminating the disturbing noise constitutes an improvement to the door.

A CLOSER LOOK AT THE SIDDUR

We continue our discussion of *Shir HaMaalos* (Psalm 126), which we recite before *Bircas HaMazon* on Shabbos and Yom Tov.

The Psalm states (v. 2) that when the redemption occurs: אָז יֹאמְרוּ בַגּוֹיִם הִגְדִּיל ה׳ לַעֲשׂוֹת עִם־אֵלֶּה, *Then it will be declared among the nations, "HASHEM has done greatly with these."* The revelation of Hashem's glory that will accompany the ultimate redemption will be such that all the nations will recognize that Hashem is the Master of all creation, and they will acknowledge the fact that Hashem has redeemed His nation.

This general acknowledgment of Hashem's Kingship is in fact the reason for the great joy that is mentioned earlier in the psalm (see our discussion of last week). The Gemara in *Berachos* (31a) states: R' Yochanan said in the name of R' Shimon bar Yochai that a person is forbidden to fill his mouth with joy in this world (that is, he is forbidden to express total, unbridled happiness) until the day that all the nations declare, *"HASHEM had done greatly with these"* (the verse in our psalm). No matter how joyous the occasion, a Jew's happiness must always be somewhat tempered by the fact that the ultimate cause for joy — the total revelation of Hashem's glory — has not yet occurred. Only when Hashem's love for the Jews is manifestly clear to all, and His Majesty is accepted and acknowledged by everyone, can we be truly and completely happy.

The psalm continues: הִגְדִּיל ה׳ לַעֲשׂוֹת עִמָּנוּ הָיִינוּ שְׂמֵחִים, *HASHEM has done greatly with us; we were joyous.* This verse, which speaks of the Jews, contrasts the newfound understanding of Hashem's glory that the nations will gain, with the knowledge of it that the Jews have always possessed. Unlike the nations, who will be surprised at the ascendancy of Israel, we have *always* been assured of Hashem's watchful providence; thus, הָיִינוּ שְׂמֵחִים, *we were joyous,* in the past tense — even before the ultimate redemption.

The psalm then turns to a prayer to bring the redemption: שׁוּבָה ה׳ אֶת־שְׁבִיתֵנוּ כַּאֲפִיקִים בַּנֶּגֶב, *HASHEM, return [us from] our captivity, like springs in the desert.* We pray that the redemption will come swiftly, although we may not yet see signs of its impending arrival, just as a spring can sometimes burst forth from the arid desert sand (see *Malbim*). This verse also hints at the overwhelming joy that will accompany the redemption; when a spring suddenly arises in a desert, the person who is the beneficiary of its waters is especially joyous, because he did not plan on having this happen (*Radak*). Furthermore, just as water can transform a desert into fertile land, the redemption will transform the world (*Rashi*).

We will conclude our discussion of this psalm next week.

QUESTION OF THE DAY:

Are the Jews considered children of Hashem, or His servants?

For the answer, see page 236.

ANSWERS TO QUESTIONS OF THE DAY

Sunday:

Shemittah must be kept even if there is only a single Jew in Eretz Yisrael, but *Yovel* is kept only if many Jews are residing there.

Monday:

וִישַׁבְתֶּם לָבֶטַח בְּאַרְצְכֶם includes the added *berachah* that there will be no need to get food from outside Eretz Yisrael (*Chizkuni*).

Tuesday:

The crop will actually be the same size, but if the people truly believe, it will satisfy them for three years. Thus, the miracle is hidden, not open.

Wednesday:

Since a poor person is viewed as if he were dead, lending him money is considered giving him life (*Alshich*).

Thursday:

One who lends money without interest will merit *techiyas hameisim* [resurrection of the dead] (*Nachal Eisan*).

Friday:

This alludes to the fact that a בֶּן דָוִד (which has the same letters as בֶּן ד׳דוֹ) will redeem us all (*Baal HaTurim*).

Shabbos:

We are both — but *Sfas Emes* suggests that on Shabbos Hashem views us with the special love reserved for sons.

פרשת בחקתי

Parashas Bechukosai

פרשת בחקתי

SUNDAY

PARASHAS BECHUKOSAI

A TORAH THOUGHT FOR THE DAY

אִם־בְּחֻקֹּתַי תֵּלֵכוּ וְאֶת־מִצְוֹתַי תִּשְׁמְרוּ וַעֲשִׂיתֶם אֹתָם
If you will go in My statutes, and you will observe My commandments and perform them . . . (*Vayikra* 26:3).

Rashi notes that the phrase *If you will go in My statutes* cannot refer to the observance of all the mitzvos of the Torah, for that is the subject of the second phrase, *and you will observe My commandments and perform them.* He therefore explains that "going in the statutes" of Hashem refers here to diligent labor (*ameilus*) in Torah study.

While *Rashi* proves by inference that the words cannot be understood at face value, we must still endeavor to understand how the idea of diligently laboring in Torah study is alluded to with these words.

The *sefer HaKesav VeHaKabbalah* explains that the root form of the word ח״ק means *interior.* Thus, חֵיק is on the inside of a person, and to be חוֹקֵק means to make an indentation. Pursuing the חֻקִּים thus means that one is involved in that part of Torah that demands an intense search to reach its meaning. This cannot be a reference to the תּוֹרָה שֶׁבִּכְתָב, *the Written Part of the Torah,* whose superficial meaning is readily apparent, but which cannot yield the full meaning and intention of the Torah. It must therefore refer to the pursuit of the Oral Law, which is the part of the Torah that teaches how to fulfill the mitzvos, and illuminates the underlying concepts that animate them. This is not a study that comes easily, for to understand the Oral Law demands serious effort and toil.

To "go in the חֻקִּים" therefore means that one is to be constantly on a path of penetrating beyond the superficial meaning of the laws and lessons of the Torah, and reaching toward their inner significance.

Another explanation is offered by the *Beis Yisrael.* The mitzvos that are referred to by the Torah as חֻקִּים, *statutes* (in contrast to מִצְוֹת or מִשְׁפָּטִים), are those for which there is no readily understandable reason. At least at the outset, these mitzvos are unfathomable and seemingly illogical. A comparison may be made between חֻקִּים and the endeavor of toiling in the study of Torah, a task that is difficult at first. Without hard work, one will not readily find satisfaction in Torah learning. To succeed at it, one must be prepared to give up the pleasures of the world and to completely abandon relaxation as a goal. Only after extended and persistent effort does the true sweetness of Torah study begin to be felt. This activity is thus referred to as a *chok,* for it is similar to the *chok* whose reasons and logic are not easily understood (see also *Ohr HaChaim*).

פרשת בחקתי

SUNDAY

PARASHAS BECHUKOSAI

The *Admor of Slonim,* in his *Nesivos Shalom,* explains that the term to "go in My statutes" implies that one is "going" upon the path of his life in a way that is consistent with the statutes of the Torah. This does not refer to the technical fulfillment of the mitzvos. Rather, the Torah with all of its mitzvos teaches a Jew how he must live and think. This Torah attitude can then be applied to every aspect of one's life, even those not governed by a specific law.

How does one reach the level of being able to intuit the true will of Hashem in one's everyday actions? How can one learn to identify what the spirit of the law dictates when there is no letter of the law to instruct? Only through constant and honest toil in the study of the laws of the Torah. Such study has the effect of refining its student to the point where even his personal and mundane activities will be informed by the spirit of the Torah and executed for the sake of Heaven.

MISHNAH OF THE DAY: ERUVIN 10:1

T*efillin* consists of two components: בָּתִּים, thick black leather *casings,* and פָּרָשִׁיּוֹת, *passages* of the Torah written on parchment and inserted into the casings. It is a mitzvah (*Devarim* 6:8) to wear two *tefillin* — one on the head (*tefillin shel rosh*) and one on the arm (*tefillin shel yad*).

Our Mishnah discusses the law of one who finds abandoned *tefillin* on the Sabbath, in a place where he is not permitted to carry:

הַמּוֹצֵא תְּפִילִין — ***One who finds tefillin*** on the Sabbath in a field, where one is not permitted to carry and where the *tefillin* are in danger of being destroyed or desecrated,[1] מַכְנִיסָן זוּג זוּג — ***should bring them in*** to a house in the city ***pair*** by ***pair.***[2] רַבָּן גַּמְלִיאֵל אוֹמֵר — ***Rabban Gamliel***

NOTES

1. For example, by stray dogs.

2. He should don them as he would to perform the mitzvah of *tefillin,* and walk, while wearing them, to a safe shelter in the city, remove them, and then repeat this procedure until he has secured all the *tefillin* (*Rashi*).

The Mishnah in *Shabbos* teaches that one is not permitted to wear *tefillin* in a *reshus harabim* on the Sabbath, but if one does, he is not liable to a *chatas* and he has not transgressed any Biblical prohibition. The Gemara there states that this is even according to the view that *tefillin* are supposed to be donned on the Sabbath [שַׁבָּת זְמַן תְּפִילִין; this is a matter of dispute, see *Gems from the Gemara*], because there is a Rabbinic concern that one wearing *tefillin* in the *reshus harabim* might come to carry them. The implication is that according to the view that *tefillin* are not to be worn on the Sabbath [שַׁבָּת לַאו זְמַן תְּפִילִין], this reason is unnecessary; it is forbidden to wear *tefillin* in the *reshus harabim* simply because they are not a normal article of attire on

says: שְׁנַיִם שְׁנַיִם — He should bring them in *two [by] two.*[3] בַּמֶּה דְּבָרִים אֲמוּרִים — *Regarding what were* these *words said?*[4] בִּישָׁנוֹת — *Regarding old tefillin.* The obligation to rescue *tefillin* found in a field applies only to old ones. אֲבָל בַּחֲדָשׁוֹת פָּטוּר — *But* if the *tefillin* are *new, he is exempt*[5] from the obligation to rescue them.[6]

מְצָאָן — If *he found* a large number of *them* [*tefillin*] צְבָתִים — tied in *pairs* אוֹ כְּרִיכוֹת — *or bundles,* מַחְשִׁיךְ עֲלֵיהֶן — *he must stay with them until dark* וּמְבִיאָן — *and* then *bring them* to safety.[7] וּבַסַּכָּנָה — *But in* a time of *danger,* when one cannot guard the *tefillin* until the Sabbath ends,[8] מְכַסֶּן — *he may cover them* וְהוֹלֵךְ לוֹ — *and leave.*

NOTES

the Sabbath. The Gemara there adds that even according to the view that *tefillin* are not worn on the Sabbath, one who wears them in the *reshus harabim* is not liable to a *chatas* for doing so, because he is nonetheless transporting the *tefillin* in the manner of an article of attire [דֶּרֶךְ מַלְבּוּשׁ] (since *tefillin* are worn on weekdays).

According to both opinions, the Rabbis relaxed the prohibition against wearing *tefillin* in a *reshus harabim* in order to save them from desecration.

3. He should wear two arm *tefillin* and two head *tefillin* for each trip into the city.

4. I.e., in what case did the Rabbis permit the transport of *tefillin* on the Sabbath in this manner to prevent their possible desecration?

5. Actually, he is prohibited from doing so (*Tosafos*). [As mentioned above (in note 2), wearing *tefillin* in a *reshus harabim* is prohibited by Rabbinic decree, which was suspended to safeguard *tefillin* from desecration. Consequently, wearing these "new" *tefillin* in a *reshus harabim* may involve a transgression of this Rabbinic decree.]

6. The Gemara (97a) defines "old" *tefillin* as those that have their straps and knots in place, so that they are ready to be worn. If there are no straps, or they are not knotted, he cannot be obligated to bring them in, because it is impossible for him to put these *tefillin* on without making the requisite knots, and it is prohibited to make these knots on the Sabbath.

7. If the number of *tefillin* found is so great that he will not be able to transfer all of them to safety before the Sabbath ends, he must stay in the field and watch over them until dark, and then bring them all in together.

8. I.e., when the non-Jewish government has banned the performance of mitzvos, and it would be dangerous for him to remain and be discovered with the *tefillin* or to take them with him.

QUESTION OF THE DAY:

Why is a person called a הוֹלֵךְ, while an angel is called an עוֹמֵד?

For the answer, see page 295.

GEMS FROM THE GEMARA

The Mishnah taught that when one finds *tefillin* on the Sabbath in a field where he is not permitted to carry, the Sages allowed him to bring the *tefillin* into the private domain by wearing just one pair of *tefillin* at a time, while Rabban Gamliel permits wearing two pairs of *tefillin* at one time. The Gemara suggests a number of explanations for the dispute:

(1) They argue over whether the Sabbath is a time when one can fulfill the mitzvah of *tefillin*: The Tanna Kamma is of the opinion that the Sabbath is a time when one can fulfill the mitzvah of *tefillin.* If so, the dispensation to don *tefillin* in a *reshus harabim* derives from the mitzvah to wear *tefillin* on the Sabbath, not based on their status as an ornament. And since no special permit is being employed, there is no reason to say that the Rabbis permitted wearing more than one pair at a time for the purpose of their rescue. Furthermore, comments *Rashi,* since the mitzvah of *tefillin* applies on the Sabbath, the accompanying prohibition of בַּל תּוֹסִיף (not to add to a mitzvah — i.e., not to wear more than one pair of *tefillin*) also pertains. Thus, the prohibition of בַּל תּוֹסִיף certainly renders each additional *tefillin* a burden.

But Rabban Gamliel maintains that the Sabbath is not a time for fulfilling the mitzvah of *tefillin.* Hence, the dispensation to rescue even one pair of *tefillin* at a time must be based on their "ornament" status. Therefore, it follows that the Rabbis permitted more than one pair to be worn in order to effect their rescue (since there is no limit to the number of ornaments a person may choose to wear). [However, only those *tefillin* worn in the areas designated for the mitzvah are considered ornaments. Hence, Rabban Gamliel is restrained from permitting more than two pairs of *tefillin* at any one time, for that is the maximum number that fit at once on the designated areas of the arm and head (*Rashi*).]

(2) All agree that the Sabbath is a time when one can fulfill the mitzvah of *tefillin,* and all agree that *tefillin* are considered ornaments even if wearing them does not constitute a mitzvah; they argue only over whether in order to discharge an obligation imposed by the Torah, one need actually have intent that he is fulfilling a commandment of the Torah when he performs the mitzvah act, or does the mere performance of the mitzvah act, without such intent, suffice:

The Tanna Kamma is of the opinion that in order for one to discharge his mitzvah obligation, specific intent to fulfill a command of the Torah is not required. Since the Sabbath is a time when one can fulfill the mitzvah of *tefillin,* and since the Tanna Kamma does not require specific intent, when one dons two pairs of *tefillin* — even solely for the purpose of saving them — he nevertheless performs the mitzvah of *tefillin* with both pairs, instead of with one as the Torah prescribes. Since this constitutes a violation (albeit inadvertent) of the prohibition בַּל תּוֹסִיף (not to add to a mitzvah act), the Tanna Kamma restricted the rescuer to only one pair of *tefillin* at a time (*Rashi*).

Rabban Gamliel maintains that specific intent is required. Even though all agree that the mitzvah of *tefillin* can be performed on the Sabbath, they also concede that *tefillin* nonetheless qualify as ornaments as well. Since Rabban Gamliel holds that one cannot perform a mitzvah unless he intends specifically to do so, as long as one's sole intent is to save the *tefillin* there is no violation of בַּל תּוֹסִיף, even if two pairs of *tefillin* are worn simultaneously. Nor are the two pairs considered a burden, because in this interpretation it is universally accepted that *tefillin* qualify as ornaments. Hence, Rabban Gamliel permits the rescuer to don two pairs of *tefillin* for each trip into the city (*Rashi*).

(3) All agree that to discharge one's mitzvah obligation, no intent to fulfill a command of the Torah is required. But they argue over whether one transgresses the prohibition of בַּל תּוֹסִיף if he has no intent to perform the action as a mitzvah act:

The Tanna Kamma maintains that transgressing the prohibition of בַּל תּוֹסִיף also requires no intent. According to the Tanna Kamma, just as one fulfills a mitzvah obligation even though he does not intend to do so, so too he may transgress the prohibition against adding to the mitzvah even though he has no intention of performing it. Hence, the Tanna Kamma allows the rescuer to wear only one pair of *tefillin* at a time, lest he transgress בַּל תּוֹסִיף.

But Rabban Gamliel holds that transgressing the prohibition of בַּל תּוֹסִיף does require intent. He maintains that it is impossible to violate בַּל תּוֹסִיף unless one has intent to perform a mitzvah act, even thought he is in fact fulfilling a mitzvah at the time. Hence, Rabban Gamliel permits the rescuer to don two pairs of *tefillin* simultaneously.

A MUSSAR THOUGHT FOR THE DAY

The prophet Yirmiyah cries: עַל־מָה אָבְדָה הָאָרֶץ, *For what reason was the land lost?* What was the ultimate cause for the downfall of Eretz Yisrael and its subsequent utter destruction? The prophet answers in the Name of Hashem: עַל־עָזְבָם אֶת־תּוֹרָתִי . . . וְלֹא הָלְכוּ בָהּ, *Because of their forsaking My Torah . . . and they did not go in it* (*Yirmiyah* 9:11,12). The phrase *and they did not go in it* is explained by the Gemara (*Nedarim* 81a) as referring to the people's neglect regarding the recitation of the blessings that must be made each morning over the study of Torah.

This lapse seems to us to be a minor infraction indeed, one that cannot possibly be the reason for the exile. Moreover, we know that this was certainly not the only sin that the people of that time were guilty of. The most basic prohibitions of the Torah were being violated, and the prophets constantly pointed this out. What are we to make of the Gemara's interpretation of this verse, assigning the blame for the loss of the land to the people's neglect of reciting blessings upon the Torah?

Taz (*Orach Chaim* 47:1) explains as follows: Torah study has the power to protect the Jewish people from misfortune despite numerous and severe sins. If punishment eventually befalls them, it can only have been due to their negligence in Torah study. That generation had lost their connection to the study of Torah, because they did not study it as it is meant to be studied. They attempted to learn Torah at the same time that they were pursuing their own pleasures. Instead of expending serious effort in searching for the innermost meaning of the Torah they were studying, they studied superficially and merely perused the texts. Torah cannot be properly acquired in this manner, and it was indeed eventually lost to them. And as soon as they were bereft of the protection of the Torah, the consequences of their other sins bore down upon them.

All this is hinted at by the prophet with the words, וְלֹא הָלְכוּ בָהּ, *they did not go in it.* For, as we have seen above (*A Torah Thought for the Day*), "going" in Torah refers to the toil of Torah study. The Gemara implied just this criticism by faulting their omission of the blessing on Torah, which contains the formulation, וְצִוָּנוּ לַעֲסוֹק בְּדִבְרֵי תוֹרָה, *Who commanded us **to engross ourselves** in the words of Torah.* These words indicate that toil in Torah is the only way to truly fulfill that obligation, and it was this fact that they chose to ignore.

R' Meshullam Igra, one of the greatest Torah scholars of his time, was once asked to adjudicate a dispute between two businessmen who were

passing through his town. Due to the halachic intricacy of the case, R' Meshullam asked them to return the following day. The men did not have time to wait, and decided to take their case to the rabbi of their hometown, who decided the case immediately.

Some time later, the men met R' Meshullam and told him what their rabbi had answered them. Realizing that this was exactly the answer he himself had arrived at after much difficult work, he decided that he must go and pay his respects to a scholar of such stature.

When they met, the rabbi explained to R' Meshullam what had happened. When the men came to him, he did not know what to tell them, and he feared that he would be greatly embarrassed in his town. Without any option, he went to his inner chamber and cried to Hashem to help him. In answer to his prayers, he pulled a random book of responsa from the shelf and discovered in it exactly the case that had just been brought before him, along with a determination of the final halachah.

R' Meshullam's esteem for the rabbi's erudition vanished instantly. "To cry and pray is not difficult. True accomplishment in Torah, however, must be acquired only with diligent study."

HALACHAH OF THE DAY

The third category of *finishing* activities mentioned above is that of creating or assembling a utensil. To illustrate, the Gemara teaches that one who takes a small piece of wood and fashions a toothpick out of it violates the *melachah* of *finishing.*

Likewise, one who molds clay into a usable shape, such as a cup, has violated the *melachah* of *finishing* by creating a utensil. This applies also to one who crafts a utensil by peeling, shaving, or carving a hard substance.

Assembling two separate items that are not usable individually, but become usable when combined, is also a form of "creating" a utensil. This applies even in cases where the items in question are only loosely connected. For example, one may not insert a pair of laces into a new pair of shoes on Shabbos. Since the insertion of the laces renders the shoes usable, it is considered akin to the creation of the shoes and is thus forbidden as an act of *finishing.* Other examples of this form of *finishing* would be stuffing feathers into a pillow, or placing a new clasp on a necklace. In all these cases one is combining or assembling parts in order to create a usable finished item — an act forbidden on Shabbos.

There are instances, however, where assembly is permitted on Shabbos.

In cases where it is necessary for two separate items to be joined in order to facilitate their use, but they are generally separated after use, the initial joining is not seen as the creation of a finished item and is not prohibited.

For example, one may insert a belt into a new pair of pants on Shabbos without violating the *melachah* of *finishing.* While the pants may not be wearable without the belt, since a belt is typically inserted for its use and then removed after the pants have been worn, the belt and the pants are never considered to have become one unified object. They are simply two individual items meant to be used together when necessary and separated after use. Since no new usable item is being created, no *melachah* has been violated.

Having mentioned the example of a belt, we must note that if a belt is intended to be inserted into a garment permanently, it may not be inserted for the first time on Shabbos. For example, the belt of a coat is generally meant to be left in place permanently. This being the case, it should not be put in its place for the first time on Shabbos.

A CLOSER LOOK AT THE SIDDUR

As we have seen above (*A Mussar Thought for the Day*), the wording of the blessing on the Torah does not follow the format of most other blessings. We do not say *"Who commanded us* ***regarding the mitzvah of learning Torah,"*** but *"Who commanded us* ***to engross ourselves in the words of Torah"*** [לַעֲסוֹק בְּדִבְרֵי תוֹרָה]. We learned that according to the *Taz,* this reflects the nature of the mitzvah to learn Torah, which is properly fulfilled only when done with effort and dedication.

The *Alter of Kelm* explains in a similar vein. The word עֵסֶק can mean *business.* When a person is involved in his business, that which earns him his livelihood, all other errands and chores must take a back seat. One's business is the first priority. This is also understood by those around him; when he is working, he cannot be bothered by other things, no matter how important they may be.

A person must treat his Torah study as if it were his business. The time set aside for study must be sacrosanct. When a person conducts himself

in this way, those around him will also understand that he cannot be disturbed while learning. Thus, לַעֲסוֹק בְּדִבְרֵי תוֹרָה means to be involved in the "business" of learning Torah.

The *Sefer HaChaim* (by the brother of the *Maharal*) offers a different explanation of this phrase. מִתְעַסֵּק, he explains, refers to inadvertent action. One who is עוֹסֵק in Torah is one who is involved in the learning, but without a true understanding of the reasons for the mitzvos. Since we are enjoined to learn the mitzvos even if we do not perceive the reasons behind them, we word the commandment in the blessing "to be involved," even without true understanding, "in the words of the Torah."

However, this is followed immediately by a prayer that we should merit to ultimately feel a connection with the underlying reasons for the various mitzvos. וְהַעֲרֶב נָא . . . אֶת דִּבְרֵי תוֹרָתְךָ בְּפִינוּ . . . וְנִהְיֶה אֲנַחְנוּ . . . יוֹדְעֵי שְׁמֶךָ, *Please sweeten . . . the words of Your Torah in our mouth . . . May we . . . know Your Name . . .* The inner knowledge of the reasons and ideas behind the mitzvos is referred to in kabbalistic sources as "knowledge of the Name of Hashem."

R' Tzadok of Lublin explains that the word "Torah," which literally means *instruction* or *guide,* refers to the learning of Torah for its own sake. Such learning has the power to guide a person with the inner light of the Torah and protect him from sin. One who does not learn Torah for its own sake does not receive this spiritual guidance from the Torah and cannot be considered to be learning "Torah," but only speaking "the words of Torah."

Since we do not presume to be on the level of learning Torah for its own sake, we begin the day's prayers with a blessing on the commandment to "involve ourselves in the words of Torah." However, we immediately pray that from this level we eventually merit to reach the level of those who *study Your **Torah,*** לוֹמְדֵי תוֹרָתֶךָ, not merely the "words of Torah," לִשְׁמָהּ, *for its own sake.*

A TORAH THOUGHT FOR THE DAY

פרשת בחקתי

MONDAY

PARASHAS BECHUKOSAI

אֲנִי ה' אֱלֹהֵיכֶם אֲשֶׁר הוֹצֵאתִי אֶתְכֶם מֵאֶרֶץ מִצְרַיִם מִהְיֹת לָהֶם עֲבָדִים וָאֶשְׁבֹּר מֹטֹת עֻלְּכֶם וָאוֹלֵךְ אֶתְכֶם קוֹמְמִיּוּת

I am HASHEM, your God, Who took you out of the land of Egypt from being their slaves; I broke the staves of your yoke and I led you erect (*Vayikra* 26:13).

According to the simple meaning of the verse, the phrase וָאוֹלֵךְ אֶתְכֶם קוֹמְמִיּוּת, *and I led you erect,* is a continuation of the metaphor regarding the yoke of slavery that Hashem had removed from the Jewish people. Once the yoke of slavery had been lifted, the Jews could walk erect and without stooping (see *Rashbam*). Accordingly, the verse evokes imagery conveying the idea of total freedom (see *Targum Onkelos*). The Midrash, however, comments cryptically that this phrase alludes to the height of Adam HaRishon. *Edus Bihosef* explains the Midrash as follows:

Originally Adam HaRishon was of such extraordinary height that there was no room for him on earth. However, since he resided in Gan Eden, this did not pose a problem. Once he sinned and had to be expelled from Gan Eden, his great size was diminished (see *Tosafos* to *Chagigah* 12a).

The blessing immediately preceding our verse is: וְהִתְהַלַּכְתִּי בְּתוֹכְכֶם, *I will walk among you,* which is explained by *Rashi* as referring to Hashem's association with Adam in Gan Eden. The culmination of the blessings in this passage is that the people will reach the level of actually living in Gan Eden together with Hashem. Since the only reason for the reduction in Adam's size was the lack of place for him outside of Gan Eden, when the people will once again reach the level of living in Gan Eden they will be able to return to the size of Adam HaRishon!

R' Yerucham Levovitz explains that the concept of "walking erect" reflects the essential nature of the spirituality of man. Man is essentially a spiritual creature, always striving heavenward. He comes from the heavens, and it is to the heavens that he is to return. In contrast, a beast is a creature of the earth, and that is also his final destination. Its essence is one of complete physicality, with all of its energies focused on its physical survival and welfare. The true nature of each is reflected in their natural postures. Man, who is spiritual and of the heavens, stands upright, with his head facing upward, reflecting his nature of perpetual spiritual growth. The beast faces the ground, the physical representation of its true essence.

Pride can cause one to walk erect. We speak here of a pride that is a reflection of the holiness of one's soul, where one's spirituality knows of no lowering or bending (see *A Mussar Thought for the Day*). It is this pride and spiritual aristocracy (חֵרוּתָא) of which *Onkelos* speaks in rendering the word קוֹמְמִיּוּת.

This, then, is the sense of the verse: I am Hashem Who has freed you from Egyptian bondage, and by removing you from servitude to man and bringing you to the servitude to God, I have transformed you into a true aristocrat. You now walk upright and erect as befits the servants of a king, who, by virtue of their bond with royalty, are likewise regarded.

MISHNAH OF THE DAY: ERUVIN 10:2

In the previous Mishnah, the Tanna Kamma ruled that in times of danger, one should merely cover *tefillin* found exposed on Shabbos, and leave them there. The Gemara records R' Shimon's dissenting opinion:

רַבִּי שִׁמְעוֹן אוֹמֵר — ***R' Shimon says:*** **נוֹתְנָן לַחֲבֵירוֹ** — ***He should give them to his friend,*** **וַחֲבֵירוֹ לַחֲבֵירוֹ** — ***and his friend*** gives them ***to his friend,***[1] **עַד שֶׁמַּגִּיעַ** — ***until he reaches*** **לֶחָצֵר הַחִיצוֹנָה** — ***the outermost courtyard*** of the city.[2] **וְכֵן בְּנוֹ** — ***So too,*** if he must transport ***his child,*** who was born in the field on the Sabbath and must subsequently be transported to the house, **נוֹתְנוֹ לַחֲבֵירוֹ** — ***he should give him to his friend,*** **וַחֲבֵירוֹ לַחֲבֵירוֹ** — ***and his friend*** gives the child

NOTES

1. Presumably, R' Shimon refers to the circumstances discussed by the Tanna Kamma — a time of danger — and asserts that instead of merely covering the *tefillin,* he should hand them to his friend, etc. This is puzzling, since, as mentioned in the previous Mishnah (note 8), the danger spoken of is the fear of being caught in the performance of mitzvos. This danger is seemingly heightened if the method endorsed by R' Shimon is followed, because of the number of people it involves! See *Gems from the Gemara* for the resolution of this problem.

2. I.e., to the first protected area at the outskirts of the town.

The last person to handle the *tefillin* may not place them into the courtyard himself, for by doing so he would be transferring an object from the public to the private domain, which is a Biblical *melachah.* Rather, he should extend his hand into the courtyard and let someone inside remove the *tefillin.* Thereby, he has performed only one-half of the *melachah.* Although even that is normally prohibited by Rabbinic law (see *Shabbos* 1:1), here it is permitted in order to save the *tefillin* from desecration (*Geon Yaakov*).

to his friend, אֲפִילוּ מֵאָה — *even if they are a hundred.*[3] רַבִּי יְהוּדָה אוֹמֵר — *R' Yehudah says:* נוֹתֵן אָדָם חָבִית לַחֲבֵירוֹ — *A person may give a barrel to his friend,* וַחֲבֵירוֹ לַחֲבֵרוֹ — *and his friend to his friend,*[4] אֲפִילוּ חוּץ לַתְּחוּם — *even beyond the techum.*[5] אָמְרוּ לוֹ — *They said to him:* לֹא תְהַלֵּךְ זוֹ — *This* barrel *should not go* יוֹתֵר מֵרַגְלֵי בְעָלֶיהָ — *further than the feet of its owner.*[6]

NOTES

3. "Even . . . a hundred." This expression was not used before in reference to the transfer of *tefillin.* The Gemara explains that R' Shimon maintains his opinion even in regard to a baby, where it might be thought that out of regard for the newborn baby, for whom the passage through so many hands could be uncomfortable, he would permit the first Tanna's method. R' Shimon's apprehension for potential Sabbath desecration (see *Gems from the Gemara*) overrides his concern for the child's comfort.

4. R' Yehudah endorses the view of R' Shimon and even extends it. The dispute between R' Shimon and the Rabbis concerned only which method of carrying in the *reshus harabim* was preferable in certain extenuating circumstances. R' Shimon agreed, however, that normally his method of carrying was prohibited by Rabbinic law. In contrast, R' Yehudah maintains that the method of handing from person to person is entirely permissible and may be used even for ordinary needs. Thus, he rules that one who finds a barrel of food or beverage in the *reshus harabim* on the Sabbath may bring it to his home using the "passing" method of transfer (*Ramban* in *Milchamos; Raavad* cited there; *Ritva; Rambam, Hil. Shabbos* 12:17; cf. *R' Yehonasan*).

5. The Gemara (97b) explains that R' Yehudah rules that one need not be concerned about *techum* in regard to the barrel, because the barrel and its contents were *hefker,* ownerless, and R' Yehudah maintains that ownerless objects do not have a *techum* limit imposed upon them.

6. One may not take the barrel out of the area allowed its owner by the laws of *techum.* The status of the barrel is totally dependent on the *techum* status of the owner. If he has made an *eruv,* the barrel must remain within the area defined as the *techum* of the *eruv;* and if he has not made an *eruv,* the barrel is confined to the *techum* of the dwelling (*Rashi*). The Gemara explains this anonymous opinion as claiming that even objects that were ownerless at the onset of Shabbos have a *techum* assigned to them.

QUESTION OF THE DAY:

To which* עוֹל *(burden) is this verse* (26:13) *referring?

For the answer, see page 295.

GEMS FROM THE GEMARA

The Tanna in the previous Mishnah taught that in a time of danger one may cover the *tefillin* and leave. The Gemara wonders how R' Shimon could begin our Mishnah by teaching that if one finds many pairs of *tefillin* in a field, he should give them to his friend and his friend to his friend. How could R' Shimon advocate that course of action? Certainly, such a public display would attract attention, and therefore endanger the lives of those involved in saving the *tefillin* even more!

The Gemara answers that it is as if the Mishnah were missing words, and this is what it teaches: When did the Tanna Kamma teach the ruling to cover the *tefillin* and depart? When there is a danger that non-Jews will execute anyone suspected of wearing *tefillin.* But if the danger is posed by highwaymen, then one should transport all the *tefillin* by carrying them less than 4 *amos* and then stopping, repeating this procedure as often as necessary to reach the city. By transferring the *tefillin* to safety in this manner, one avoids violating the Biblical injunction against carrying 4 *amos* in the *reshus harabim.* [Since in this case it is not dangerous for him to be discovered with *tefillin,* he cannot simply leave them in their place. However, since it is dangerous for him to stay in that place, he does not have to remain there until dark.] And it was to that latter ruling that R' Shimon objected, arguing that the preferred method of removing the *tefillin* is by passing them from hand to hand.

The Gemara then explains the underlying issue in the dispute between R' Shimon and the Rabbis regarding this latter ruling. The Tanna Kamma held that walking less than 4 *amos* at a time is preferable, because if you say that one should give the *tefillin* to his friend and his friend should pass them along to his friend until the *tefillin* eventually reach the city, the matter of disrespect for the Sabbath is needlessly publicized. And R' Shimon maintained that passing them to his friend is preferable, because if you say that one should transport the *tefillin* by walking less than 4 *amos* at a time, sometimes he might forget and come to carry them a full 4 *amos* in the *reshus harabim,* thereby committing a Biblical desecration of the Sabbath.

R' Shimon agrees, however, that where other people are not available, he may carry the *tefillin* in a series of moves less than 4 *amos* each. His disagreement with the first Tanna is only regarding which of the two methods is preferable (*Tosafos*).

A MUSSAR THOUGHT FOR THE DAY

In *A Torah Thought for the Day* we explained the meaning of the verse's statement that the Jewish people will reach the point that they go with "an erect bearing." There is, however, a basic difficulty with this verse. It is written in the Gemara (*Kiddushin* 31a) and ruled in *Shulchan Aruch* (*Orach Chaim* §2) that one is forbidden to walk with an erect bearing. To walk or even simply to stand in this manner is pretentious and is seen as a sign of excessive pride. To walk in this manner is considered as *pushing away the Divine Presence.* How, then, can this attitude be an illustration of a high spiritual level — indeed the culmination of all the blessings promised to those who would uphold the Torah in its entirety?

R' Shimon Schwab writes (in his *Iyun Tefillah*) that when he was learning as a young man in the yeshivah in Mir, his rebbi, *R' Yerucham Levovitz,* offered 10 *zloty* to any student who could answer this question. R' Schwab recounts that although he did not have an answer at the time, over the years he has come to a realization that there is more than one way to stand erectly, and that there is a great difference between the different ways.

One who is filled with arrogance will straighten himself up and carry himself in a way that mirrors his own excessive pride. However, one can also pull oneself up to one's full height in order to express his total potential. This is what one does when being measured by the doctor. This posture can serve as a positive metaphor for the fulfillment of one's potential. When the Torah describes the Jewish people as walking with erect bearing, the meaning is that as a nation they will reach the spiritual level of Adam before his sin, the highest possible level that man can reach. This is aptly described by the erect bearing of a person reaching his full height.

[R' Schwab added that he believes that this explanation would have earned him the 10 *zloty* from his rebbi!]

Sfas Emes explains that regarding an erect bearing there is a difference between this world and the next. When in this world, a person is inherently imperfect, and must therefore display submission to Hashem by assuming a less than fully-erect bearing. In the next world, when a person will be perfected, it will be possible for him to straighten up to his natural full height without diminishing his complete submission to Hashem. *R' Gedaliah Schorr* points out that this is the meaning of the phrase found in the *Nishmas* prayer (recited during *Pesukei D'Zimrah* on Shabbos and festivals) that כָּל קוֹמָה לְפָנֶיךָ תִשְׁתַּחֲוֶה, *every erect spine shall prostrate itself before You.* In the future, it will be natural to submit to Hashem even with an erect bearing.

Chasam Sofer explains that the propriety of "erect bearing" depends on what one's initial behavior is, and Hashem's reaction to that behavior. When a person raises himself above where he should be and behaves with undue pride, Hashem's reaction is to withdraw His presence from this person. However, a person who submits himself to Hashem and walks humbly merits the opposite reaction — Hashem raises him up and dwells together with him; thus, he will be able to stand erect.

HALACHAH OF THE DAY

Yesterday, we mentioned one example of permissible assembling. We will now mention one more form of assembling permitted by some *poskim.*

There are *poskim* who rule that when two separate parts need to be joined in order to facilitate their use, but their attachment is weak in nature and the finished item is intended for one-time use, the item may be assembled on Shabbos without any violation of *melachah.* This would be true even if the parts of the finished item are not separated after its use. An example of this would be the assembly of an injection syringe. Since the syringe is intended to be used once and then discarded, the needle may be attached to the body of the syringe on Shabbos, and it does not have to be broken apart before it is discarded.

The fourth category of activities included in *finishing* is the repairing or reassembling of a broken utensil. The laws governing this category vary depending on the type of repair as well as the solidity of the assembly.

The *melachah* of *finishing* can be violated when effecting a repair with or without the use of tools.

If the article being repaired cannot be used at all without first being repaired, performing the repair is Biblically forbidden. If the item still has limited functionality, the repair is Rabbinically forbidden. [It should be noted that the parts of a broken utensil that one is Biblically forbidden to repair are often considered to be *muktzeh.* We will discuss this issue in greater detail further along.]

In order to illustrate the above guidelines, we will use the example given by the Mishnah (*Beitzah* 28a). The Mishnah states: "We may not sharpen a knife on Yom Tov." A dull knife that cannot cut at all is considered to be a broken utensil. By sharpening it, one in effect "recreates" the utensil — thus violating the *melachah* of *finishing* on a Biblical level.

The same would apply to straightening out a knife that is bent. By considering different possible cases of bent knives, one can easily understand the difference between a Biblical violation and a Rabbinical one. If the knife is bent to the extent that it cannot be used, straightening it would violate the Biblical prohibition. If, however, the knife is still somewhat usable in its present condition, straightening it or sharpening it is a violation of Rabbinic law.

A CLOSER LOOK AT THE SIDDUR

The blessing of being led קוֹמְמִיּוּת, with an *erect bearing* or *upright pride,* is mentioned in the context of our prayers in the *Ahavah Rabbah* blessing, which is said prior to the recitation of the morning *Shema.* We say: וַהֲבִיאֵנוּ לְשָׁלוֹם מֵאַרְבַּע כַּנְפוֹת הָאָרֶץ וְתוֹלִיכֵנוּ קוֹמְמִיּוּת לְאַרְצֵנוּ, *Bring us in peacefulness from the four corners of the earth, and lead us with upright pride to our land.* According to *R' Shimon Schwab* (see above, *A Mussar Thought for the Day*), this blessing refers to the Jewish people reaching their highest national potential, something that is assured to us only in the World to Come. Here, in our prayers, we ask that even before the epoch of the World to Come, the nation should merit to reach this exalted level with the coming of Mashiach.

According to *Siach Yitzchak,* the term קוֹמְמִיּוּת, meaning *with upright pride,* refers to the manner in which Mashiach will come. The Gemara (*Sanhedrin* 98a) comments that two verses describing the coming of Mashiach seem to contradict each other. One (*Daniel* 7:13) describes Mashiach as coming with the clouds of the heavens; the other (*Zechariah* 9:9) describes him as a poor man riding on a donkey. The Gemara explains that if the generation is worthy, they will merit the more glorious revelation of Mashiach, and if not, he will come to them as a poor man riding on a donkey. In this prayer, as we ask for the coming of Mashiach, we add that his coming be one of pride and uprightness, the mark of the meritorious generation.

Chasam Sofer explains the two parts of this prayer — that we come in peace and that we be led in an upright manner — as referring to two separate but necessary components of the future salvation. Were we to

omit the second phrase, we would not have asked to see Eretz Yisrael while alive, since the dead too will be brought to Eretz Yisrael (through underground tunnels — see *Kesubos* 111a) at the time of *techiyas hameisim* (the resurrection of the dead). We therefore add that we be led "upright" to the land.

On the other hand, it is also important to add that we would like to come *in peacefulness,* for without that we would not be praying for the coming of Mashiach, but simply to arrive in Eretz Yisrael. We therefore say both parts of the prayer. We plead to be brought, while alive, to see the ultimate salvation in Eretz Yisrael.

A similar thought is explained by the *Dover Shalom* regarding the precision of the language of וַהֲבִיאֵנוּ לְשָׁלוֹם. The Gemara (*Berachos* 64a) writes that one who takes leave of the living says לֵךְ לְשָׁלוֹם, *go* ***to*** *peace,* while those who take leave of the dead say לֵךְ בְּשָׁלוֹם, *go* ***in*** *peace.* In this prayer too, since we are praying to be gathered to Eretz Yisrael while still alive, we say . . . וַהֲבִיאֵנוּ לְשָׁלוֹם, *bring us* ***to*** *peace,* i.e., may we merit to be led to Eretz Yisrael while still very much alive.

A TORAH THOUGHT FOR THE DAY

וְנָתַתִּי אֶת־עָרֵיכֶם חָרְבָּה וַהֲשִׁמּוֹתִי
אֶת־מִקְדְּשֵׁיכֶם וְלֹא אָרִיחַ בְּרֵיחַ נִיחֹחֲכֶם

I will lay your cities in ruin and I will make your sanctuaries desolate; I will not savor your satisfying aromas (*Vayikra* 26:31).

The above translation follows the explanation of the *Ibn Ezra,* who states that the words וַהֲשִׁמּוֹתִי אֶת־מִקְדְּשֵׁיכֶם refer to the destruction of the *Beis HaMikdash.* He explains that the previous verse had foretold that the Spirit of Hashem will reject the people (וְגָעֲלָה נַפְשִׁי אֶתְכֶם), which refers to the departure of the Divine Presence from the *Beis HaMikdash.* At that point it is no longer called מִקְדָּשִׁי, *My* Sanctuary, but מִקְדְּשֵׁיכֶם, *your* sanctuaries, and is subject to destruction and desolation.

Rashi, however, does not follow this explanation. He explains that the destruction of the *Beis HaMikdash* is described in the following phrase: וְלֹא אָרִיחַ בְּרֵיחַ נִיחֹחֲכֶם, *I will not savor your satisfying aromas.* This is a clear reference to the offerings of the *Beis HaMikdash,* which have the effect of giving a satisfying aroma to Hashem (see *Rashi* to *Vayikra* 1:9). Now, states Hashem in his *Tochachah* (Rebuke), there will no longer be any offerings to provide that satisfying aroma. It must be, then, that the previous phrase does not refer to the destruction of the *Beis HaMikdash* itself, but to another aspect of the *churban. Rashi* therefore renders מִקְדְּשֵׁיכֶם as *your prepared ones* (from קַדֵּשׁ, *to make ready*), and explains it as a reference to the throngs of pilgrims who would come to the city of Yerushalayim after purifying themselves. The verse here foretells that the city will become desolate, for these throngs of pilgrims will come no more.

A different explanation of the verse is offered by the *Netziv* in his *Haamek Davar.* He explains that the first part of the verse refers to the physical destruction of the *Beis HaMikdash* (as *Ibn Ezra* explained). However, even after the structure of the *Beis HaMikdash* is destroyed, it would be theoretically possible to bring offerings on the Altar. This verse declares that these offerings will not be accepted by Hashem. This precludes the bringing of offerings on the Altar even without the *Beis HaMikdash,* since the offerings are not valid without having the effect of providing this *satisfying aroma* to Hashem (see *Zevachim* 46b).

Interestingly, there is one exception to the above rule. The *pesach*-offering is not brought with the purpose of causing a *satisfying aroma,* and could therefore be offered even at the time when Hashem is not savoring

the satisfying aromas of the offerings. Indeed, *Haamek Davar* writes, there was a while, even after the destruction of the second *Beis HaMikdash,* when there was an Altar intact upon which they did bring the *pesach*-offering!

When will the promise of לֹא אָרִיחַ end? *Netziv* writes that when the nations will give permission to rebuild the *Beis HaMikdash,* it will be a clear signal of Divine favor, and the nullification of this curse. At that time, we will once again be able to bring all the offerings on the place of the original Altar. [Due to historical developments in the middle of the 19th century, a fascinating debate in fact developed regarding the possibility of reinstating some of the offerings on the Temple Mount. See, for example, Responsa of *Binyan Tziyon* (§1) from *R' Yaakov Ettlinger,* the *Aruch LaNer.*]

MISHNAH OF THE DAY: ERUVIN 10:3

The Mishnah discusses another instance where a Rabbinic injunction was suspended so that a sacred object could be treated with its due respect:

הָיָה קוֹרֵא בְּסֵפֶר עַל הָאִיסְקוּפָּה — If ***one was reading a book,*** i.e., a scroll of Scripture, while ***on a threshold,***[1] **וְנִתְגַּלְגֵּל הַסֵּפֶר מִיָּדוֹ** — ***and*** one end of ***the book rolled from his hand*** into the *reshus harabim* below, while the other end remained in the reader's hand, **גּוֹלְלוֹ אֶצְלוֹ** — ***he may roll it*** in ***to himself.***[2]

NOTES

1. The threshold discussed here is elevated, similar to a stoop. The Gemara initially assumes that it is a *reshus hayachid* (i.e., it is 10 *tefachim* high and 4 wide); see below. The books in Mishnaic times were written on scrolls (*Rashi*).

2. The Biblical prohibition against transferring objects between a *reshus harabim* and a *reshus hayachid* applies only if one transfers an entire object from one *reshus* to another (see *Shabbos* 91b). In our case, the scroll is only partially in the *reshus harabim,* since one end is still in his hand on the threshold; therefore, even if the threshold is a *reshus hayachid,* there is no Biblical injunction against rolling the fallen end of the scroll back onto the threshold. However, a Rabbinic prohibition is in order, to forbid one to roll in the scroll as a safeguard against the possibility that the entire scroll might fall out of his hands into the *reshus harabim* below, and he might come to transgress the Biblical violation of bringing it from the *reshus harabim* back onto the threshold.

Apparently, this clause of the Mishnah maintains that no Rabbinic law stands in the way of treating the Holy Scriptures with their due respect; therefore, this Rabbinic decree is waived so that the scroll may be rolled in and not left hanging. This follows the opinion of R' Shimon; see below.

פרשת בחקתי

TUESDAY

PARASHAS BECHUKOSAI

הָיָה קוֹרֵא בְּרֹאשׁ הַגַּג — If *one was reading on top of a roof* (which is a *reshus hayachid*), וְנִתְגַּלְגֵּל הַסֵּפֶר מִיָּדוֹ — *and* one end of *the book rolled from his hand* into the *reshus harabim* below, עַד שֶׁלֹּא הִגִּיעַ לַעֲשָׂרָה טְפָחִים גּוֹלְלוֹ אֶצְלוֹ — *as long as it has not* yet *reached to* within *ten tefachim* of the ground *he may roll it* in *to himself.*[3] מִשֶּׁהִגִּיעַ לַעֲשָׂרָה טְפָחִים הוֹפְכוֹ עַל הַכְּתָב — *Once it has reached to* within *ten tefachim* of the ground, however, he may not roll it in; rather, *he should turn it over on its written side* so that the lettering is not exposed, and leave it there until the end of the Sabbath.[4] רַבִּי יְהוּדָה אוֹמֵר — *R' Yehudah says:* אֲפִילּוּ אֵין מְסוּלָּק מִן הָאָרֶץ אֶלָּא כִּמְלֹא מַחַט — *Even if it was removed from the ground by only a pin's thickness,* גּוֹלְלוֹ אֶצְלוֹ — *he may roll* it in *to himself* — but not once it has reached the ground itself.[5] רַבִּי שִׁמְעוֹן אוֹמֵר — *R' Shimon says:* אֲפִילּוּ בָּאָרֶץ עַצְמוֹ גּוֹלְלוֹ אֶצְלוֹ — *Even* if the fallen end of the scroll is *on the ground itself, he may roll it* in *to himself,* שֶׁאֵין לְךָ דָּבָר מִשּׁוּם שְׁבוּת עוֹמֵד בִּפְנֵי כִּתְבֵי הַקּוֹדֶשׁ — *because no law which is* only of *Rabbinic* origin *stands in the way of* treating *the Holy Scriptures* with their due respect.[6]

NOTES

3. Airspace above 10 *tefachim* from the *reshus harabim* is considered a *makom petur,* an exempt area. Thus, even if he had released the scroll, no Biblical prohibition would have been involved in returning it to the roof from where the lower end of the scroll is sitting. The Sages thus permitted its retrieval as long as one end is in his hands.

4. It is a disgrace for a book of Scripture to lie open and exposed to the street. By turning the written side of the scroll to the wall, one at least minimizes the disgrace (*Rashi*). The ideal procedure would be to roll in the entire scroll; however, although this is permitted according to Biblical law (see note 2), it is nevertheless forbidden by Rabbinic decree. The Rabbis were concerned that the entire scroll might fall out of his hand into the *reshus harabim* (or its 10-*tefach* airspace), in which case retrieving it would constitute a Biblical transgression. They therefore forbade one to roll it in even in the event that one end is still in his hand.

The Gemara explains that in both of these cases, the unrolled end "came to rest" on a wall slanted toward the street. In one case, the hanging part of the scroll is sitting on the wall more than 10 *tefachim* above the *reshus harabim* (and thus is at rest in a *makom petur*), and in the other case, it rests below 10 *tefachim* (and thus is at rest in a public domain).

5. R' Yehudah does not disagree with the ruling set forth in regard to a scroll coming to rest on a slanty wall within 10 *tefachim* of the street. Rather, he is referring to an entirely different case, where the scroll did not come to rest, but was left dangling in the air. R' Yehudah rules that, in contrast to the previous case, here the scroll may be rolled back even if it enters the 10-*tefach* airspace of the *reshus harabim.* For since the scroll did not come to rest at all, retrieving it in these circumstances would not involve a Biblical prohibition even if the scroll had left his hand entirely.

6. According to R' Shimon, the decree mentioned above (note 4) is waived so that the scroll will not be left in this demeaning state until the end of the Sabbath.

GEMS FROM THE GEMARA

Simply understood, the threshold in the Mishnah's first clause is a *reshus hayachid,* and the area in front of it is a *reshus harabim.* And yet, although there is room for the Rabbis to forbid one to roll in the scroll in this case (see note 2 to the Mishnah), apparently this clause of the Mishnah follows R' Shimon, who holds that no Rabbinic law stands in the way of treating the Holy Scriptures with their due respect. But, the Gemara asks, R' Shimon's opinion is quoted again in the latter part of the Mishnah, resulting in the implausible arrangement of the first and last clauses of the Mishnah reflecting the opinion of R' Shimon, and the middle clause reflecting the opinion of R' Yehudah!

Abaye explains that the Mishnah's threshold is actually a *karmelis* [i.e., it is 4 *tefachim* wide but less than 10 *tefachim* high], and a *reshus harabim* passes in front of it. Accordingly, if the end of the scroll fell within 4 *amos* of the threshold, even if it were to fall entirely out of the person's hands and he were to bring it back to the threshold, he will not have transgressed a Biblical prohibition, since the threshold is not a *reshus hayachid.* Therefore, where one end is still in his hands, the Rabbis permitted him to roll the scroll back onto the threshold. Where the potential exists for a *Biblical* violation were the entire scroll to fall out of his hands, the Rabbis forbade him to roll it even in the event that he still holds onto one end of the scroll. But where there is no potential for a Biblical violation even if the scroll were to fall entirely out of his hands, he is allowed to roll it in provided one end is still in his hand.

According to this explanation, the first ruling of the Mishnah is a unanimous one: where the threshold is a *karmelis* and there is no possibility of a Biblical violation, R' Yehudah concedes that the scroll may be rolled in. R' Yehudah rules restrictively only where the potential for a Biblical transgression exists, such as in the latter case of the Mishnah where the man is sitting on a roof, which is certainly a *reshus hayachid.*

The Gemara asks: If R' Yehudah forbids one to roll a scroll back onto a threshold where the potential for a Biblical violation exists, then let R' Yehudah prohibit one to roll it in out of concern that the entire scroll might fall out of his hands into the *reshus harabim,* and he might bring it in from the *reshus harabim* via the threshold to the *reshus hayachid* on the other side of the threshold, which is a Biblical violation! [Generally, a threshold leads into a house or some other type of enclosed building. There should therefore be a concern that he might pick up the scroll from the *reshus harabim* and take it directly into his house.]

[And even though a *karmelis* interposes between the *reshus harabim* and the *reshus hayachid,* it is still in fact a Biblical transgression, because Rava said that one who passes an object in the *reshus harabim* from the beginning of a 4-*amah* stretch to the end of the 4 *amos,* even if he passed it over himself via the *mekom petur* (i.e., more than 10 *tefachim* above the ground), he has nevertheless transgressed a Biblical violation. This proves that the fact that an object is passed through an intervening exempt area does not alleviate the prohibition. Consequently, in our case, one who would carry a scroll from a *reshus harabim* to a *reshus hayachid* via a *karmelis* does indeed commit a Biblical transgression. If so, why was a Rabbinic decree not promulgated to prevent such a violation from occurring?]

The Gemara gives two answers to this question:

(1) We are dealing here with an elongated threshold, i.e., there is a considerable distance between the *reshus harabim* and the *reshus hayachid.* Consequently, we assume he will remember as he carries the scroll over the threshold that he will incur a Biblical violation if he takes it directly into the *reshus hayachid.* It can be presumed, therefore, that he will stop first on the threshold. [It is not necessary for him to physically put the scroll down. Merely making a complete pause on the threshold (e.g., to rest or to peruse the book) is sufficient for the scroll to be considered at rest in that domain even while it is still in his hand (*Rashi*).] Then, since the scroll came to rest on the threshold, his act of carrying is legally considered to have come to an end. When he resumes walking, he initiates a new act of carrying. Thus even if he were to continue and take the scroll into the *reshus hayachid,* we do not view his actions as a transference from a *reshus harabim* to a *reshus hayachid,* but rather as two independent acts: one act of carrying from a *reshus harabim* to a *karmelis,* and one from a *karmelis* to a *reshus hayachid.*

(2) We are not concerned that he might come to carry the entire scroll directly from the *reshus harabim* into the *reshus hayachid,* because this Mishnah follows the opinion of Ben Azzai, who said that walking is tantamount to standing. That is, an object that is carried by a person who is walking is considered to be at rest every time the person places his foot on the ground, just as an object is considered to be at rest when held by a person who stands motionless. Consequently, one who carries the scroll over the threshold, even without stopping, does not commit a Biblical violation because the scroll is considered to be at rest on the threshold with each step that he takes.

The Gemara concludes that there is no concern that he will pick up the Holy Scriptures and *throw* them from the *reshus harabim* to the *reshus hayachid* (in which case even Ben Azzai concedes that he commits a Biblical violation, since a thrown object is not considered to be at rest until it actually lands). This is because one is not allowed to throw Holy Scriptures; we are thus not concerned that he might throw the scroll, because it is forbidden to do so.

A MUSSAR THOUGHT FOR THE DAY

We have seen that as part of the *Tochachah,* Hashem promises to withdraw His Divine Presence from among the people, as the verse says (*Vayikra* 26:30): וְגָעֲלָה נַפְשִׁי אֶתְכֶם, *My Spirit will reject you.* It is interesting that the beginning of that very verse promises that Hashem will excise idolatry from the land: וְהִכְרַתִּי אֶת־חַמָּנֵיכֶם, *I will decimate your sun-idols.* The proximity of these two promises seems hard to understand. If there will no longer be any idols, then the land should be free for the Divine Spirit to flourish. Why, then, does the decimation of the idols result in the Divine Spirit leaving as well? The answer offered by *R' Simcha Bunim* of *P'shis'cha* contains a profound and relevant lesson.

R' Simcha Bunim explains that holiness and impurity must always be in a state of equilibrium. There cannot be only one without the possibility for the other. Just as there cannot be a situation where there is only the potential for evil, so too there cannot be a situation where there is only the potential for holiness without a balancing potential for impurity. Therefore, after the idols are destroyed, the Divine Presence must also take its leave.

This is a basic rule that has both communal and individual applications. The potential for evil and sin is a reflection of great spiritual potential as well. Those generations that had a desire for idolatry (before it was removed; see *Sanhedrin* 64a) also had a potential for service of Hashem that we, with our severely diminished capacity for both sin and service, cannot begin to fathom (see *Gra* to *Hoshea* 3:4; *Igros Chazon Ish* 1:209).

R' Shlomo Wolbe (in his *Alei Shur* vol. 1) elaborates on how this rule applies in the personal development of the individual. Each person possesses one area in which he has particular difficulty, "his challenge," as it were. This may be a source of embarrassment for the person, convincing him that he simply has an undue inclination to impurity, and there is nothing that he can do about it. It would be best, he thinks, to sweep it under the rug and deal with it as little as possible.

R' Wolbe writes that it is important to know that what for one person is an easy thing may be for another a source of great difficulty. The uniqueness of each individual is at the root of one's particular hardship in a particular area. To ignore this hardship is to miss an essential opportunity. A particularly strong desire in one area, or a particular character failing, should serve as a signal that this is the area that contains the greatest potential for a person to accomplish spiritually. For it is where one can grow the most that the *yetzer hara* tries the hardest to cripple him.

It takes persistence and perseverance to deal with one's hardest challenges, and one must know how to go about it. But the first step is to know that the challenge is there for him to address, not ignore.

HALACHAH OF THE DAY

Yesterday, we discussed the restrictions against repairs due to the *melachah* of *finishing.* As we learned, if an item is completely unusable without repair, the act of repair is Biblically prohibited. According to many *poskim,* this Biblical prohibition also applies to winding a watch that has stopped. Although the stopped watch is not considered "broken" in the conventional sense, the watch is not usable for its primary purpose while it is stopped. Therefore, rewinding it and rendering it usable is a violation of *finishing.*

There is a difference between the Biblical prohibition of *finishing* and its Rabbinic counterpart. In the case of a Biblical act of *finishing* — a repair where the broken item is completely unusable — the repair may not be made even if it is an act that requires little effort. By contrast, the Rabbinic restriction against improving the functionality of a usable item applies only if the repair requires some effort. An act that can be accomplished effortlessly may be done on Shabbos.

For example, if the soft wire temple of a pair of eyeglasses became bent out of shape so that the glasses have become uncomfortable but they are still usable, one may bend the temple back into shape. If, however, a firm item that would require a lot of effort to bend was bent out of shape, bending it back into shape would be a violation of Rabbinic law.

Another exception to the Rabbinic restriction is the case of an article

that requires reshaping on a regular basis. When such an article becomes bent out of shape it is not seen as being broken, and therefore reshaping it is seen as a part of its regular use. For example, it is permitted on Shabbos to reshape a soft felt hat that has been dented or crushed. Since these hats commonly become dented during their regular use, they may be reshaped on Shabbos.

In some cases, the repair of an item requires the reassembly of its parts. If, in order to repair an item that has become disassembled, one needs to reattach the components tightly, the act of reassembly is Biblically prohibited. To reattach the components in a loose manner is Rabbinically prohibited. As a case in point, if a pot handle fell off, screwing it on tightly on Shabbos is a violation of Biblical law. [Even tightening a loose screw before the handle falls off is a violation of Biblical law.] However, loosely screwing on the pot handle is a violation of Rabbinic law only, based on the principle we have just discussed.

A CLOSER LOOK AT THE SIDDUR

The phrase (*Vayikra* 26:31): וְלֹא אָרִיחַ בְּרֵיחַ נִיחֹחֲכֶם, *and I will not savor your satisfying aromas,* precludes the bringing of offerings in the time of the exile (see above, *A Torah Thought for the Day*). And yet, according to one reading of the blessing of *Avodah,* the Temple Service, in *Shemoneh Esrei,* we pray even today for Hashem to accept our offerings: וְאִשֵּׁי יִשְׂרָאֵל וּתְפִלָּתָם בְּאַהֲבָה תְקַבֵּל בְּרָצוֹן, *the fire-offerings of Israel and their prayer accept with love and favor.* What is the meaning of this prayer in the context of our lack of a *Beis HaMikdash*?

Some explain the words by placing the punctuation of the sentence differently. Accordingly, the words וְאִשֵּׁי יִשְׂרָאֵל are viewed as part of the previous phrase, asking for the return of the Temple service *and the fire-offerings of Israel.* The next sentence begins by asking for our prayers to be accepted with love and favor (*Tosafos* to *Menachos* 110a ד״ה ומיכאל; *Tur, Orach Chaim* §120 and glosses of the *Gra* ibid.).

In keeping with the first punctuation mentioned above, *Tur* explains that the fire-offerings here are a reference to the prayers of the Jewish people, which take the place of the offerings in the Temple. Thus, "the fire-offerings of Israel, [which are] their prayers, accept with love and favor" (*Beis Yosef, Perishah*). Alternatively, but following the same idea, we can explain that there are two types of prayers. The three standard daily prayers, which were enacted to parallel the daily offerings in the

Temple, are called אִשֵּׁי יִשְׂרָאֵל, "fire offerings of Israel." Other prayers, such as individual voluntary prayers or those that are not parallel to the daily offerings in the Temple, are referred to with the words וּתְפִלָּתָם, "and their prayers" (*Bach; see Taz*).

Another explanation of these words is based on a Midrash that says that the angel Michael serves as the High Priest in heaven, and offers daily offerings to Hashem. These offerings consist of the souls of the righteous. The word אִשֵּׁי can be rendered as אַנְשֵׁי, *the people of,* i.e., may You accept with favor the souls of the righteous people of Israel when they are offered by Michael (*Beis Yosef* based on *Tur, Tosafos* ibid.). Alternatively, and in keeping with the simple meaning of the words: "The fire offering [that is comprised] of the [righteous of] Israel may You accept with favor" (*Perishah*).

Eitz Yosef explains that this does not mean that Hashem is offered the souls of the righteous as they die, for we would not pray for the death of the righteous. Rather, it is a prayer that the souls of the righteous who may have died long ago be accepted by Hashem as an offering. It is said in the name of the *Arizal* that the final and ultimate reward of the righteous is this very experience of being brought as an offering to Hashem. The joy and pleasure that this entails is unfathomable to any human being. At times the soul is not prepared to reach this level, due to imperfections or sin. We thus pray that these souls be cleansed and elevated so that they can be offered to Hashem, and that Hashem accept this sublime offering with love and favor.

QUESTION OF THE DAY:

Once the Torah foretold the punishment of destroying the cities of Eretz Yisrael if the Jews would sin, what is the additional punishment of making the "land" desolate?

For the answer, see page 295.

פרשת בחקתי

WEDNESDAY

PARASHAS BECHUKOSAI

A TORAH THOUGHT FOR THE DAY

וְזָכַרְתִּי אֶת־בְּרִיתִי יַעֲקוֹב וְאַף אֶת־בְּרִיתִי יִצְחָק
וְאַף אֶת־בְּרִיתִי אַבְרָהָם אֶזְכֹּר וְהָאָרֶץ אֶזְכֹּר

I will remember My covenant with Yaakov,
and also My covenant with Yitzchak,
and also My covenant with Avraham will I remember,
and I will remember the land (*Vayikra* 26:42).

The Gemara (*Shabbos* 55a) records two opinions regarding the effects of the merit of our patriarchs, Avraham, Yitzchak and Yaakov (זְכוּת אָבוֹת), and the extent of its benefit for their children. Shmuel holds that the merit of the patriarchs has already expired, and no longer affords us protection. R' Yochanan says that the merit of the patriarchs continues to afford us with grace from Heaven. *Tosafos* (ibid. ד״ה ושמואל) claim, however, that the above verse clearly states that the Jewish people will have deliverance because of Hashem's remembering their forefathers. How does Shmuel explain this verse? Furthermore, why do we constantly mention the *Avos* in our prayers if their merit has already expired?

According to one answer in *Tosafos,* there is a difference between the merit of the patriarchs, which according to Shmuel has been used up, and the *covenant* with the patriarchs. The covenant, sworn by Hashem to the *Avos* regarding their children, is never broken. The covenant is the subject of the above verse, and it is to this covenant that we refer in our prayers.

In the second answer, *Tosafos* suggest that in fact there is no disagreement between Shmuel and R' Yochanan. Shmuel, who says that the merit of the patriarchs no longer has any effect, is referring to its power to protect the wicked, while R' Yochanan is referring to its power to protect the righteous. As explained by *Dvar Avraham,* one can justly take pride in the greatness of one's ancestors as long as his actions do not belie the very greatness in which he purports to take pride. Those who do not follow the Torah cannot take any refuge in the righteousness of the patriarchs, for their actions repudiate the source of their merit.

R' Moshe Feinstein (in his *Dibros Moshe* to 43:15) offers another explanation of how we can rely on the merit of the patriarchs even according to Shmuel. It is true that the patriarchs had a special place in the eyes of Hashem, one that afforded merit for their descendants for a number of generations. However, even after this special merit of the patriarchs had been spent, we can still ask Hashem to help us in their merit. This is due to their standing as righteous people, aside from their special status as *Avos.* The Torah promises to reward every righteous person for up to 2,000 generations (*Shemos* 34:7). We can thus benefit from that promise,

since we are still within that number of generations from these righteous people.

It is true that in order to access this merit one must also be considered righteous, and not every member of the Jewish people is able to make that claim regarding himself. However, the nation as a whole is considered to be righteous and observes the mitzvos of the Torah; thus, it can still benefit from the merit of the patriarchs. This is how, even according to Shmuel, we can evoke the merit of our righteous forebears — Avraham, Yitzchak and Yaakov.

MISHNAH OF THE DAY: ERUVIN 10:4

This Mishnah deals with the laws of using an area that is above another domain on the Sabbath, and the use of one domain while standing in another domain:

זִיז שֶׁלִּפְנֵי חַלּוֹן — If there was ***a ledge*** 4 *tefachim* wide and 10 *tefachim* above the ground ***in front of a window,*** i.e., it juts out of the exterior wall of a building below a window, **נוֹתְנִין עָלָיו וְנוֹטְלִין מִמֶּנּוּ בַּשַּׁבָּת** — ***one*** who is in the building ***may put*** things ***on it and remove*** things ***from it on the Sabbath,*** because it has the status of a *reshus hayachid.* [1]

עוֹמֵד אָדָם בִּרְשׁוּת הַיָּחִיד וּמְטַלְטֵל בִּרְשׁוּת הָרַבִּים — ***A person may stand in a reshus hayachid and move*** things ***in a reshus harabim,*** [2] **בִּרְשׁוּת הָרַבִּים וּמְטַלְטֵל בִּרְשׁוּת הַיָּחִיד** — or stand ***in a reshus harabim and move*** things ***in a reshus hayachid,*** **וּבִלְבַד שֶׁלֹּא יוֹצִיא חוּץ מֵאַרְבַּע אַמּוֹת** — ***provided he does not take them beyond four amos*** from their original location in the *reshus harabim.* [3]

NOTES

1. The ledge is considered an extension of the window and the house. Thus, it comes under the category of חוֹרֵי רְשׁוּת הַיָּחִיד, *crevices of a reshus hayachid,* which, if they are 10 *tefachim* above the ground, are treated as *reshus hayachid.*

2. E.g., he stands in a house [and reaches through an opening in the wall], or he stands on a roof, and bends down and moves objects in the *reshus harabim* below (*Rashi*). The Mishnah teaches that the Rabbis did not forbid these activities out of concern that one might bring the object into the domain in which he is standing (*Rashi*). See below, Mishnah 6.

3. This qualification applies to the first case, where the object is in a *reshus harabim.*

The Biblical prohibition not to move objects 4 *amos* in the *reshus harabim* is more closely defined here. Note that the Mishnah does not say, "provided he does not take them 4 *amos,*" but rather it says, "take them *beyond* 4 *amos.*" When one moves an object exactly 4 *amos,* he has not transgressed (see *Rambam, Hil. Shabbos* 12:19; *Mishnah Berurah* 239:9).

GEMS FROM THE GEMARA

The Gemara notes a difficulty with the Mishnah's ruling concerning a ledge. Into what type of domain does this ledge extend? If you say that it extends over a *reshus harabim,* why in fact is one permitted to use it — let us be concerned that something might fall off the ledge into the *reshus harabim,* and one might come to bring it back into the *reshus hayachid*! A Rabbinic decree is certainly appropriate to safeguard against the possibility of this Biblical transgression. And if the case of the Mishnah is that of a ledge that extends into a *reshus hayachid* (e.g., a *chatzeir*), if so, the Mishnah's ruling is obvious! There is no reason to assume that one may not use a ledge that extends into a *reshus hayachid.*

Abaye explains that actually the ledge does extend over a *reshus harabim,* but the Mishnah allowed one to put only breakable utensils (e.g., of earthenware or glass) on it. Since they will break if they fall off the ledge, there is no concern that one might retrieve them. The Gemara then adduces a Baraisa in support of this explanation of the Mishnah, for a Baraisa taught: If there is a ledge in front of a window and it extends over a *reshus harabim,* one may put breakable items on it such as plates, cups, pitchers, and flasks.

That Baraisa continued, stating in the end that one may only make use of a ledge that is directly opposite the window. The Gemara wonders about this last clause. What are the circumstances of this ledge? If it is not 4 *tefachim* wide, one may not make use of it even if it is opposite the window. Since it is so narrow, most objects placed on it will fall off, and therefore one who uses it appears to be throwing objects directly into the *reshus harabim.* [Generally, when there is a *mekom petur* lying between a *reshus harabim* and a *reshus hayachid,* it is in fact permissible for people in the *reshus hayachid* or the *reshus harabim* to put things on it — and this ledge, being less than 4 *tefachim* wide, is a *mekom petur.* However, since it is narrow and not really fit for this type of use, it may be used on only an occasional basis (e.g., to adjust one's load by resting one's burden upon it momentarily). Using it on a regular basis is forbidden, because of the concern that objects placed on it are likely to fall off into the *reshus harabim,* and it appears as if one is throwing them into a *reshus harabim.*] Accordingly, a ledge that is less than 4 *tefachim* wide may not be used even for breakable items (*Rashi*). And if it *is* 4 *tefachim* wide, let him use the ledge along the entire length of the wall, and not just opposite the window!

Abaye explains that the ledge in the Baraisa's last clause is not itself

4 *tefachim* wide, but the window sill completes its width to 4 *tefachim;* i.e., the combined width of the ledge together with the window sill is 4 *tefachim.* Therefore, one may make use of the ledge where it is opposite the window, because that part of the ledge is an extension of the window sill, and their combined surface is 4 *tefachim* wide. However, one is forbidden to make use of the ledge on either side of the window, since those parts of the ledge are narrower than 4 *tefachim.*

A MUSSAR THOUGHT FOR THE DAY

We may ask: What is the rationale behind the phenomenon of זְכוּת אָבוֹת (merit of the patriarchs)? Where is the justice in Hashem's forgiving our sins or sending us salvation, not in the merit of our personal deeds, but because of deeds done by people whom we do not even know, just because we are lucky enough to be their descendants?

R' Dessler, in the beginning of his *Michtav MeiEliyahu,* explains this concept at length, and the obligation that it places upon us.

Imagine that two thieves are brought before a judge for sentencing. Both have certainly committed crimes punishable by a lengthy prison sentence. The judge, not being vindictive, would like to find a way to rehabilitate the criminals without having them face the full brunt of the law. He therefore decides to find out whatever he can about each of them. His investigations yield the following: One of the thieves comes from an upstanding family and usually keeps company with law-abiding friends. This one time, he had fallen in with a bad friend who had influenced him to commit this crime. The judge decides that if, instead of sending the man to prison, he releases him to the jurisdiction of his family, it can be hoped that under their influence and direction he will not violate the law again. This will have a better long-term effect on him than a lengthy term of incarceration.

The second thief, on the other hand, has none of this vital social safety net. If he were returned to his own society, he would almost inevitably return to criminal behavior. In his case, there is no choice but to enforce the law that he be sent to prison, so that he will at least learn the negative effects of his deeds.

In both of these cases justice was served, and the goal of correcting the criminal behavior was pursued. With regard to the first, this goal was able to be accomplished through מִדַּת הָרַחֲמִים, *the attribute of mercy,* whereas the second had to feel the attribute of דִּין, strict *justice.*

Our forefathers bequeathed to us a rich spiritual legacy. *R' Chaim of Volozhin* writes that the phenomenon of millions of simple Jews throughout the ages giving their lives so as not to violate the Torah is a result of the great accomplishment of Avraham in consenting to give his life for Hashem in *Ur Kasdim.* That which was a great spiritual feat for Avraham is for his children part of their nature and legacy. This is true with regard to the other accomplishments of the patriarchs as well. We have a naturally elevated spiritual character due to the efforts of our fathers.

When do we merit to rely on זְכוּת אָבוֹת? When we identify with that rich legacy, when we allow the noble character traits that they implanted in our nation to resonate inside us. When we work on strengthening ourselves in the characteristic of sacrificing all our natural desires for Hashem, we connect with the forefathers and show that we are able to repent from any sins that were merely the results of an aberration of our true natures. Then Hashem can decide that it is worth giving us another chance. Hashem can "return us to the company of" our fathers, whose legacy will have a good influence on us and cause us to remain on the proper path.

HALACHAH OF THE DAY

Yesterday, we learned that reassembling an item comprised of different components is prohibited; if one attaches the components loosely, he is in violation of a Rabbinic prohibition, while if one reassembles them tightly, he violates Biblical law.

This pertains, however, only to reassembling items that are normally tightly assembled. In such cases, the Sages prohibited even loosely assembling the parts, out of concern that one might come to attach them tightly and thus violate Biblical law. A more lenient law applies to items that are typically only loosely fastened, as we will now describe.

Although it is forbidden to *initially* assemble separate parts in a loose manner on Shabbos in order to create a usable item, *reassembling* them is permitted. Thus, although on Shabbos one may not insert a set of laces into a new pair of shoes for the first time, one is permitted to *reinsert* a shoelace into a shoe on Shabbos, even though doing so still makes the shoe usable. However, inserting a fresh shoelace that has never been in the shoe before is forbidden, since this is not reassembling parts that had already previously been joined as one utensil; rather, it is the creation of a new one.

Strengthening a damaged article to prevent further damage is considered a "repair" and is therefore forbidden. For example, applying nail polish to a stocking with a run in it to prevent the run from spreading is prohibited as an act of *finishing.* Since the nail polish strengthens the hosiery and thereby improves it, it is forbidden to apply it.

Even strengthening an article that is not yet damaged is prohibited under this *melachah.* Thus, one may not spray hair spray onto a wig to strengthen the coiffure, even when the wig is properly shaped.

There are instances when it is permissible to make a repair. When an article has nothing inherently wrong with it, but there is an external factor that prevents it from being used, removing the external factor is *not* prohibited under the *melachah* of *finishing.* The item is not viewed as being broken, since it has no internal defect. For example, it is permissible to remove the price tag from a new garment in order to wear it. Since the garment is inherently fit for use, and the tag is an external element that interferes with use of the garment, it may be removed. It is important to note that although one may tear off the tag, one must avoid ripping any words or letters that are printed on it, so as not to violate the *melachah* of *erasing.*

A CLOSER LOOK AT THE SIDDUR

In the very first blessing of the *Shemoneh Esrei,* known as the blessing of *Avos,* Patriarchs, we invoke the merit of the patriarchs, specifically Avraham Avinu. In the blessing, we speak of Hashem, saying: וְזוֹכֵר חַסְדֵי אָבוֹת וּמֵבִיא גוֹאֵל לִבְנֵי בְנֵיהֶם לְמַעַן שְׁמוֹ בְּאַהֲבָה, *And He recalls the kindnesses of the patriarchs, and brings a redeemer to their children's children, for His Name's sake, with love.* This seems difficult to understand. The first phrase implies that the redeemer will come due to the kindness of the patriarchs. The sentence ends, however, that it is for His Name's sake (to end the desecration of the Name of Hashem that is the result of the exile of the Jewish people). Furthermore, if it is for His Name's sake, then why do we say that it is "with love"?

R' Yehoshua Heller (in his *Beis Tefillah*) explains the words of this prayer by setting it against the background of Avraham's special relationship with Hashem.

Avraham served Hashem with love (see *Yeshayah* 41:8: אַבְרָהָם אֹהֲבִי, *Avraham who loved Me*). The nature of a relationship built on love is that each partner seeks the betterment of the other, even to the negation of his own interest. Thus, the highest expression of love of Hashem is giving up one's life for Hashem's honor. This relationship between Avraham and Hashem is expressed in the Midrash where Hashem asks Avraham which punishment he would choose for his children to suffer for their sins — exile or Gehinnom. The Midrash reports that Avraham chose Gehinnom while Hashem chose exile.

R' Heller explains: The punishment of exile is in fact the "better" punishment. First of all, it does not require the death of the violator. Furthermore, the Name of Hashem is desecrated when the Jewish people are exiled. Therefore, their eventual redemption is assured, if only to stop the desecration of His Name. Gehinnom, on the other hand, is harder for the ones who are enduring it but does not entail any desecration of the Name of Hashem. To the contrary, when the soul is punished in that way, the sinner himself proclaims the justice of Hashem, and the Name of Hashem is glorified.

Avraham, when faced with the choice of the easier or harder punishment for his children, in his love for Hashem chose the one that would be harder for his children but would yield greater honor to Hashem. Hashem dealt with Avraham in kind, by accepting upon Himself, as it were, the desecration of His Name, so that Avraham's descendants could suffer less and be assured of an eventual redemption.

This, then, is the meaning of the words of the blessing. Hashem זוֹכֵר חַסְדֵי אָבוֹת, *recalls the kindnesses of the patriarchs* — the love of Avraham, who took upon himself the more difficult punishment; and in that merit וּמֵבִיא גּוֹאֵל לִבְנֵי בְנֵיהֶם לְמַעַן שְׁמוֹ, *He brings a redeemer to their children's children, for His Name's sake.* As explained above, in reflection of Avraham's love Hashem gave his descendants exile, from which they must eventually be redeemed לְמַעַן שְׁמוֹ, *for His Name's sake,* which is desecrated while they are there. Thus, the redemption that is for the sake of the Name of Hashem is actually a result of the "kindness of the partriarch," Avraham.

And both of these causes of the redemption — the kindness of Avraham, and the prevention of the desecration of the Name of Hashem — are a result of the relationship that existed between Hashem and Avraham — בְּאַהֲבָה, *with love.*

QUESTION OF THE DAY:

Why does the Torah not use the word "remembrance" in connection with Yitzchak?

For the answer, see page 295.

A TORAH THOUGHT FOR THE DAY

פרשת בחקתי

THURSDAY

PARASHAS BECHUKOSAI

דַּבֵּר אֶל־בְּנֵי יִשְׂרָאֵל וְאָמַרְתָּ אֲלֵהֶם אִישׁ כִּי
יַפְלִא נֶדֶר בְּעֶרְכְּךָ נְפָשֹׁת לַה'. וְהָיָה עֶרְכְּךָ הַזָּכָר
מִבֶּן עֶשְׂרִים שָׁנָה וְעַד בֶּן־שִׁשִּׁים שָׁנָה . . .
וְאִם־נְקֵבָה הִוא . . . וְאִם מִבֶּן־חָמֵשׁ שָׁנִים
וְעַד בֶּן־עֶשְׂרִים שָׁנָה . . . וְאִם מִבֶּן־חֹדֶשׁ
וְעַד בֶּן־חָמֵשׁ שָׁנִים . . . וְאִם מִבֶּן־שִׁשִּׁים שָׁנָה וָמַעְלָה

Speak to the Children of Israel and say to them:
If a man articulates a vow to Hashem regarding a valuation
of living beings. The valuation of a male shall be:
for someone twenty years of age to sixty years of age . . .
If she is female . . . And if from five to twenty years of age . . .
And if from a month to five years of age . . .
And if from sixty years and older . . . (Vayikra 27:2-7).

C*humash Vayikra* concludes with the laws of gifts and pledges to the *Beis HaMikdash.* The first of the series of different types of donations that are discussed in this chapter are the laws of *arachin,* valuations. The Torah tells us that if a person wishes to contribute to the *Beis HaMikdash,* one of the ways he may do so is by donating his own or a different person's *erech* valuation — which is determined on a sliding scale based on age and gender, as listed in the relevant verses — to the Temple treasury. The different *arachin* brackets are as follows: the first *erech* bracket of a person's life is from one month of age until 5 years, the second is from 5 years until 20, the third from 20 until 60, and the fourth and final *erech* bracket is for a person who is more than 60 years old. For each of these age groups, the Torah assigns a different *erech* valuation for a man and for a woman. Thus, when a person pledges to donate "the *erech* value of So and so" (or of himself), the Torah commands the Kohen to assess the valuation of the person whose *erech* has been pledged; the person who made the commitment to donate is then required to fulfill this debt.

It is clear that a person's *erech* valuation is in no way meant to be seen as his or her actual "value," for it is not based on physical strength, righteousness, earning ability, or the myriad of other gauges through which a person may normally be assessed. Indeed, the *erech* valuation of every person within the same *erech* bracket of age and gender is the same. The laws of *arachin* are a unique creation of the Torah, in which we are told that when the pledge to donate the *erech* valuation of a person is made, the way to fulfill this promise is by giving the *Beis HaMikdash* a set amount that corresponds to this person's *erech* value.

The commentaries struggle to explain what the Torah is teaching us by introducing the concept of donations through *arachin.* One might reason that the entire passage is unnecessary; if a person wishes to contribute to the Temple treasury, why can't he simply pledge to give the amount of money that the *erech* declaration requires him to contribute, without identifying this gift as being the *erech* of a certain person? What is achieved by making the donation to the *Beis HaMikdash* specifically through the method of a person's *erech* valuation?

Mishmar HaLevi suggests an answer to this question based on *Shiltei HaGiborim* (to *Avodah Zarah* 13a), who explains that although it is true that the Temple treasury receives the same sum whether this money is given as an ordinary donation or in fulfillment of an *erech* pledge, an *erech* pledge nevertheless does something that a regular contribution does not — it spiritually uplifts the person who is being valuated. [It is for this reason, rules *Shiltei HaGiborim,* that an *erech* donation may not be vowed on Shabbos, for although it is permitted to pledge donations to *tzedakah* or to the *Beis HaMikdash* on Shabbos, this includes only pledges that do not specify that a particular item will be given. Promising to give a specified item, however, is forbidden by Rabbinic law because it resembles a business transaction. Since *arachin* are not monetary pledges, but actually serve to "consecrate" the person whose valuation is being promised, they too are viewed as specifying particular items, and are thus forbidden.] *Netziv* offers a similar approach in understanding *arachin;* he states that the act of donating the valuation of a person to the *Beis HaMikdash* is meant to serve as a merit for this person.

Haflaas Arachin explains how an *erech* pledge elevates the person whose value is being given by pointing out that *arachin* are in truth not simply financial gifts. Rather, just as an animal may be sanctified for use as a *korban* or money may be consecrated to be used to buy supplies for the *Beis HaMikdash,* the Torah is telling us that a person may be sanctified for Temple use as well. However, since there is of course no use for a person in the *Beis HaMikdash* service, the Torah decreed that the person be redeemed and the money be given to the Temple treasury. When this amount is paid and the *Beis HaMikdash* gains by receiving the money, the person whose value has been used to assist the Temple treasury is elevated through his role of having being "used" in the *Beis HaMikdash.* It is for this reason, concludes *Mishmar HaLevi,* that the *Midrash Tanchuma* tells us that Hashem considers the *arachin* vows of the Jewish people as if they really offered themselves before Him, for donating the *erech* of a person to the *Beis HaMikdash* actually includes a person in the Temple service. [It is also for this reason, *Chazon Ish*

(*Kodashim* §29) explains, that the requirement to fulfill an *erech* vow does not take effect until the person is valuated by a Kohen; like all other gifts to the *Beis HaMikdash,* the action of giving a sanctified item to a Temple representative is needed to effect the gift and sanctify the item that is being donated.]

MISHNAH OF THE DAY: ERUVIN 10:5

The Mishnah continues with a similar case of a person standing in one domain and performing some deed in another domain: **לֹא יַעֲמוֹד אָדָם בִּרְשׁוּת הַיָּחִיד וְיַשְׁתִּין בִּרְשׁוּת הָרַבִּים** — ***A person may not stand in a reshus hayachid and urinate into a reshus harabim,*** **בִּרְשׁוּת הָרַבִּים וְיַשְׁתִּין בִּרְשׁוּת הַיָּחִיד** — or stand ***in a reshus harabim and urinate into a reshus hayachid,*** **וְכֵן לֹא יָרוֹק** — ***and similarly, one may not expectorate*** from one domain to another.[1] **רַבִּי יְהוּדָה אוֹמֵר** — ***R' Yehudah says:*** **אַף מִשֶּׁנִּתְלַשׁ רוּקוֹ בְּפִיו לֹא יְהַלֵּךְ אַרְבַּע אַמּוֹת עַד שֶׁיָּרוֹק** — ***Even when one's saliva collects***[2] ***in one's mouth one may not walk four amos*** in the *reshus harabim* ***until one expectorates.*** Since the saliva is ready to be expelled from the body, it is no longer considered a part of the body; rather, it is a load that one carries in one's mouth.[3]

NOTES

1. Urinating or expectorating from the *reshus harabim* to the *reshus hayachid* or vice versa falls into the category of the *melachah* of *transferring* (the urine or saliva) from one domain to another.

2. Literally: becomes detached. R' Yehudah asserts that saliva, after it has accumulated in the mouth and is ready to be spit out, is no longer considered part of the body, but is viewed as something being carried in the mouth. Thus, if one were to walk 4 *amos* in a *reshus harabim* with the saliva in his mouth, he would have transferred it 4 *amos* in the *reshus harabim.*

3. *Shulchan Aruch* (*Orach Chaim* 350:3) rules in accordance with this opinion.

GEMS FROM THE GEMARA

The Mishnah taught that a person may not stand in a private domain and urinate into a public domain. Rav Yosef said that one who did urinate or expectorate from one domain to another is obligated to bring a *chatas*-offering to atone for a Biblical violation.

The Gemara challenges Rav Yosef's ruling. The law is that in regard to the prohibition against carrying, we require that the object being carried be removed from, and placed down upon, an area that is 4 *tefachim* square. But there is no such area in this case, since the object [i.e., the urine or saliva] is being removed from a place that is less than 4 *tefachim* square [i.e., his bladder or mouth]!

The Gemara explains Rav Yosef's ruling by saying that a man's intent makes it a significant area. That is, since he has a need for this object to leave this particular place, his act of transference from one *reshus* to another is considered to be of legal significance, despite the fact that technically it began from a surface that is less than 4 *tefachim* square.

The Gemara proves that this principle must be valid, for otherwise we would not be able to explain the following statement made by Rava: If one threw an object 4 *amos* in a *reshus harabim,* and it landed in the mouth of a dog or in the opening of a furnace, and was consumed before ever reaching the ground, he is nevertheless obligated to bring a *chatas*-offering to atone for a Biblical violation. Now, there too one may ask: Since the object landed in a dog's mouth or in the flames of a furnace, the object was not placed on an area that is 4 *tefachim* square! Rather, one must say that his intent makes it a significant area; i.e., since he had a need for the object to land in the dog's mouth or in the furnace, his act of throwing is considered to be of legal significance. [That is, he *benefits* more from the object landing in this particular location than in any other location; e.g., he wanted to feed the dog, or to burn the object in the furnace. However, if he merely intended that an object land in a specific spot, his intent alone does not make his act a legally significant one (*Tosafos*).]

Therefore, here too, in the case of our Mishnah, we can apply the same principle: His intent makes it a significant area, despite the fact that, in reality, it is less than 4 *tefachim* square.

A MUSSAR THOUGHT FOR THE DAY

We explained in *A Torah Thought for the Day* that the valuation of each *erech* bracket mentioned in the Torah includes everyone in this age and gender group. Thus, since these valuations are in no way dependent upon a person's achievements or abilities, *arachin* cannot be seen as a way of appraising the person's actual worth.

R' Moshe Feinstein (*Kol Ram*) points out that the Mishnah (*Arachin* 1:1) tells us that there is a way in which the actual "value" of a person may be donated to the *Beis HaMikdash*: instead of declaring that he will donate "the *erech* of So and so," a benefactor pledges to contribute a person's "worth" to the Temple treasury. If this declaration is made, the sum that must be given is the Kohen's assessment of the person's earning power. Unlike *arachin* that are a set amount for everyone in the same bracket, the sum of money that must be paid to fulfill a vow of "worth" will depend on the strength, success or capabilities of the person whose "worth" was promised; the "price" of a stronger or more successful person will naturally be more than the amount given to the *Beis HaMikdash* if the "worth" of a weaker person is promised.

R' Moshe comments that several messages may be learned from these two different types of "values" that are used to assess a person. On the one hand, the laws of set *arachin* brackets tell us that although everyone enjoys his own areas of strength in which he excels, there is nevertheless an objective minimum level of *avodas Hashem* that may be easily fulfilled, and in fact must be maintained at all times. No matter what happens to a person, he is not permitted to ignore these basic obligations. And since this level of mitzvah performance is indispensable, one who fails to maintain it will be punished more severely than a person who did not achieve higher levels of *avodas Hashem.*

On the other hand, in allowing vows of "worth," where a person is assessed based on his actual accomplishments, the Torah is sending us the message that a person should never become complacent and satisfied with the minimum required level of *avodas Hashem,* but must always strive to grow and develop into the best possible servant of Hashem that he can be.

R' Moshe concludes that these two perspectives work together, for one is built on the other. When we are embarking on a new course in mitzvah observance, or teaching our students or children, the first area to be addressed is the basic obligation that must be fulfilled. After this level is achieved and maintained, we should not feel that we can now stop growing. Rather, we must try to do as much as possible, and constantly add to our spiritual "worth."

QUESTION OF THE DAY:

How is it possible for a 33-year-old man in good health to have no erech value?

For the answer, see page 295.

HALACHAH OF THE DAY

Yesterday, we discussed one instance where it is permissible to make a repair on Shabbos, namely, when there is an external factor that causes the article to be unusable, but the item itself is inherently usable.

Another instance where it is permissible to repair an item is when it is evident that the repair is of a temporary nature. For instance, although, as we stated earlier, one may not ordinarily insert a new shoelace into a shoe on Shabbos, it would be permissible to insert a brown shoelace into a black shoe. This is permitted because it is obvious that the brown lace is being used only as a temporary stopgap measure.

Also, if the normal manner of use of an item requires certain adjustments to be made from time to time, these adjustments are not considered "repairs," and making them does not violate the *melachah* of *finishing.* Thus, it is permissible for one to shake down a thermometer in order to use it on Shabbos, even though this action prepares the thermometer for use. Since the normal usage of a thermometer requires this adjustment before each use, the thermometer is not deemed "broken" prior to being shaken down, nor is it considered "repaired" after being shaken.

The fifth and final category of activities that are classified as acts of *finishing* is that of making a new opening in a container. Making an opening in a container is a finishing touch, since it facilitates the removal of items contained inside, as well as the insertion of new items — the basic use of a container. This is therefore considered part of the *melachah* of *finishing.*

It is Biblically prohibited to make an opening in a container when the opening is intended to facilitate the two-way transfer of items. Such an opening is a full-fledged opening, for it accomplishes the full role of an opening to a useful vessel. However, when an opening is intended only for one-way transfer — i.e., to remove *or* insert things — creating it is prohibited only Rabbinically.

The Sages did not, however, prohibit one from making an opening for one-way transfer if the opening is made in a place where it is unusual to make a real opening. The example provided by the Talmud is that of one making a hole in the stopper of a barrel. If one wanted the barrel to have a bona fide "opening," one would remove the stopper. He would not make a hole in the stopper, thus ruining it and allowing dirt to fall into the barrel through the hole. We therefore view the hole that he bored in the stopper merely as a passage through which the contents of the barrel can be extracted from it, not as a true opening that perfects the container.

A CLOSER LOOK AT THE SIDDUR

We continue to discuss the third of the Six Remembrances — the actions of Amalek, which we are bidden to remember daily by reciting the verse (*Devarim* 25:17-18):

זָכוֹר אֵת אֲשֶׁר־עָשָׂה לְךָ עֲמָלֵק בַּדֶּרֶךְ בְּצֵאתְכֶם מִמִּצְרָיִם. אֲשֶׁר קָרְךָ בַּדֶּרֶךְ וַיְזַנֵּב בְּךָ כָּל־הַנֶּחֱשָׁלִים אַחֲרֶיךָ וְאַתָּה עָיֵף וְיָגֵעַ וְלֹא יָרֵא אֱלֹהִים.

Remember what Amalek did to you on the way as you were leaving Egypt, that he happened upon you on the way, and he struck those of you who were hindmost, all the weaklings at your rear when you were faint and exhausted, and he did not fear God.

Last week, we discussed the purpose of remembering Amalek's intention and their punishment. We will now take a look at another aspect of this episode, and discuss how remembering this daily will help us to improve our ways and grow in our service of Hashem.

The *Tanchuma* (*Parashas Beshalach*) tells us a rule: The enemy can attack the Jewish people only when there is some sin or shortcoming in our service of Hashem. The *Mechilta* interprets the word רְפִידִם (the name of the location where Amalek's attack took place — see *Shemos* 17:8) as an allusion to the reason for the attack: שֶׁרָפוּ יְדֵיהֶם מִן הַתּוֹרָה, *for they loosened their grip on the Torah.* This means that the Jews became lax in their Torah study. There were signs of laziness and a lack of enthusiasm, and as a result Amalek had the ability to attack (*Iyun Tefillah*).

The Talmud (*Megillah* 11a) tells us that the same thing occurred in the days of Haman, who was a descendant of Amalek: He had the ability to endanger the Jewish nation only because of their laziness in Torah study.

Ohr HaChaim explains that this is why Moshe chose Yehoshua to lead the battle against Amalek. It was not because he had a reputation as an outstanding warrior. On the contrary, he is singled out as the student who never left the study hall (*Shemos* 33:11). His prowess in Torah, however, was the more important factor, for the only way to chase away Amalek is by returning to a high level of Torah study. Yehoshua's diligence in Torah ensured that Amalek would be driven away.

Thus, the episode of Amalek cautions us to uphold the Torah's precious stature in every situation. Our remembrance of it is a daily reminder that it does not suffice to study Torah or perform mitzvos coldly, without zeal. They must be performed with love for the mitzvos, and with feeling for the מְצַוֶּה — the One Who commanded us to do them. As the *Rambam* says (*Hilchos Lulav* 8:15): The happiness that should overtake a person while performing mitzvos, and the love he should direct to Hashem Who commanded them, is a great service.

[Incidentally, the *sefarim* elaborate as to how Amalek was able to cool off the enthusiasm of the Jewish people in serving Hashem. Indeed, the verse describes Amalek's attack as אֲשֶׁר קָרְךָ בַּדֶּרֶךְ (see *Rashi* to *Devarim* 25:18, third explanation). The word קָרְךָ denotes "cooling off" — Amalek chilled you and cooled you down from your fervent level of devotion. To counteract Amalek, we must always strive to keep the flame of Torah and the fire of serving Hashem burning brightly.]

A TASTE OF LOMDUS

The Gemara in *Arachin* (4a) comments that a close reading of the verse (27:2) reveals that the word בְּעֶרְכְּךָ, *a valuation,* seems to be superfluous. [Many commentaries (see *Rashi, Malbim, Rash MiShantz, Torah Temimah*) explain that proper Hebrew grammar would require that this verse should state: כִּי יַפְלִא נֶדֶר בְּעֶרֶךְ, not בְּעֶרְכְּךָ. The added ךָ implies that in addition to the simple translation of this verse, another message is also being taught.] This added nuance, explains the Gemara, teaches us that the laws of *arachin* are stated with respect to the evaluation of an *entire* person. [*Torah Temimah* explains that the Gemara seemingly understands בְּעֶרְכְּךָ as a contraction of בְּעֵרֶךְ כֻּלְּךָ, *the valuation of all of you,* as opposed to only part of the body.] Thus, the Gemara concludes, if a person would vow to give "the *erech* valuation of limbs," his declaration would be meaningless and he would not be obligated to give any amount of money to the *Beis HaMikdash.* [Of course, this exclusion applies only when the person declares his intention to give an *erech* value. If, however, he would commit to donating the *worth* of a particular limb, he must fulfill this obligation. See *A Mussar Thought for the Day* for the difference between gifts of *arachin* and gifts of actual worth.]

Commenting on this Gemara, *Tosafos* (ד״ה ערך כולו) ask why a specific Scriptural exegesis of בְּעֶרְכְּךָ is needed to tell us that the laws and obligations that are introduced in the *parashah* of *arachin* take effect only when the person vows the *erech* value of the entire body, which implies that if not for this exegesis, we would have understood otherwise. However, since the only source of *erech* valuations is our Torah passage, which assigns a particular monetary value to each era of a

person's life and makes no mention of anything less than full *living beings,* there would seemingly be no reason to think that an *erech* declared on a limb would have any *arachin* validity. Why does the Torah see the need to tell us this seemingly obvious fact — that the only *erech* declaration that carries weight is when a person states that he wishes to give the *erech* of the entire body? *Tosafos* answer their own question by explaining that since it is clear to all that a declaration of *arachin* declared on a limb is worthless, a person who declares this meaningless statement obviously realizes that he is accomplishing nothing. Thus, the only way to interpret his declaration is to say that he agrees to donate the *erech* value of the entire body. However, the Torah, in writing בְּעֶרְכְּךָ, is telling us that although this person's intention may be to donate the full amount, since his *erech* declaration did not say so explicitly, the declaration is invalid and non-binding.

R' Yosef Shalom Elyashiv (*He'aros L'Maseches Arachin*) asks a question on *Tosafos'* explanation. The Gemara (*Shevuos* 26b) tells us that although explicit speech is normally needed in order to create an obligation — a person who merely thinks about selling or giving someone an item is under no legal commitment to actually do so until he commits by giving his word — there are several exceptions to this rule. One of these, states the Gemara, is *hekdesh* — consecrating items for donation to the *Beis HaMikdash.* A person is halachically obligated to fulfill his pledged donation to *hekdesh* even if he only mentally made up his mind to do so. [Designating produce as *terumah* is another exception, and food becomes forbidden to non-Kohanim as soon as the owner even silently decides to consecrate it as *terumah.*] With this in mind, asks R' Elyashiv, how can *Tosafos* understand the Gemara to be telling us that there is no binding act of *arachin* when the person pledges to give the *erech* of limbs if he mentally intends to give the full *erech*? The unspoken decision to give the *erech* of the entire person to the *Beis HaMikdash* should indeed obligate him to do so!

R' Elyashiv answers his question by explaining that although it is true that the undeclared decision to donate the *erech* of the full body — or any gift — to the *Beis HaMikdash* obligates the person to do so, this rule is true only as long as the person does not explicitly state anything to the contrary — such as the desire to donate only the valuation of limbs. If, however, a person's spoken word contradicts what he is thinking — even in instances, such as *hekdesh* and *terumah,* where a person is normally responsible to fulfill even his unspoken decision — it is clear that nothing has been accomplished.

Keren Orah and *Shalmei Nedarim* (*Nedarim* 2a) explain why this is so by pointing out that there are in essence two types of *machshavos* (thoughts) — designations and preparations. For example, a person can mentally decide to *designate* a fruit as *terumah*, or an animal as *hekdesh*. Or, his thought process can be a decision that he *will* take action — by verbally declaring this item holy. There is an inherent difference, they explain, between these two types of thoughts. Unlike a mental *designation*, which itself effects a result on its own, the second type of thought — *planning* to carry out the action of speech — is only *preparation*. And since in such a case the person has decided to use the vehicle of verbal declaration, and not unspoken designation, to consecrate the item, the *machshavah* (thought) does not accomplish anything beyond creating a plan of action. Accordingly, the thought is meaningless until this planned course of action is actually carried out.

The same is true when a person declares that he wishes to donate "the *erech* valuation of limbs." Although it may be true, as *Tosafos* explains, that this person in truth wishes to donate the full *erech* of the entire body to the *Beis HaMikdash*, the fact that he said something shows that he did not want this *erech* to take effect with *machshavah* alone; thus, his *machshavah* does not require him to carry out his pledge before he verbally utters his thoughts. However, since the declaration was invalid — for there is no *erech* value for limbs — this too is non-binding. Consequently, no act of *arachin* has taken place.

A TORAH THOUGHT FOR THE DAY

**וְכָל־מַעְשַׂר בָּקָר וָצֹאן כֹּל אֲשֶׁר־יַעֲבֹר
תַּחַת הַשָּׁבֶט הָעֲשִׂירִי יִהְיֶה־קֹּדֶשׁ לַה׳**

*Any tithe of cattle or of the flock,
any that passes under the staff,
the tenth one shall be holy to* H*ASHEM* (*Vayikra* 27:32).

The process of tithing one's livestock (*maasar beheimah*) is different from that of tithing one's produce. With the latter, one can simply calculate the volume of a tenth of one's total yield and separate that amount for his tithe. Animal tithing, however, requires staging an elaborate procedure.

The owner herds all of the year's young livestock into a corral that has an opening that allows only one to leave at a time. The mothers of the young livestock are positioned outside the corral, so that the animals will all head out through the narrow opening. The owner stands at the opening holding a stick with red dye on it, and counts the animals as they leave, "One, two, three," and so on. When the tenth leaves the corral, he declares, "This is *maaser* (the tithe)," and marks it with his stick. He then begins the count again. An interesting explanation for this procedure was offered by R' Shlomo Aronson, the Rav of Kiev, in connection with an appeal he made to the wealthy Brodsky brothers.

It happened that the Rav asked for a sizable donation from the brothers and received it. Three days later he returned with a new appeal for a donation. The brothers made no secret of their surprise that he would return so soon with another request. He then elaborated on the *maasar beheimah* requirement by way of explaining his behavior.

Imagine an owner of 500 sheep who must separate his tithes. Were he obligated to come and directly remove from his herd 50 sheep, he might be pained by the large number of sheep that he is required to separate. The Torah therefore prescribes the following method. One sheep leaves under the eyes of the owner, and the owner counts to himself, "There is one sheep for me." The second sheep passes by and he says, "There goes a second sheep for me," and so on, until he has done this nine times. After appreciating how many sheep he has for himself, it will not be hard for him to then separate one sheep for Hashem.

In fact, this is the proper way for a person to give charity. One must start by literally counting all of one's blessings. After enumerating the clothing, house, furniture and profit that one has, it will not be such a difficult task to separate some of it for Hashem.

"If you were to count all the profits that you made since the last time I approached you," concluded R' Shlomo, "you would not have a hard time giving a fresh pledge."

The *Ohel Yaakov* suggests another explanation for this sheep-counting procedure. By putting all the animals in a position where any one of them could end up being consecrated, the owner, in effect, has dedicated all of his animals to Hashem, for each one could potentially be marked as a tithe. In this way, the tithe that he gives is a representation of his willingness to give all of them to Hashem.

MISHNAH OF THE DAY: ERUVIN 10:6

The Mishnah continues dealing with the topic of a person standing in one domain and performing deeds in another domain:

לֹא יַעֲמוֹד אָדָם בִּרְשׁוּת הַיָּחִיד וְיִשְׁתֶּה בִּרְשׁוּת הָרַבִּים — ***A person may not stand in a reshus hayachid,*** bend forward, ***and drink in a reshus harabim;*** בִּרְשׁוּת הָרַבִּים וְיִשְׁתֶּה בִּרְשׁוּת הַיָּחִיד — nor may he stand ***in a reshus harabim*** and bend forward ***and drink in a reshus hayachid,*** because he might inadvertently bring the water cup into the domain in which he is standing,[1] אֶלָּא אִם כֵּן הִכְנִיס רֹאשׁוֹ וְרוּבּוֹ לַמָּקוֹם שֶׁהוּא שׁוֹתֶה — ***unless he brings his head and most of his body into the domain in which he is drinking.*** In this position, he is unlikely to forget and remove the cup from its domain. וְכֵן בְּגַת — ***And the same*** applies ***in*** the case of ***a winepress.***[2]

קוֹלֵט אָדָם מִן הַמַּזְחִילָה לְמַטָּה מֵעֲשָׂרָה טְפָחִים — ***A person*** standing in a *reshus harabim* ***may*** hold up a vessel in the air and ***catch*** water that is falling ***from a gutter*** — the gutter being ***lower than ten tefachim*** from

NOTES

1. A person standing in one *reshus* may not bend over into another *reshus* to drink water or beverages that are in the other domain. We are concerned that he may forget himself while drinking and transfer the liquid into his domain (*Rashi*).

The Gemara (99a) explains that this is not comparable to Mishnah 4, where a person is permitted to move objects in the *reshus harabim* although he himself remains in the *reshus hayachid.* The ruling in that Mishnah refers only to objects that are not presently needed by the person; thus, there is little reason to fear that he may transfer them to his own domain. In our case, however, he needs the water in his domain now, so we are concerned that he will bring it there.

2. See *Gems from the Gemara* for two interpretations of this phrase.

the ground.[3] וּמִן הַצִּינּוֹר מִכָּל מָקוֹם שׁוֹתֶה — ***And from a** drain**pipe one may drink in any manner;*** i.e., one may even place one's mouth (or a vessel) directly against the pipe itself and drink the water.[4]

NOTES

3. In Mishnaic times roofs were, as a rule, flat. Rainwater accumulating on the roof would be channeled toward the side of the roof by means of a large number of small pipes. It would then spill from these pipes onto a sloping gutter that lay along the side of the house and directed the water away from the house, so as to prevent damage to the walls. The Mishnah rules that one may stand in a *reshus harabim* and hold a vessel to collect water falling from this gutter. In the case of the Mishnah, the gutter from which the water drops is within 10 *tefachim* of the ground, and thus no transference into the *reshus harabim* is involved in collecting the falling water, since it is already in the *reshus harabim.* See diagram.

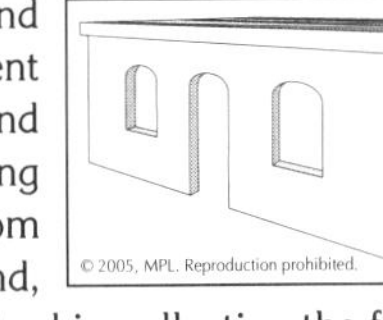

He may not, however, place his mouth or container directly to the open end of the gutter, because the gutter, being within 3 *tefachim* of the roof, is considered an extension of it, and as a result it is a *reshus hayachid.* Thus, taking the water directly from the gutter would constitute transferring from a *reshus hayachid* (the gutter) to a *reshus harabim* (where the person is standing) (*Rashi*).

4. Unlike a gutter, a drainpipe juts out at right angles from the house and therefore its open end is assumed to be more than 3 *tefachim* from the roof. Consequently, it does not have the status of a *reshus hayachid,* and thus one is allowed to take water directly from it (*Rashi*). See diagram.

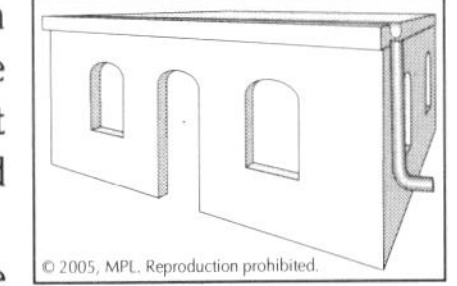

Actually, since the drainpipe is not an extension of the roof, its status is determined by (a) its width and length, and (b) its height above the ground. Thus, if it is less than 4 by 4 *tefachim,* then regardless of its elevation it is a *mekom petur.* If it is more than 4 by 4 *tefachim,* then within 10 *tefachim* above the ground it is a *karmelis;* if it is more than 10 *tefachim* above the ground it is a *reshus hayachid.* Accordingly, the Gemara (99b) adds that only when the pipe's dimensions are less than 4 by 4 *tefachim* may one place his mouth or container directly to the pipe.

GEMS FROM THE GEMARA

The Gemara posed a legal query: What is the law in regard to a *karmelis* — is it permissible to stand in a *karmelis* and drink in a *reshus hayachid* or in a *reshus harabim* (and vice versa)? Abaye said that the restrictive law that applies to the Biblical domains also applies to the Rabbinic domain of *karmelis.*

Rava challenged Abaye's view, based on the fact that the law of *karmelis* is itself only a Rabbinic decree (to safeguard against the possibility of one committing the Biblical violation of transferring an object between a *reshus harabim* and a *reshus hayachid*). And, as a general rule, we never legislate another Rabbinic decree to protect the first Rabbinic decree! [If the Rabbis were to ban standing in a *karmelis* while drinking in a different domain to prevent the possibility of bringing the vessel into the *karmelis,* it would be a safeguard to a safeguard (*Rashi*).]

[Abaye ruled stringently in our case, for one of various reasons given by the *Rishonim.* Either, (a) the laws of carrying are an exception (*Tosafos* to Shabbos 11b). Since people do not regard the prohibition against carrying as seriously as they do the other categories of labor, the Rabbis had to be unusually strict to counter this attitude (*Ritva* ibid.). Or, (b) Abaye does not consider this a safeguard to a safeguard. In his view it is merely a logical extension of the original safeguard. Once the Sages enacted the rule that a *karmelis* must be treated as stringently as a public domain, if we permit an action in a *karmelis,* people will not differentiate and will come to perform that act even in a Biblical *reshus harabim* (*Rashba* and *Pnei Yehoshua* ibid.). And (c), as it is so easy to make a mistake and inadvertently bring the water into one's own domain, the Sages considered it necessary to be extra stringent (*Tosafos*).]

Abaye cites support for his position from the Mishnah's statement, "And the same applies in the case of a winepress." Presumably, this means that one may not stand in a *reshus harabim,* lean over a winepress and drink wine from it with a vessel. However, so as not to be merely a restatement of the first clause, the winepress referred to here must be a *karmelis* (i.e., it is less than 10 *tefachim* deep, but 4 *tefachim* wide), rather than a *reshus hayachid.* This is proof, therefore, that one may not stand in a *reshus harabim* and drink in a *karmelis.*

Rava, however, says that this clause refers to the subject of *maaser,* and is not related to the laws of the Sabbath at all. The Biblical obligation to separate *terumah* and *maaser,* and the resulting prohibition to consume the untithed produce, take effect only once the produce has been fully processed. Produce that is not yet fully processed, although permitted for consumption by Biblical law, is forbidden by Rabbinic decree. However, the Rabbis prohibited only regular consumption — the produce *may* be eaten as a casual snack. The Mishnah discusses untithed wine that is still in the winepress, and so is not yet considered fully processed until it is drawn into the holding pit (*Rashi,* Shabbos 11b). It therefore may be drunk casually but not in a formal manner. To drink the wine over the press is considered casual drinking and is permitted, but drinking outside the press is considered to be regular drinking and is prohibited.

Rava cites R' Meir's opinion in a Mishnah (*Maasros* 4:4) that rules that a person may not stand outside the press, lean forward and drink the untithed wine over the press, because he might bring the wine to where he is standing and drink it there, which is prohibited. However, if his head and most of his body are situated over the press, he may drink, because this removes the concern that he might inadvertently retract his head and body and drink outside the winepress. Our Mishnah thus follows the view of R' Meir, that drinking untithed wine directly over a winepress is permitted, and it teaches that one's head and most of one's body must be over the winepress for this leniency to apply. Otherwise we are concerned lest he bring the wine to where he is standing and drink it there — which is forbidden.

A MUSSAR THOUGHT FOR THE DAY

We have seen above (*A Torah Thought for the Day*) that the optimal way to give charity is by beginning with an appreciation of the fact that all one has is from Hashem. This must serve as the basis for any giving that a person does. This concept was succinctly put by none other than Dovid HaMelech, with the words: כִּי־מִמְּךָ הַכֹּל וּמִיָּדְךָ נָתַנּוּ לָךְ, *for everything is from You, and from Your hand have we given to You* (*I Divrei HaYamim* 29:14). A fascinating explanation is given to these words in *Sefer HaMiknah* (to *Kiddushin* 32a).

One of the legal methods of transferring ownership of movable objects is with מְשִׁיכָה, where the buyer draws the object toward himself. *Meshichah,* however, does not work when it is performed while the object being acquired is still in the property of the seller. It is only in a neutral area that one can use this method of acquisition.

We know that we receive everything that we have from Hashem. However, we must understand that we have never actually acquired it from Him; no transference of ownership has ever taken place. This is due to the fact that there is no place in which to make that acquisition, for anywhere that we would go is the domain of Hashem. There is no neutral area in which to make the transfer! It follows, then, that while Hashem has given us our possessions, we do not have them as owners, but rather as those who use another's belongings with his permission. When giving charity, we must understand that we are not actually giving away anything of ours at all; it is the property and the money of Hashem that we are merely returning to Him.

This is the meaning of the verse mentioned above. The word יָד is often used figuratively to mean *domain.* Thus, the words וּמִיָּדְךָ נָתַנּוּ לָךְ explain why we feel that we are merely giving back to Hashem what is His — *from Your domain we have given to You.* We never actually acquired the possession from You, for it was always in Your domain.

Becoming accustomed to this attitude is also the key to one's being happy with his lot. It is natural to be happy when one first receives something, but then as time goes on, one gets used to the idea that it is his, and the excitement fades. One who understands that he does not actually own any of his possessions, but they are merely given to him to use as long as he has them, will feel that all the time he has the use of these items he is profiting. In this way he will be constantly happy with his lot.

In the Mishnah in *Avos* (3:8), R' Elazar paraphrases the above statement of Dovid HaMelech thus: תֶּן לוֹ מִשֶּׁלּוֹ שֶׁאַתָּה וְשֶׁלְּךָ שֶׁלּוֹ, *Give Him from His own, for you and your possessions are His.* With these words R' Elazar is expanding the above idea to include not only one's possessions but also all of one's talents and energies. Understanding that even these actually belong to Hashem will encourage one to use these gifts generously in His service (see *Tiferes Yisrael*).

HALACHAH OF THE DAY

As we have learned earlier, when a broken utensil is unfit for its proper use, and the repair of the utensil is Biblically prohibited, its components are often considered *muktzeh.* When the components are unfit for any use whatsoever in their current state, they are inherently *muktzeh.* Even if the disassembled components are still somewhat individually usable, if there is a concern that the owner might use them to repair the utensil and thus violate the Biblical *melachah,* the Sages decreed that they be considered *muktzeh.* To illustrate, if a leg became detached from a chair so that the chair is no longer usable in the usual fashion, both the leg and the chair are considered *muktzeh.*

Since the prohibition of *muktzeh* is imposed in this case only to ensure that one not repair a broken item, it is applicable only where the concern that one might do so exists. Thus, only when the detached leg is available and fit to be used to reattach to the chair are the chair and the leg considered *muktzeh.* If the leg of the chair is missing or broken, the chair is not deemed *muktzeh.* This is because a broken chair is still somewhat fit to be used. As we stated earlier, the Sages prohibited only a broken item that is somewhat usable in a case where the owner might use the components to fix the utensil and thus violate the Biblical prohibition. Since in this case the leg is missing or not fit to be used for the repair, we do not prohibit the chair and deem it *muktzeh.*

This is certainly true if the chair was used without the leg prior to Shabbos. In this case, the concern that one might use the leg to fix the chair is mitigated by the fact that it was already used in its current state, and the chair is not deemed to be *muktzeh.*

Having discussed all the various types of actions that may be restricted by this *melachah,* we will now begin to analyze the *melachah* from the standpoint of practical application.

The *melachah* of *finishing* applies to hard materials or soft materials, to garments, cutlery and books. It applies to both large and small items, to new ones as well as old ones. It applies even to an item that will be used only once and then discarded. For example, whittling a piece of wood into a toothpick is forbidden, even if it will be discarded after a single use.

Some *poskim* rule that the *melachah* of *finishing* does not apply to food items. Therefore, it is permissible to wash or soak a salty piece of fish that is inedible due to its saltiness. However, although the Biblical *melachah* of *finishing* does not apply to foods, the Sages prohibited certain improvements to food items that resemble repairs. We will discuss these in detail tomorrow.

A CLOSER LOOK AT THE SIDDUR

Toward the end of his life, Dovid HaMelech gathered together the entire congregation and announced to them the dedication of his treasures to the *Beis HaMikdash.* He then asked the people themselves to donate to this cause. A passage in *Divrei HaYamim* (I, Ch. 29) describes how the leaders of the people donated generously of their own resources to the fund of the *Beis HaMikdash.* וַיִּשְׂמְחוּ הָעָם עַל־הִתְנַדְּבָם כִּי בְּלֵב שָׁלֵם הִתְנַדְּבוּ לַה׳ וְגַם דָּוִיד הַמֶּלֶךְ שָׂמַח שִׂמְחָה גְדוֹלָה, *The people rejoiced in their donations, for they donated wholeheartedly to* H*ASHEM; King David also rejoiced with great gladness* (v. 9). When David saw that they gave with such joy, he prayed that the joy and enthusiasm the people had in their hearts in doing this mitzvah should remain with them always: ה׳ . . . שָׁמְרָה־זֹּאת לְעוֹלָם לְיֵצֶר מַחְשְׁבוֹת לְבַב עַמֶּךָ וְהָכֵן לְבָבָם אֵלֶיךָ, *HASHEM . . . preserve this forever to be the product of the thoughts of the hearts of*

Your people, and set their hearts toward You (v. 18).

There are two places in our daily prayers in which the events or words of that gathering are referred to.

The first is in *Pesukei D'Zimrah,* where David's blessing to the people is recorded (וַיְבָרֶךְ דָּוִיד). It is the custom (based on the *Arizal*) to give some charity while saying these verses. The *Admor of Ozrov* explains that we do this to connect to the sublime level of giving that the people reached on that day. They did not take any credit for themselves for their donation, but thanked Hashem for the opportunity to give Him from that with which He had blessed them (see above, *A Mussar Thought for the Day;* see also *A Closer Look at the Siddur, Parashas Behar,* Wednesday, for another explanation of this custom).

The second place where this is mentioned is in *U'va LeTzion,* where we recite the verse cited above: ה' . . . שָׁמְרָה־זֹּאת לְעוֹלָם. In that context, we are asking Hashem to help us preserve the fervent declaration of His holiness in our hearts forever (*Abudraham*).

R' Tzadok of Lublin (*Tzidkas HaTzaddik* §252) writes that we must appreciate that not only are all of our physical blessings from Hashem, but even the very will that we have to serve Hashem is from Him. He writes that this is the intention of David's declaration: כִּי־מִמְּךָ הַכֹּל, *for everything is from You* — "everything" includes the very inspiration to donate to You and to serve You (see above, *A Mussar Thought for the Day*). And because our inspiration and joy also come from Hashem, we can ask Him to preserve it for us forever. After David declared that even this aspect of the service of Hashem is from Him, he prayed that He continue to inspire us to His service.

After experiencing a special spiritual inspiration, it behooves us to pray that that inspiration and enthusiasm, which are a gift from Hashem just as all other blessings, remain with us always. *Sefer Chassidim* writes that if a person experiences a sudden burst of joy and devotion to Hashem while in the middle of the blessing of שְׁמַע קוֹלֵנוּ (*Acceptance of Prayer*), he should recite the following prayer before he finishes his *Shemoneh Esrei*: "May it be Your will that this love should remain planted firmly in my heart, and in the hearts of all my descendants." He should ask for nothing else at this time except for this.

QUESTION OF THE DAY:

How was the maaser animal distinguished from the others?

For the answer, see page 295.

A TORAH THOUGHT FOR THE DAY

פרשת בחקתי

SHABBOS

PARASHAS BECHUKOSAI

לֹא יְבַקֵּר בֵּין־טוֹב לָרַע וְלֹא יְמִירֶנּוּ וְאִם־הָמֵר יְמִירֶנּוּ וְהָיָה־הוּא וּתְמוּרָתוֹ יִהְיֶה קֹּדֶשׁ לֹא יִגָּאֵל

He shall not distinguish between good and bad, and he should not substitute for it; and if he does substitute for it, then it and its substitute shall both be holy; it may not be redeemed (*Vayikra* 27:33).

The first part of this verse teaches us that the tenth animal, which becomes sanctified as *maaser,* must be selected by chance; whichever one comes through the opening of the corral as the tenth is *maaser.* One is not allowed to arrange matters so that an inferior animal exits tenth; nor is he even allowed to ensure that a *superior* specimen is the tenth. The choice is left to Hashem (see *Rashi*).

The second part of the verse teaches the law of *temurah,* attempted *substitution* for a consecrated animal. If an animal is consecrated and one wishes to substitute another animal for it, whether it is better or worse, this is forbidden. Nevertheless, the substitution is valid to the extent that the second animal also becomes consecrated; however, the first animal remains consecrated as well.

The rule of *temurah* applies to all *korbanos,* not only to *maaser;* it is stated in the Torah earlier (see *Vayikra* Ch. 12). We may ask: Why was it necessary to repeat the law of *temurah* with respect to *maaser* specifically?

In order to understand the answer, we must realize that there is a basic difference between *maaser* and other types of *korbanos.* When one consecrates an animal as an *olah,* there is no process that the animal must undergo; the very statement, "This animal shall be an *olah,*" is sufficient to invest it with holiness. This is not the case with *maaser.* In order for an animal to become *maaser,* it must be included in the count of ten animals, and it becomes *maaser* when it leaves the corral as the tenth one. Because of this intrinsic difference, one might think that when an attempt is made to substitute a second animal for an animal designated as *maaser,* the second one would not become consecrated. Since it did not undergo the proper process, it would be reasonable to assume that it could not become consecrated through mere words. The Torah therefore tells us that this is not the case. Although the animal did not undergo the counting process, the substitution is successful even in this case, to the extent that the second animal does become sanctified. The first animal, however, does not lose its sanctity.

For further discussion of *temurah,* see *A Mussar Thought for the Day.*

MISHNAH OF THE DAY: ERUVIN 10:7

This Mishnah continues the discussion of cases where one stands in one domain and moves objects about in the other domain:

בּוֹר בִּרְשׁוּת הָרַבִּים וְחוּלְיָיתוֹ גָּבוֹהַּ עֲשָׂרָה טְפָחִים — *If* there is ***a water hole in the reshus harabim, and its embankment is ten tefachim high,***[1] חַלּוֹן שֶׁעַל גַּבָּיו מְמַלְּאִין הֵימֶנּוּ בְּשַׁבָּת — ***one*** who is in a nearby *reshus hayachid* **may draw** water ***from it*** [the water hole] ***on the Sabbath*** via ***a window that is above it.***[2]

אַשְׁפָּה בִּרְשׁוּת הָרַבִּים גָּבוֹהַּ עֲשָׂרָה טְפָחִים — *If* there is ***a trash heap in the reshus harabim ten tefachim high,*** חַלּוֹן שֶׁעַל גַּבָּיו שׁוֹפְכִין לְתוֹכָהּ מַיִם בְּשַׁבָּת — ***one may pour water onto it on the Sabbath*** from ***a window that is above it.***[3]

NOTES

1. A water hole that is 10 *tefachim* deep and 4 *tefachim* square is a *reshus hayachid* even if it is located in the middle of a *reshus harabim.* If a *reshus harabim* passing in front of a house has a water hole in it, a person standing at the window of the house may not draw water from the hole to the house on the Sabbath. Although both the house and the hole are private domains, the area between them is a *reshus harabim,* and, by Rabbinic decree, one may not transfer between one *reshus hayachid* and another through a *reshus harabim.*

The Mishnah, however, discusses a case where there is a 10-*tefach* high embankment around the water hole, which changes the ruling.

2. Since the embankment is 10 *tefachim* high, the water-bucket will never pass over the *reshus harabim* within 10 *tefachim* of the ground. Since a *reshus harabim* rises to a height of only 10 *tefachim,* and airspace above is considered a *mekom petur,* the person drawing water to the window will be transferring from one *reshus hayachid* to another through an exempt area, not a *reshus harabim.*

3. The ruling regarding the trash heap is identical with that concerning the water hole. Furthermore, we are not concerned that the trash will someday be removed, thereby transforming the area into a *reshus harabim* — and resulting in people desecrating the Sabbath as they continue to pour out their water from this window. See *Gems from the Gemara.*

QUESTION OF THE DAY:

What happens if the temurah animal is blemished?

For the answer, see page 295.

GEMS FROM THE GEMARA

The Gemara discusses the second case of the Mishnah, of a trash heap in the *reshus harabim.* The Gemara asks: Why are we not concerned that the trash heap might someday be partially removed so that its height is diminished to less than 10 *tefachim,* and yet people will continue to throw garbage onto it as they had been accustomed to do before? The Gemara quotes a Baraisa that relates an actual incident concerning a certain *mavoi* whose one side terminated at the sea, and whose other side terminated at a trash heap. The sea wall (i.e., the slope of land descending from the water's edge until the seabed — see below) had a height of 10 *tefachim* or more, so that it constituted a partition for that side of the *mavoi.* The trash heap stood at least 10 *tefachim* high, forming a partition for the *mavoi's* second side. See diagram. In addition, one end of the *mavoi* was closed, and the other end opened to the street, but was adjusted with a *lechi* or *korah.* In that case, the matter came before Rebbi to decide whether it was permitted to carry in the *mavoi,* or not.

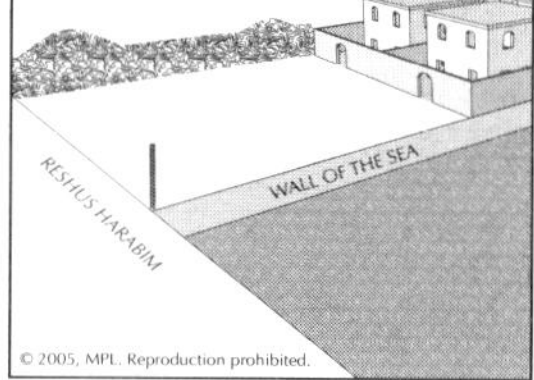

In the end, Rebbi refused to rule on the matter one way or the other. He would not permit carrying in it, because we are concerned that the trash heap might be removed, or that the sea might bring up sediment creating an area of silt against the present wall of the sea, thereby depriving the *mavoi* of that wall. See diagram. For the partition formed by a sea wall is negated in a case where the floor of the sea begins at the shore and gradually slopes downward; such a wall does not constitute a partition even though it eventually descends to a great depth. [Only a slope so steep that one, walking 4 *amos* along it, would rise 10 *tefachim* above his starting point, is considered vertical enough to qualify as a partition. And when the wall of the sea is not sufficiently steep, it no longer serves as a wall for a *mavoi.*]

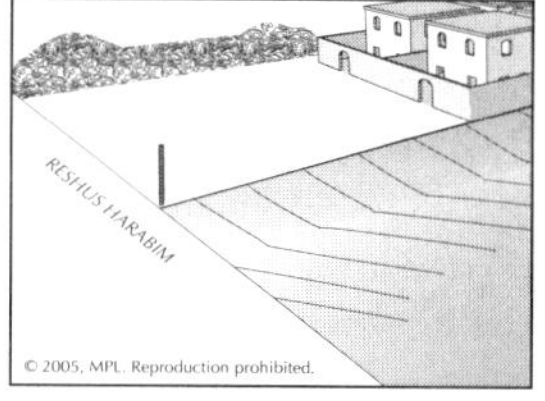

But Rebbi did not prohibit carrying in it either, because partitions do currently exist. These were valid partitions that gave the *mavoi* a fully enclosed status.

We see from this Baraisa that while carrying in this *mavoi* was technically permissible, Rebbe would not sanction it for fear that these changes would occur, and yet people would continue to carry in the *mavoi* as they were accustomed to previously. How, then, could our Mishnah permit carrying into the trash heap, inasmuch as the trash heap could be removed?

The Gemara answers that the case that came before Rebbi dealt with a trash heap owned by an individual, which is liable to be removed at any time. The case of our Mishnah, however, was of a trash heap owned by many people; a publicly owned trash heap is much less likely to be removed.

A MUSSAR THOUGHT FOR THE DAY

In *A Torah Thought for the Day* we discussed the prohibition against substituting a non-consecrated animal in the place of a *maaser* animal, and stated that in such a case both animals remain consecrated. *R' Moshe Feinstein,* noting that there are two prohibitions in the verse, asks: Once the Torah has taught that one cannot ensure that a certain animal comes out tenth, is it not obvious that he cannot substitute for the animal that did come out tenth? If one cannot even attempt to influence the arrival of the sanctity, certainly he cannot remove it once it has descended!

R' Moshe explains that the lesson here is to be extended to a person's choices in life. A person is never supposed to say, "It is not for me to aspire to a life as a Torah scholar; there are others who are smarter and more diligent than I am." This would be a case of attempting to influence the decision before it occurs. Every person has the capacity to be "sanctified" in this sense; the argument that others are more qualified is simply a tactic of the *yetzer hara,* to deter him from reaching his true potential. Each person must do his utmost to make the attempt to reach greatness, and Hashem will choose if he is to "come out tenth," as it were.

[This is true with regard to children as well. One may not decide that a certain child is not "cut out" for greatness in Torah. Every child is a candidate for greatness.]

The second prohibition may be likened to a person who has indeed studied and grown in Torah, but feels that he has reached the point where he may leave the toil for others and begin to become more involved in worldly matters. The Torah teaches us here that there is never a time when this is proper. The Torah studies of others can never substitute for personal growth; both must remain holy. [This is true even in a case where the person feels that by removing himself from the Torah world he will be enabling others to learn in his stead by supporting them. Even in situations where one has to learn a livelihood, this is not a license to depart from Torah study; it merely shortens the time each day that is available for one to study. The obligation to study when the time presents itself remains exactly the same.]

HALACHAH OF THE DAY

Yesterday, we discussed the fact that some *poskim* rule that the *melachah* of *finishing* does not apply to food; nonetheless, there are certain improvements that are prohibited, as they resemble repairs.

It is therefore forbidden on Shabbos to separate *terumos* and *maasros* from fruits and vegetables grown in Eretz Yisrael. Since these foods cannot be eaten unless they are tithed, by separating the *terumos* and *maasros* one renders them fit to be eaten. He is thus, in effect, "repairing" the food, and this is prohibited.

It is also forbidden for one to remove the *challah* portion from bread or cake on Shabbos. Since the baked item may not be eaten until the *challah* has been separated, taking *challah* is considered to be effecting a "repair," similar to taking *terumos* and *maasros.*

In the event that one forgot to separate *terumos* and *maasros* or *challah* prior to Shabbos, one should consult a competent halachic authority.

We will now discuss some of the other practical applications of *finishing.*

As stated earlier, it is permissible to remove a tag from a garment, since the garment is inherently usable, and the tag is simply an external factor. Likewise, one may remove the pins from a new shirt; since the shirt is complete and ready for use, and the pins are external things that stand in the way of wearing it, this is permissible. In a similar vein, one may remove a thorn that became attached to an item of clothing, since it is an item external to the garment.

On the other hand, it is forbidden to remove a tailor's chalk marks from a completed garment, since the chalk marks constitute a defect in the garment itself.

As mentioned earlier, it is permissible to reshape a soft hat, even if it completely loses its shape, since this is common with soft hats, and the reshaping is effortless. Nonetheless, it is forbidden to steam or brush a hat.

It is permissible to insert shoe trees into shoes in order to retain the shape of the shoes. If the shoes have become completely misshapen, it is prohibited to insert shoe trees on Shabbos.

SHABBOS

PARASHAS BECHUKOSAI

It is forbidden to insert a new shoelace into a shoe on Shabbos, because one thereby completes the shoe. It is permissible, however, to reinsert a shoelace that was in the shoe prior to Shabbos.

In the event that one's shoelace tore on Shabbos, there are two solutions that he can employ. Either he should insert a shoelace of a different color than the shoe, so that it is obvious that this is a temporary repair. Or, he should put in a shoelace of the same color as the shoe, but only lace it through the first two eyelets. In this case, it is also obvious that this is a temporary measure, and therefore permissible.

A CLOSER LOOK AT THE SIDDUR

We continue our discussion of *Shir HaMaalos* (Psalm 126), which we recite before *Bircas HaMazon* on the Sabbath and festivals.

Last week, we discussed the fact that the ultimate redemption will transform the world as rain can transform a barren land into a fertile garden. Continuing the metaphor of one who plants, the psalm states: הַזֹּרְעִים בְּדִמְעָה בְּרִנָּה יִקְצֹרוּ, *Those who plant with tears will reap with song.* The "planting" being discussed here is not the planting of crops, but the planting of values — the implanting of morals, honesty, and integrity into ourselves, our children, and our fellows. The verse tells us here that although the process of doing so can be painful and frustrating, the rewards will be clear and abundant in the end; the tears will be changed to glad song.

Indeed, there is a direct correlation between the effort and the tears that are invested in this critical work, and the success and *nachas* that are the ultimate result. The Mishnah in *Avos* (5:26) tells us: לְפוּם צַעֲרָא אַגְרָא, *the reward is commensurate with the pain* experienced in the service of Hashem.

The psalm continues, fleshing out the metaphor more completely: הָלוֹךְ יֵלֵךְ וּבָכֹה נֹשֵׂא מֶשֶׁךְ־הַזָּרַע, *He walks, weeping, as he carries the measured seed.* As one plants in the desert, he weeps for fear that his few measured seeds may not survive in the harsh environment, depriving him of the crop he needs. So too, as the Jews move through the various exiles, they bear the arduous task of ensuring that the generations remain true to their *mesorah.* The job is a difficult one, and it is accompanied by much prayer and many tears. Yet, we know that Hashem smiles upon us as we strive to do His work, and that He will bless us with success. Thus, the psalm concludes: בֹּא־יָבוֹא בְרִנָּה נֹשֵׂא אֲלֻמֹּתָיו, *He will surely come in song, carrying his sheaves.* The seeds will indeed survive and flourish — because Hashem wills it to be so. Thus, when the final redemption is at hand, one who struggled through the difficult times with faith in Hashem will be richly rewarded. Instead of bearing only a measured amount of seeds, he will be carrying sheaves, full armloads of grain that have sprouted from his meager beginnings. This, too, foretells of the splendor that will be ours when Hashem's true majesty is revealed to the world.

ANSWERS TO QUESTIONS OF THE DAY

Sunday:

A person, who can move up and down in his spiritual levels, is called a הוֹלֵךְ, while an angel, who is fixed in place, is called an עוֹמֵד.

Monday:

It is the עול placed upon the *Avos* that their descendants would be exiled and moved from place to place (*Netziv*).

Tuesday:

It implies that people will not even be passing through the land at all (*Rashi*).

Wednesday:

Hashem does not need to *remember* Yitzchak, for because of the *Akeidah,* his memory is *always* before Hashem (see *Toras Kohanim* 8:7).

Thursday:

This is possible in a case where the courts have condemned him to execution for his sins (*Rambam, Hil. Arachin* 1:13).

Friday:

The red dye on the stick that was used to hit it left a mark that was its identifier (*Rashi*).

Shabbos:

It becomes sanctified, but cannot be offered as a *korban;* nevertheless, it is subject to the same restrictions as a genuine *maaser* animal that was blemished (see *Rashi*).